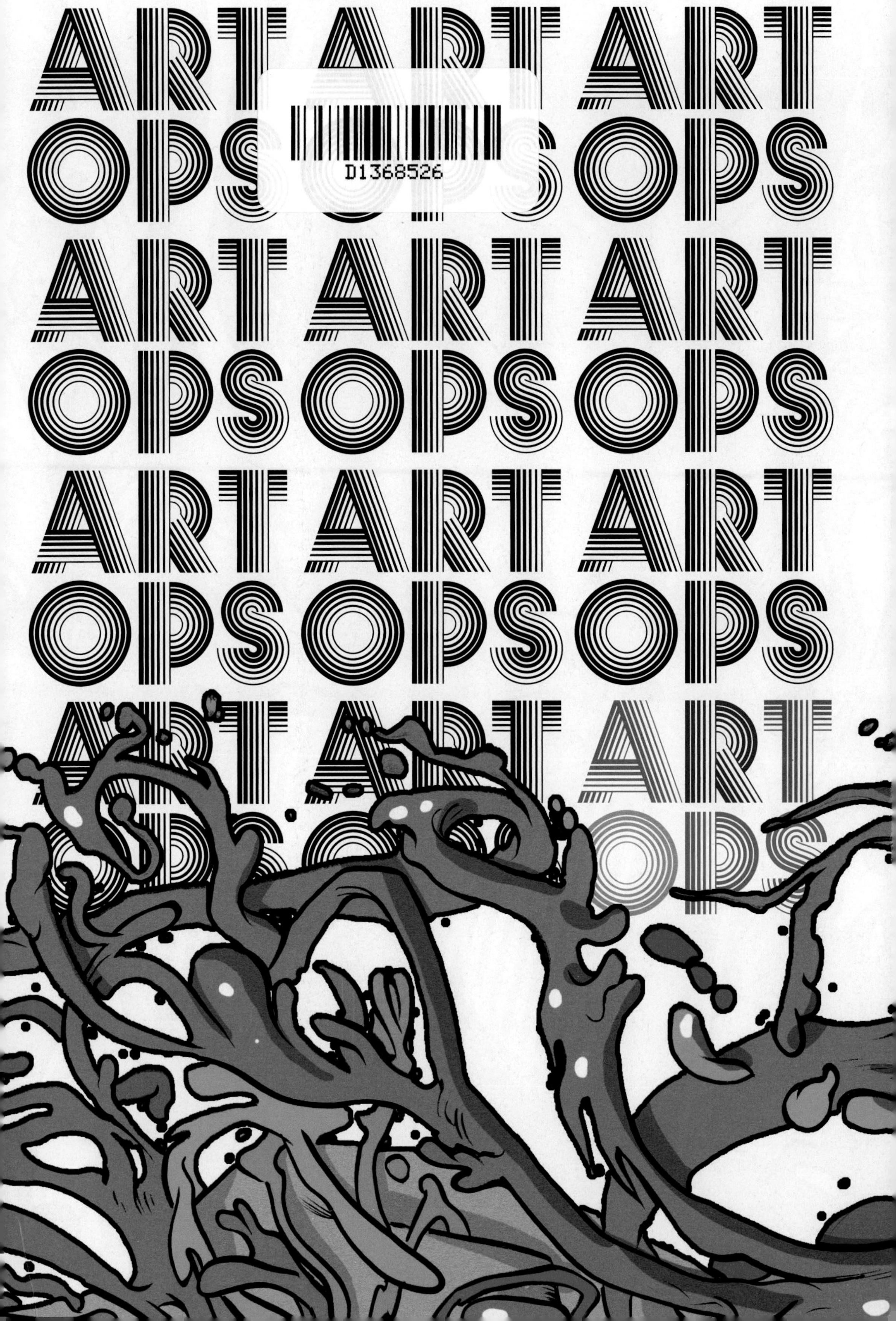
ART ART ART
OPS OPS OPS
ART ART ART
OPS OPS OPS
ART ART ART
OPS OPS OPS
ART ART ART
OPS OPS OPS

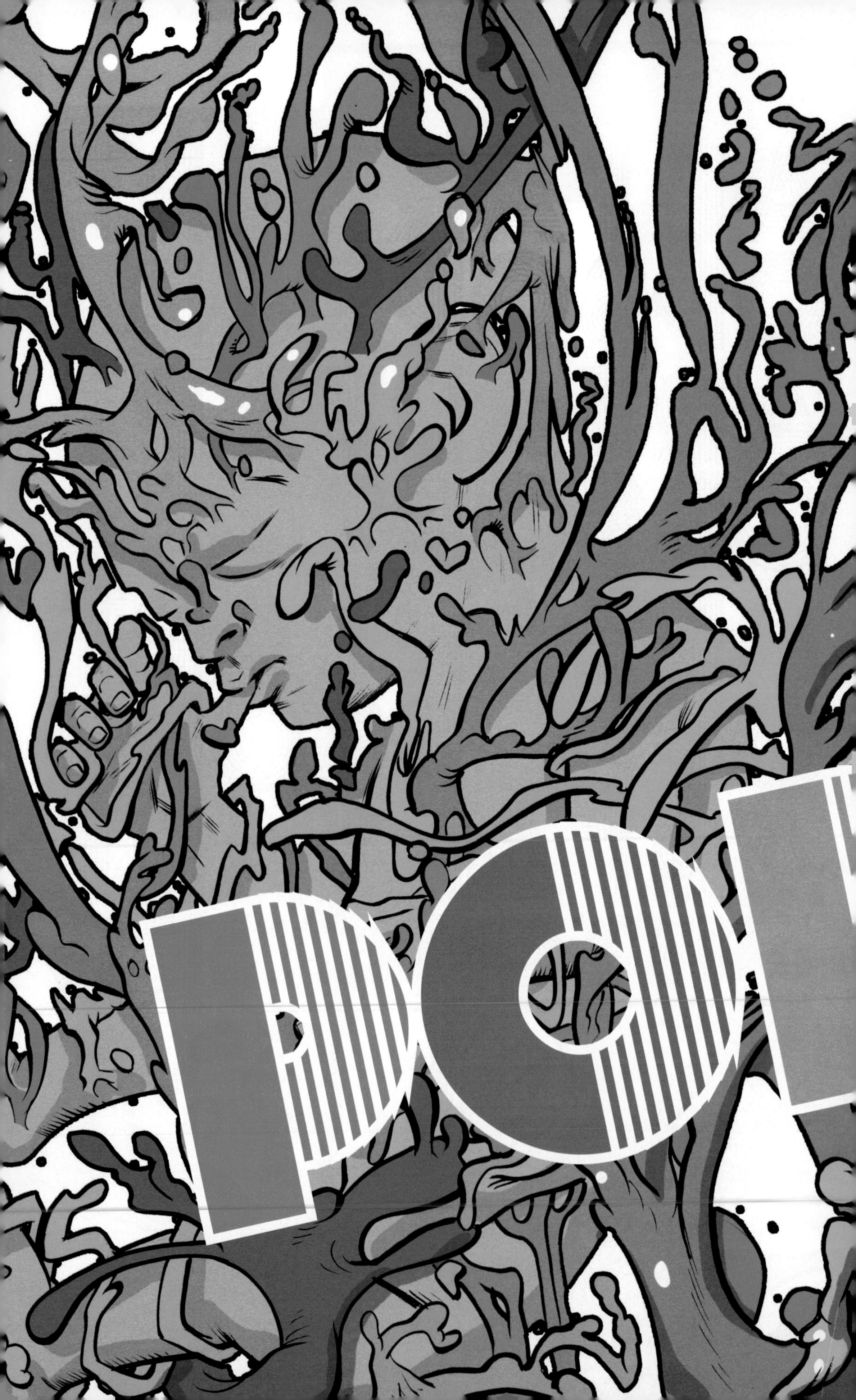

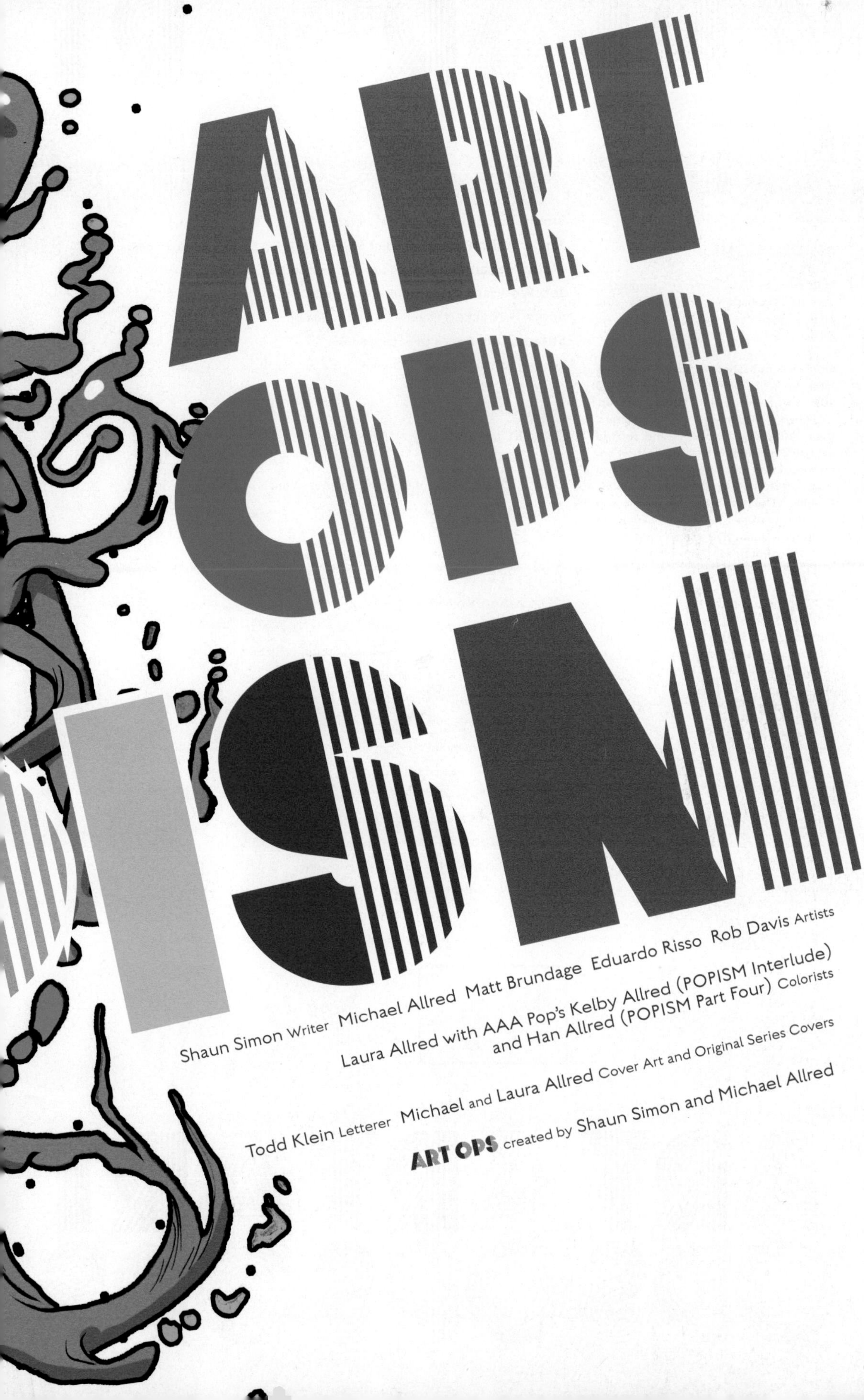

ART OPS POPISM

Shaun Simon Writer Michael Allred Matt Brundage Eduardo Risso Rob Davis Artists

Laura Allred with AAA Pop's Kelby Allred (POPISM Interlude) and Han Allred (POPISM Part Four) Colorists

Todd Klein Letterer Michael and Laura Allred Cover Art and Original Series Covers

ART OPS created by Shaun Simon and Michael Allred

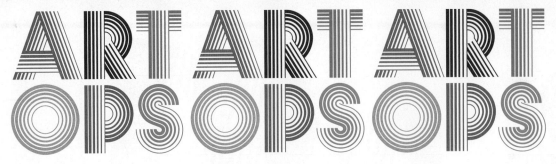

Logo design by Steve Cook

ART OPS: POPISM

DC Comics
2900 West Alameda Avenue
Burbank, CA 91505
Printed in the USA. First Printing.
ISBN: 978-1-4012-6741-4

Library of Congress Cataloging-in-Publication Data

Names: Simon, Shaun, author. | Allred, Mike (Mike Dalton) artist. | Brundage, Matt, artist. | Davis, Rob, artist. | Allred, Laura, colorist, artist. | Klein, Todd, letterer.
Title: Art Ops : popism / Shaun Simon, writer ; Michael Allred, Matt Brundage, Rob Davis, artists ; Laura Allred, colorist ; Todd Klein, letterer ; Michael and Laura Allred, cover art and original series covers.
Other titles: Popism
Description: Burbank, CA : DC Comics/Vertigo, [2016] | "Originally published in single magazine form as ART OPS 6-10." | "ART OPS created by Shaun Simon and Michael Allred"
Identifiers: LCCN 2016035914 | ISBN 9781401267414 (paperback)
Subjects: LCSH: Comic books, strips, etc. | BISAC: COMICS & GRAPHIC NOVELS / Superheroes.
Classification: LCC PN6728.A75 S58 2016 | DDC 741.5/973—dc23
LC record available at https://lccn.loc.gov/2016035914

Shelly Bond Editor – Original Series
Jamie S. Rich Editor – Original Series and Group Editor – Vertigo Comics
Molly Mahan Associate Editor – Original Series
Jeb Woodard Group Editor – Collected Editions
Scott Nybakken Editor – Collected Edition
Steve Cook Design Director – Books
Louis Prandi Publication Design

Diane Nelson President
Dan DiDio Publisher
Jim Lee Publisher
Geoff Johns President & Chief Creative Officer
Amit Desai Executive VP – Business & Marketing Strategy, Direct to Consumer & Global Franchise Management
Sam Ades Senior VP – Direct to Consumer
Bobbie Chase VP – Talent Development
Mark Chiarello Senior VP – Art, Design & Collected Editions
John Cunningham Senior VP – Sales & Trade Marketing
Anne DePies Senior VP – Business Strategy, Finance & Administration
Don Falletti VP – Manufacturing Operations
Lawrence Ganem VP – Editorial Administration & Talent Relations
Alison Gill Senior VP – Manufacturing & Operations
Hank Kanalz Senior VP – Editorial Strategy & Administration
Jay Kogan VP – Legal Affairs
Thomas Loftus VP – Business Affairs
Jack Mahan VP – Business Affairs
Nick J. Napolitano VP – Manufacturing Administration
Eddie Scannell VP – Consumer Marketing
Courtney Simmons Senior VP – Publicity & Communications
Jim (Ski) Sokolowski VP – Comic Book Specialty Sales & Trade Marketing
Nancy Spears VP – Mass, Book, Digital Sales & Trade Marketing

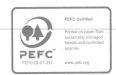

PEFC Certified
Printed on paper from sustainably managed forests and controlled sources
PEFC
PEFC/29-31-337
www.pefc.org

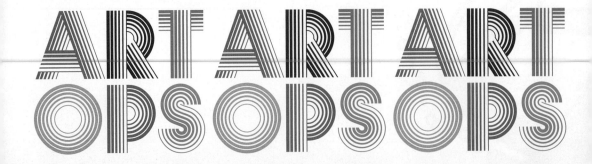

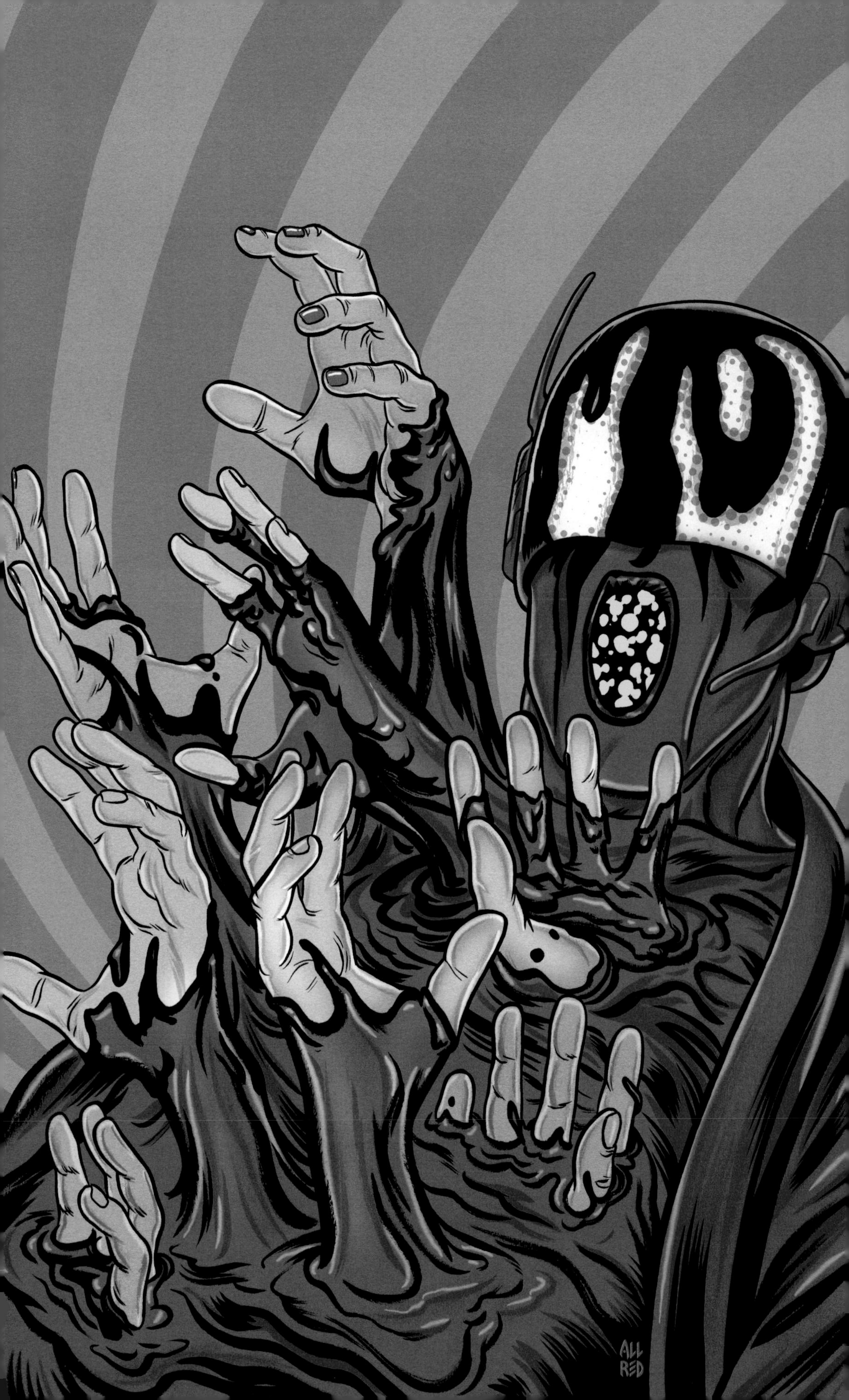
ALL
RED

MODERN LOVE

Art by EDUARDO RISSO

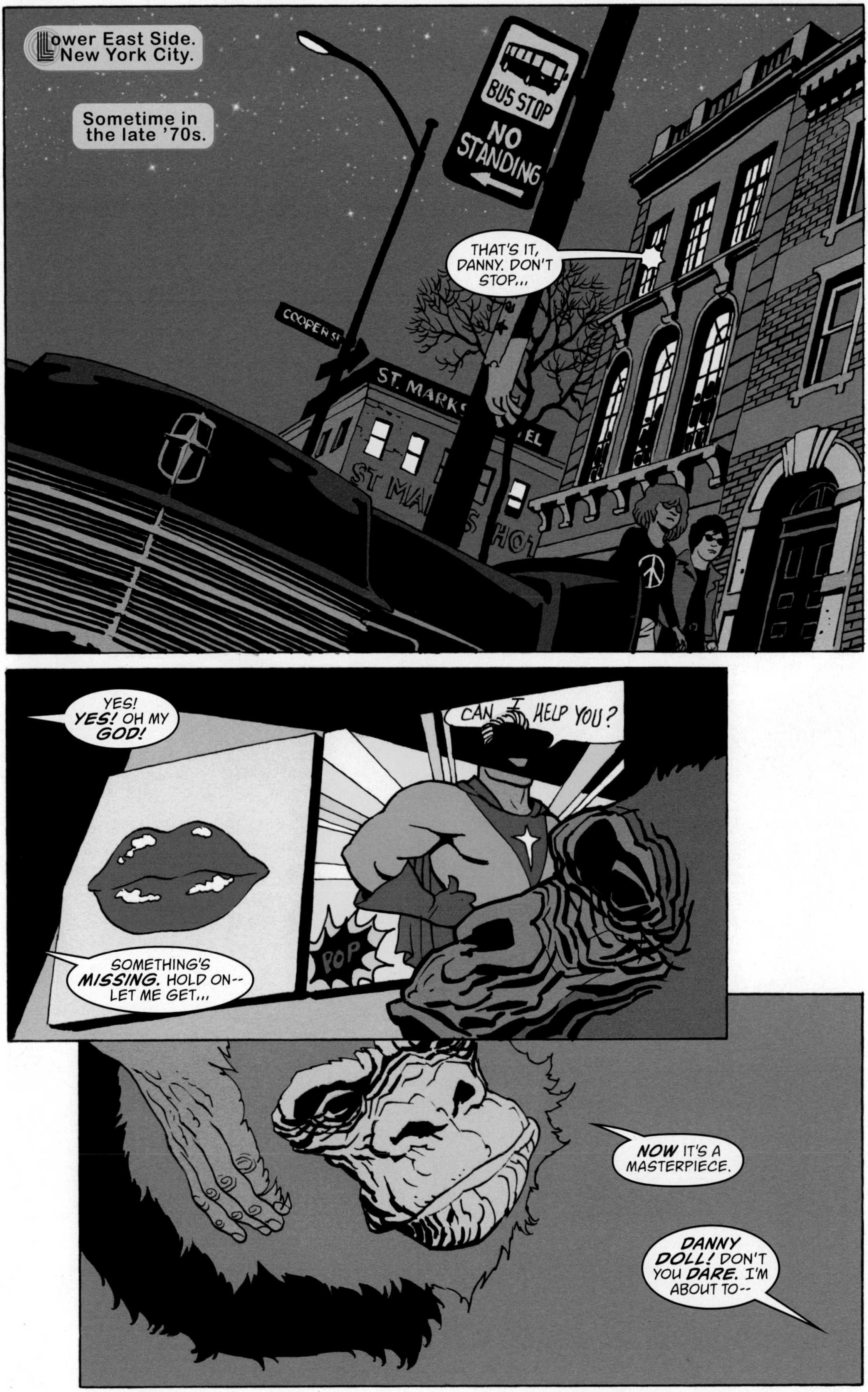
Lower East Side. New York City.
Sometime in the late '70s.
BUS STOP
NO STANDING
COOPER ST
ST. MARKS
THAT'S IT, DANNY. DON'T STOP...
YES! YES! OH MY GOD!
CAN I HELP YOU?
POP
SOMETHING'S MISSING. HOLD ON-- LET ME GET...
NOW IT'S A MASTERPIECE.
DANNY DOLL! DON'T YOU DARE. I'M ABOUT TO--

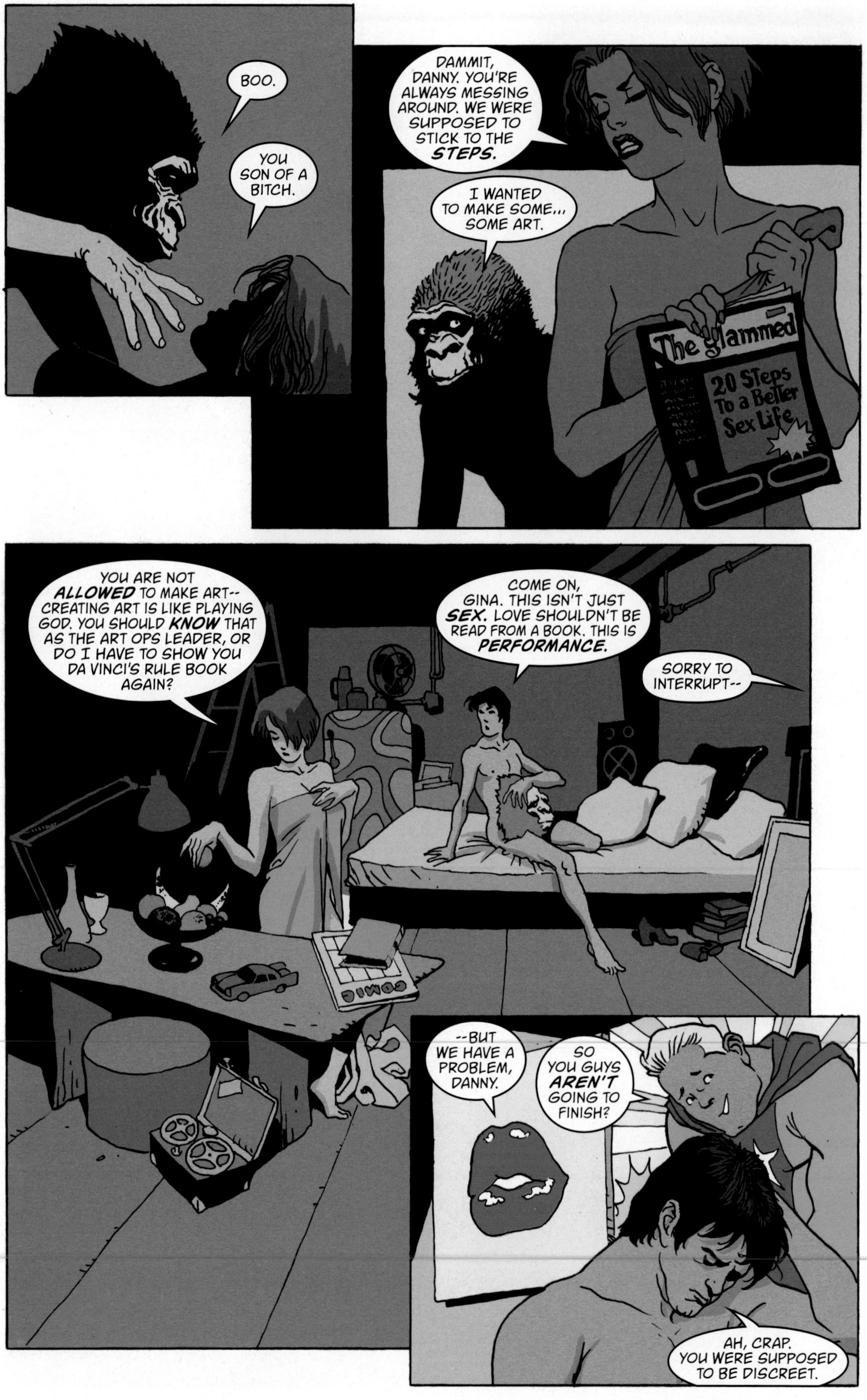
BOO.
YOU SON OF A BITCH.
DAMMIT, DANNY. YOU'RE ALWAYS MESSING AROUND. WE WERE SUPPOSED TO STICK TO THE STEPS.
I WANTED TO MAKE SOME... SOME ART.
The glammed
20 STeps To a Better Sex Life
YOU ARE NOT ALLOWED TO MAKE ART-- CREATING ART IS LIKE PLAYING GOD. YOU SHOULD KNOW THAT AS THE ART OPS LEADER, OR DO I HAVE TO SHOW YOU DA VINCI'S RULE BOOK AGAIN?
COME ON, GINA. THIS ISN'T JUST SEX. LOVE SHOULDN'T BE READ FROM A BOOK. THIS IS PERFORMANCE.
SORRY TO INTERRUPT--
COMIC
--BUT WE HAVE A PROBLEM, DANNY.
SO YOU GUYS AREN'T GOING TO FINISH?
AH, CRAP. YOU WERE SUPPOSED TO BE DISCREET.

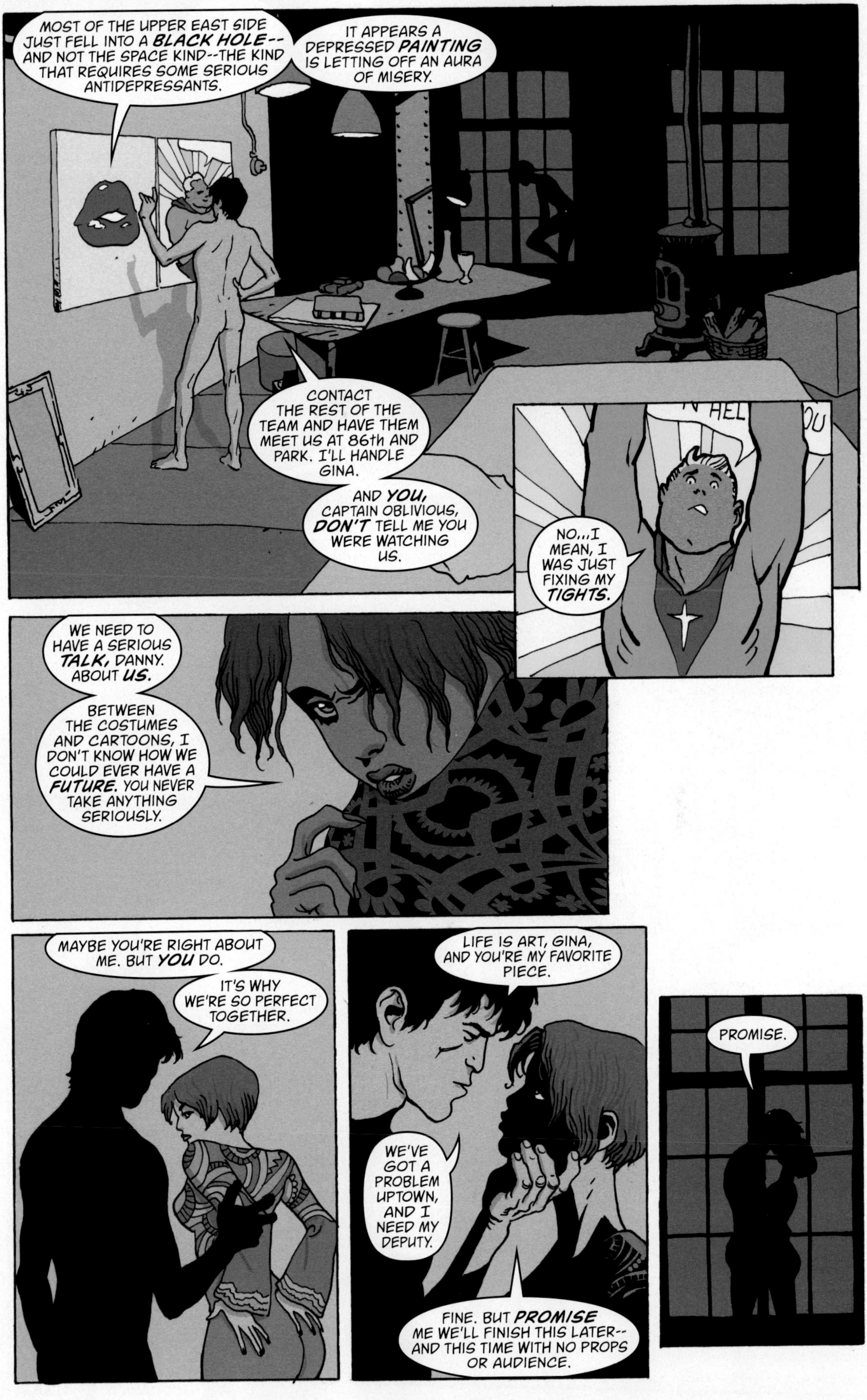
MOST OF THE UPPER EAST SIDE JUST FELL INTO A BLACK HOLE-- AND NOT THE SPACE KIND--THE KIND THAT REQUIRES SOME SERIOUS ANTIDEPRESSANTS.
IT APPEARS A DEPRESSED PAINTING IS LETTING OFF AN AURA OF MISERY.
CONTACT THE REST OF THE TEAM AND HAVE THEM MEET US AT 86th AND PARK. I'LL HANDLE GINA.
AND YOU, CAPTAIN OBLIVIOUS, DON'T TELL ME YOU WERE WATCHING US.
NO...I MEAN, I WAS JUST FIXING MY TIGHTS.
WE NEED TO HAVE A SERIOUS TALK, DANNY. ABOUT US.
BETWEEN THE COSTUMES AND CARTOONS, I DON'T KNOW HOW WE COULD EVER HAVE A FUTURE. YOU NEVER TAKE ANYTHING SERIOUSLY.
MAYBE YOU'RE RIGHT ABOUT ME. BUT YOU DO.
IT'S WHY WE'RE SO PERFECT TOGETHER.
LIFE IS ART, GINA, AND YOU'RE MY FAVORITE PIECE.
WE'VE GOT A PROBLEM UPTOWN, AND I NEED MY DEPUTY.
FINE. BUT PROMISE ME WE'LL FINISH THIS LATER-- AND THIS TIME WITH NO PROPS OR AUDIENCE.
PROMISE.

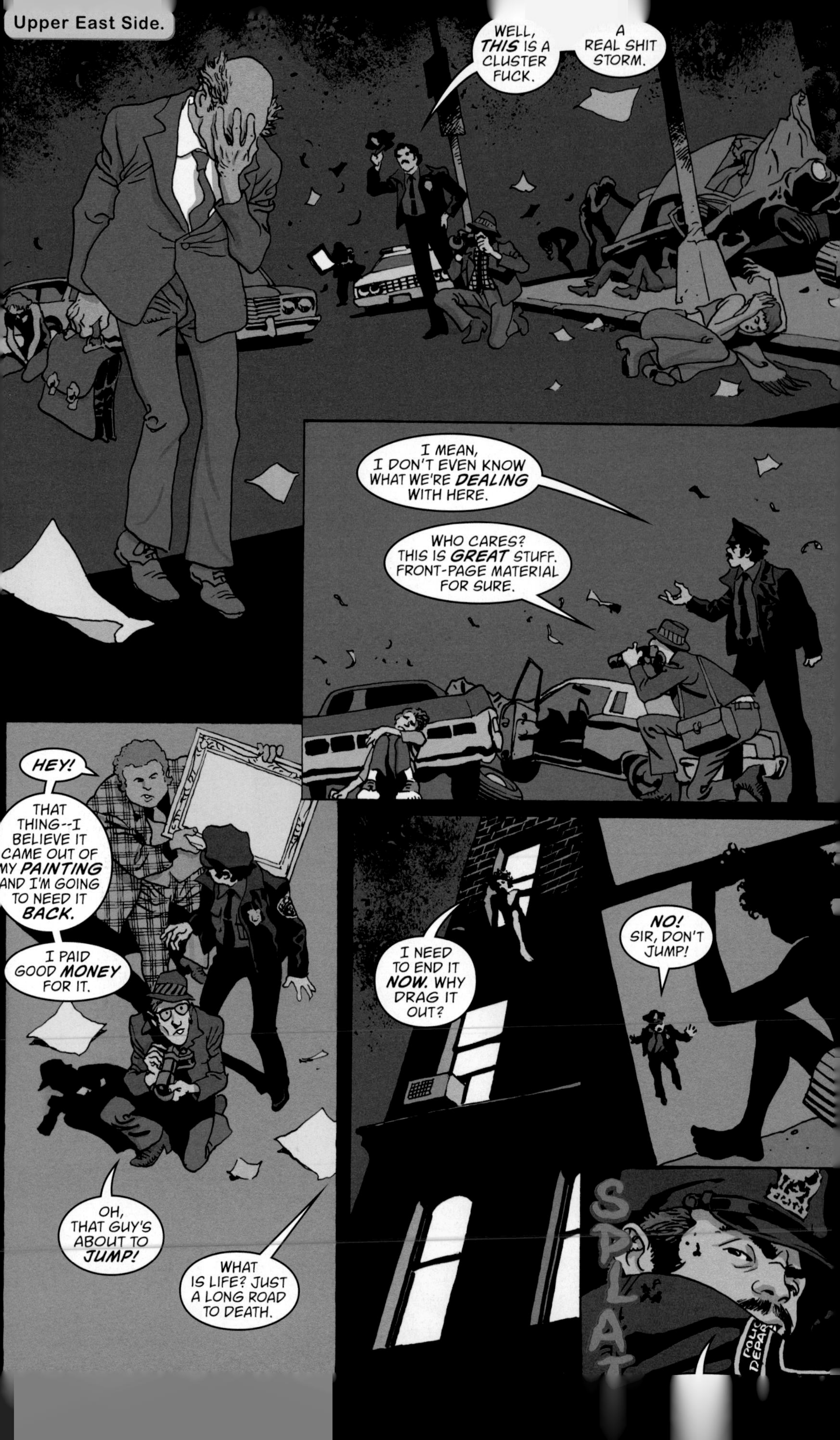
Upper East Side.
WELL, THIS IS A CLUSTER FUCK.
A REAL SHIT STORM.
I MEAN, I DON'T EVEN KNOW WHAT WE'RE DEALING WITH HERE.
WHO CARES? THIS IS GREAT STUFF. FRONT-PAGE MATERIAL FOR SURE.
HEY!
THAT THING--I BELIEVE IT CAME OUT OF MY PAINTING AND I'M GOING TO NEED IT BACK.
I PAID GOOD MONEY FOR IT.
OH, THAT GUY'S ABOUT TO JUMP!
WHAT IS LIFE? JUST A LONG ROAD TO DEATH.
I NEED TO END IT NOW. WHY DRAG IT OUT?
NO! SIR, DON'T JUMP!
SPLAT

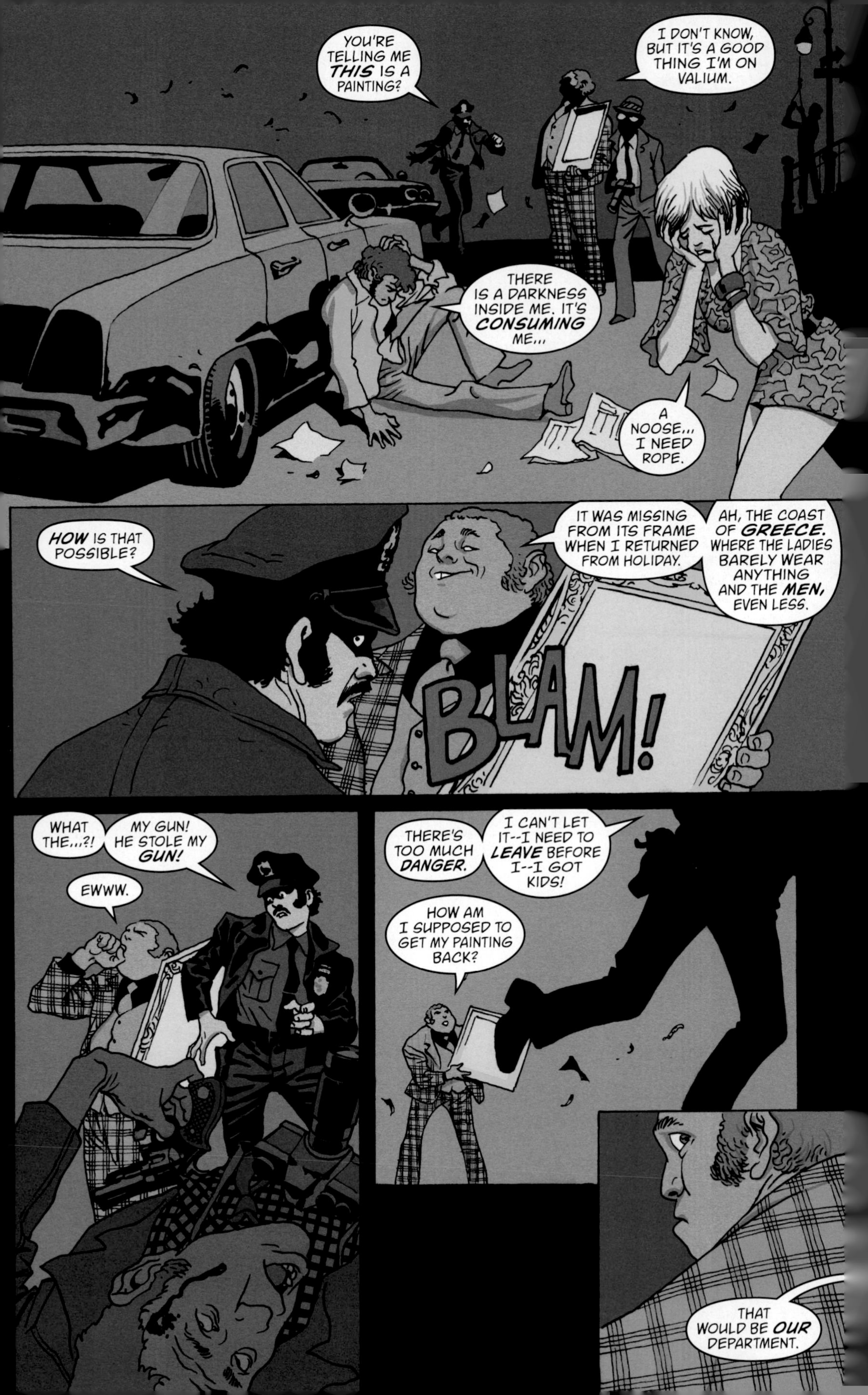
YOU'RE TELLING ME THIS IS A PAINTING?
I DON'T KNOW, BUT IT'S A GOOD THING I'M ON VALIUM.
THERE IS A DARKNESS INSIDE ME. IT'S CONSUMING ME...
A NOOSE... I NEED ROPE.
HOW IS THAT POSSIBLE?
IT WAS MISSING FROM ITS FRAME WHEN I RETURNED FROM HOLIDAY.
AH, THE COAST OF GREECE. WHERE THE LADIES BARELY WEAR ANYTHING AND THE MEN, EVEN LESS.
BLAM!
WHAT THE...?!
MY GUN! HE STOLE MY GUN!
EWWW.
THERE'S TOO MUCH DANGER.
I CAN'T LET IT--I NEED TO LEAVE BEFORE I--I GOT KIDS!
HOW AM I SUPPOSED TO GET MY PAINTING BACK?
THAT WOULD BE OUR DEPARTMENT.

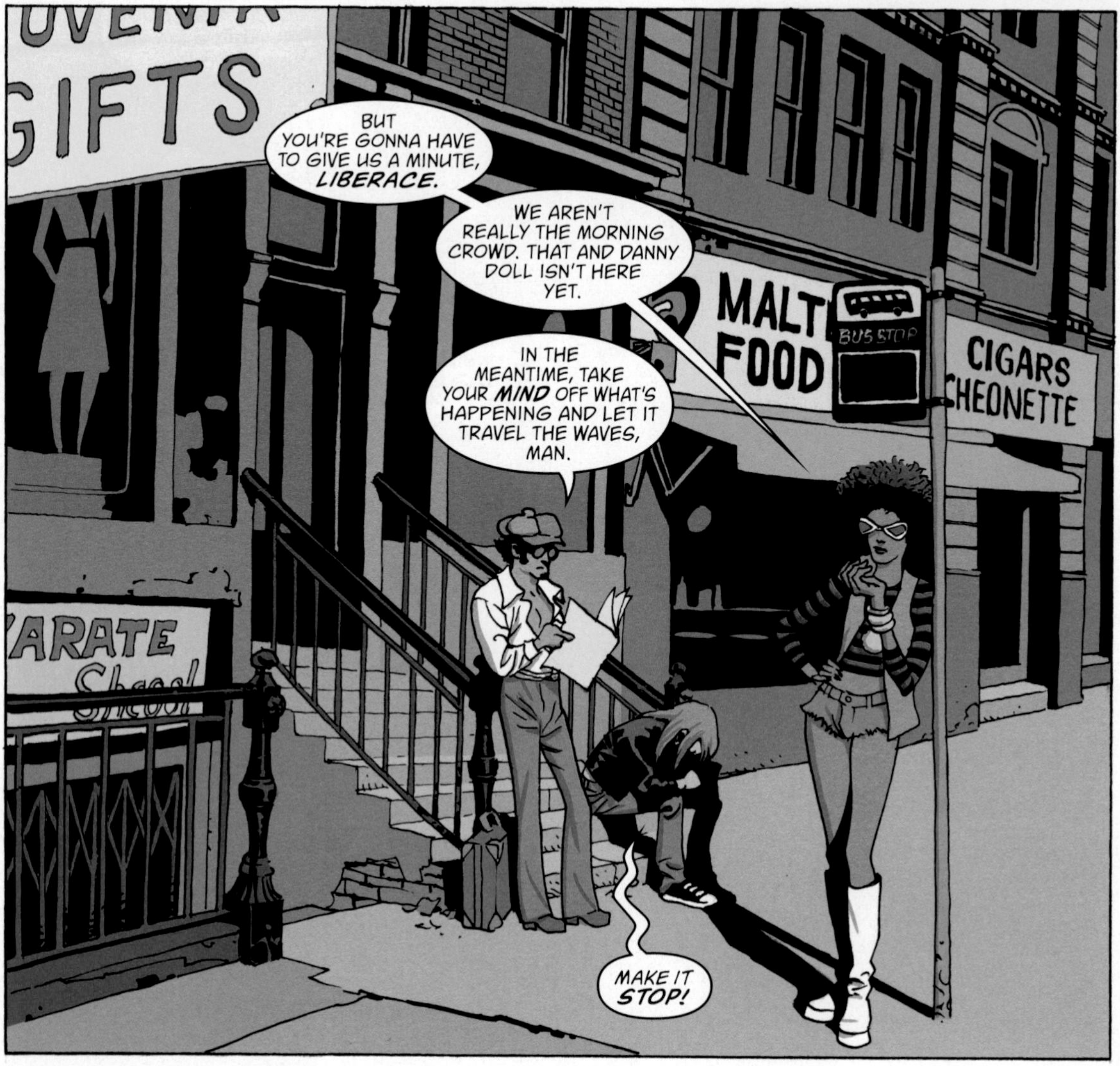
GIFTS
BUT YOU'RE GONNA HAVE TO GIVE US A MINUTE, LIBERACE.
WE AREN'T REALLY THE MORNING CROWD. THAT AND DANNY DOLL ISN'T HERE YET.
IN THE MEANTIME, TAKE YOUR MIND OFF WHAT'S HAPPENING AND LET IT TRAVEL THE WAVES, MAN.
MALT FOOD
BUS STOP
CIGARS
CHEONETTE
KARATE School
MAKE IT STOP!

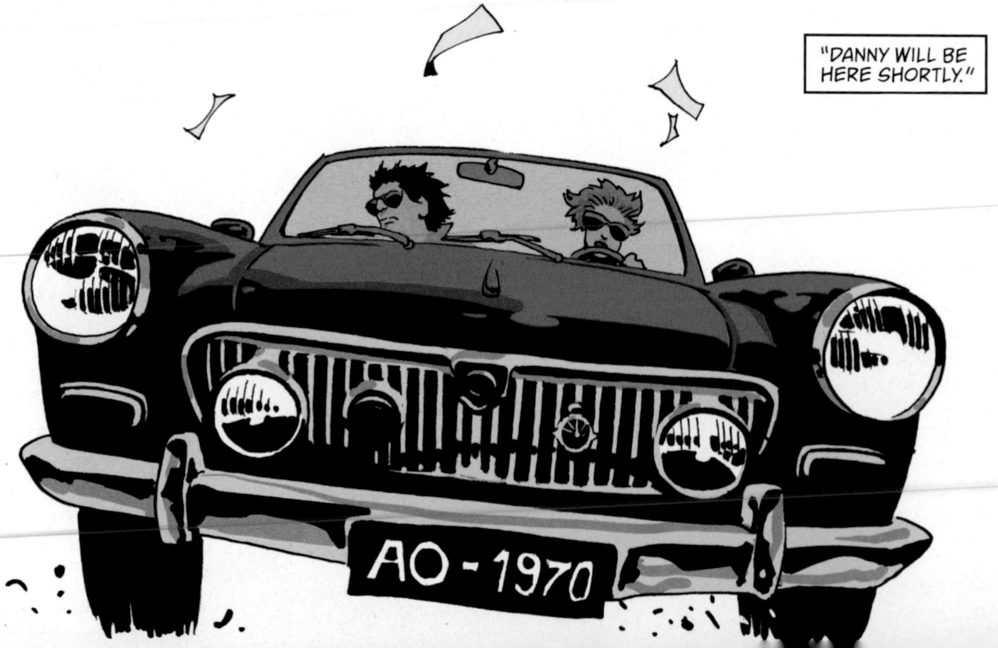
"DANNY WILL BE HERE SHORTLY."
AO - 1970

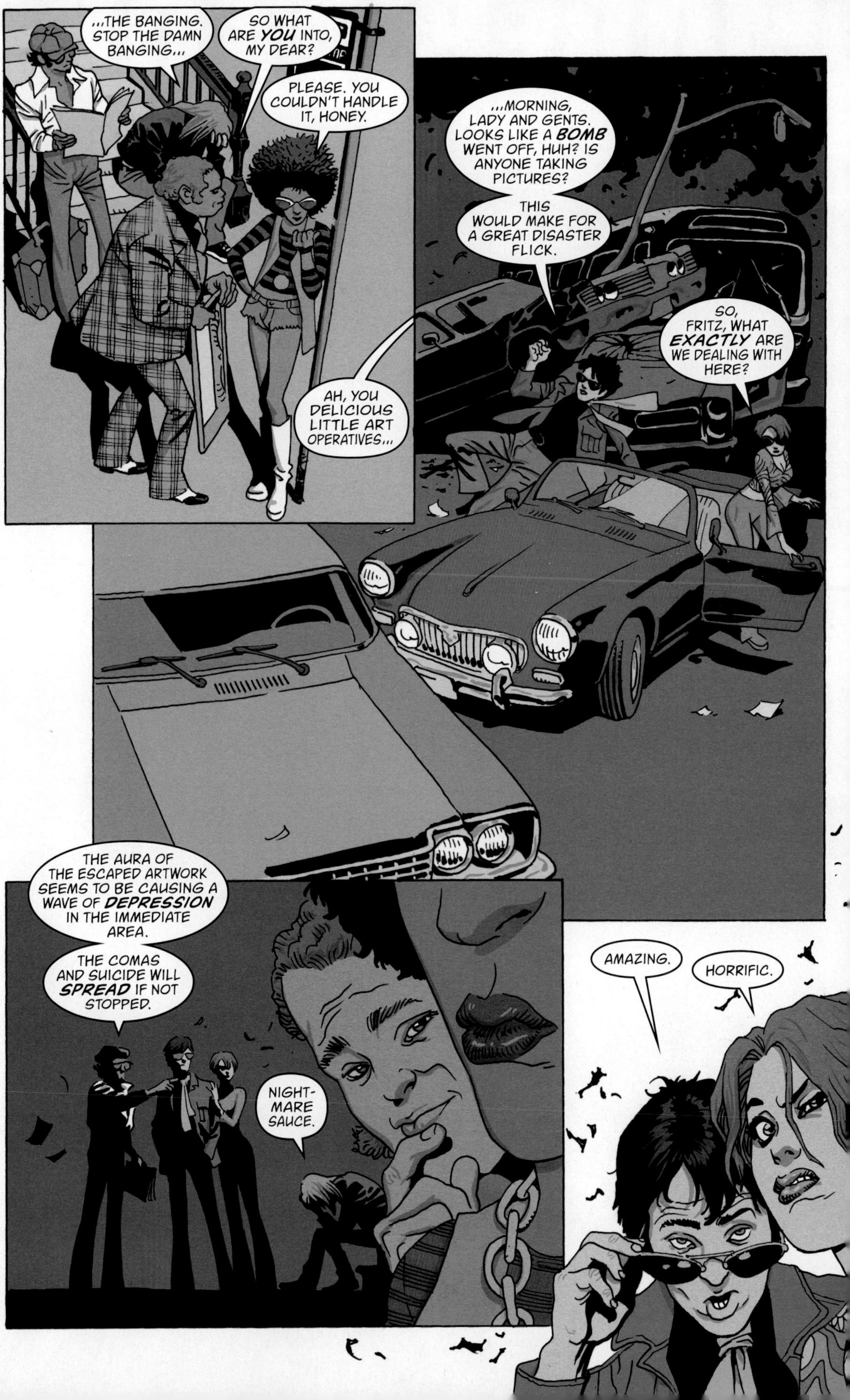
...THE BANGING. STOP THE DAMN BANGING...
SO WHAT ARE YOU INTO, MY DEAR?
PLEASE. YOU COULDN'T HANDLE IT, HONEY.
AH, YOU DELICIOUS LITTLE ART OPERATIVES...
...MORNING, LADY AND GENTS. LOOKS LIKE A BOMB WENT OFF, HUH? IS ANYONE TAKING PICTURES?
THIS WOULD MAKE FOR A GREAT DISASTER FLICK.
SO, FRITZ, WHAT EXACTLY ARE WE DEALING WITH HERE?
THE AURA OF THE ESCAPED ARTWORK SEEMS TO BE CAUSING A WAVE OF DEPRESSION IN THE IMMEDIATE AREA.
THE COMAS AND SUICIDE WILL SPREAD IF NOT STOPPED.
NIGHT-MARE SAUCE.
AMAZING.
HORRIFIC.

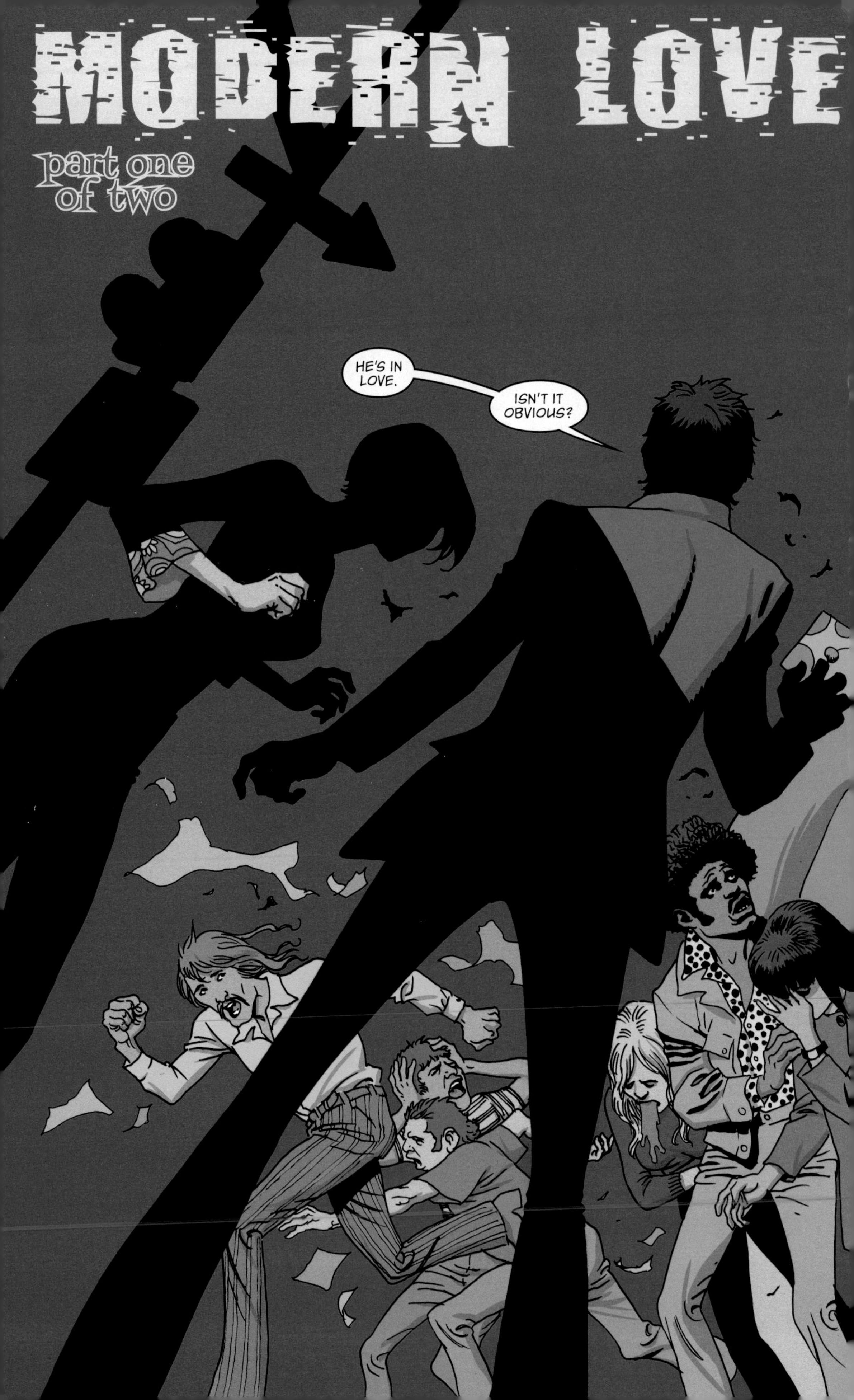
MODERN LOVE
part one of two
HE'S IN LOVE.
ISN'T IT OBVIOUS?

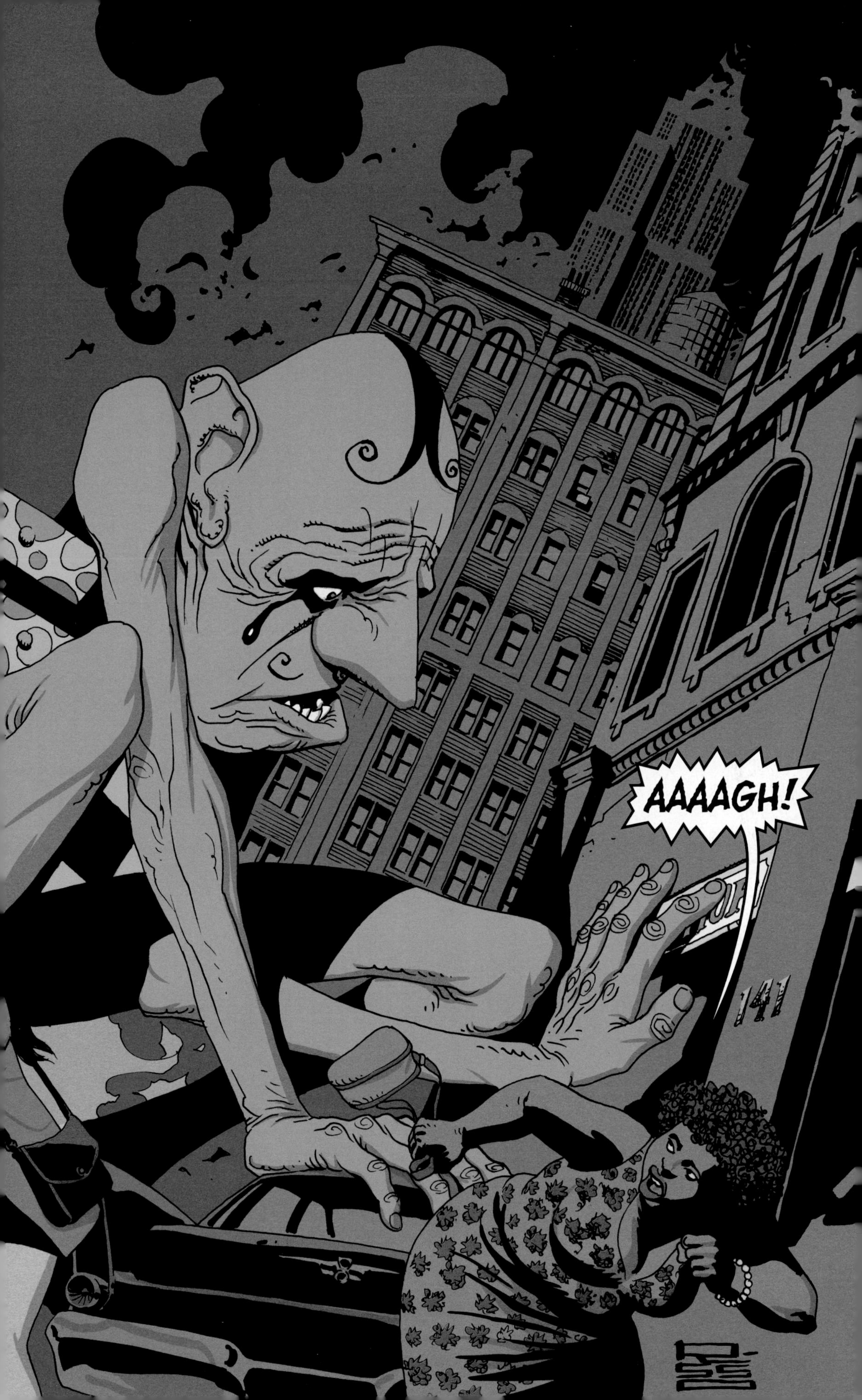
AAAAGH!
141

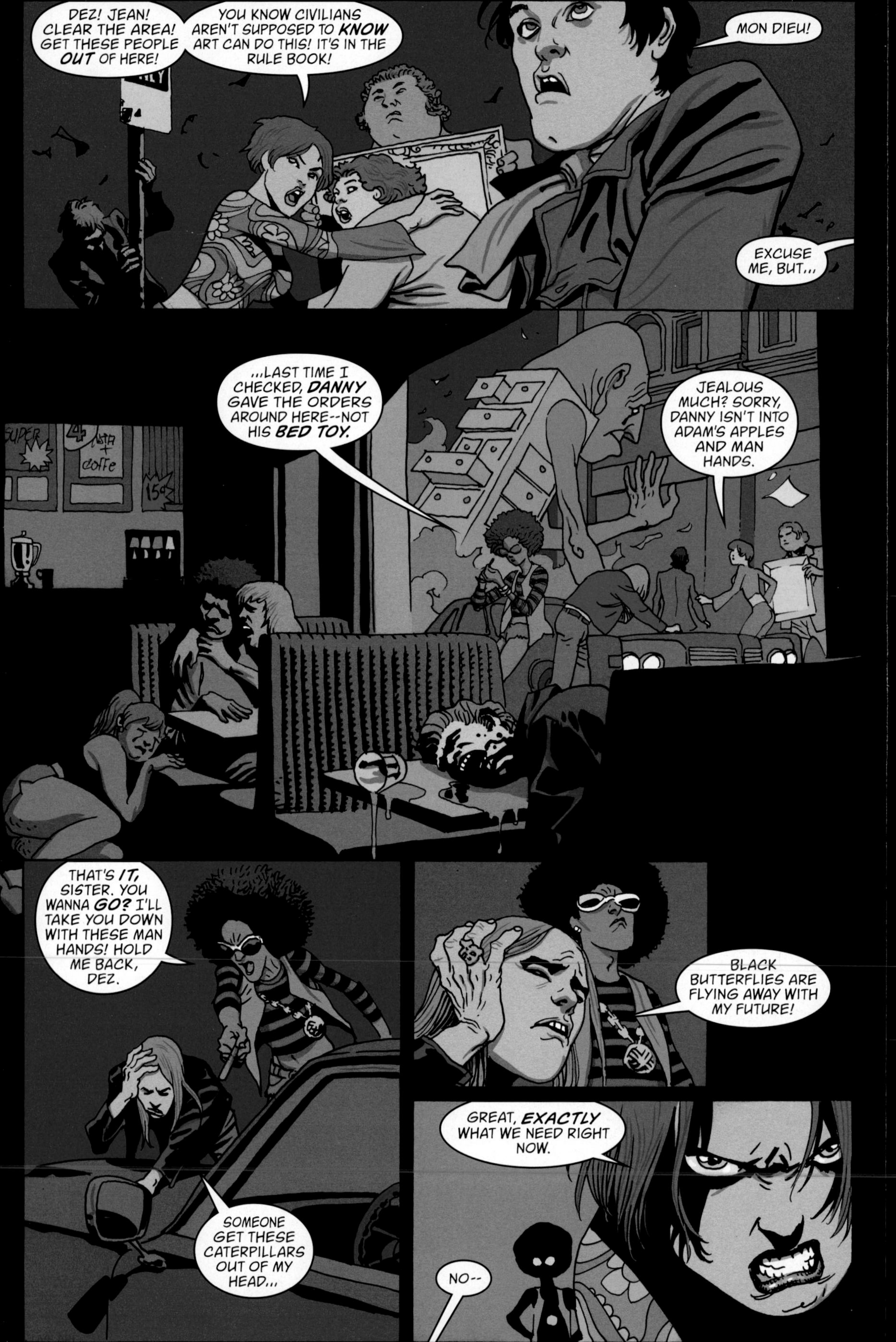
DEZ! JEAN! CLEAR THE AREA! GET THESE PEOPLE OUT OF HERE!
YOU KNOW CIVILIANS AREN'T SUPPOSED TO KNOW ART CAN DO THIS! IT'S IN THE RULE BOOK!
MON DIEU!
EXCUSE ME, BUT...
...LAST TIME I CHECKED, DANNY GAVE THE ORDERS AROUND HERE--NOT HIS BED TOY.
JEALOUS MUCH? SORRY, DANNY ISN'T INTO ADAM'S APPLES AND MAN HANDS.
THAT'S IT, SISTER. YOU WANNA GO? I'LL TAKE YOU DOWN WITH THESE MAN HANDS! HOLD ME BACK, DEZ.
SOMEONE GET THESE CATERPILLARS OUT OF MY HEAD...
BLACK BUTTERFLIES ARE FLYING AWAY WITH MY FUTURE!
GREAT, EXACTLY WHAT WE NEED RIGHT NOW.
NO--

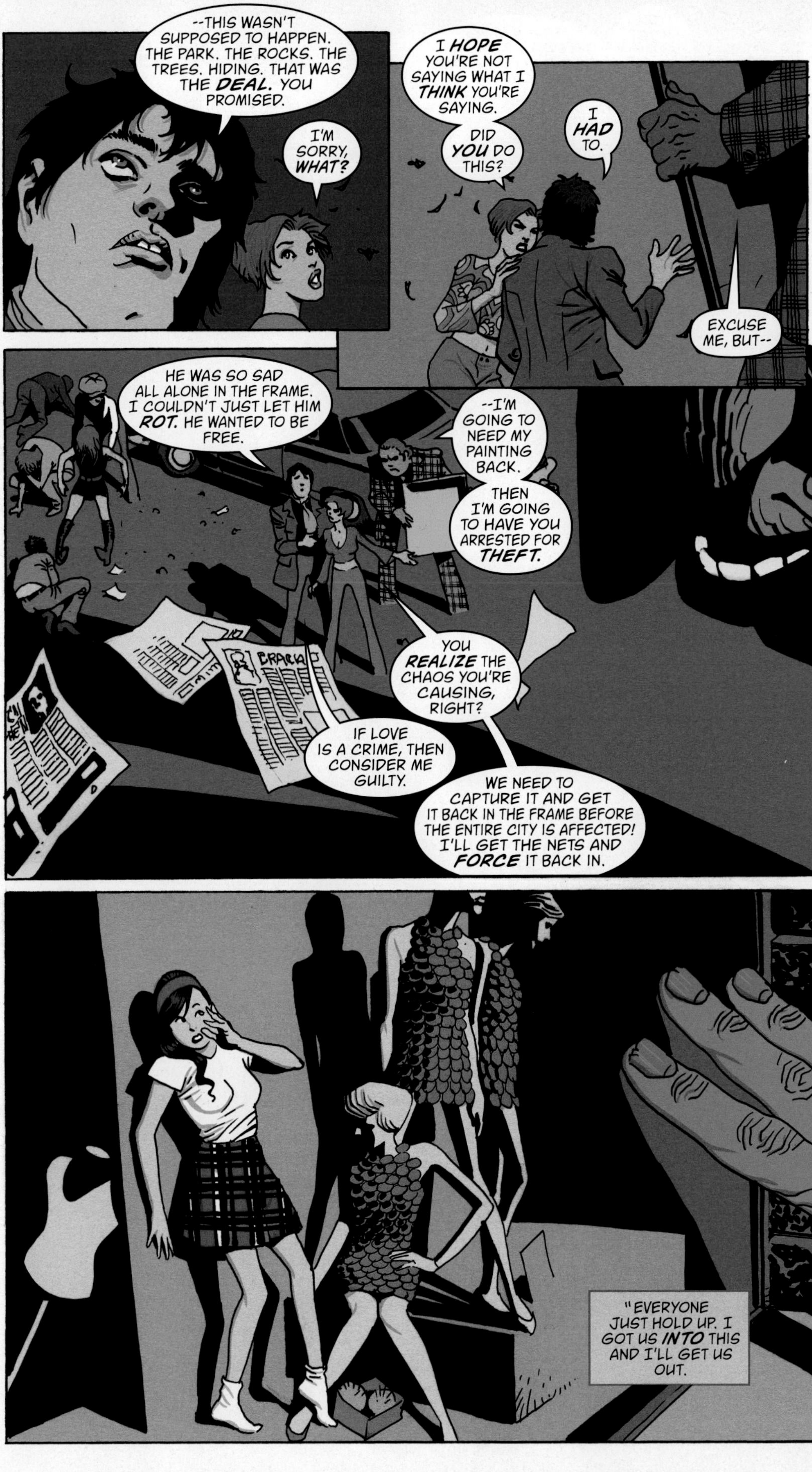
--THIS WASN'T SUPPOSED TO HAPPEN. THE PARK. THE ROCKS. THE TREES. HIDING. THAT WAS THE DEAL. YOU PROMISED.
I'M SORRY, WHAT?
I HOPE YOU'RE NOT SAYING WHAT I THINK YOU'RE SAYING.
DID YOU DO THIS?
I HAD TO.
EXCUSE ME, BUT--
HE WAS SO SAD ALL ALONE IN THE FRAME. I COULDN'T JUST LET HIM ROT. HE WANTED TO BE FREE.
--I'M GOING TO NEED MY PAINTING BACK.
THEN I'M GOING TO HAVE YOU ARRESTED FOR THEFT.
YOU REALIZE THE CHAOS YOU'RE CAUSING, RIGHT?
IF LOVE IS A CRIME, THEN CONSIDER ME GUILTY.
WE NEED TO CAPTURE IT AND GET IT BACK IN THE FRAME BEFORE THE ENTIRE CITY IS AFFECTED! I'LL GET THE NETS AND FORCE IT BACK IN.
"EVERYONE JUST HOLD UP. I GOT US INTO THIS AND I'LL GET US OUT.

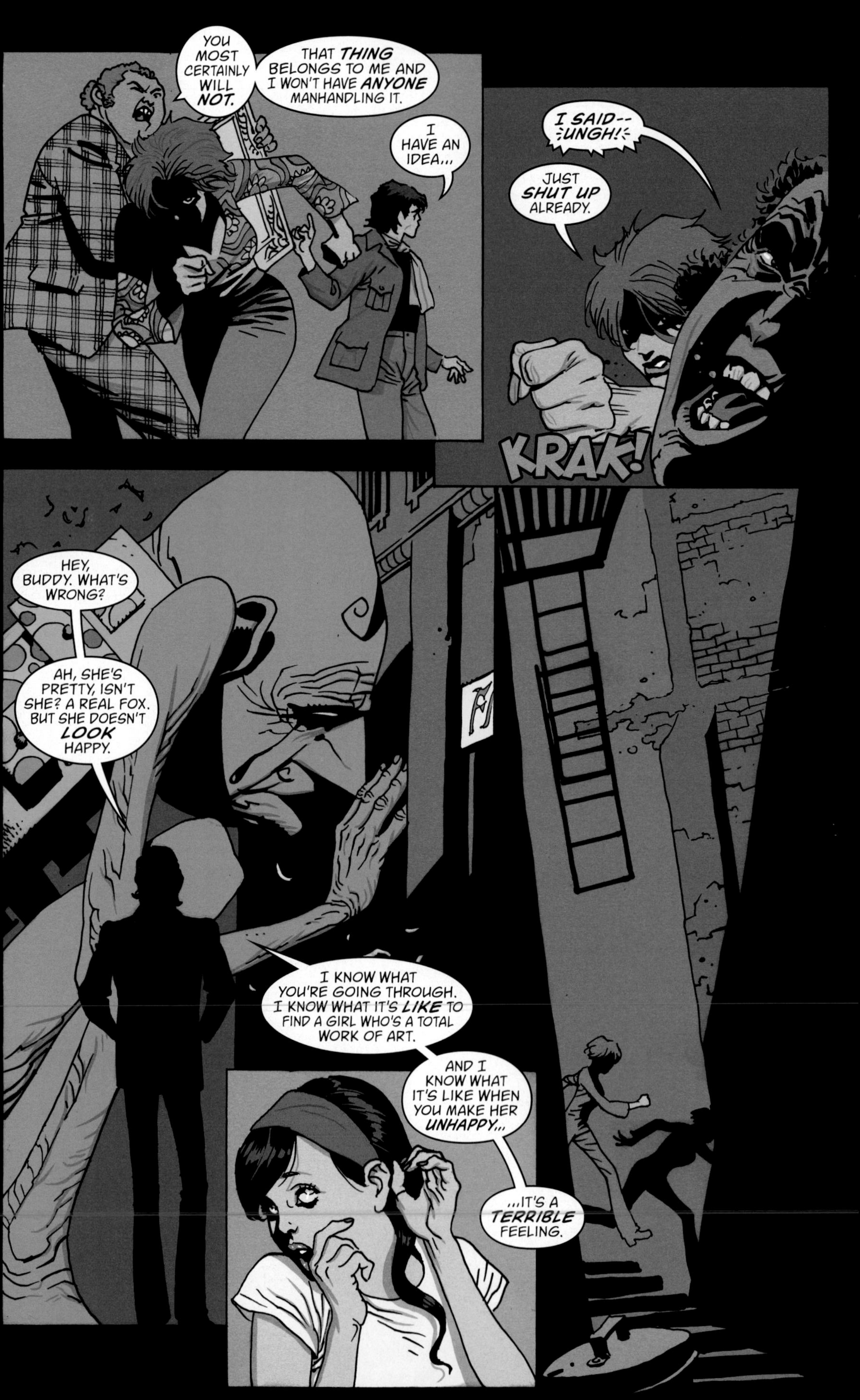
YOU MOST CERTAINLY WILL NOT.
THAT THING BELONGS TO ME AND I WON'T HAVE ANYONE MANHANDLING IT.
I HAVE AN IDEA...
I SAID-- UNGH!
JUST SHUT UP ALREADY.
KRAK!
HEY, BUDDY. WHAT'S WRONG?
AH, SHE'S PRETTY, ISN'T SHE? A REAL FOX. BUT SHE DOESN'T LOOK HAPPY.
I KNOW WHAT YOU'RE GOING THROUGH. I KNOW WHAT IT'S LIKE TO FIND A GIRL WHO'S A TOTAL WORK OF ART.
AND I KNOW WHAT IT'S LIKE WHEN YOU MAKE HER UNHAPPY...
...IT'S A TERRIBLE FEELING.

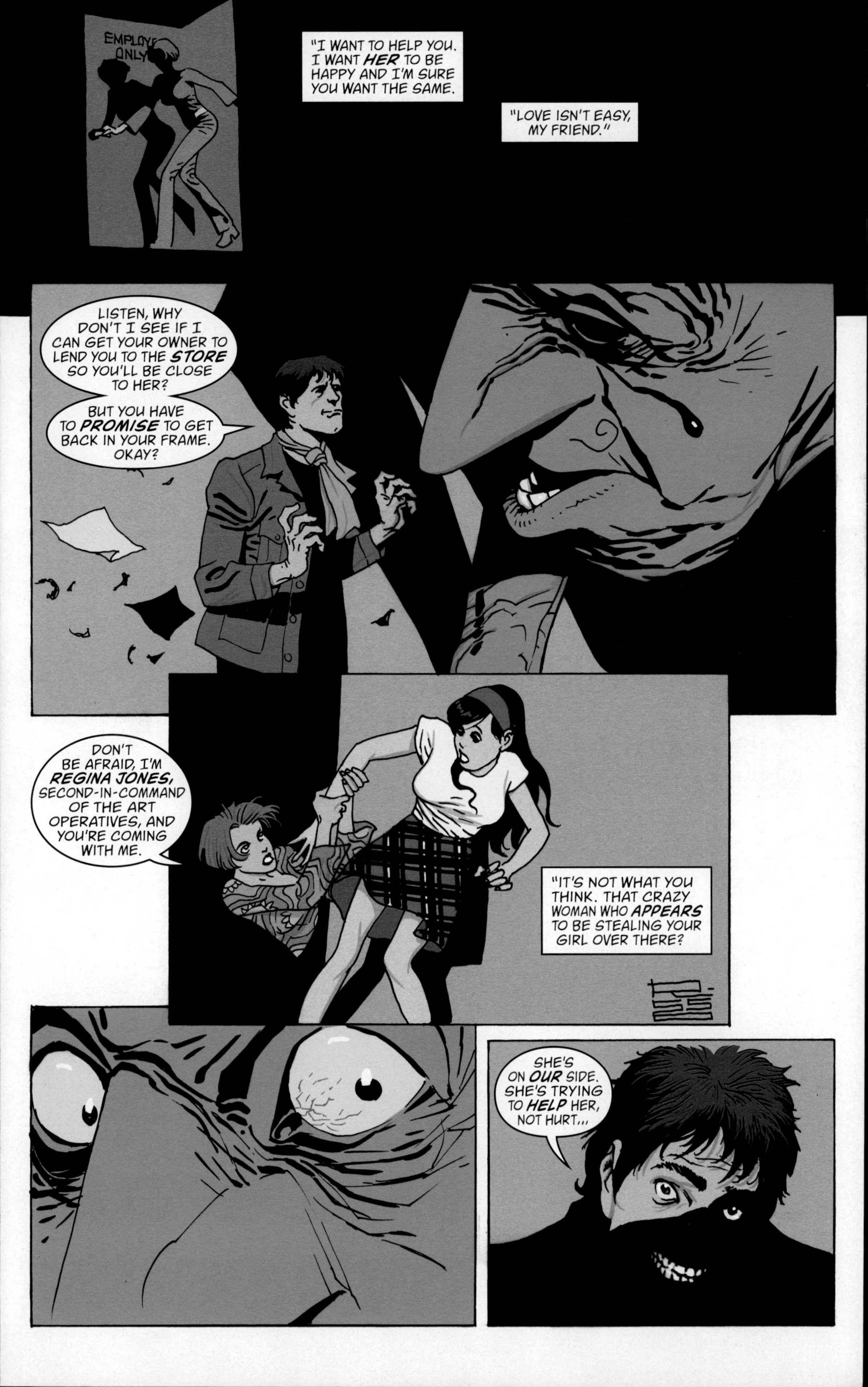
EMPLOYEES ONLY
"I WANT TO HELP YOU. I WANT HER TO BE HAPPY AND I'M SURE YOU WANT THE SAME.
"LOVE ISN'T EASY, MY FRIEND."
LISTEN, WHY DON'T I SEE IF I CAN GET YOUR OWNER TO LEND YOU TO THE STORE SO YOU'LL BE CLOSE TO HER?
BUT YOU HAVE TO PROMISE TO GET BACK IN YOUR FRAME. OKAY?
DON'T BE AFRAID, I'M REGINA JONES, SECOND-IN-COMMAND OF THE ART OPERATIVES, AND YOU'RE COMING WITH ME.
"IT'S NOT WHAT YOU THINK. THAT CRAZY WOMAN WHO APPEARS TO BE STEALING YOUR GIRL OVER THERE?
SHE'S ON OUR SIDE. SHE'S TRYING TO HELP HER, NOT HURT...

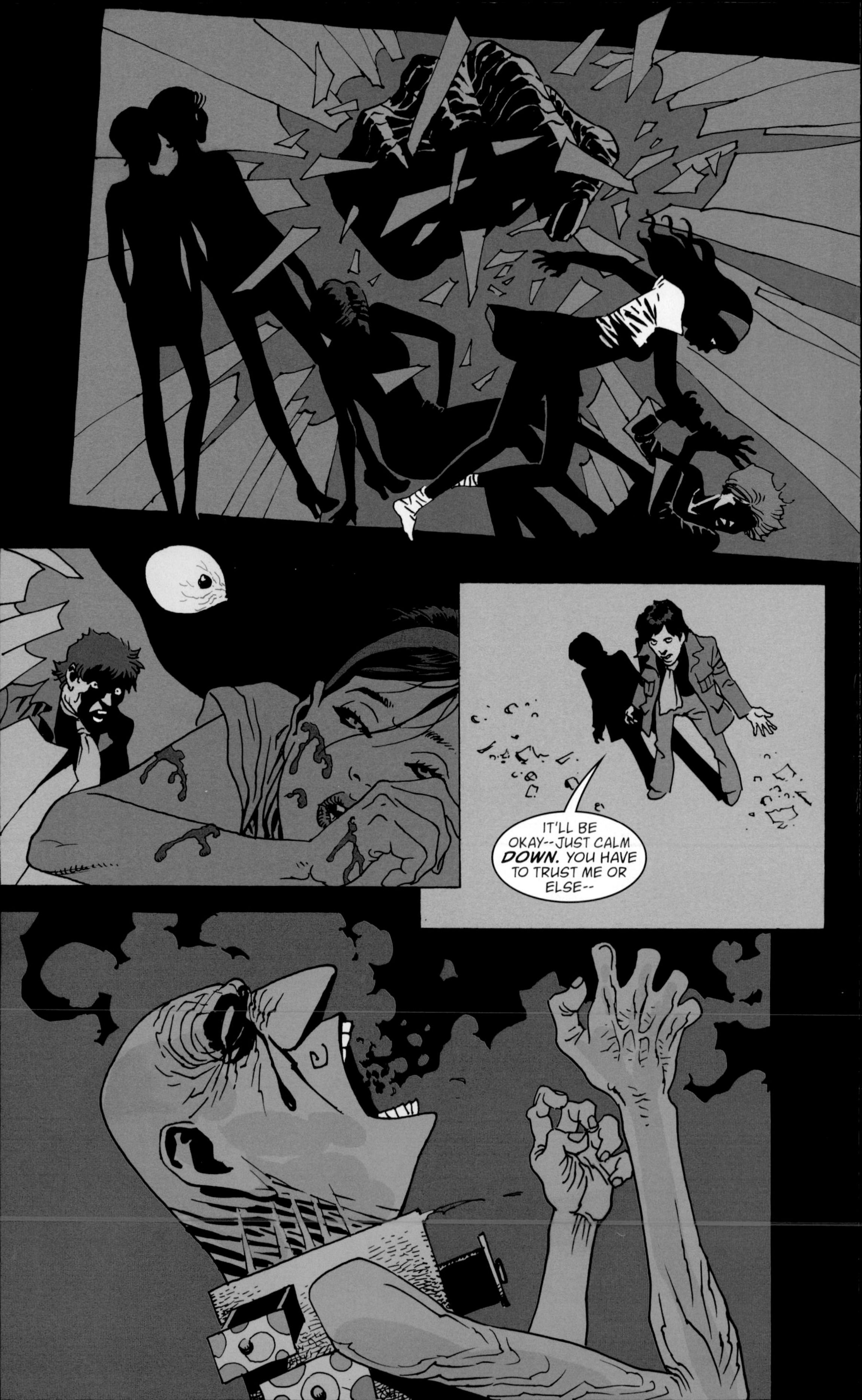
IT'LL BE OKAY--JUST CALM **DOWN.** YOU HAVE TO TRUST ME OR ELSE--

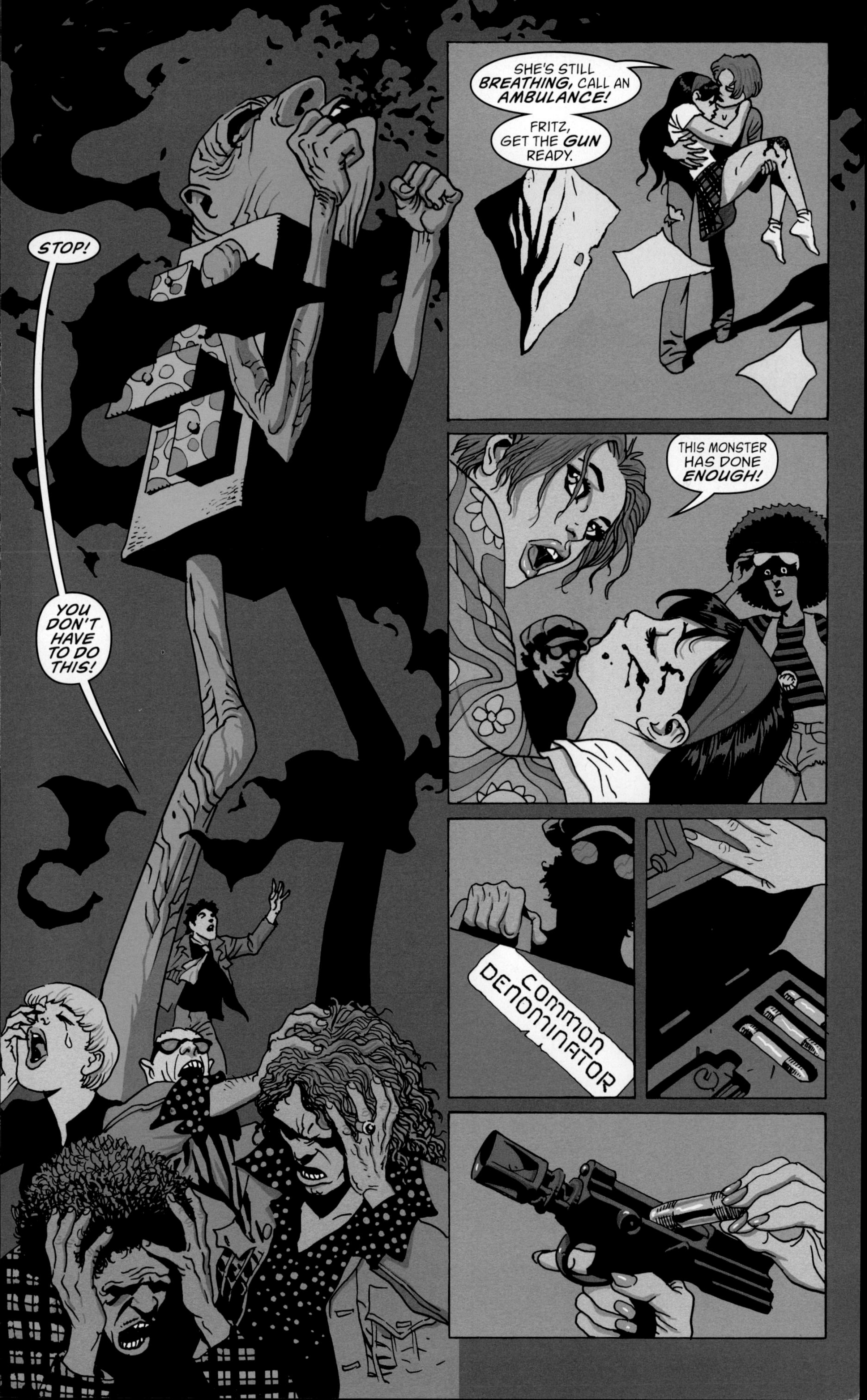
STOP!
YOU DON'T HAVE TO DO THIS!
SHE'S STILL BREATHING, CALL AN AMBULANCE!
FRITZ, GET THE GUN READY.
THIS MONSTER HAS DONE ENOUGH!
COMMON DENOMINATOR

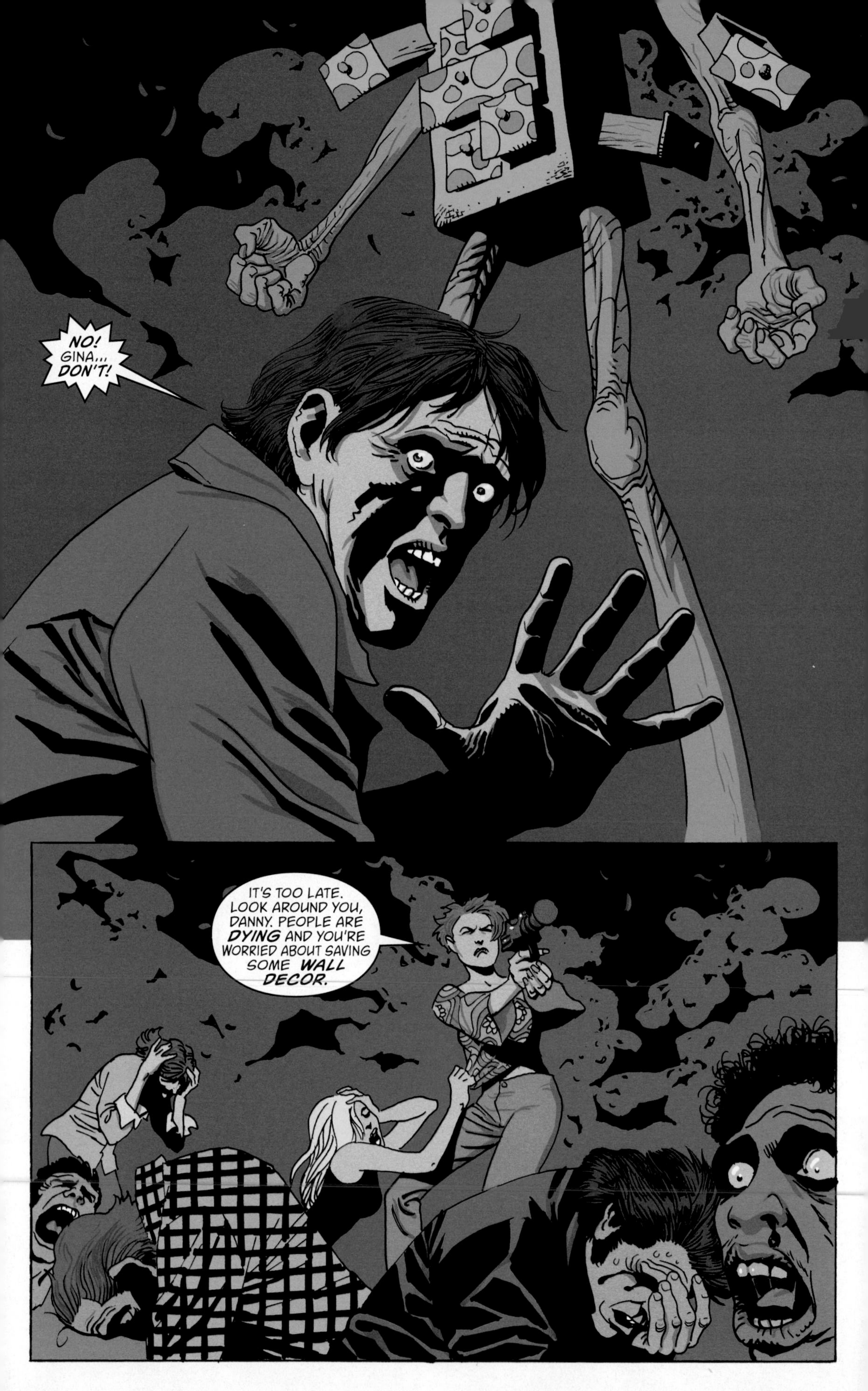
NO! GINA... DON'T!
IT'S TOO LATE. LOOK AROUND YOU, DANNY. PEOPLE ARE DYING AND YOU'RE WORRIED ABOUT SAVING SOME WALL DECOR.

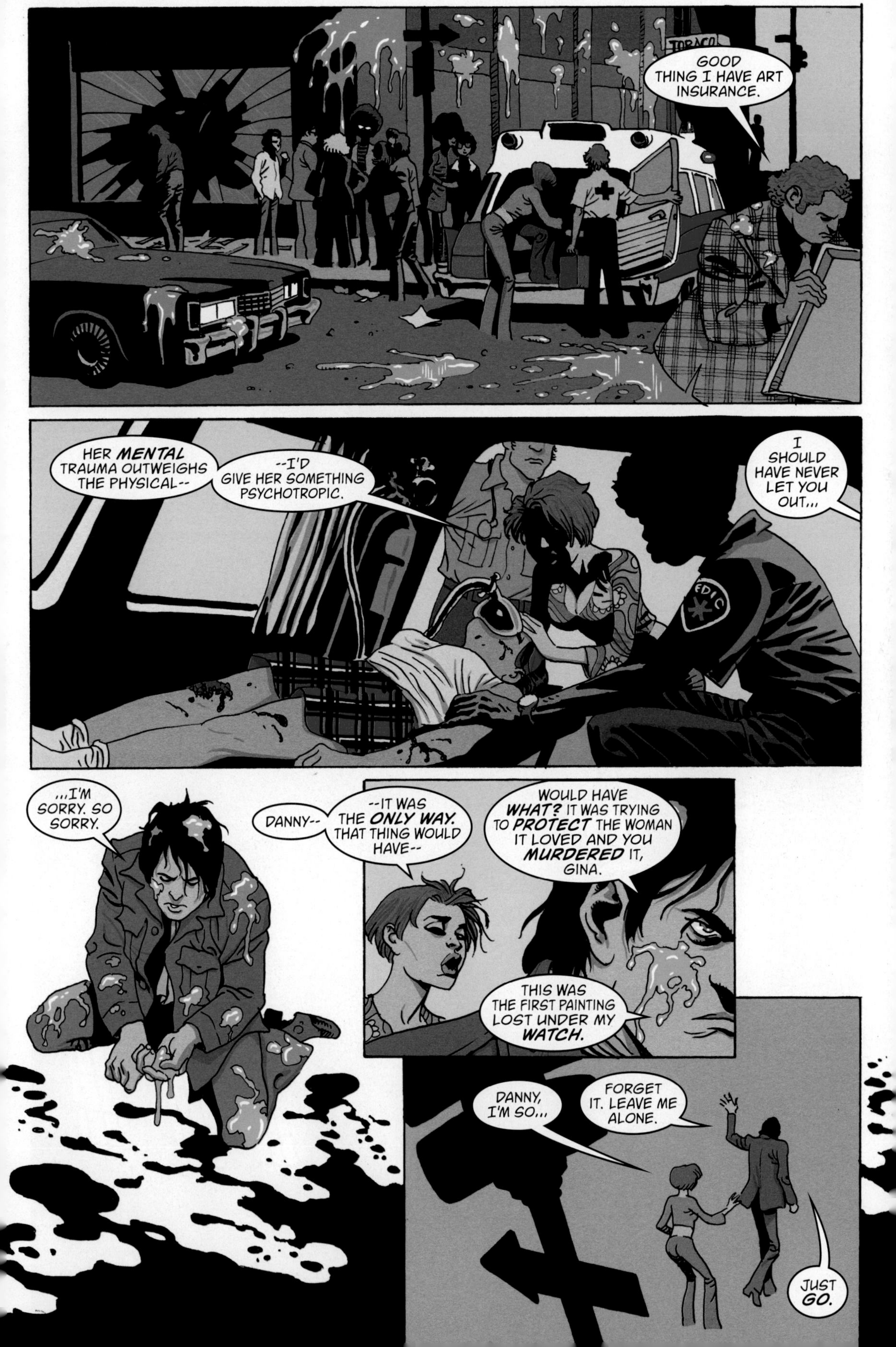
GOOD THING I HAVE ART INSURANCE.
HER MENTAL TRAUMA OUTWEIGHS THE PHYSICAL--
--I'D GIVE HER SOMETHING PSYCHOTROPIC.
I SHOULD HAVE NEVER LET YOU OUT...
...I'M SORRY. SO SORRY.
DANNY--
--IT WAS THE ONLY WAY. THAT THING WOULD HAVE--
WOULD HAVE WHAT? IT WAS TRYING TO PROTECT THE WOMAN IT LOVED AND YOU MURDERED IT, GINA.
THIS WAS THE FIRST PAINTING LOST UNDER MY WATCH.
DANNY, I'M SO...
FORGET IT. LEAVE ME ALONE.
JUST GO.

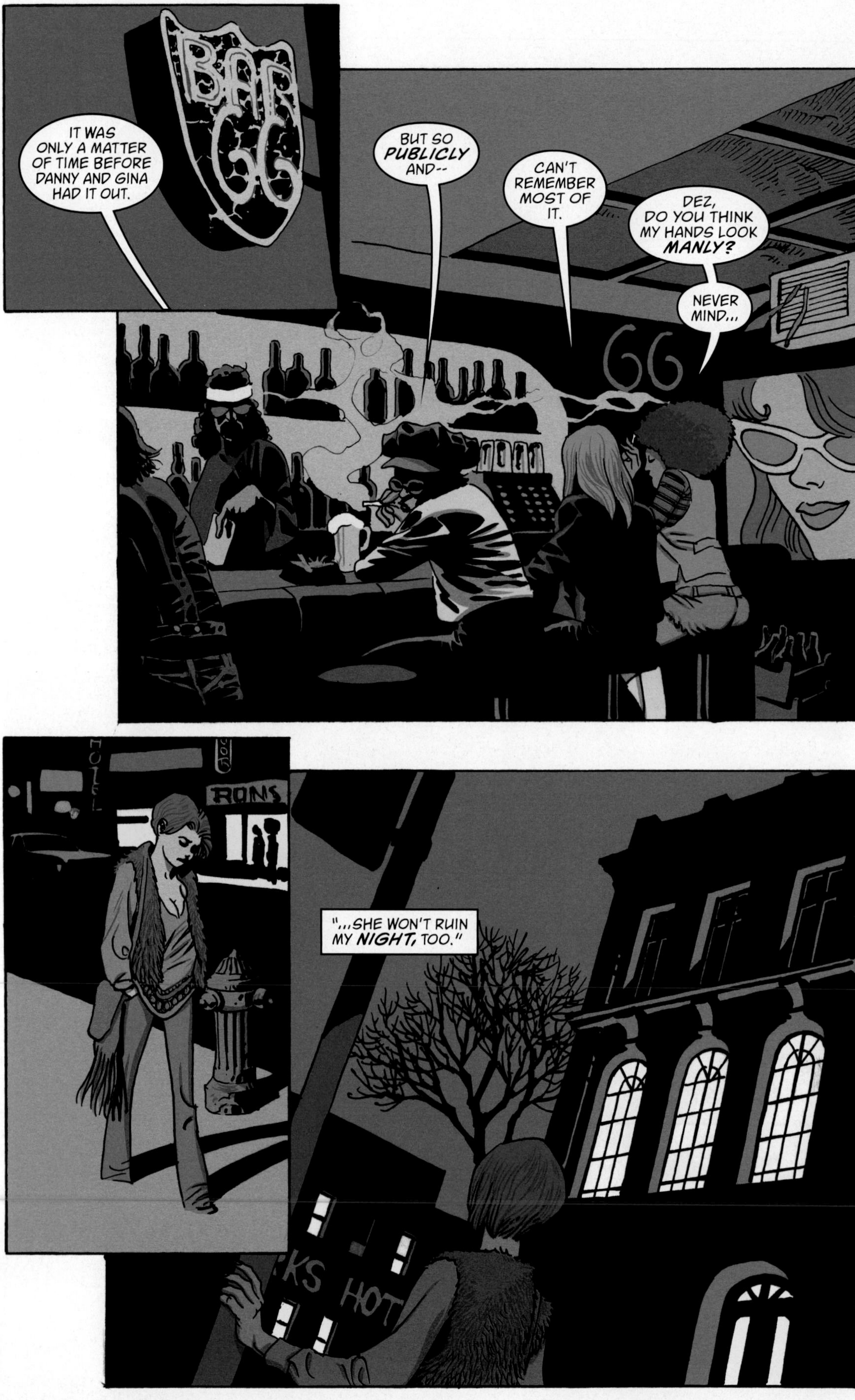
BAR 66
IT WAS ONLY A MATTER OF TIME BEFORE DANNY AND GINA HAD IT OUT.
BUT SO *PUBLICLY* AND--
CAN'T REMEMBER MOST OF IT.
DEZ, DO YOU THINK MY HANDS LOOK ***MANLY?***
NEVER MIND...
66
HOTEL
RONS
"...SHE WON'T RUIN MY ***NIGHT,*** TOO."
KS HOT

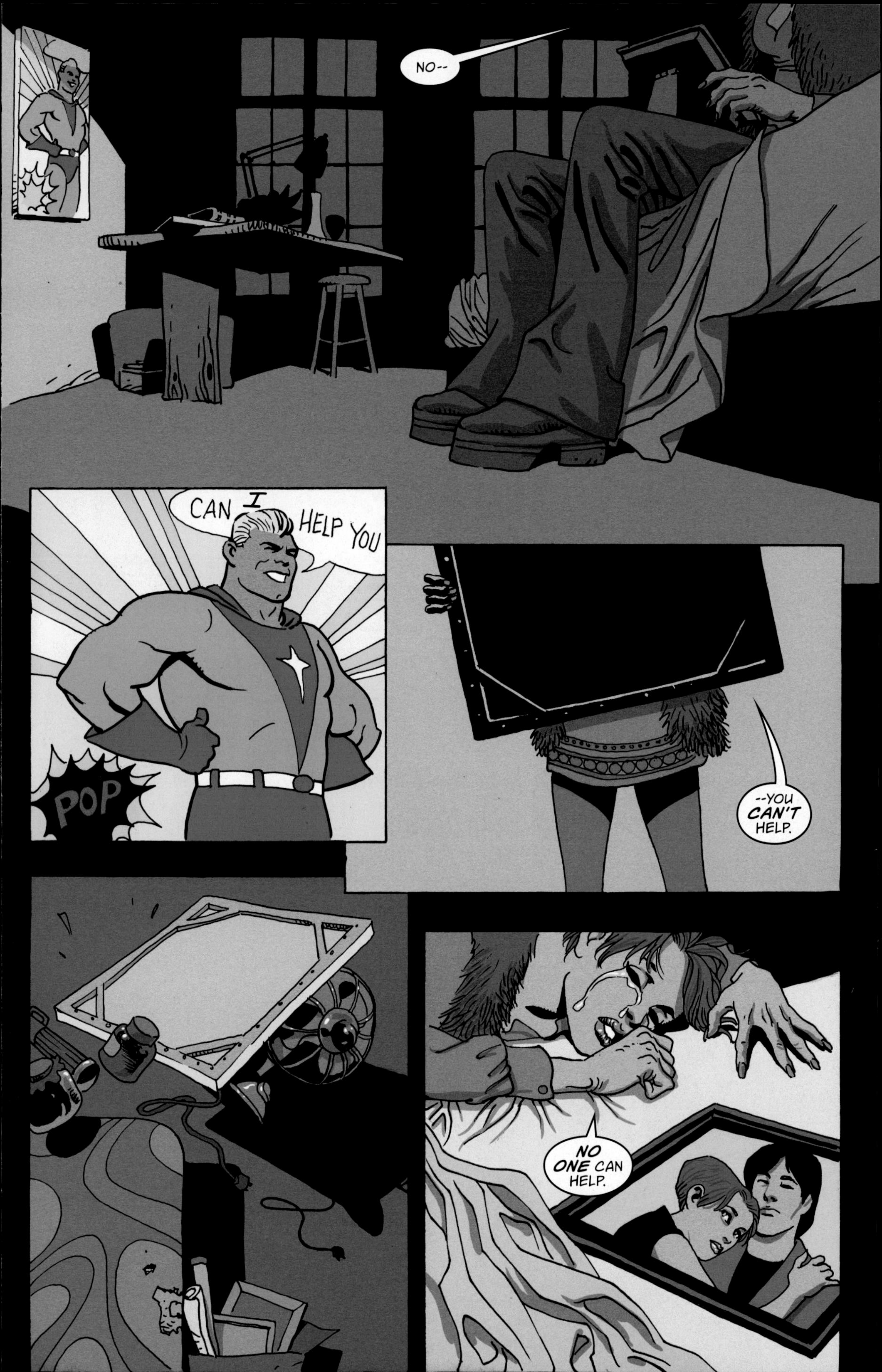

NO--
CAN I HELP YOU
POP
--YOU CAN'T HELP.
NO ONE CAN HELP.

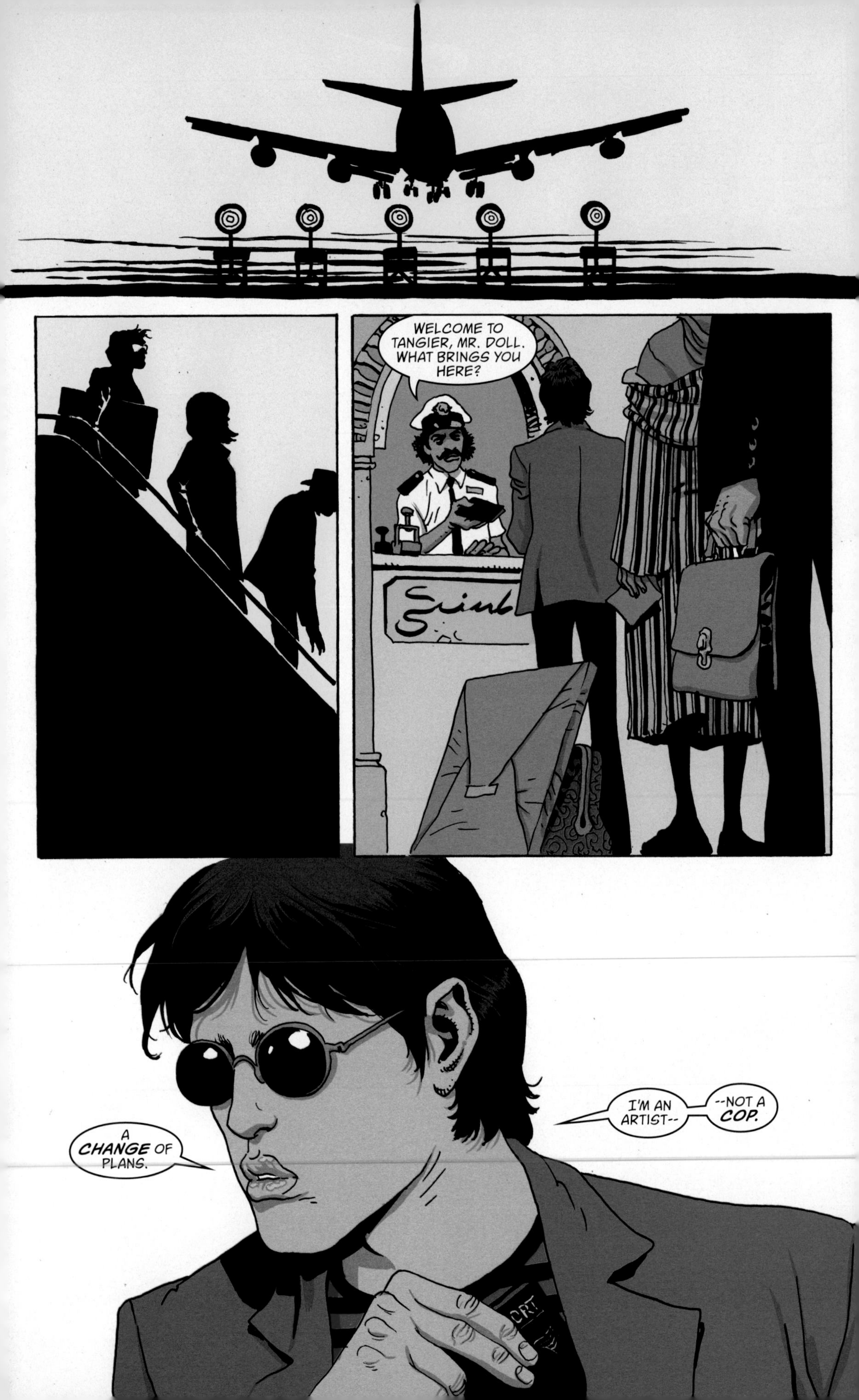
WELCOME TO TANGIER, MR. DOLL. WHAT BRINGS YOU HERE?
A CHANGE OF PLANS.
I'M AN ARTIST--
--NOT A COP.

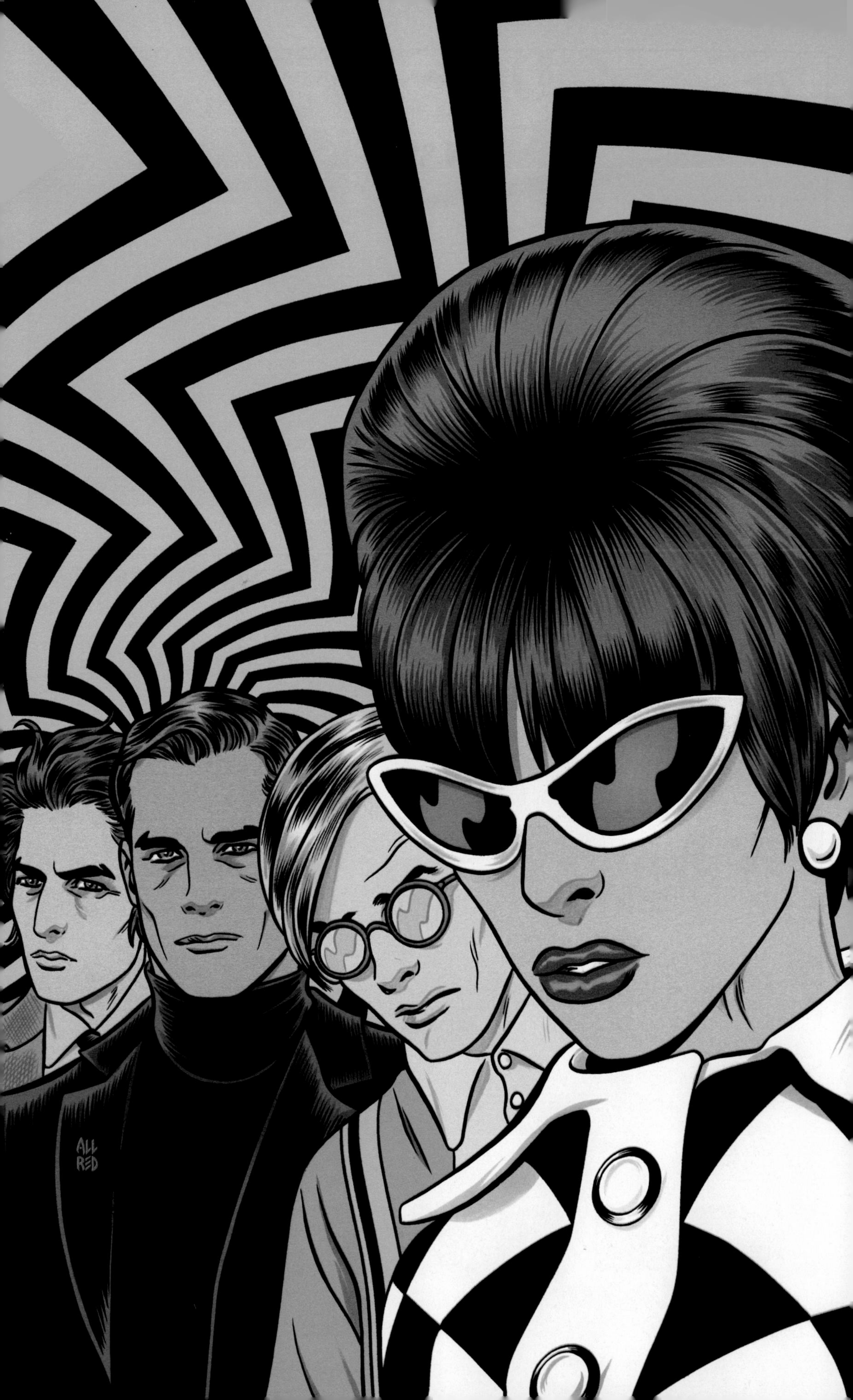
ALL RED

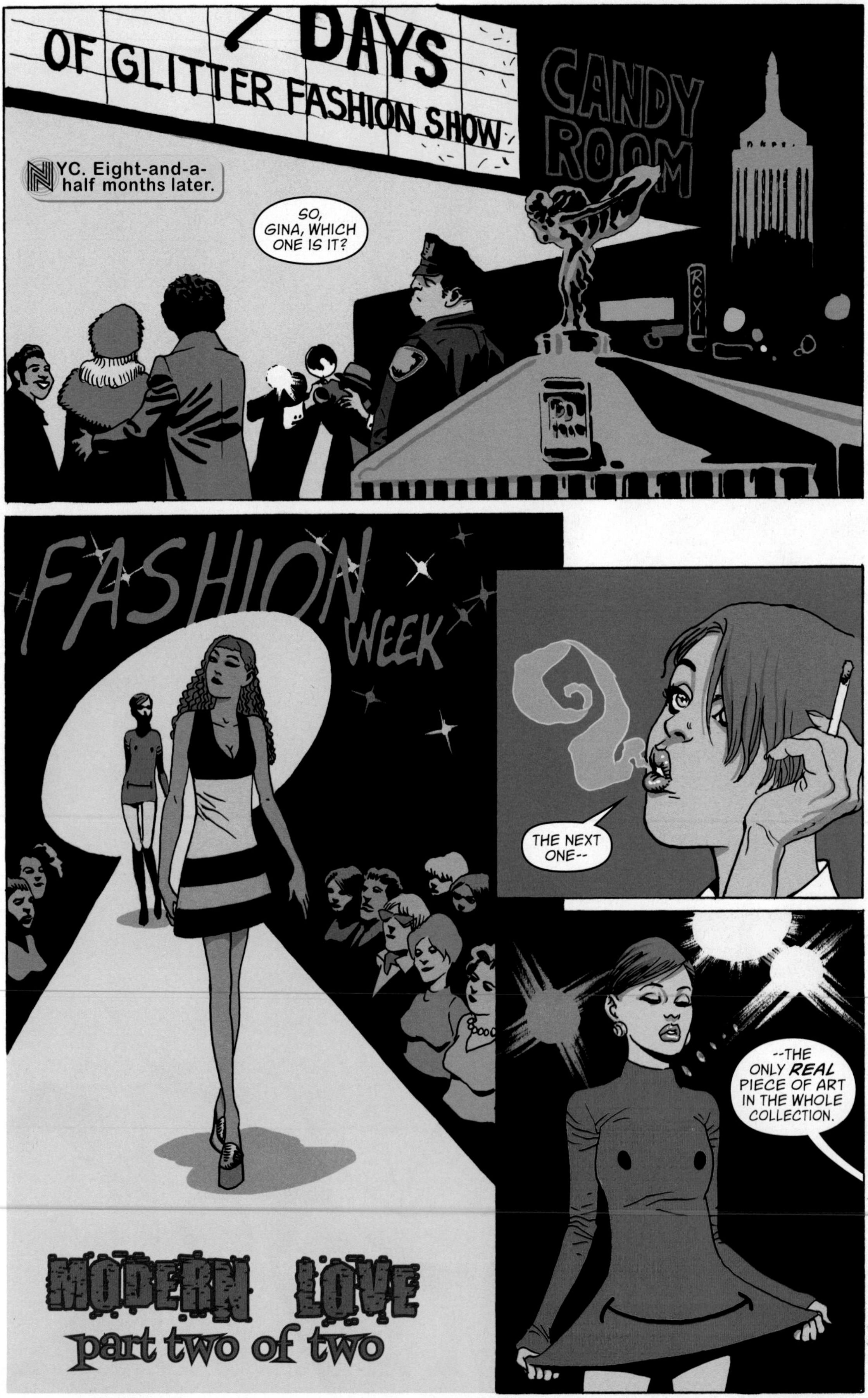
7 DAYS
OF GLITTER FASHION SHOW
CANDY ROOM
NYC. Eight-and-a-half months later.
SO, GINA, WHICH ONE IS IT?
ROXI
FASHION WEEK
THE NEXT ONE--
--THE ONLY *REAL* PIECE OF ART IN THE WHOLE COLLECTION.
MODERN LOVE
part two of two

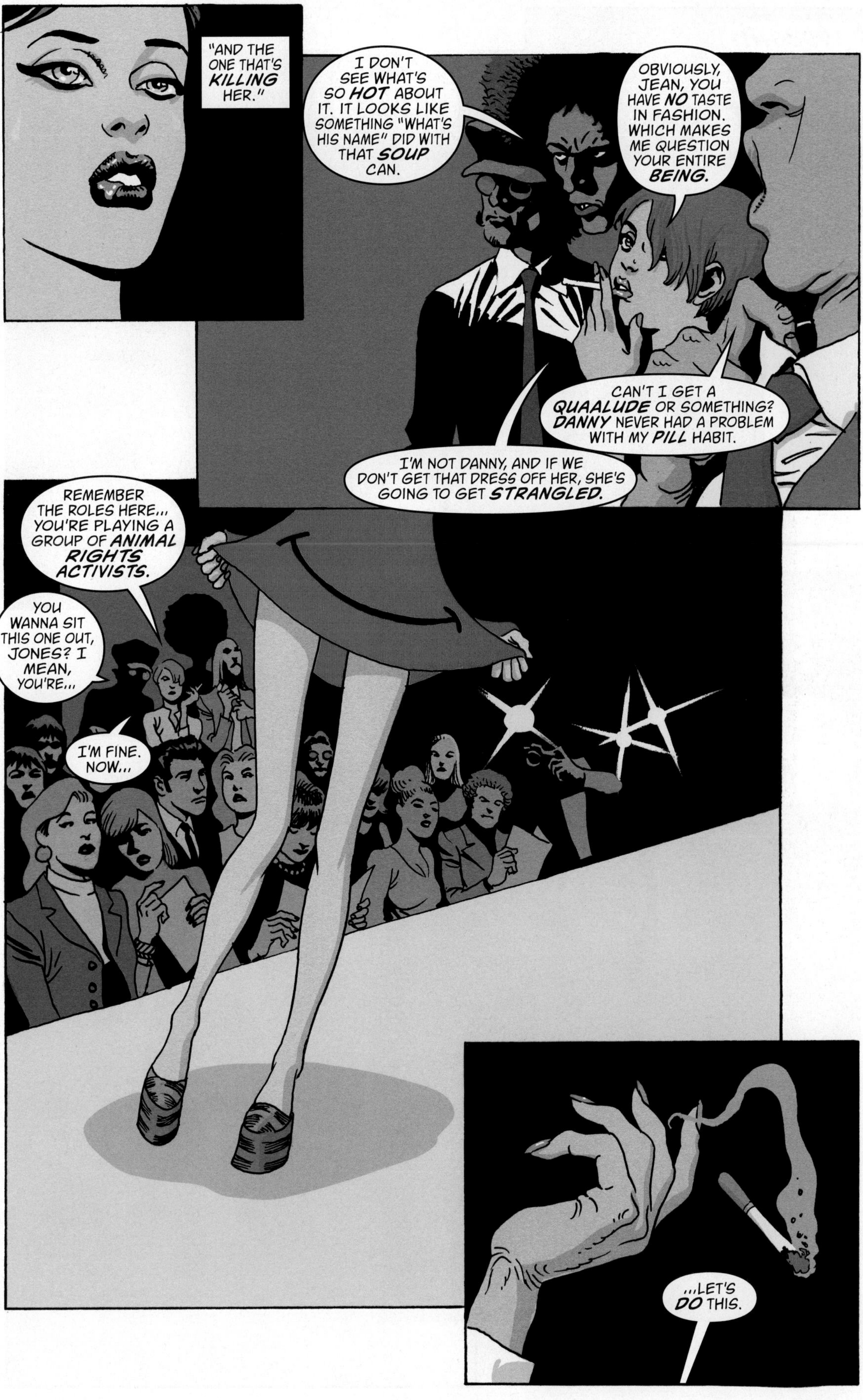
"AND THE ONE THAT'S KILLING HER."
I DON'T SEE WHAT'S SO HOT ABOUT IT. IT LOOKS LIKE SOMETHING "WHAT'S HIS NAME" DID WITH THAT SOUP CAN.
OBVIOUSLY, JEAN, YOU HAVE NO TASTE IN FASHION. WHICH MAKES ME QUESTION YOUR ENTIRE BEING.
CAN'T I GET A QUAALUDE OR SOMETHING? DANNY NEVER HAD A PROBLEM WITH MY PILL HABIT.
I'M NOT DANNY, AND IF WE DON'T GET THAT DRESS OFF HER, SHE'S GOING TO GET STRANGLED.
REMEMBER THE ROLES HERE... YOU'RE PLAYING A GROUP OF ANIMAL RIGHTS ACTIVISTS.
YOU WANNA SIT THIS ONE OUT, JONES? I MEAN, YOU'RE...
I'M FINE. NOW...
...LET'S DO THIS.

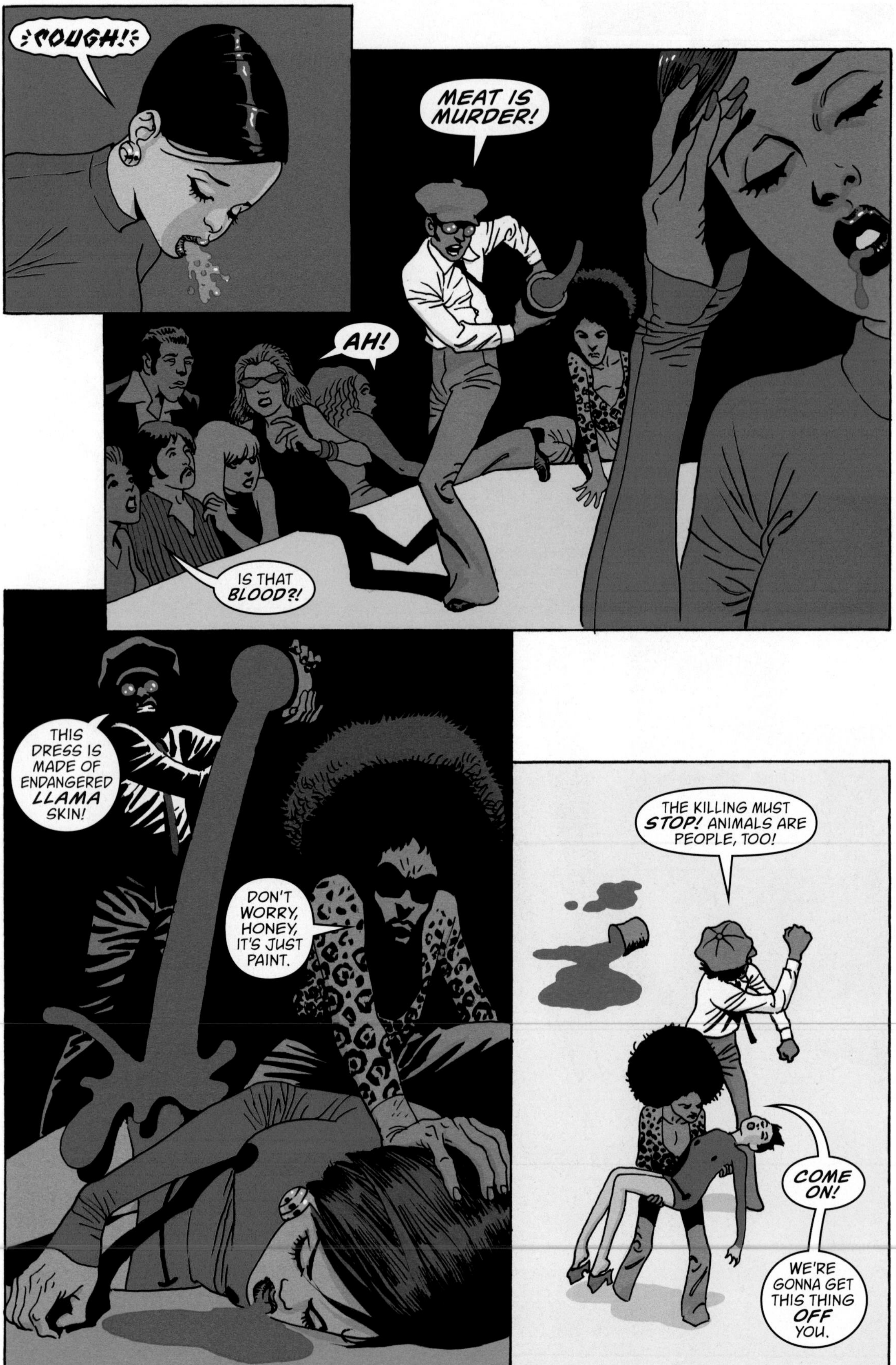
COUGH!
MEAT IS MURDER!
AH!
IS THAT BLOOD?!
THIS DRESS IS MADE OF ENDANGERED LLAMA SKIN!
DON'T WORRY, HONEY, IT'S JUST PAINT.
THE KILLING MUST STOP! ANIMALS ARE PEOPLE, TOO!
COME ON!
WE'RE GONNA GET THIS THING OFF YOU.

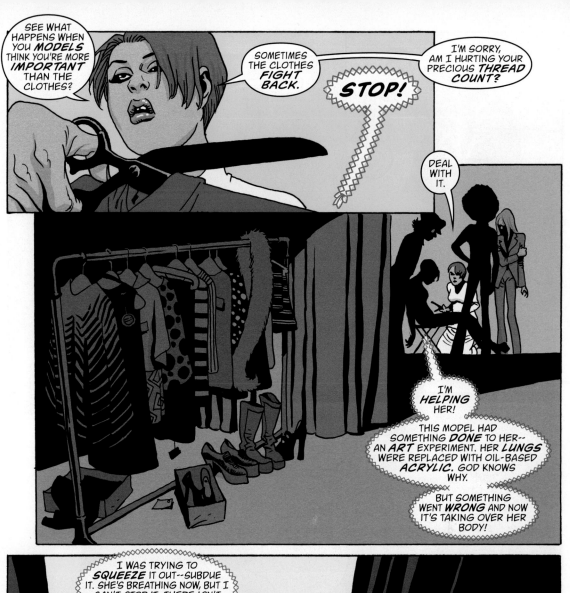

SEE WHAT HAPPENS WHEN YOU *MODELS* THINK YOU'RE MORE *IMPORTANT* THAN THE CLOTHES?

SOMETIMES THE CLOTHES *FIGHT BACK.*

STOP!

I'M SORRY, AM I HURTING YOUR PRECIOUS *THREAD COUNT?*

DEAL WITH IT.

I'M *HELPING* HER!

THIS MODEL HAD SOMETHING *DONE* TO HER-- AN *ART* EXPERIMENT. HER *LUNGS* WERE REPLACED WITH OIL-BASED *ACRYLIC.* GOD KNOWS WHY.

BUT SOMETHING WENT *WRONG* AND NOW IT'S TAKING OVER HER BODY!

I WAS TRYING TO *SQUEEZE* IT OUT--SUBDUE IT. SHE'S BREATHING NOW, BUT I CAN'T STOP IT. THERE ISN'T MUCH TIME. SHE'S *DYING.*

WHERE WAS THIS DONE?

TANGIER. THERE'S A PASSPORT IN HER PURSE.

JEAN, HAND ME MY BAG.

EXCUSE ME?

OR WOULD YOU *PREFER* I THROW UP DOWN YOUR BLOUSE?

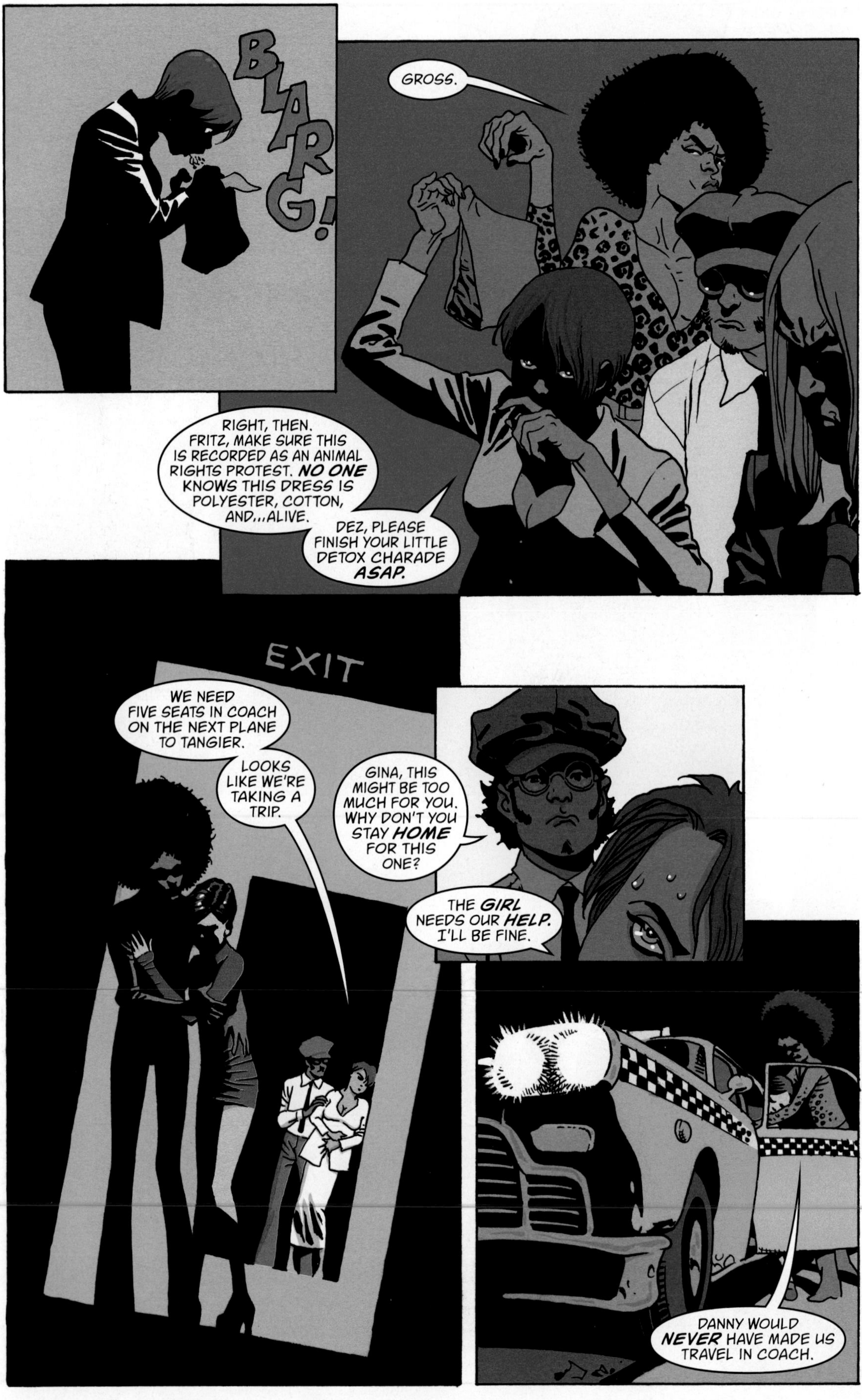
BLARG!
GROSS.
RIGHT, THEN. FRITZ, MAKE SURE THIS IS RECORDED AS AN ANIMAL RIGHTS PROTEST. NO ONE KNOWS THIS DRESS IS POLYESTER, COTTON, AND...ALIVE.
DEZ, PLEASE FINISH YOUR LITTLE DETOX CHARADE ASAP.
EXIT
WE NEED FIVE SEATS IN COACH ON THE NEXT PLANE TO TANGIER.
LOOKS LIKE WE'RE TAKING A TRIP.
GINA, THIS MIGHT BE TOO MUCH FOR YOU. WHY DON'T YOU STAY HOME FOR THIS ONE?
THE GIRL NEEDS OUR HELP. I'LL BE FINE.
DANNY WOULD NEVER HAVE MADE US TRAVEL IN COACH.

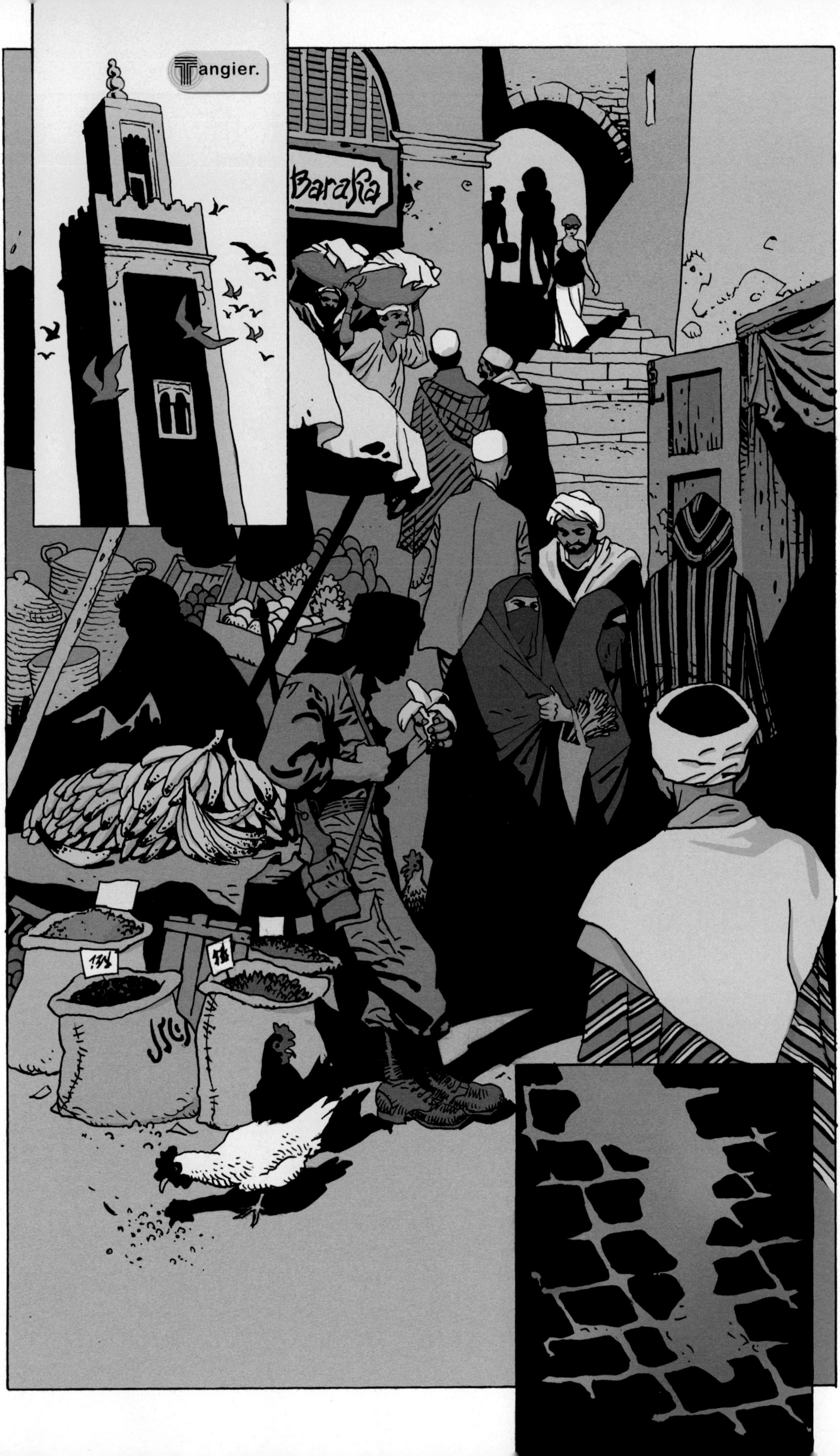
Tangier.
Baraka

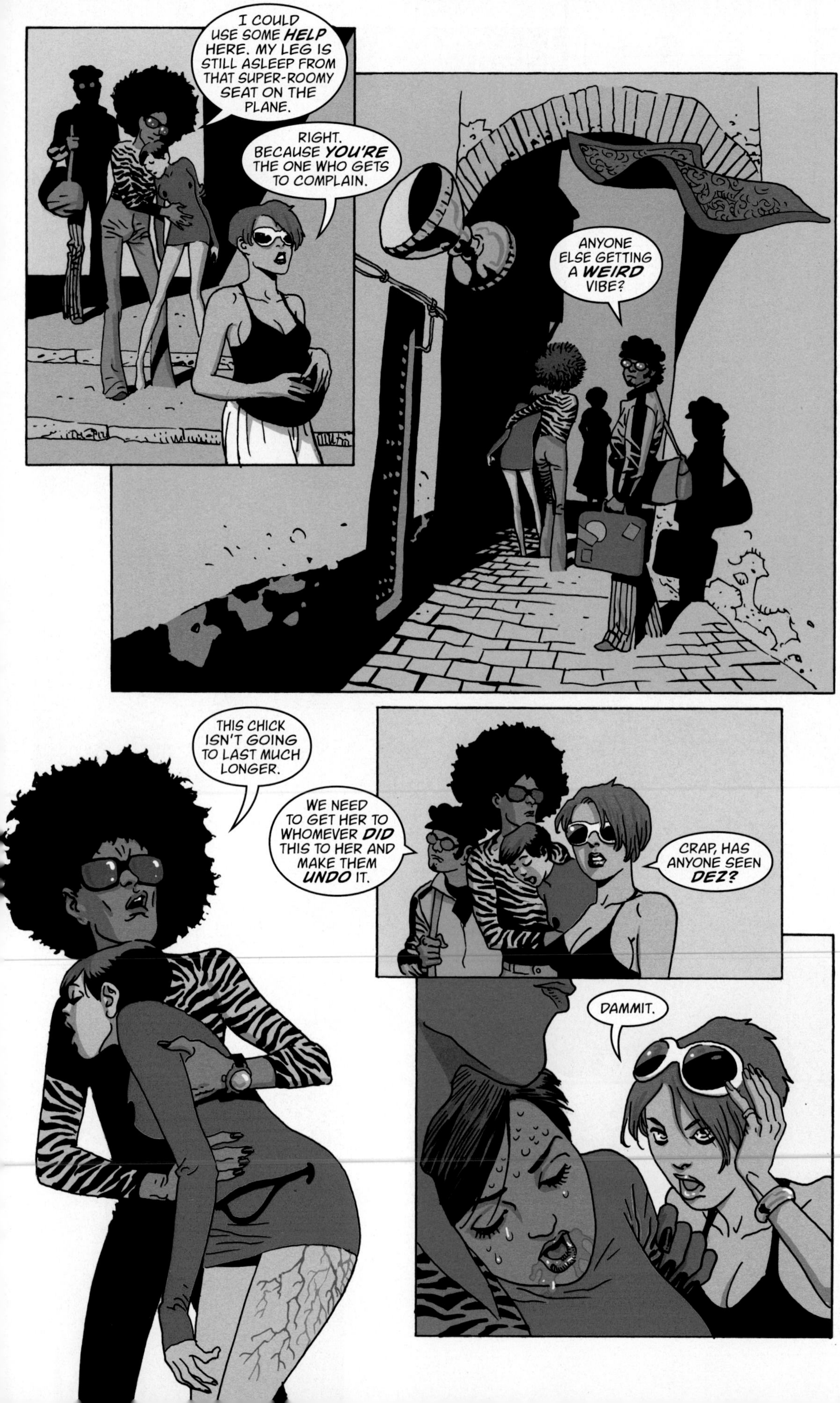
I COULD USE SOME HELP HERE. MY LEG IS STILL ASLEEP FROM THAT SUPER-ROOMY SEAT ON THE PLANE.
RIGHT. BECAUSE YOU'RE THE ONE WHO GETS TO COMPLAIN.
ANYONE ELSE GETTING A WEIRD VIBE?
THIS CHICK ISN'T GOING TO LAST MUCH LONGER.
WE NEED TO GET HER TO WHOMEVER DID THIS TO HER AND MAKE THEM UNDO IT.
CRAP, HAS ANYONE SEEN DEZ?
DAMMIT.

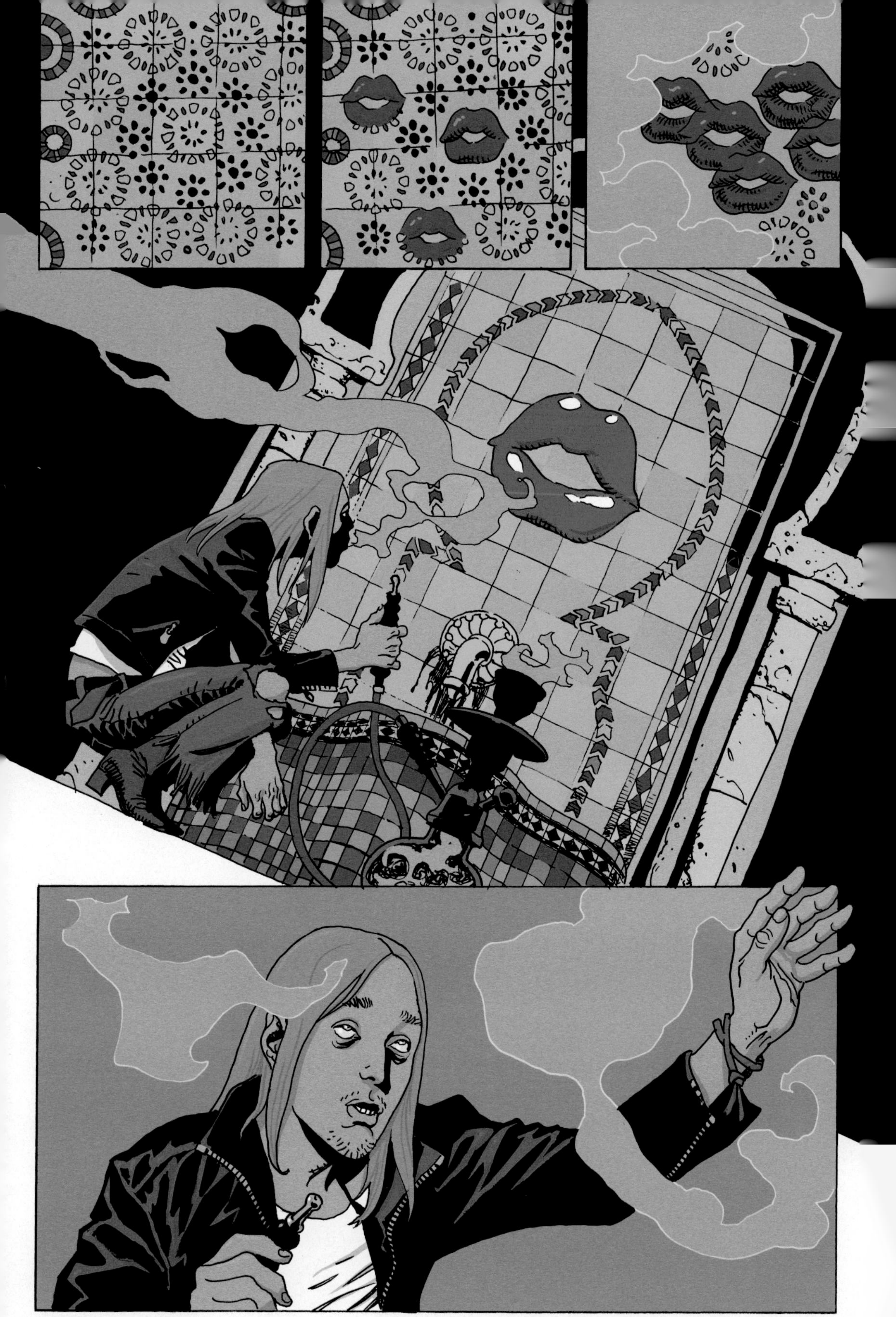

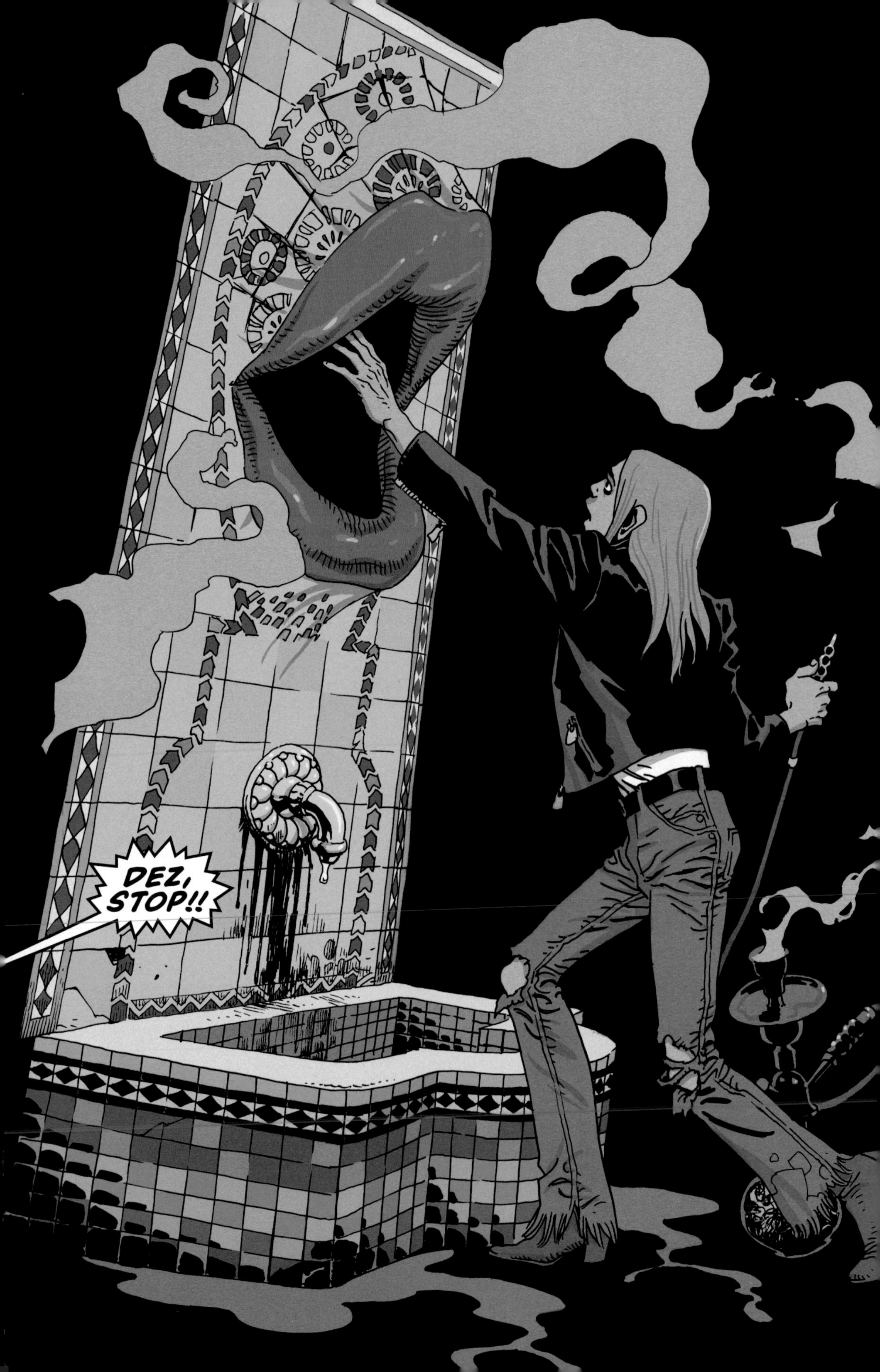
DEZ, STOP!!

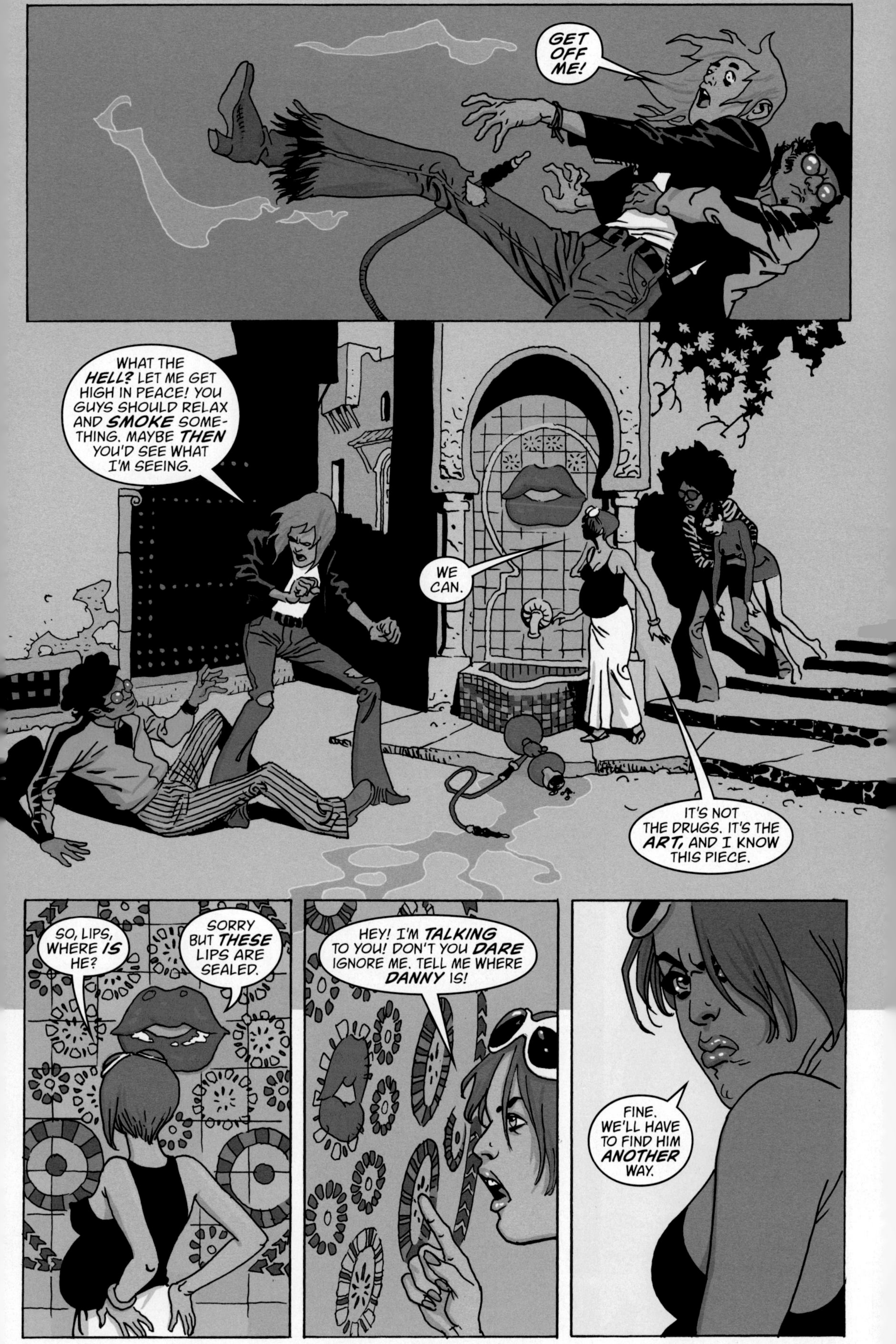
GET OFF ME!
WHAT THE HELL? LET ME GET HIGH IN PEACE! YOU GUYS SHOULD RELAX AND SMOKE SOMETHING. MAYBE THEN YOU'D SEE WHAT I'M SEEING.
WE CAN.
IT'S NOT THE DRUGS. IT'S THE ART, AND I KNOW THIS PIECE.
SO, LIPS, WHERE IS HE?
SORRY BUT THESE LIPS ARE SEALED.
HEY! I'M TALKING TO YOU! DON'T YOU DARE IGNORE ME. TELL ME WHERE DANNY IS!
FINE. WE'LL HAVE TO FIND HIM ANOTHER WAY.

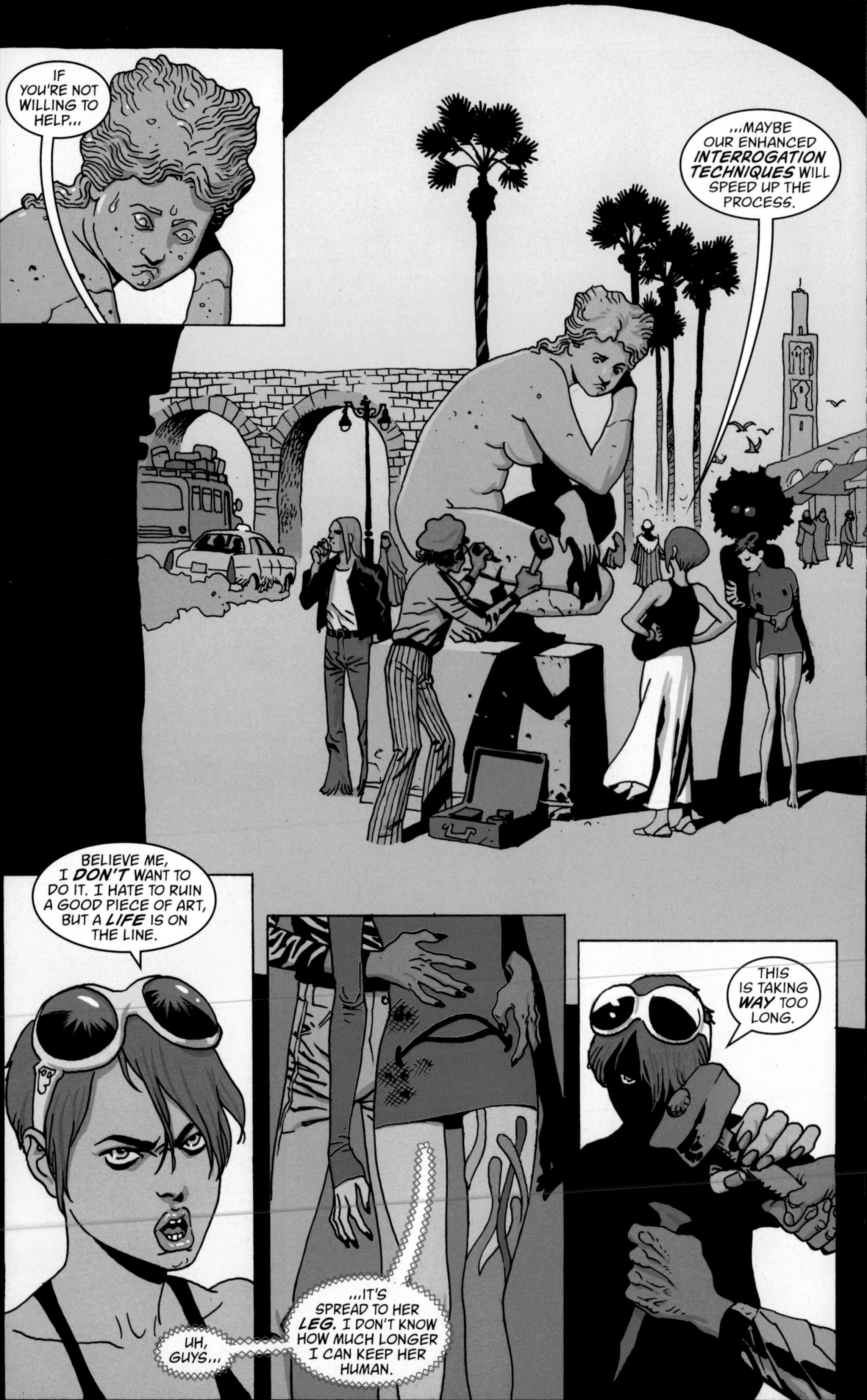
IF YOU'RE NOT WILLING TO HELP...
...MAYBE OUR ENHANCED INTERROGATION TECHNIQUES WILL SPEED UP THE PROCESS.
BELIEVE ME, I DON'T WANT TO DO IT. I HATE TO RUIN A GOOD PIECE OF ART, BUT A LIFE IS ON THE LINE.
UH, GUYS...
...IT'S SPREAD TO HER LEG. I DON'T KNOW HOW MUCH LONGER I CAN KEEP HER HUMAN.
THIS IS TAKING WAY TOO LONG.

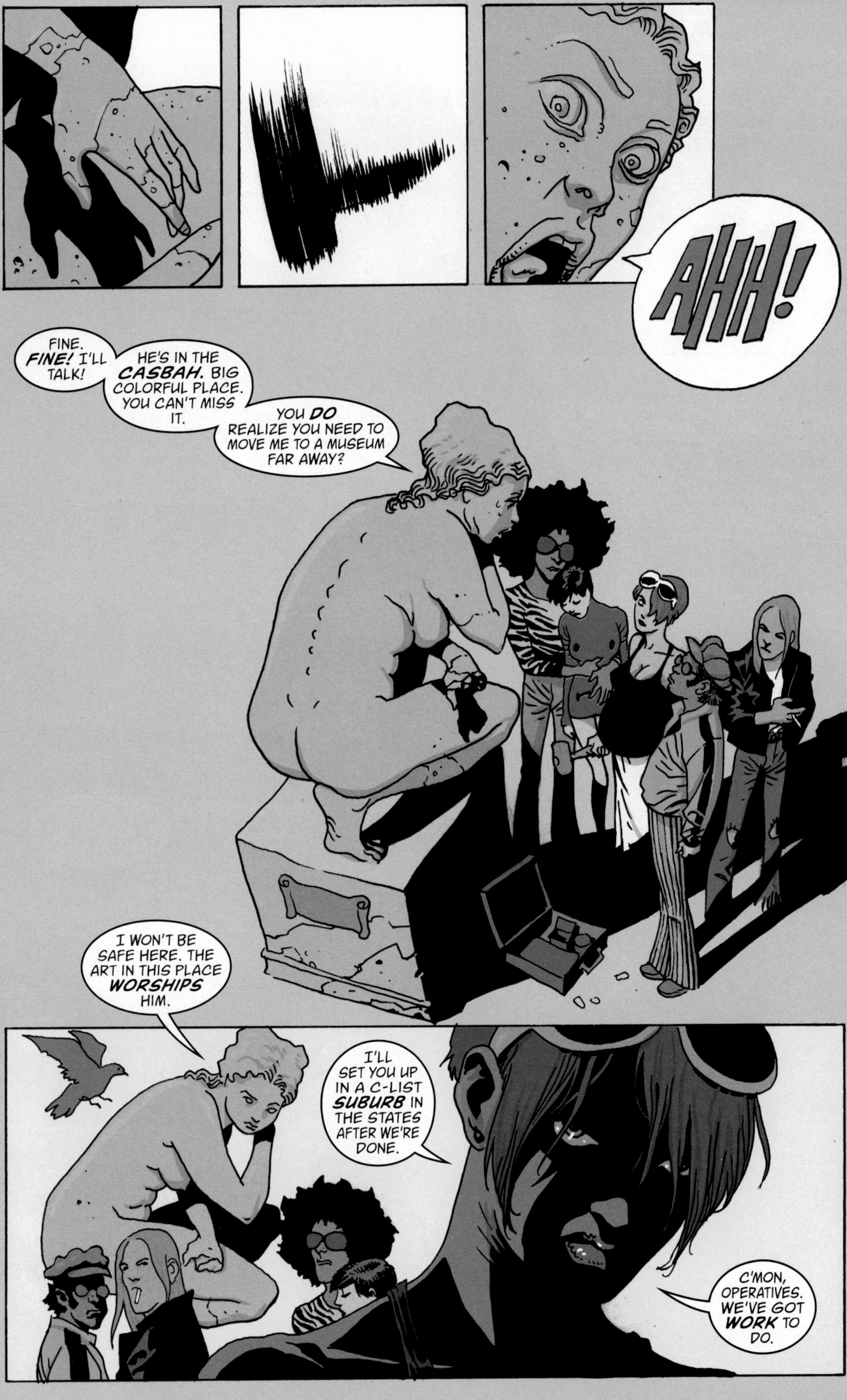
AHH!
FINE. FINE! I'LL TALK!
HE'S IN THE CASBAH. BIG COLORFUL PLACE. YOU CAN'T MISS IT.
YOU DO REALIZE YOU NEED TO MOVE ME TO A MUSEUM FAR AWAY?
I WON'T BE SAFE HERE. THE ART IN THIS PLACE WORSHIPS HIM.
I'LL SET YOU UP IN A C-LIST SUBURB IN THE STATES AFTER WE'RE DONE.
C'MON, OPERATIVES. WE'VE GOT WORK TO DO.

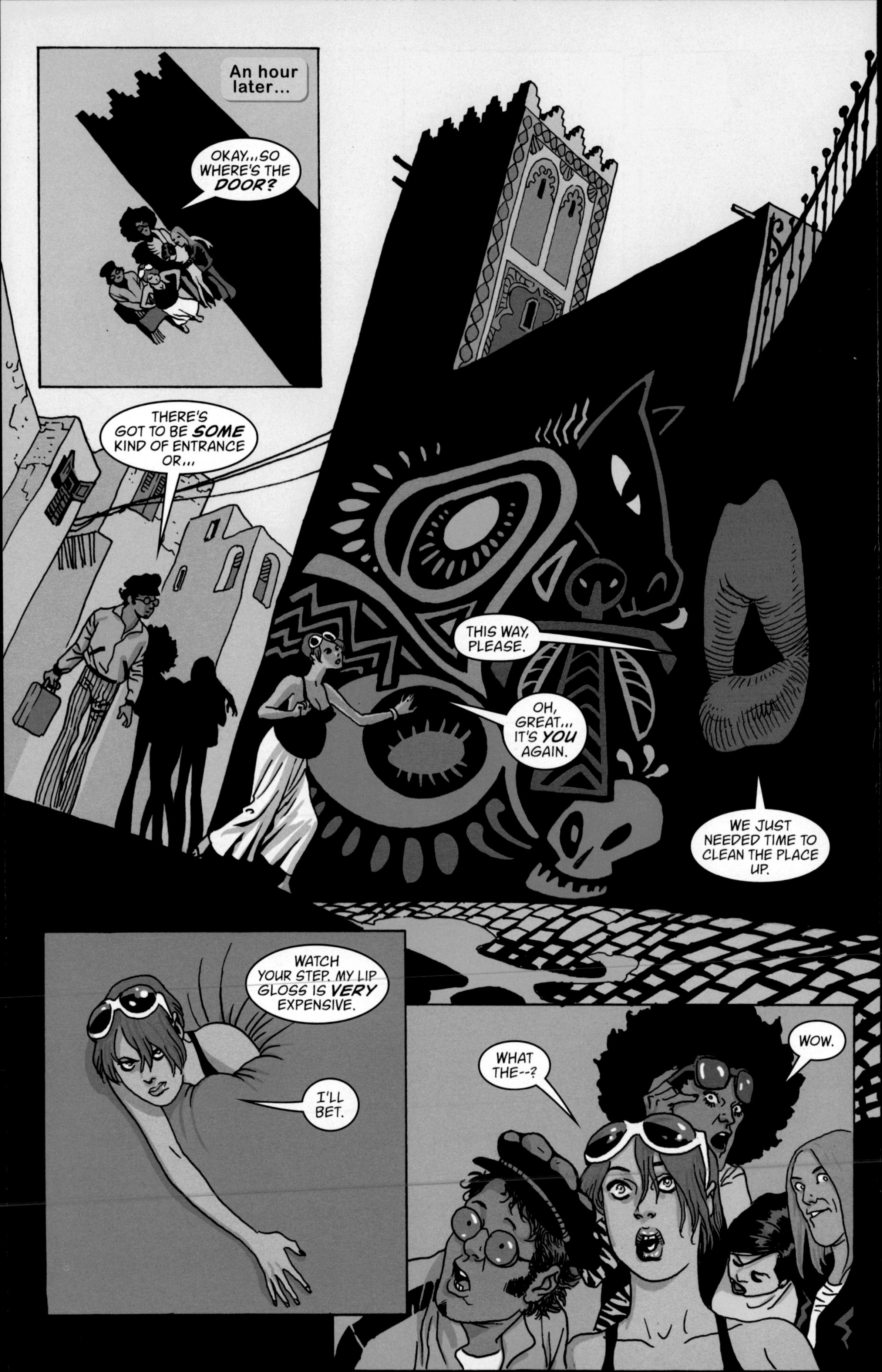
An hour later...
OKAY...SO WHERE'S THE DOOR?
THERE'S GOT TO BE SOME KIND OF ENTRANCE OR...
THIS WAY, PLEASE.
OH, GREAT... IT'S YOU AGAIN.
WE JUST NEEDED TIME TO CLEAN THE PLACE UP.
WATCH YOUR STEP. MY LIP GLOSS IS VERY EXPENSIVE.
I'LL BET.
WHAT THE--?
WOW.

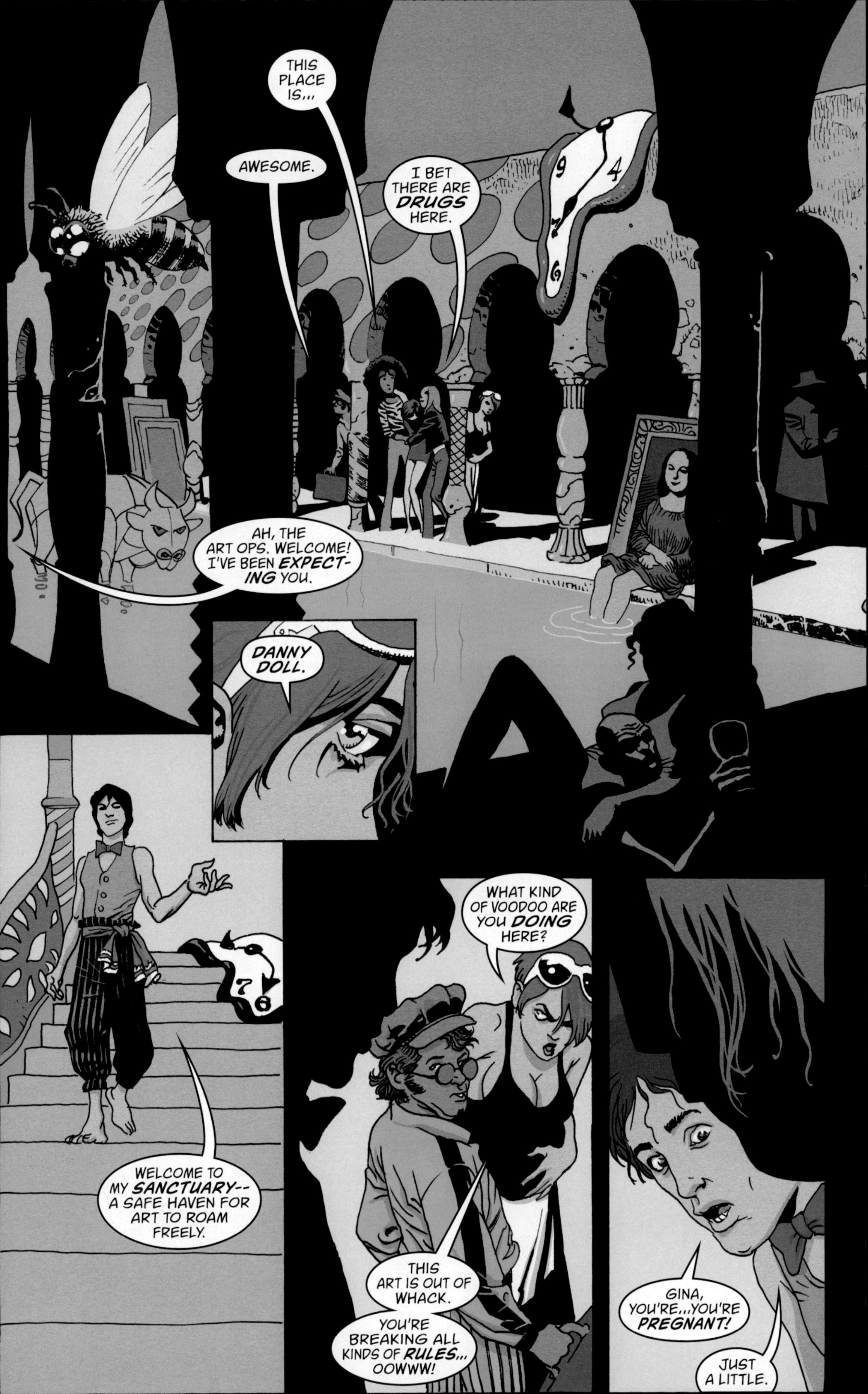
THIS PLACE IS...
AWESOME.
I BET THERE ARE DRUGS HERE.
AH, THE ART OPS. WELCOME! I'VE BEEN EXPECTING YOU.
DANNY DOLL.
WELCOME TO MY SANCTUARY-- A SAFE HAVEN FOR ART TO ROAM FREELY.
WHAT KIND OF VOODOO ARE YOU DOING HERE?
THIS ART IS OUT OF WHACK.
YOU'RE BREAKING ALL KINDS OF RULES... OOWWW!
GINA, YOU'RE... YOU'RE PREGNANT!
JUST A LITTLE.

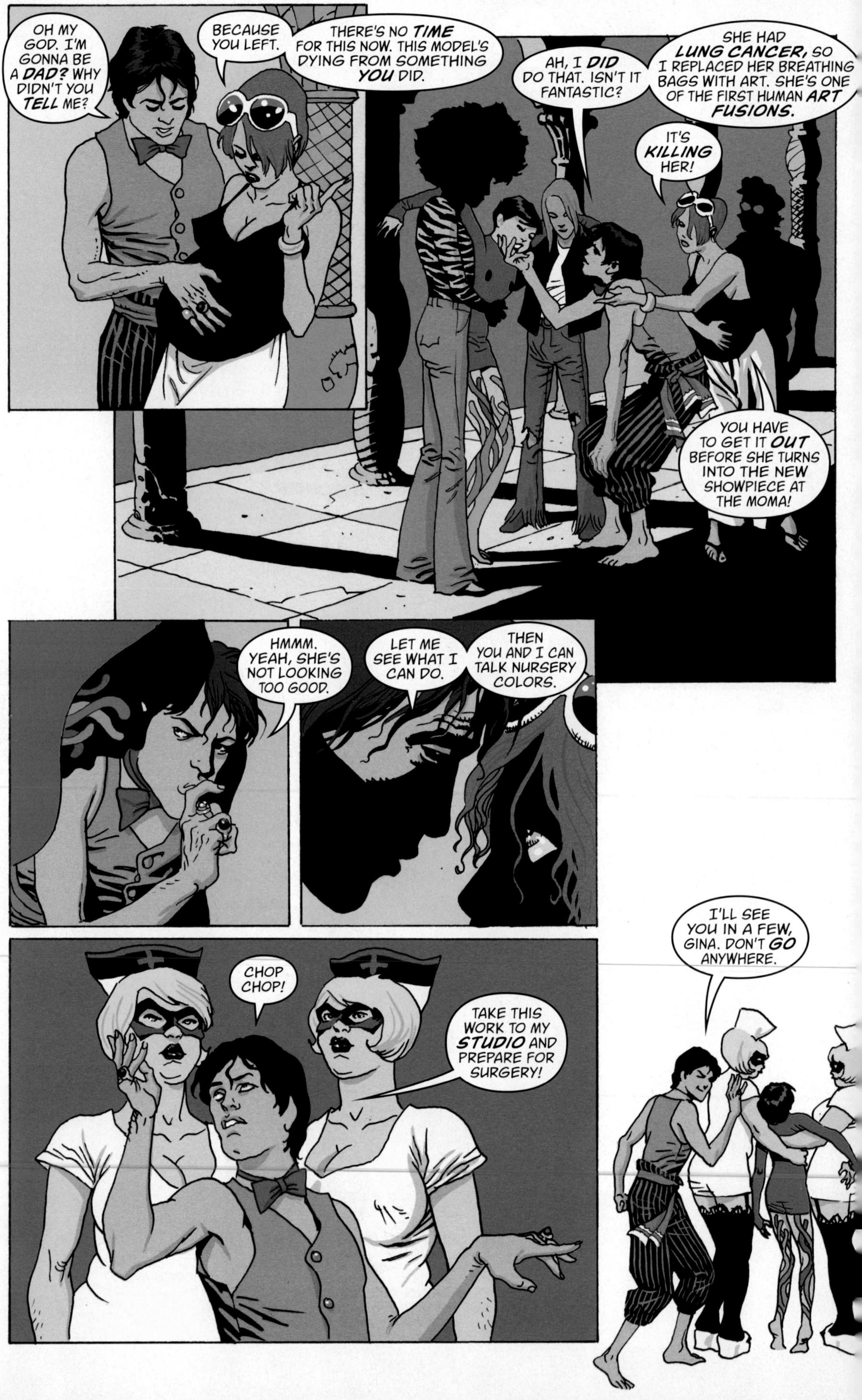
OH MY GOD. I'M GONNA BE A DAD? WHY DIDN'T YOU TELL ME?
BECAUSE YOU LEFT.
THERE'S NO TIME FOR THIS NOW. THIS MODEL'S DYING FROM SOMETHING YOU DID.
AH, I DID DO THAT. ISN'T IT FANTASTIC?
SHE HAD LUNG CANCER, SO I REPLACED HER BREATHING BAGS WITH ART. SHE'S ONE OF THE FIRST HUMAN ART FUSIONS.
IT'S KILLING HER!
YOU HAVE TO GET IT OUT BEFORE SHE TURNS INTO THE NEW SHOWPIECE AT THE MOMA!
HMMM. YEAH, SHE'S NOT LOOKING TOO GOOD.
LET ME SEE WHAT I CAN DO.
THEN YOU AND I CAN TALK NURSERY COLORS.
CHOP CHOP!
TAKE THIS WORK TO MY STUDIO AND PREPARE FOR SURGERY!
I'LL SEE YOU IN A FEW, GINA. DON'T GO ANYWHERE.

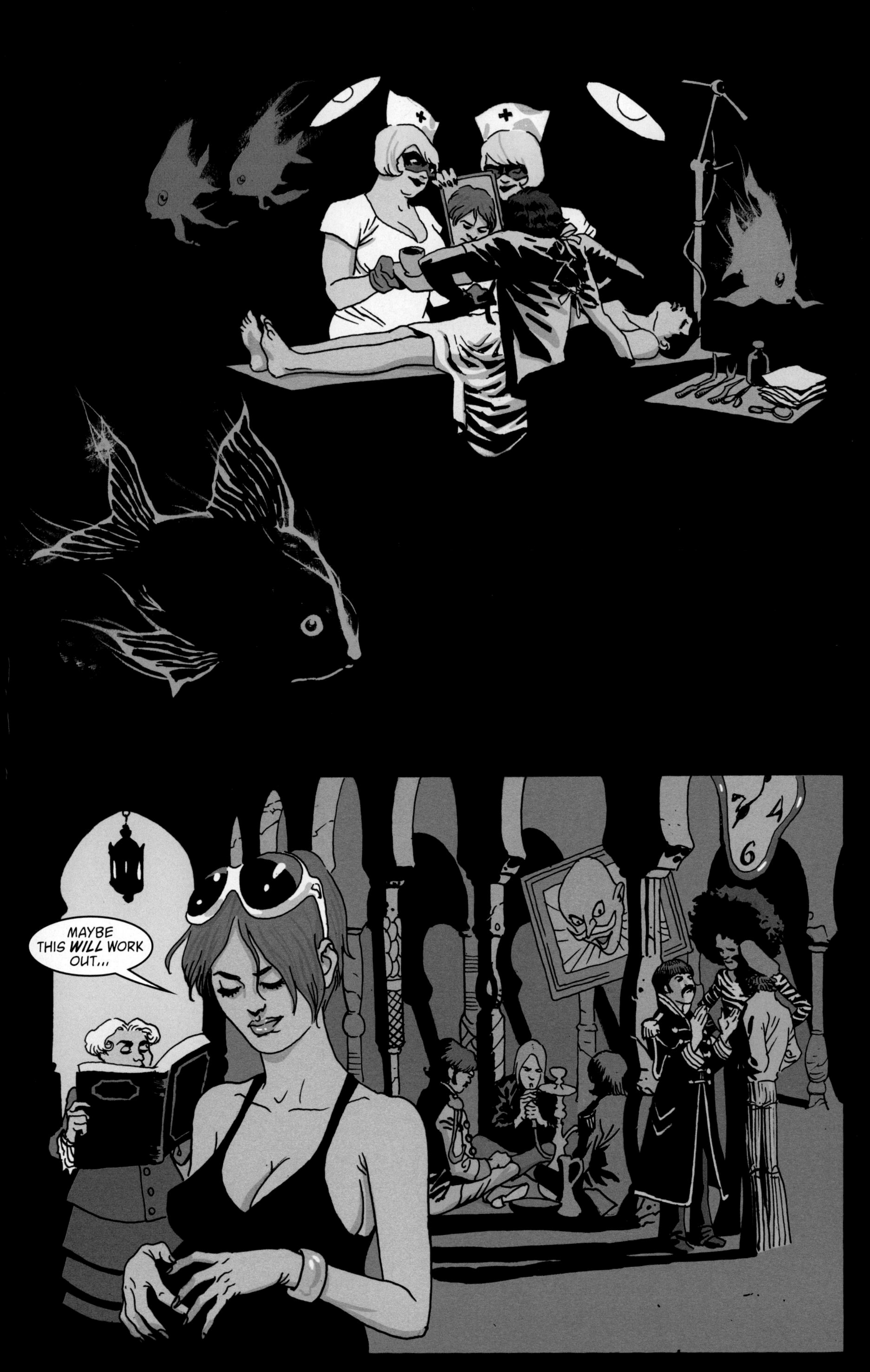
MAYBE THIS WILL WORK OUT...

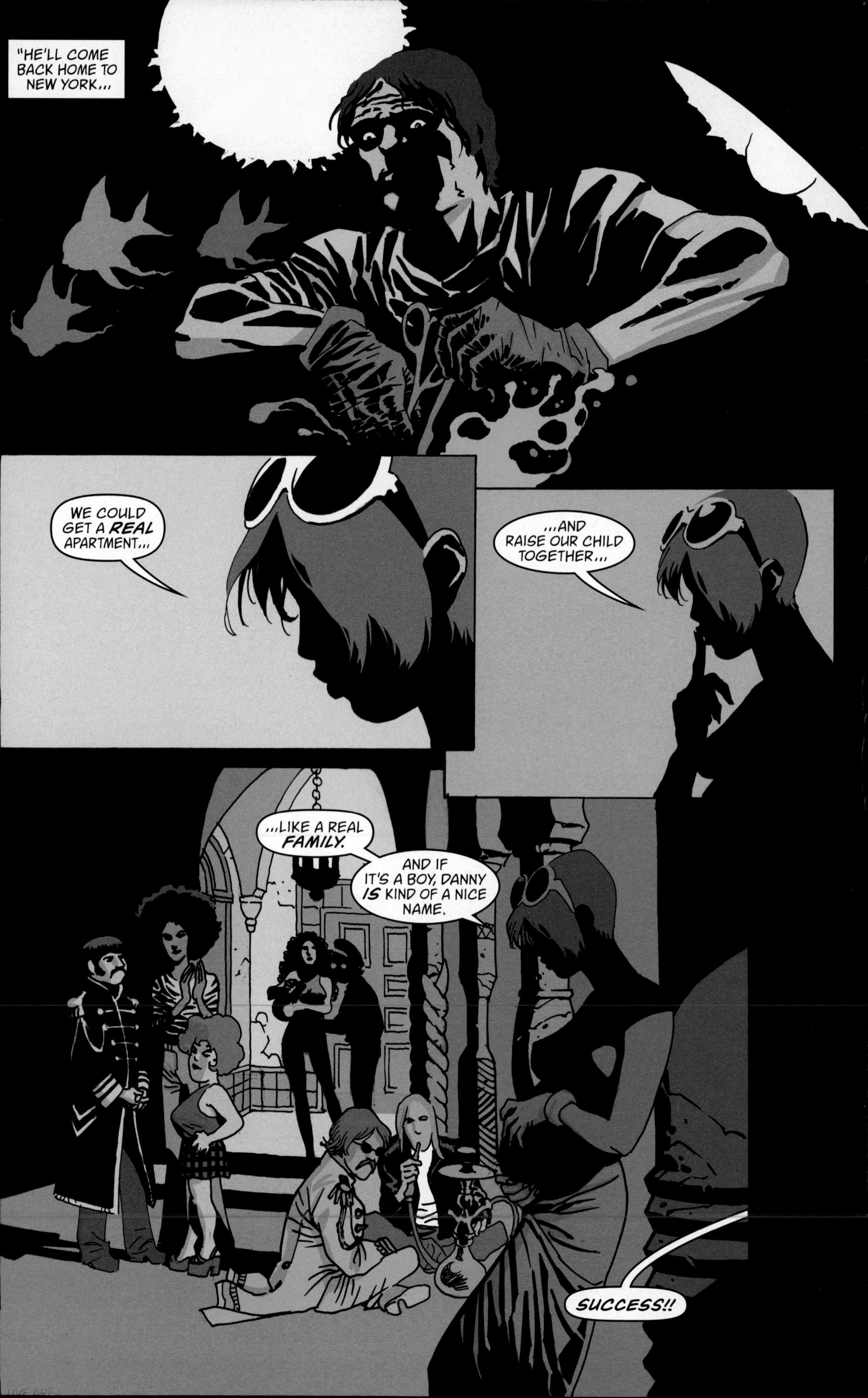
"HE'LL COME BACK HOME TO NEW YORK...
WE COULD GET A REAL APARTMENT...
...AND RAISE OUR CHILD TOGETHER...
...LIKE A REAL FAMILY.
AND IF IT'S A BOY, DANNY IS KIND OF A NICE NAME.
SUCCESS!!

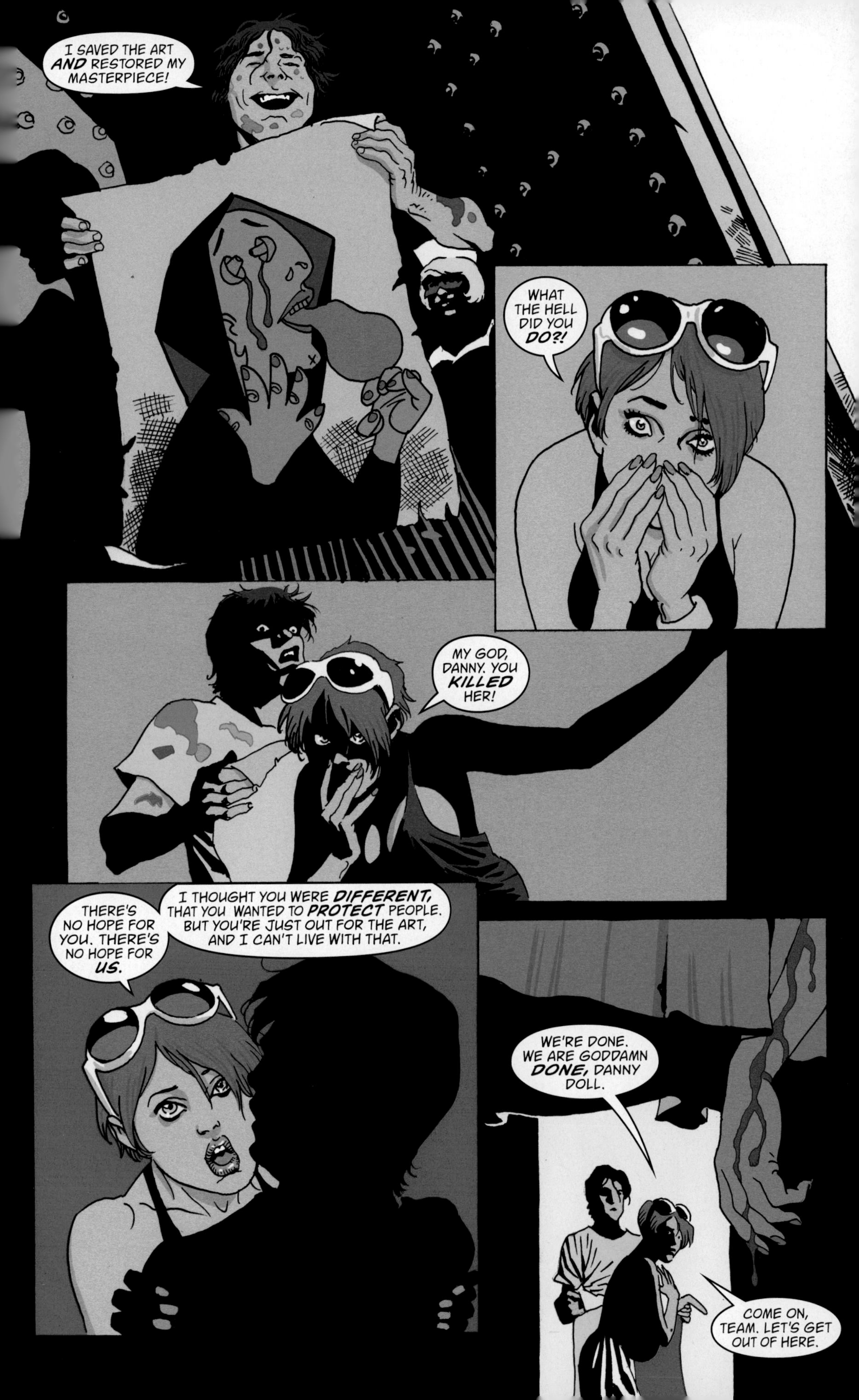
I SAVED THE ART AND RESTORED MY MASTERPIECE!
WHAT THE HELL DID YOU DO?!
MY GOD, DANNY. YOU KILLED HER!
THERE'S NO HOPE FOR YOU. THERE'S NO HOPE FOR US.
I THOUGHT YOU WERE DIFFERENT, THAT YOU WANTED TO PROTECT PEOPLE. BUT YOU'RE JUST OUT FOR THE ART, AND I CAN'T LIVE WITH THAT.
WE'RE DONE. WE ARE GODDAMN DONE, DANNY DOLL.
COME ON, TEAM. LET'S GET OUT OF HERE.

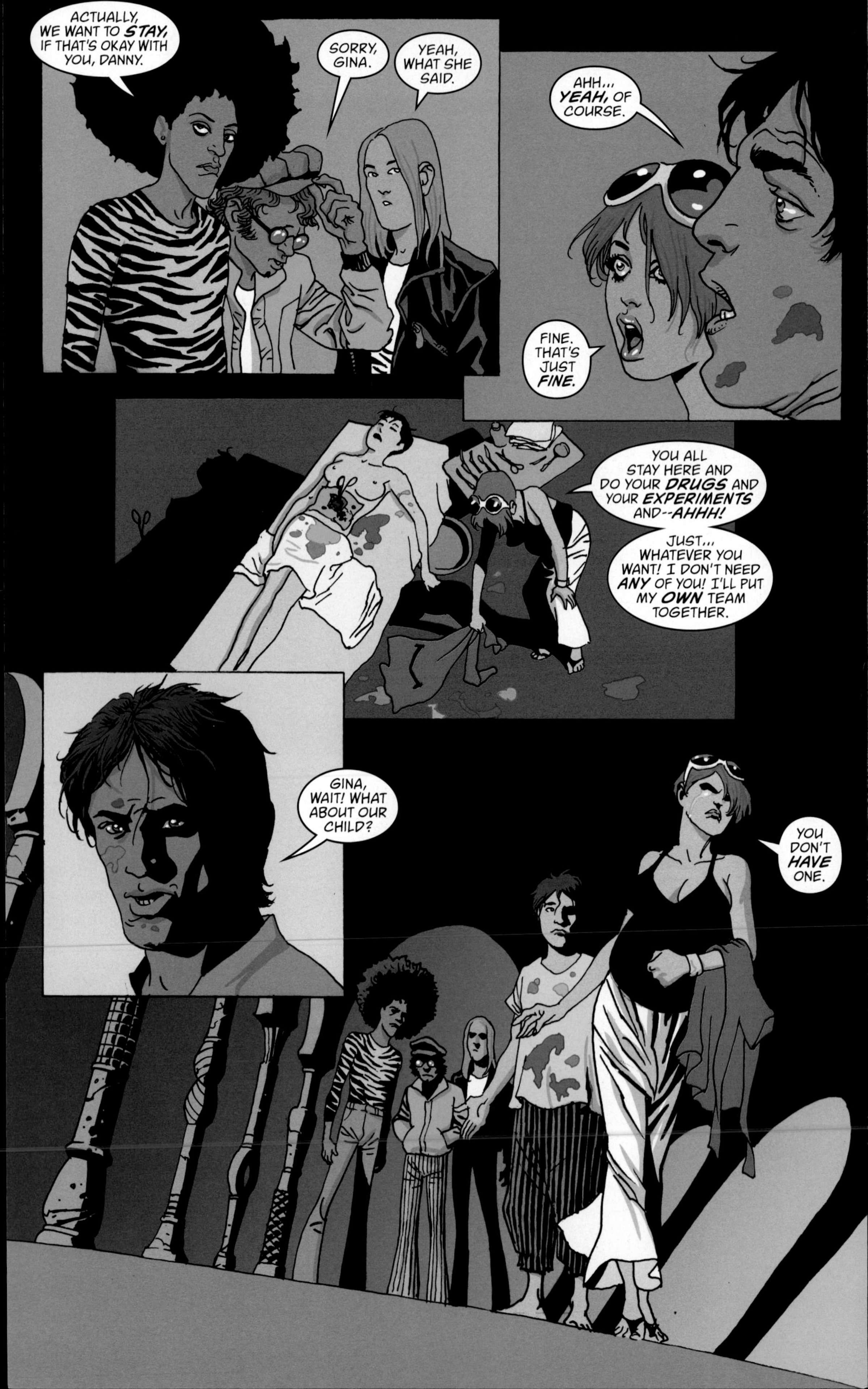
ACTUALLY, WE WANT TO STAY, IF THAT'S OKAY WITH YOU, DANNY.
SORRY, GINA.
YEAH, WHAT SHE SAID.
AHH... YEAH, OF COURSE.
FINE. THAT'S JUST FINE.
YOU ALL STAY HERE AND DO YOUR DRUGS AND YOUR EXPERIMENTS AND--AHHH!
JUST... WHATEVER YOU WANT! I DON'T NEED ANY OF YOU! I'LL PUT MY OWN TEAM TOGETHER.
GINA, WAIT! WHAT ABOUT OUR CHILD?
YOU DON'T HAVE ONE.

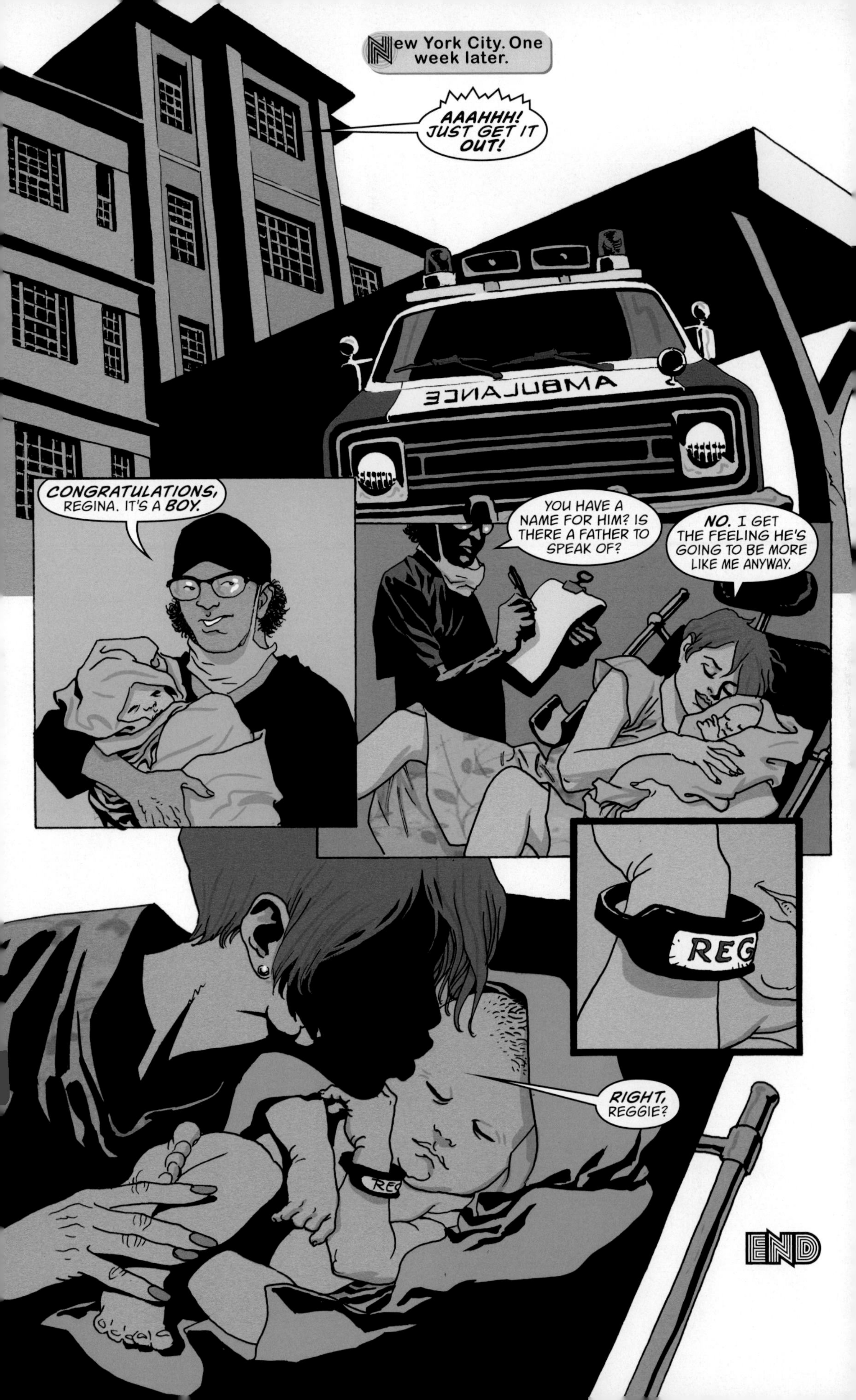
New York City. One week later.
AAAHHH! JUST GET IT OUT!
AMBULANCE
CONGRATULATIONS, REGINA. IT'S A BOY.
YOU HAVE A NAME FOR HIM? IS THERE A FATHER TO SPEAK OF?
NO. I GET THE FEELING HE'S GOING TO BE MORE LIKE ME ANYWAY.
REG
RIGHT, REGGIE?
REG
END

ART ART ART
OPS OPS OPS
ART ART ART
OPS OPS OPS
ART ART ART
OPS OPS OPS
ART ART ART
OPS OPS OPS
ART ART ART
OPS OPS OPS
ART ART ART
OPS OPS OPS

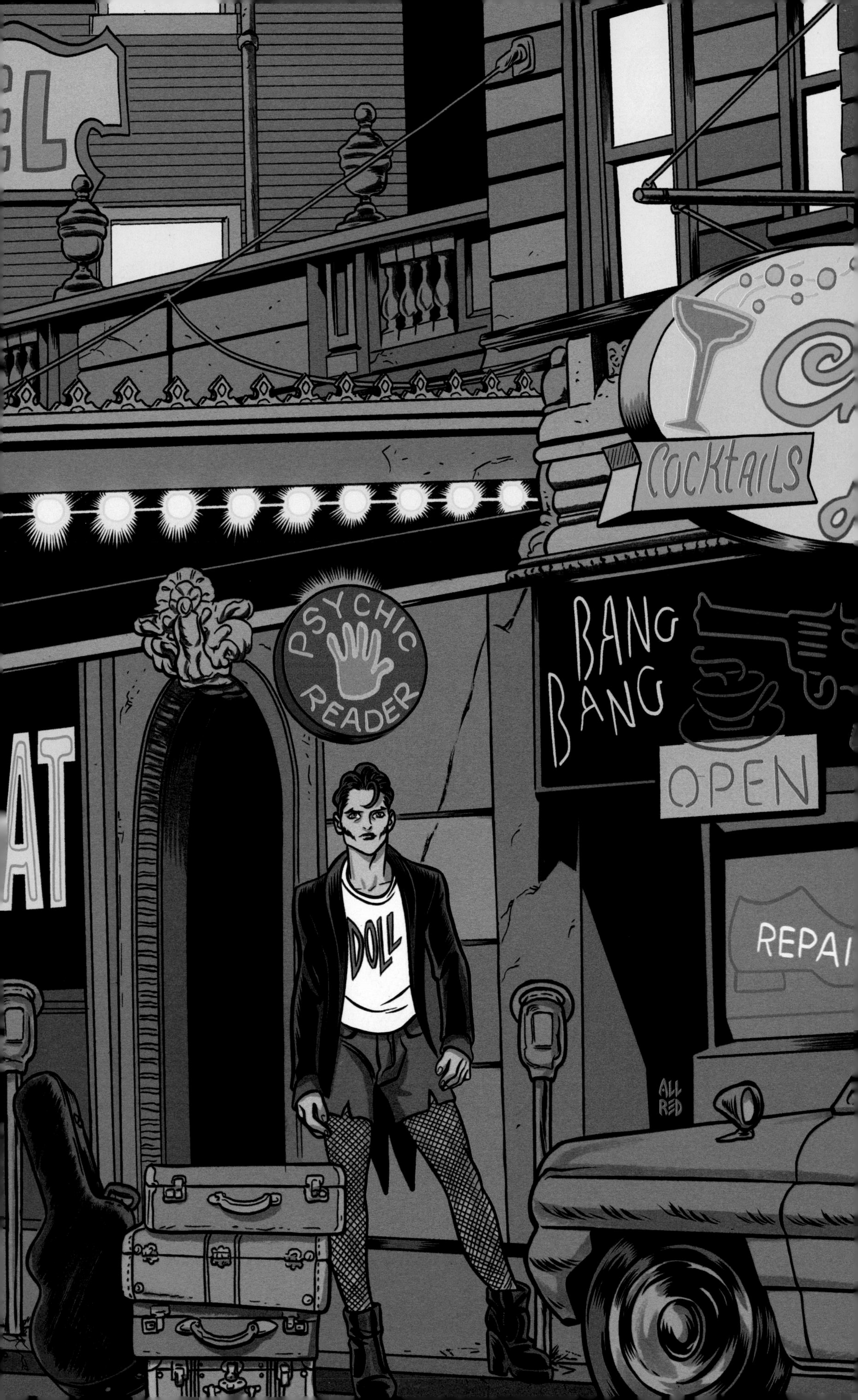
COCKTAILS
PSYCHIC READER
BANG BANG
OPEN
REPAI
DOLL
ALLRED

POPISM

Art by **MICHAEL ALLRED** and **MATT BRUNDAGE** (Part One)
MATT BRUNDAGE (Parts Two and Three)
ROB DAVIS (Interlude)
MICHAEL ALLRED (Part Four)

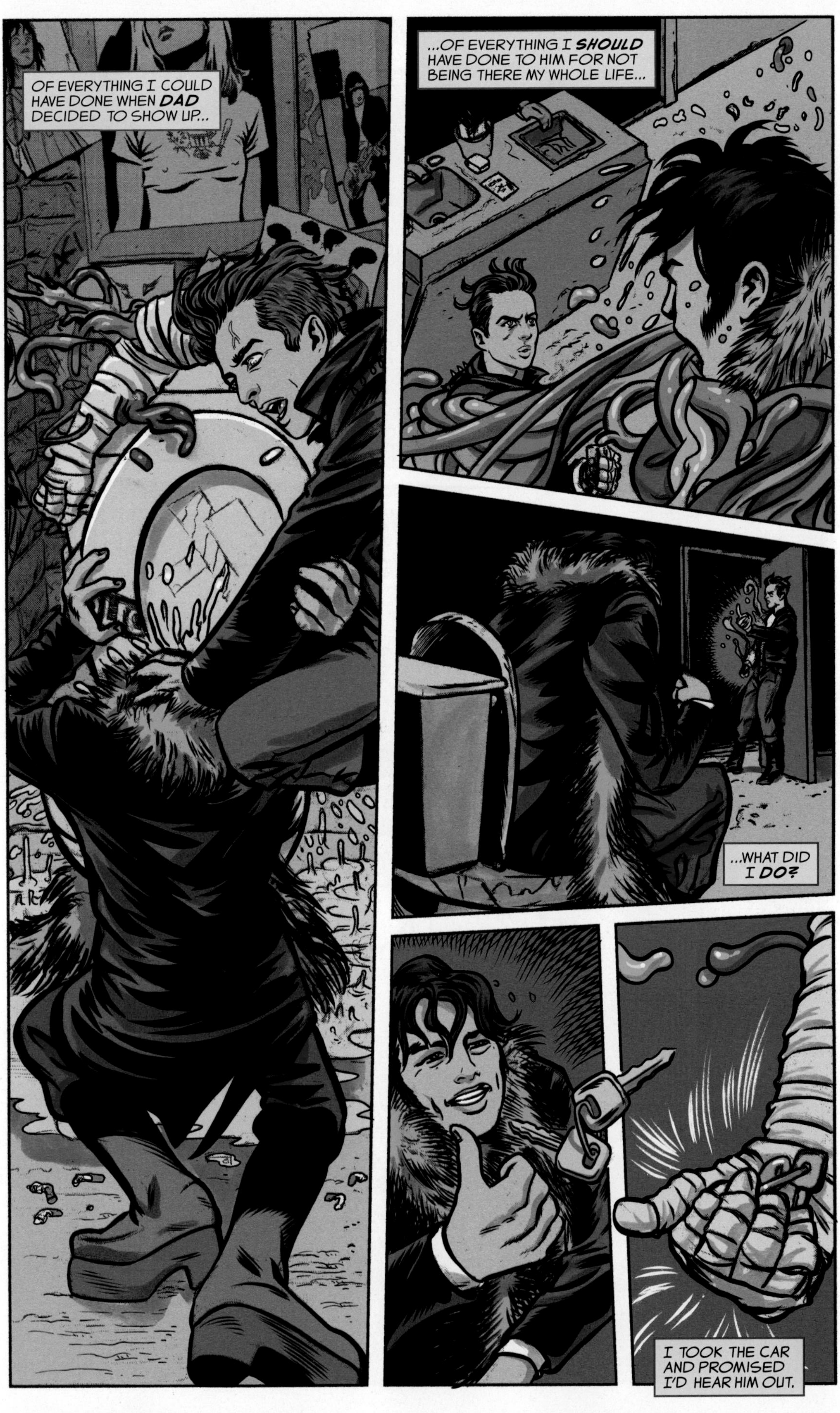

OF EVERYTHING I COULD HAVE DONE WHEN DAD DECIDED TO SHOW UP...
...OF EVERYTHING I SHOULD HAVE DONE TO HIM FOR NOT BEING THERE MY WHOLE LIFE...
...WHAT DID I DO?
I TOOK THE CAR AND PROMISED I'D HEAR HIM OUT.

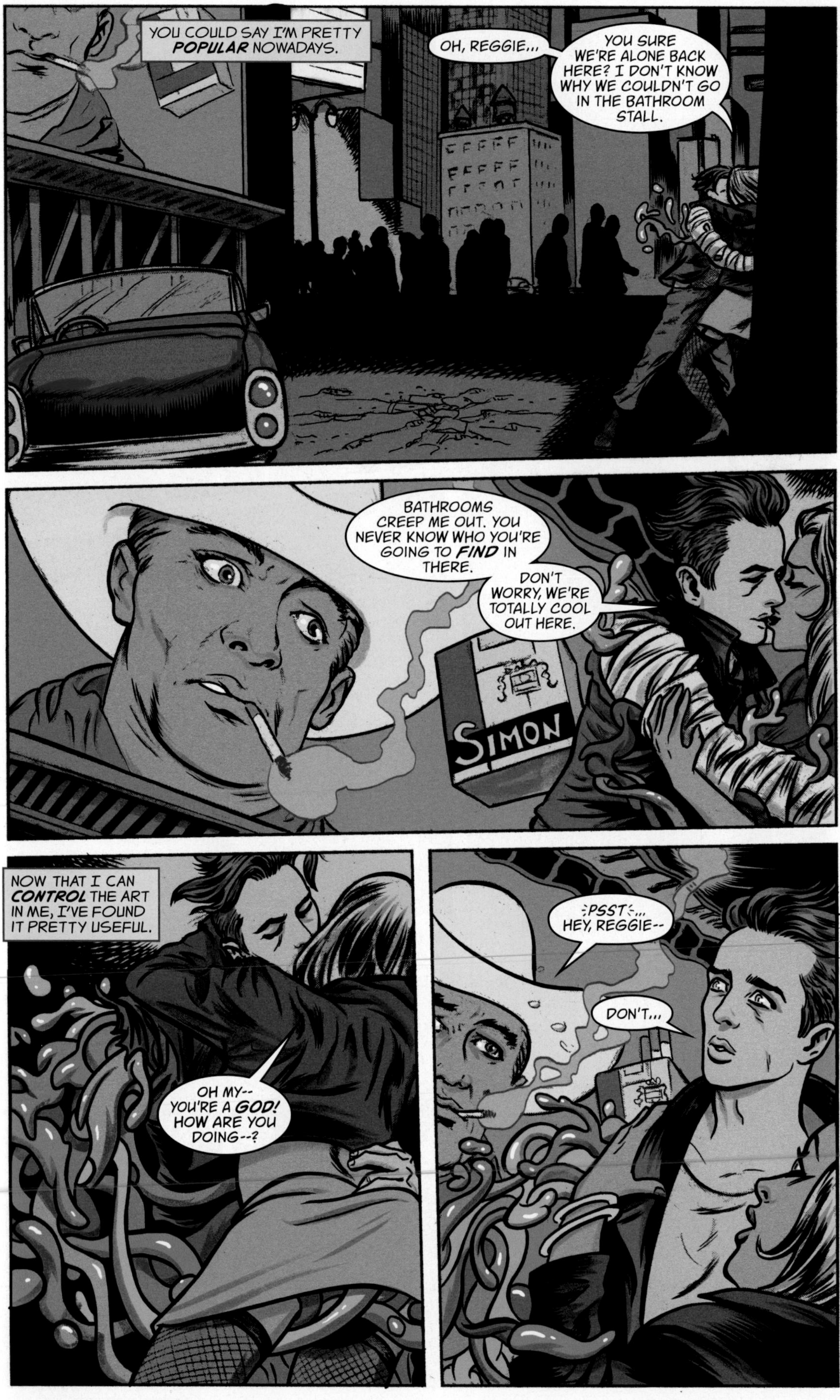
YOU COULD SAY I'M PRETTY POPULAR NOWADAYS.
OH, REGGIE...
YOU SURE WE'RE ALONE BACK HERE? I DON'T KNOW WHY WE COULDN'T GO IN THE BATHROOM STALL.
BATHROOMS CREEP ME OUT. YOU NEVER KNOW WHO YOU'RE GOING TO FIND IN THERE.
DON'T WORRY, WE'RE TOTALLY COOL OUT HERE.
SIMON
NOW THAT I CAN CONTROL THE ART IN ME, I'VE FOUND IT PRETTY USEFUL.
OH MY-- YOU'RE A GOD! HOW ARE YOU DOING--?
PSST... HEY, REGGIE--
DON'T...

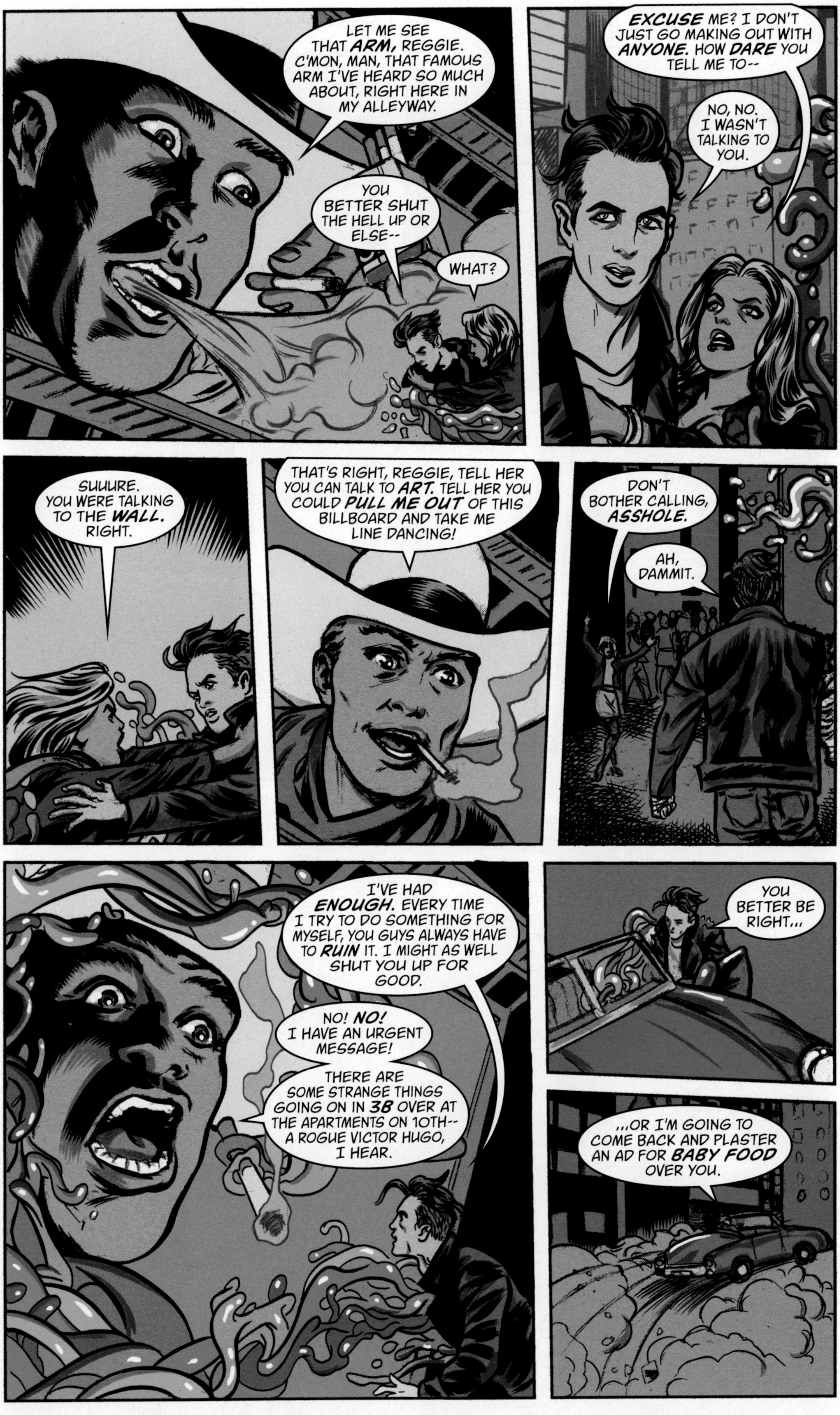
LET ME SEE THAT ARM, REGGIE. C'MON, MAN, THAT FAMOUS ARM I'VE HEARD SO MUCH ABOUT, RIGHT HERE IN MY ALLEYWAY.
YOU BETTER SHUT THE HELL UP OR ELSE--
WHAT?
EXCUSE ME? I DON'T JUST GO MAKING OUT WITH ANYONE. HOW DARE YOU TELL ME TO--
NO, NO. I WASN'T TALKING TO YOU.
SUUURE. YOU WERE TALKING TO THE WALL. RIGHT.
THAT'S RIGHT, REGGIE, TELL HER YOU CAN TALK TO ART. TELL HER YOU COULD PULL ME OUT OF THIS BILLBOARD AND TAKE ME LINE DANCING!
DON'T BOTHER CALLING, ASSHOLE.
AH, DAMMIT.
I'VE HAD ENOUGH. EVERY TIME I TRY TO DO SOMETHING FOR MYSELF, YOU GUYS ALWAYS HAVE TO RUIN IT. I MIGHT AS WELL SHUT YOU UP FOR GOOD.
NO! NO! I HAVE AN URGENT MESSAGE!
THERE ARE SOME STRANGE THINGS GOING ON IN 3B OVER AT THE APARTMENTS ON 10TH-- A ROGUE VICTOR HUGO, I HEAR.
YOU BETTER BE RIGHT...
...OR I'M GOING TO COME BACK AND PLASTER AN AD FOR BABY FOOD OVER YOU.

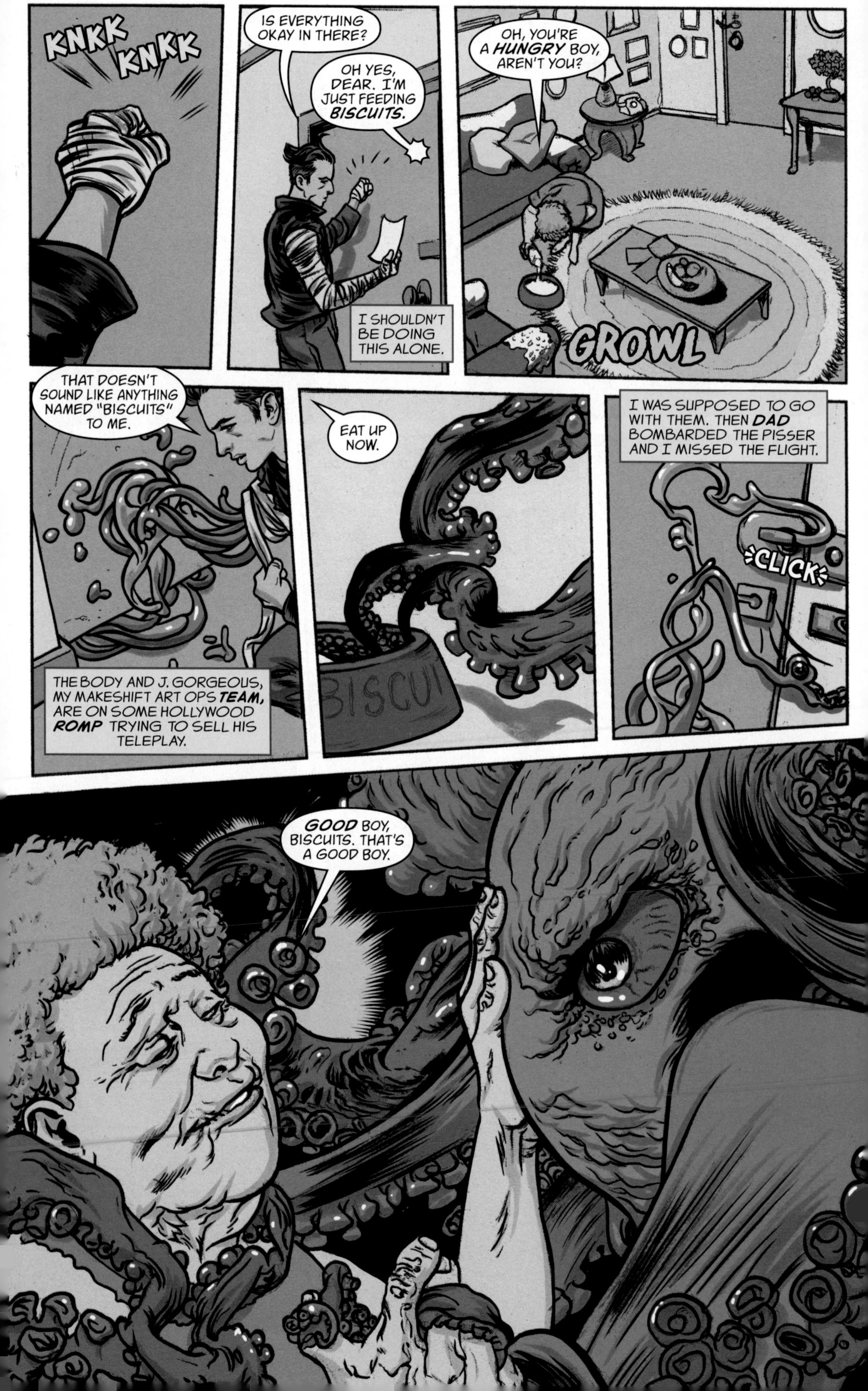
KNKK KNKK
IS EVERYTHING OKAY IN THERE?
OH YES, DEAR. I'M JUST FEEDING BISCUITS.
I SHOULDN'T BE DOING THIS ALONE.
OH, YOU'RE A HUNGRY BOY, AREN'T YOU?
GROWL
THAT DOESN'T SOUND LIKE ANYTHING NAMED "BISCUITS" TO ME.
THE BODY AND J. GORGEOUS, MY MAKESHIFT ART OPS TEAM, ARE ON SOME HOLLYWOOD ROMP TRYING TO SELL HIS TELEPLAY.
EAT UP NOW.
BISCUI
I WAS SUPPOSED TO GO WITH THEM. THEN DAD BOMBARDED THE PISSER AND I MISSED THE FLIGHT.
CLICK
GOOD BOY, BISCUITS. THAT'S A GOOD BOY.

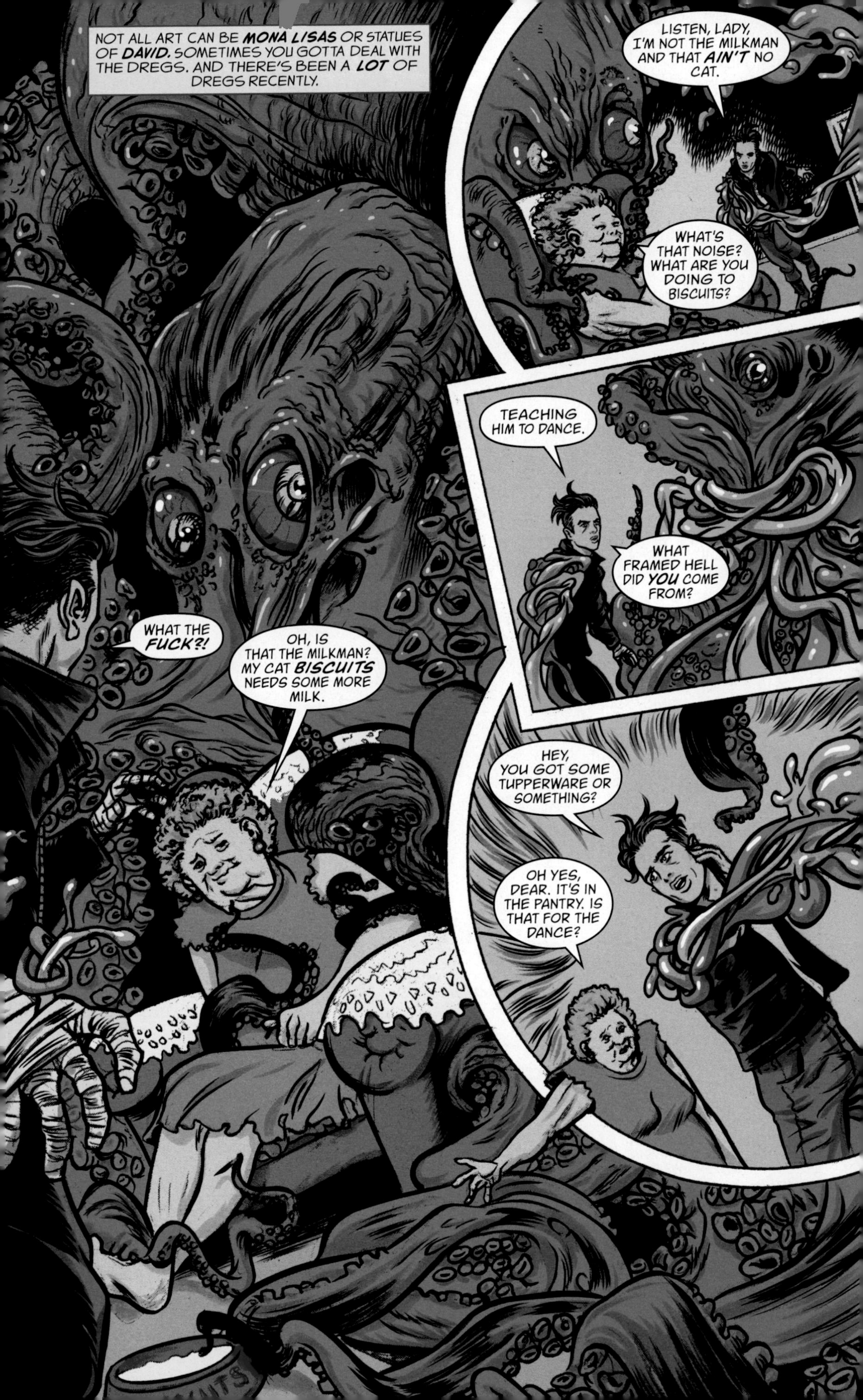
NOT ALL ART CAN BE MONA LISAS OR STATUES OF DAVID. SOMETIMES YOU GOTTA DEAL WITH THE DREGS. AND THERE'S BEEN A LOT OF DREGS RECENTLY.
WHAT THE FUCK?!
OH, IS THAT THE MILKMAN? MY CAT BISCUITS NEEDS SOME MORE MILK.
LISTEN, LADY, I'M NOT THE MILKMAN AND THAT AIN'T NO CAT.
WHAT'S THAT NOISE? WHAT ARE YOU DOING TO BISCUITS?
TEACHING HIM TO DANCE.
WHAT FRAMED HELL DID YOU COME FROM?
HEY, YOU GOT SOME TUPPERWARE OR SOMETHING?
OH YES, DEAR. IT'S IN THE PANTRY. IS THAT FOR THE DANCE?

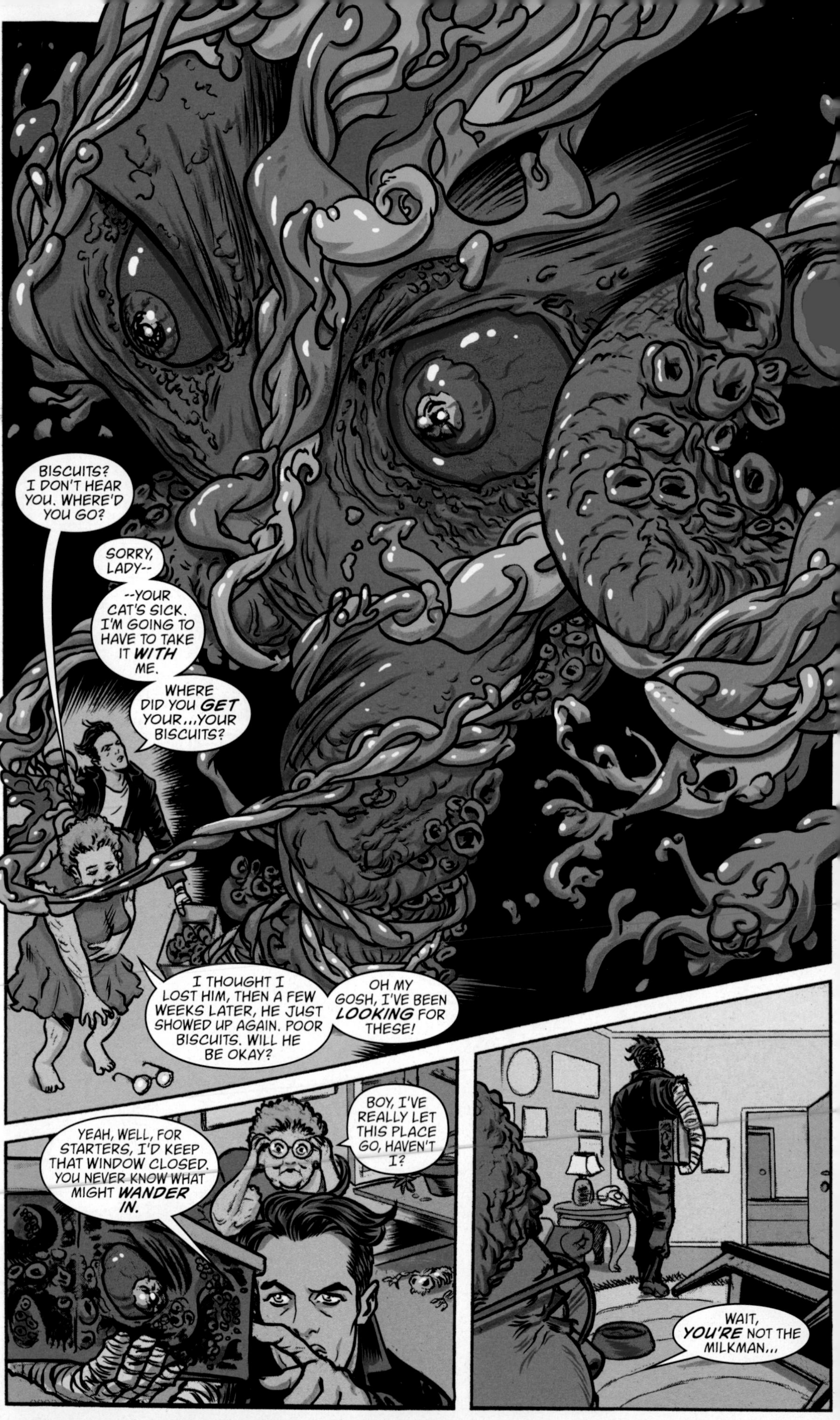
BISCUITS? I DON'T HEAR YOU. WHERE'D YOU GO?
SORRY, LADY--
--YOUR CAT'S SICK. I'M GOING TO HAVE TO TAKE IT **WITH** ME.
WHERE DID YOU **GET** YOUR...YOUR BISCUITS?
I THOUGHT I LOST HIM, THEN A FEW WEEKS LATER, HE JUST SHOWED UP AGAIN. POOR BISCUITS. WILL HE BE OKAY?
OH MY GOSH, I'VE BEEN **LOOKING** FOR THESE!
BOY, I'VE REALLY LET THIS PLACE GO, HAVEN'T I?
YEAH, WELL, FOR STARTERS, I'D KEEP THAT WINDOW CLOSED. YOU NEVER KNOW WHAT MIGHT **WANDER IN.**
WAIT, **YOU'RE** NOT THE MILKMAN...

"...YOU DON'T LOOK LIKE *ANYONE* I KNOW!"

"WE JUST WANT YOU TO CONSIDER SOMETHING A LITTLE MORE *NOW*..."

...AUDIENCES HAVE BEEN *VERY* KEEN ON SUPERNATURAL SHOWS RECENTLY.

WHAT IF THE HUSBAND IS *SECRETLY* A VAMPIRE?

WELL, I NEVER THOUGHT--

OR SHE ISN'T HIS MISTRESS, SHE'S A WEREWOLF?

YOU HAVE SOME GREAT STUFF THERE. WE WANT TO MAKE IT BETTER-- MAKE IT *POP!*

WE'D LOVE TO TAKE YOUR SHOW TO OUR PRESIDENT THE *NEXT* TIME WE MEET.

JUST THINK ABOUT IT.

YES. SEE YOU AT OUR NEXT MEETING THEN.

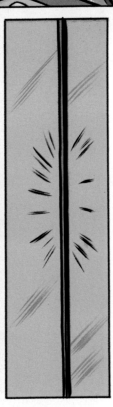

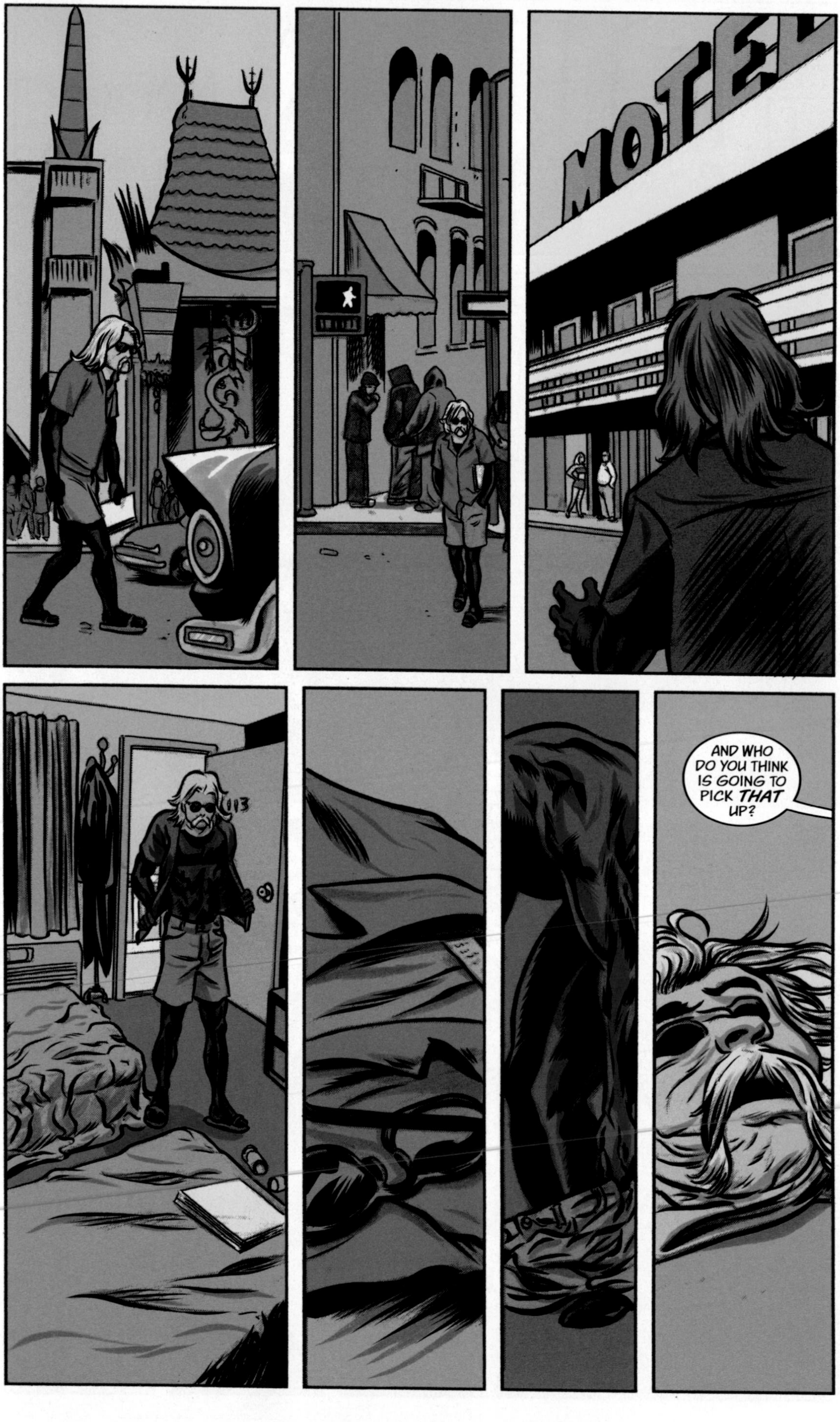
MOTEL
AND WHO DO YOU THINK IS GOING TO PICK *THAT* UP?

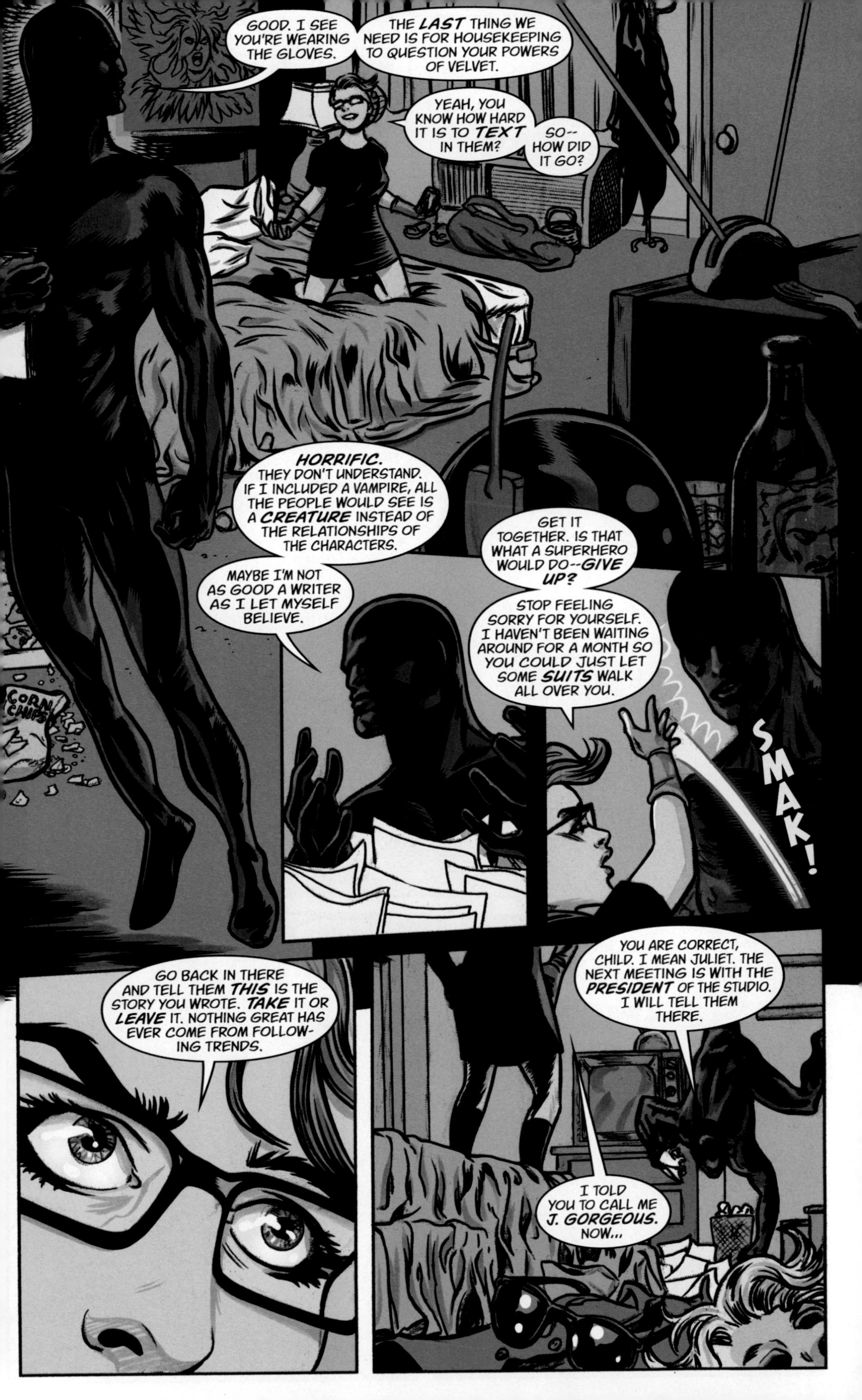
GOOD. I SEE YOU'RE WEARING THE GLOVES.
THE LAST THING WE NEED IS FOR HOUSEKEEPING TO QUESTION YOUR POWERS OF VELVET.
YEAH, YOU KNOW HOW HARD IT IS TO TEXT IN THEM?
SO-- HOW DID IT GO?
HORRIFIC. THEY DON'T UNDERSTAND. IF I INCLUDED A VAMPIRE, ALL THE PEOPLE WOULD SEE IS A CREATURE INSTEAD OF THE RELATIONSHIPS OF THE CHARACTERS.
MAYBE I'M NOT AS GOOD A WRITER AS I LET MYSELF BELIEVE.
GET IT TOGETHER. IS THAT WHAT A SUPERHERO WOULD DO--GIVE UP?
STOP FEELING SORRY FOR YOURSELF. I HAVEN'T BEEN WAITING AROUND FOR A MONTH SO YOU COULD JUST LET SOME SUITS WALK ALL OVER YOU.
SMAK!
CORN CHIPS
GO BACK IN THERE AND TELL THEM THIS IS THE STORY YOU WROTE. TAKE IT OR LEAVE IT. NOTHING GREAT HAS EVER COME FROM FOLLOWING TRENDS.
YOU ARE CORRECT, CHILD. I MEAN JULIET. THE NEXT MEETING IS WITH THE PRESIDENT OF THE STUDIO. I WILL TELL THEM THERE.
I TOLD YOU TO CALL ME J. GORGEOUS. NOW...

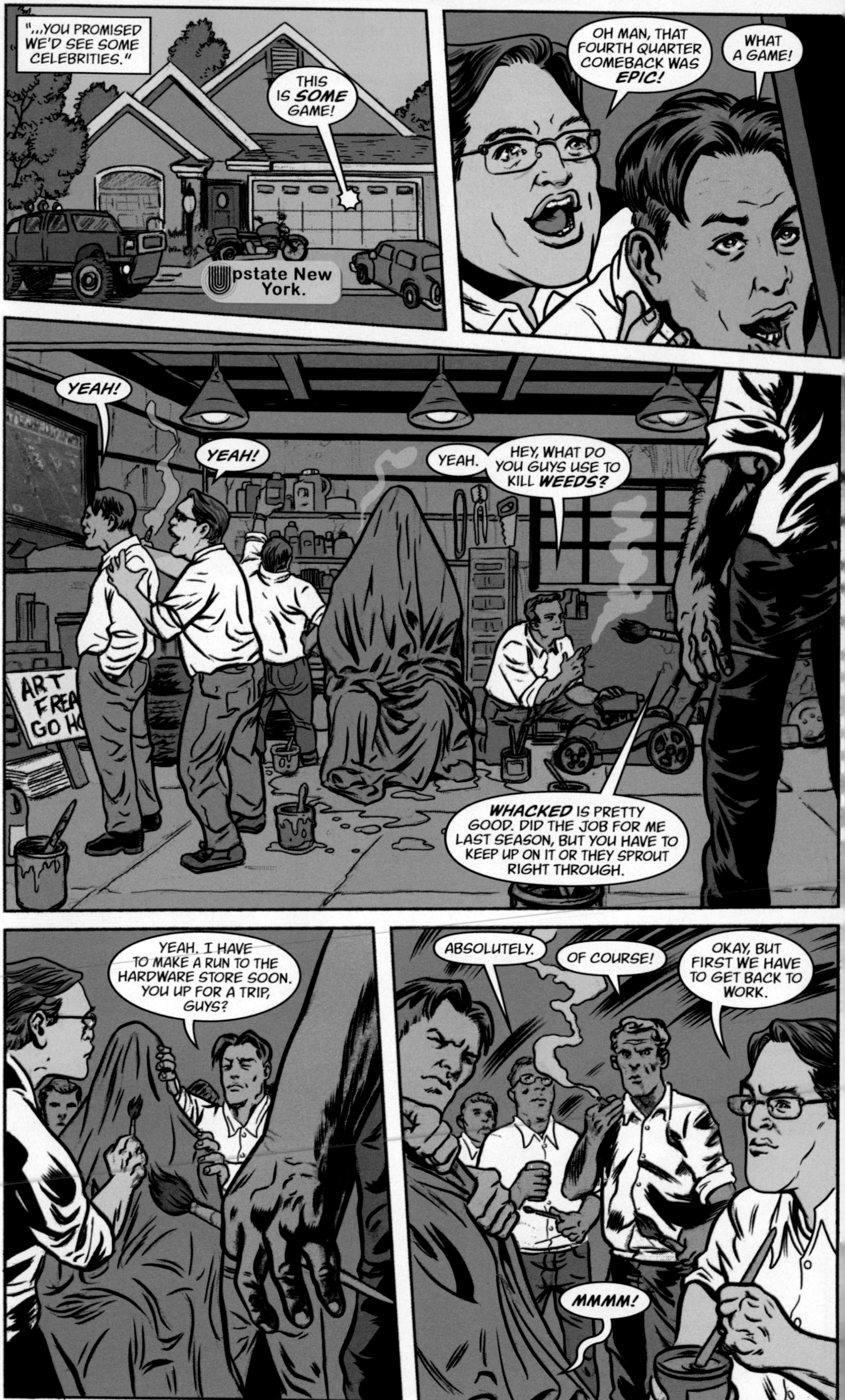
"...YOU PROMISED WE'D SEE SOME CELEBRITIES."
THIS IS SOME GAME!
Upstate New York.
OH MAN, THAT FOURTH QUARTER COMEBACK WAS EPIC!
WHAT A GAME!
YEAH!
YEAH!
YEAH.
HEY, WHAT DO YOU GUYS USE TO KILL WEEDS?
ART FREA GO H
WHACKED IS PRETTY GOOD. DID THE JOB FOR ME LAST SEASON, BUT YOU HAVE TO KEEP UP ON IT OR THEY SPROUT RIGHT THROUGH.
YEAH. I HAVE TO MAKE A RUN TO THE HARDWARE STORE SOON. YOU UP FOR A TRIP, GUYS?
ABSOLUTELY.
OF COURSE!
OKAY, BUT FIRST WE HAVE TO GET BACK TO WORK.
MMMM!

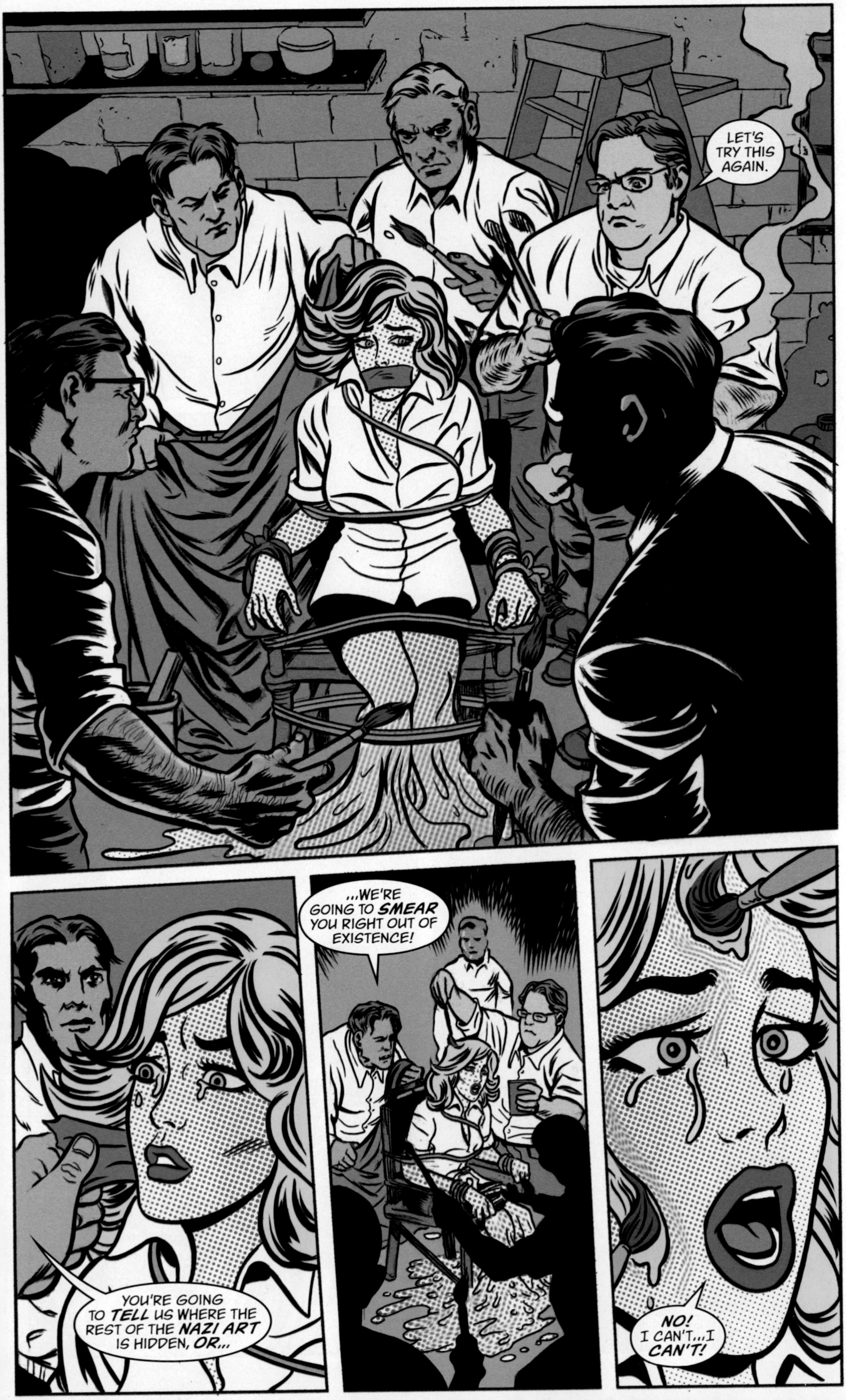
LET'S TRY THIS AGAIN.
YOU'RE GOING TO TELL US WHERE THE REST OF THE NAZI ART IS HIDDEN, OR...
...WE'RE GOING TO SMEAR YOU RIGHT OUT OF EXISTENCE!
NO! I CAN'T...I CAN'T!

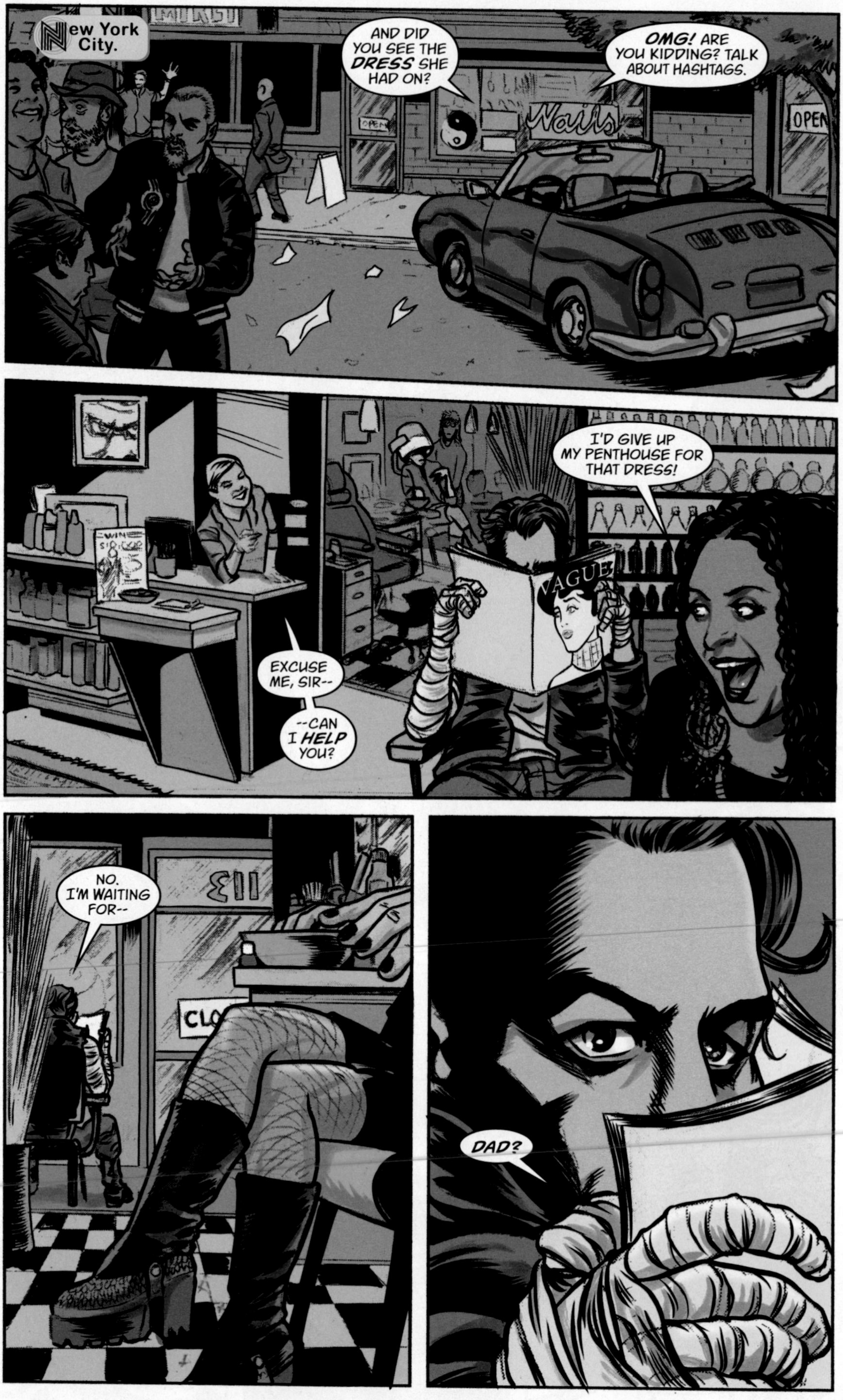
New York City.
AND DID YOU SEE THE DRESS SHE HAD ON?
OMG! ARE YOU KIDDING? TALK ABOUT HASHTAGS.
OPEN
Nails
OPEN
I'D GIVE UP MY PENTHOUSE FOR THAT DRESS!
VAGUE
EXCUSE ME, SIR--
--CAN I HELP YOU?
NO. I'M WAITING FOR--
DAD?

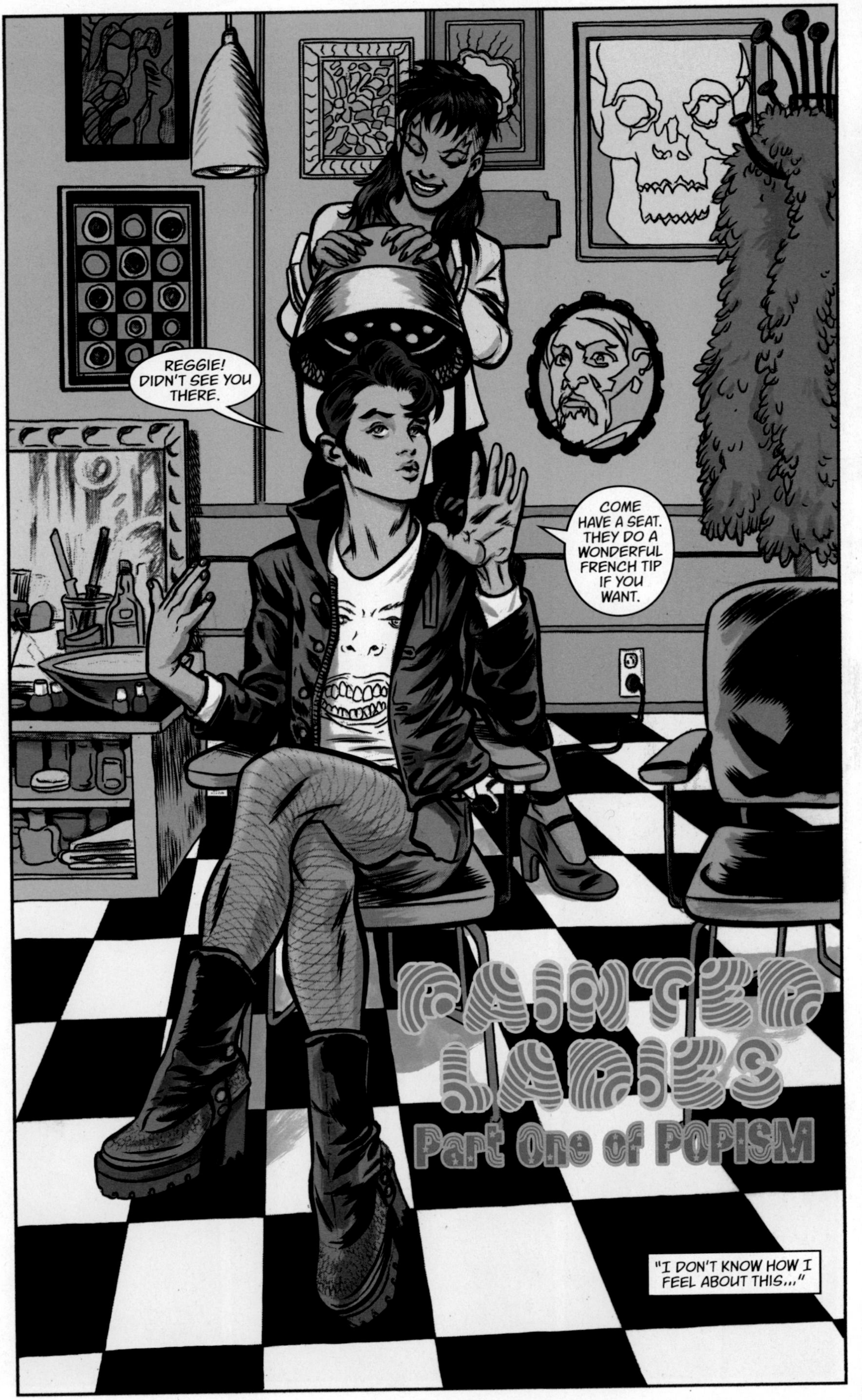
REGGIE! DIDN'T SEE YOU THERE.
COME HAVE A SEAT. THEY DO A WONDERFUL FRENCH TIP IF YOU WANT.
PAINTED LADIES
Part One of POPISM
"I DON'T KNOW HOW I FEEL ABOUT THIS..."

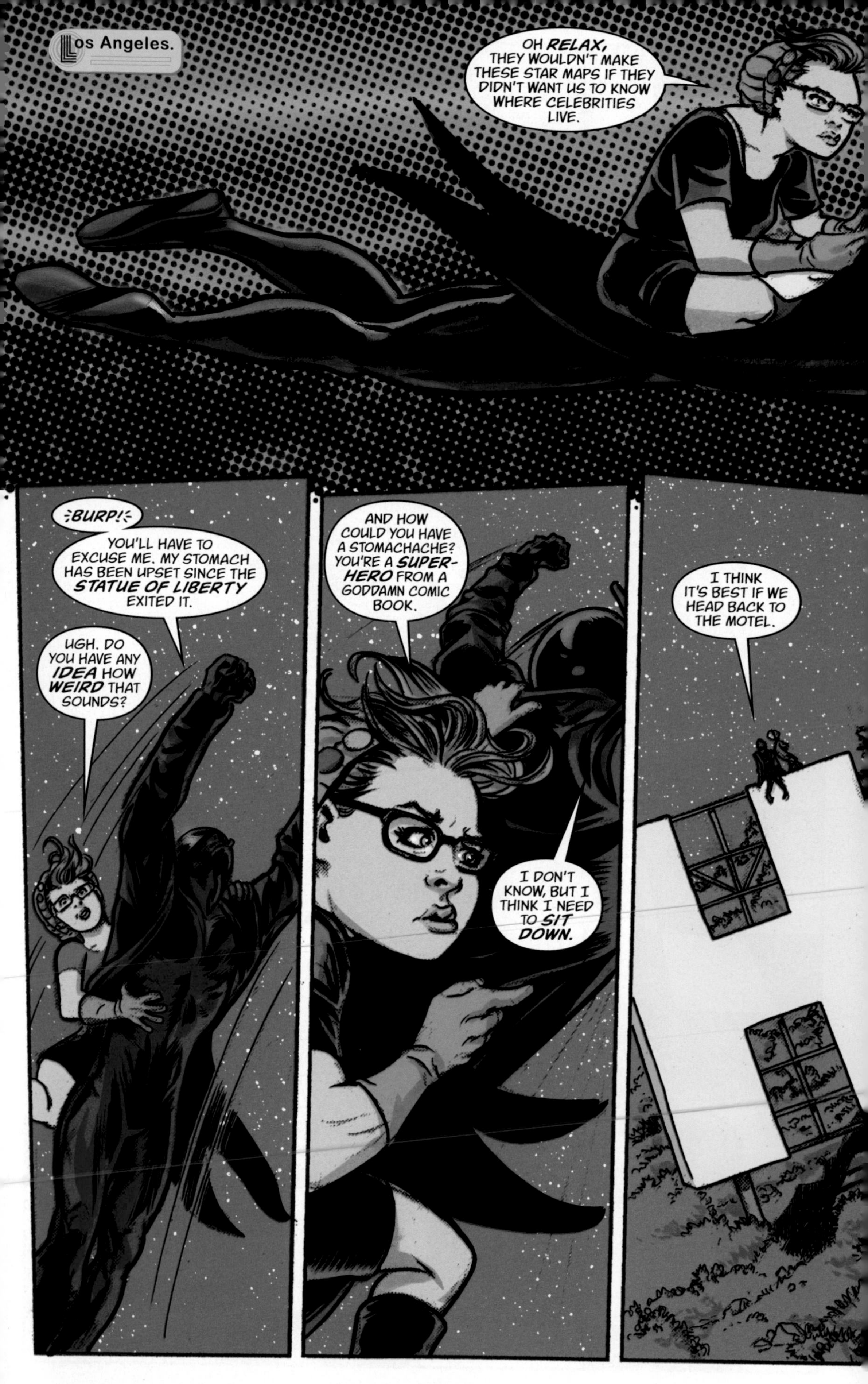
Los Angeles.
OH RELAX, THEY WOULDN'T MAKE THESE STAR MAPS IF THEY DIDN'T WANT US TO KNOW WHERE CELEBRITIES LIVE.
BURP!
YOU'LL HAVE TO EXCUSE ME. MY STOMACH HAS BEEN UPSET SINCE THE STATUE OF LIBERTY EXITED IT.
UGH. DO YOU HAVE ANY IDEA HOW WEIRD THAT SOUNDS?
AND HOW COULD YOU HAVE A STOMACHACHE? YOU'RE A SUPER-HERO FROM A GODDAMN COMIC BOOK.
I DON'T KNOW, BUT I THINK I NEED TO SIT DOWN.
I THINK IT'S BEST IF WE HEAD BACK TO THE MOTEL.

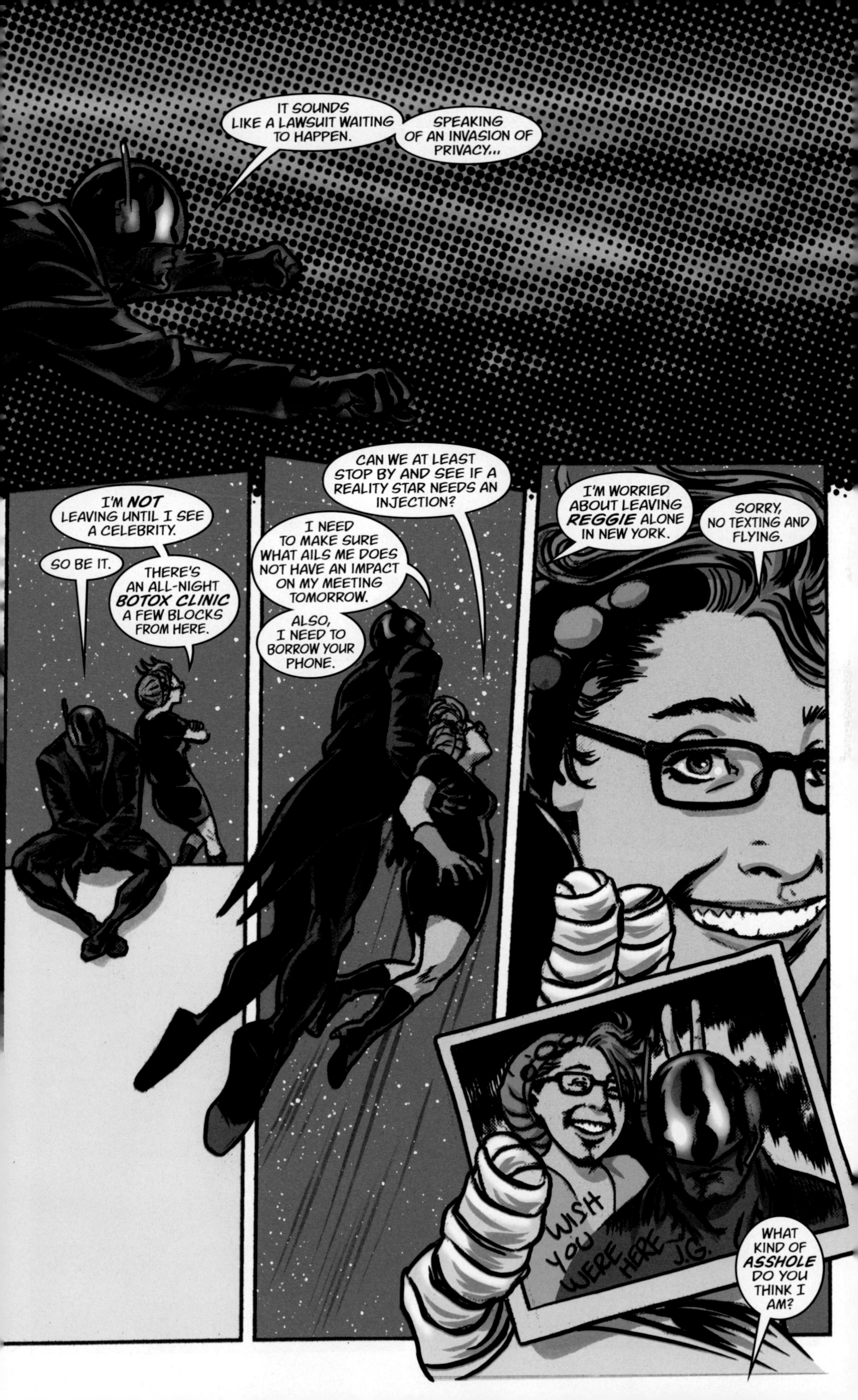
IT SOUNDS LIKE A LAWSUIT WAITING TO HAPPEN.
SPEAKING OF AN INVASION OF PRIVACY...
I'M NOT LEAVING UNTIL I SEE A CELEBRITY.
SO BE IT.
THERE'S AN ALL-NIGHT BOTOX CLINIC A FEW BLOCKS FROM HERE.
CAN WE AT LEAST STOP BY AND SEE IF A REALITY STAR NEEDS AN INJECTION?
I NEED TO MAKE SURE WHAT AILS ME DOES NOT HAVE AN IMPACT ON MY MEETING TOMORROW.
ALSO, I NEED TO BORROW YOUR PHONE.
I'M WORRIED ABOUT LEAVING REGGIE ALONE IN NEW YORK.
SORRY, NO TEXTING AND FLYING.
WISH YOU WERE HERE — J.G.
WHAT KIND OF ASSHOLE DO YOU THINK I AM?

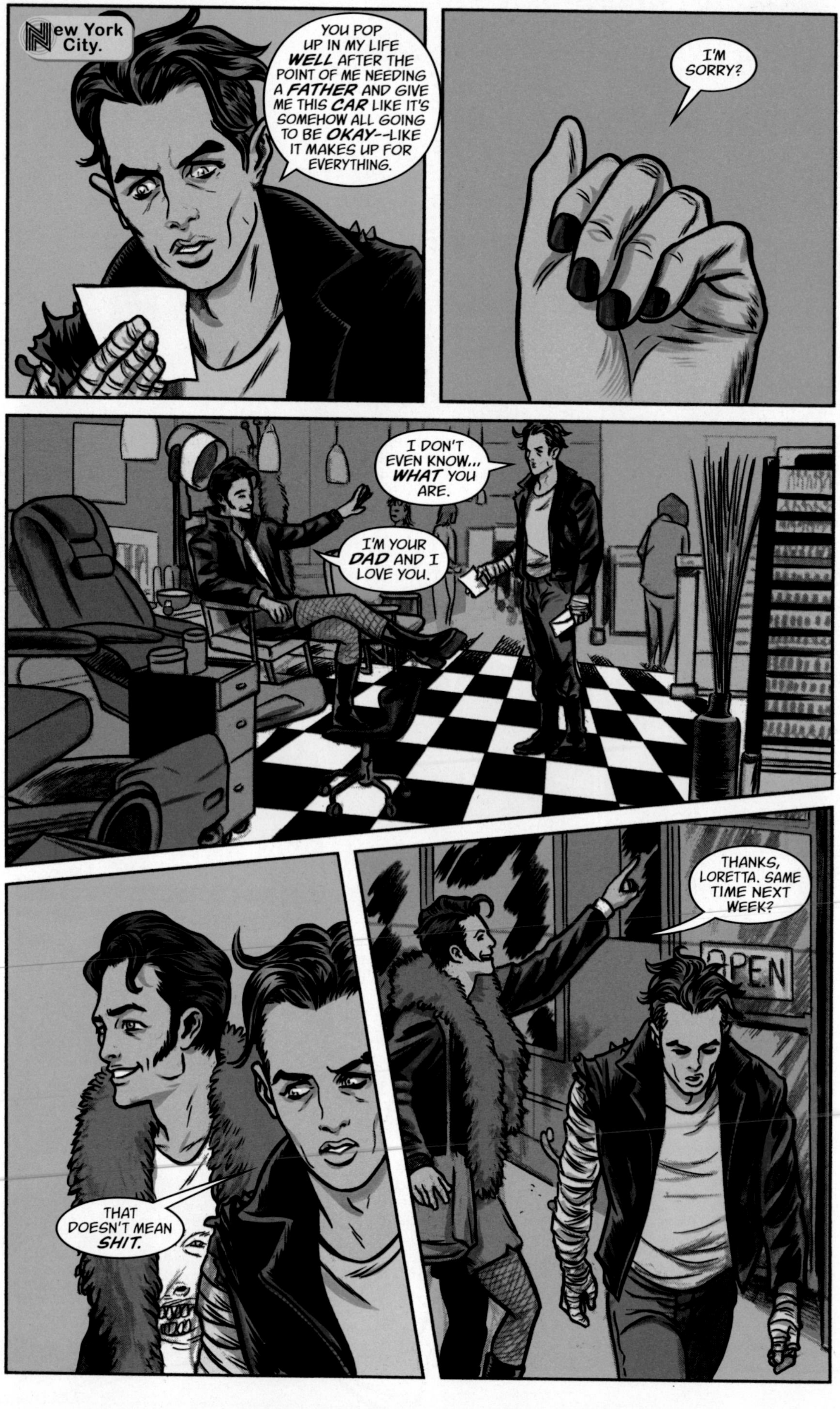
New York City.
YOU POP UP IN MY LIFE WELL AFTER THE POINT OF ME NEEDING A FATHER AND GIVE ME THIS CAR LIKE IT'S SOMEHOW ALL GOING TO BE OKAY--LIKE IT MAKES UP FOR EVERYTHING.
I'M SORRY?
I DON'T EVEN KNOW... WHAT YOU ARE.
I'M YOUR DAD AND I LOVE YOU.
THAT DOESN'T MEAN SHIT.
THANKS, LORETTA. SAME TIME NEXT WEEK?
OPEN

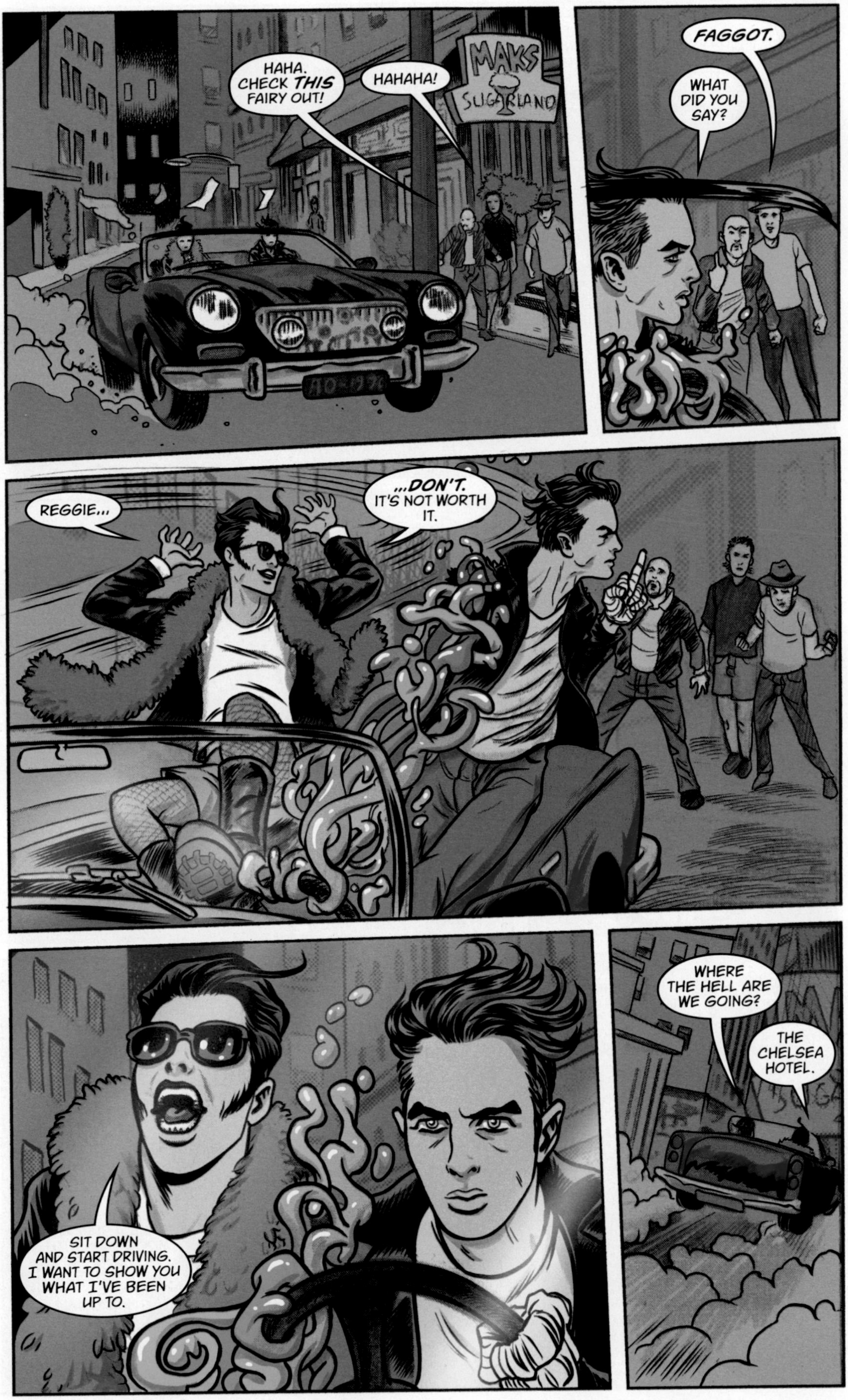
HAHA. CHECK THIS FAIRY OUT!
HAHAHA!
MAKS SUGARLAND
FAGGOT.
WHAT DID YOU SAY?
REGGIE...
...DON'T. IT'S NOT WORTH IT.
SIT DOWN AND START DRIVING. I WANT TO SHOW YOU WHAT I'VE BEEN UP TO.
WHERE THE HELL ARE WE GOING?
THE CHELSEA HOTEL.

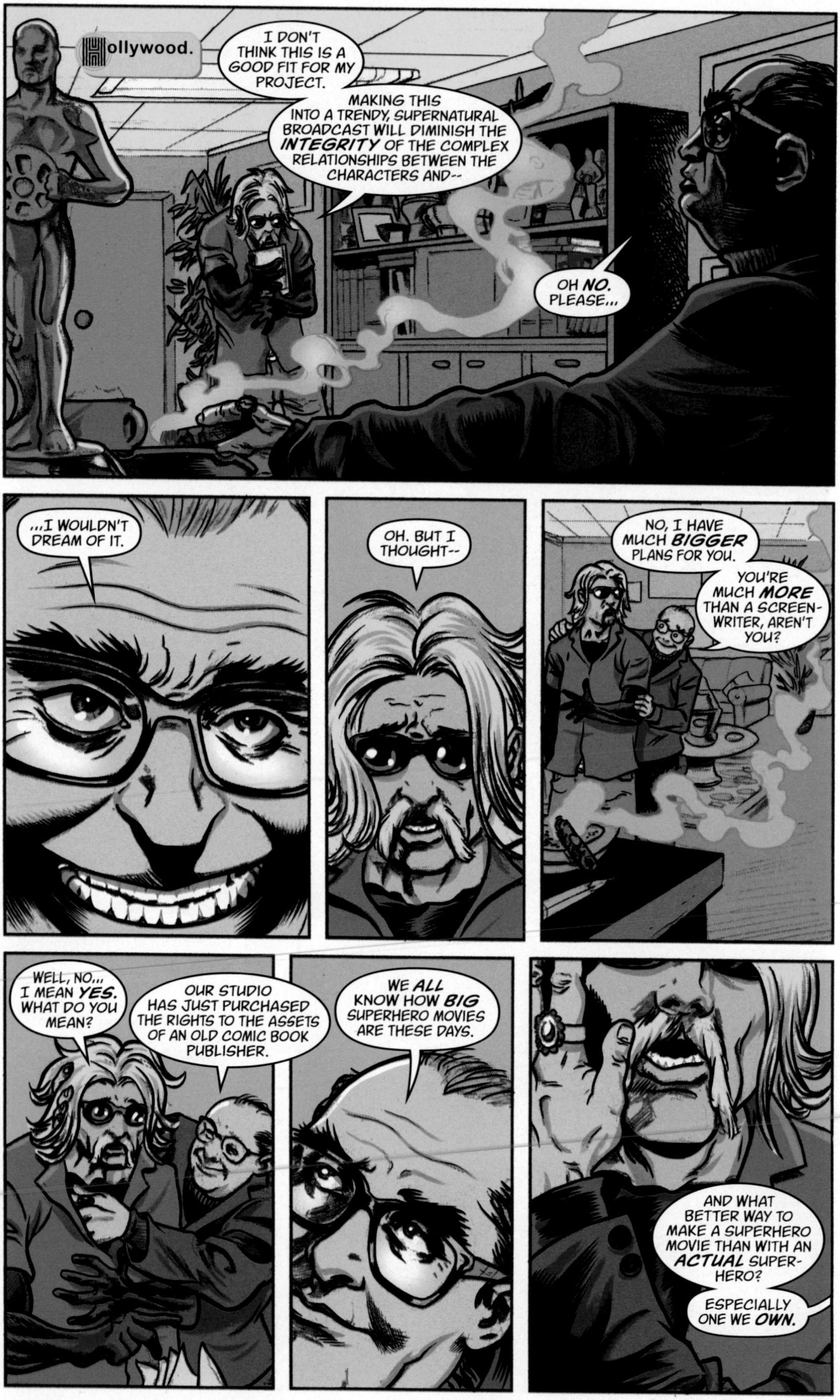

Hollywood.
I DON'T THINK THIS IS A GOOD FIT FOR MY PROJECT.
MAKING THIS INTO A TRENDY, SUPERNATURAL BROADCAST WILL DIMINISH THE INTEGRITY OF THE COMPLEX RELATIONSHIPS BETWEEN THE CHARACTERS AND--
OH NO. PLEASE...
...I WOULDN'T DREAM OF IT.
OH. BUT I THOUGHT--
NO, I HAVE MUCH BIGGER PLANS FOR YOU.
YOU'RE MUCH MORE THAN A SCREEN-WRITER, AREN'T YOU?
WELL, NO... I MEAN YES. WHAT DO YOU MEAN?
OUR STUDIO HAS JUST PURCHASED THE RIGHTS TO THE ASSETS OF AN OLD COMIC BOOK PUBLISHER.
WE ALL KNOW HOW BIG SUPERHERO MOVIES ARE THESE DAYS.
AND WHAT BETTER WAY TO MAKE A SUPERHERO MOVIE THAN WITH AN ACTUAL SUPER-HERO?
ESPECIALLY ONE WE OWN.

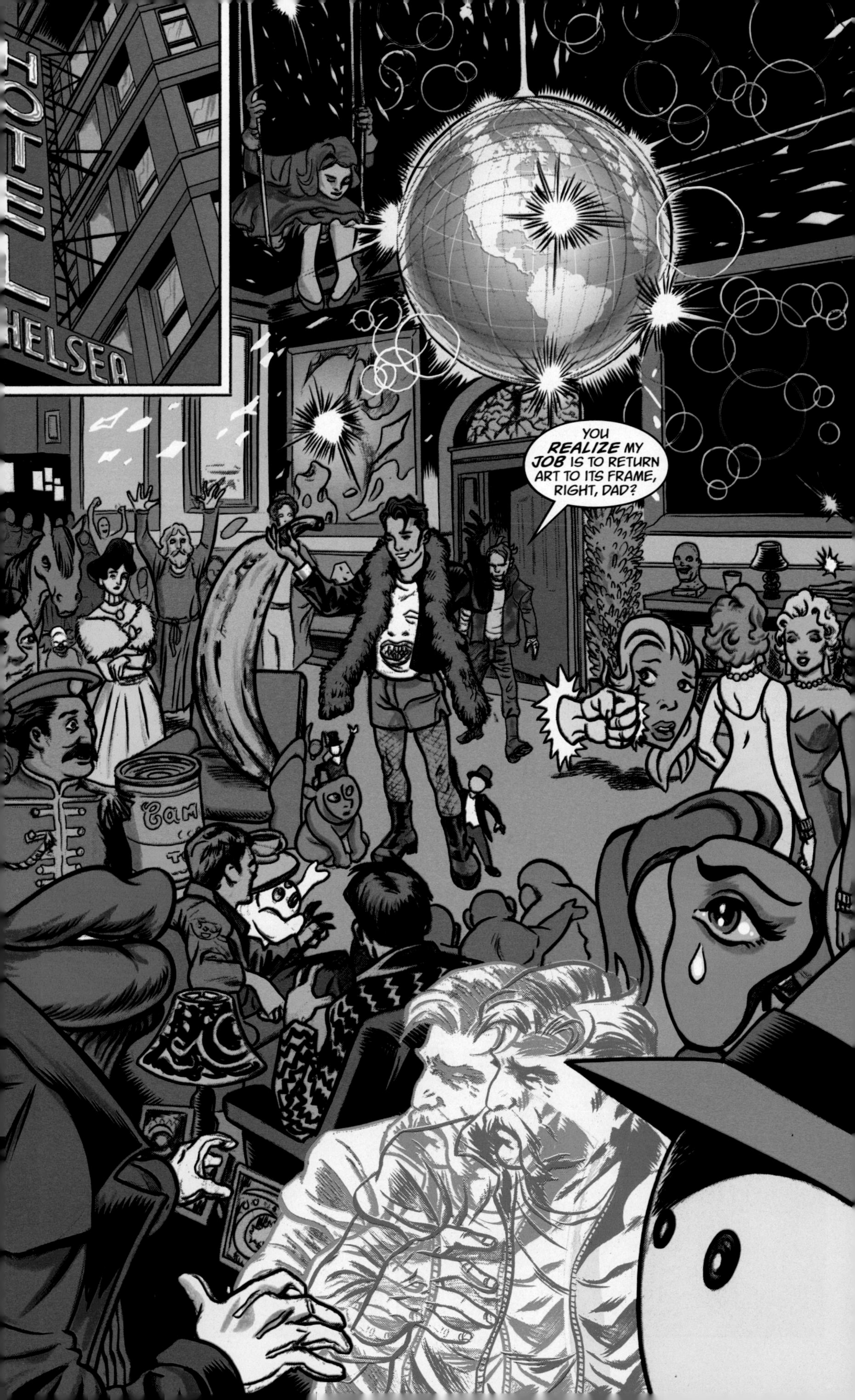
HOTEL
HELSEA
YOU REALIZE MY JOB IS TO RETURN ART TO ITS FRAME, RIGHT, DAD?

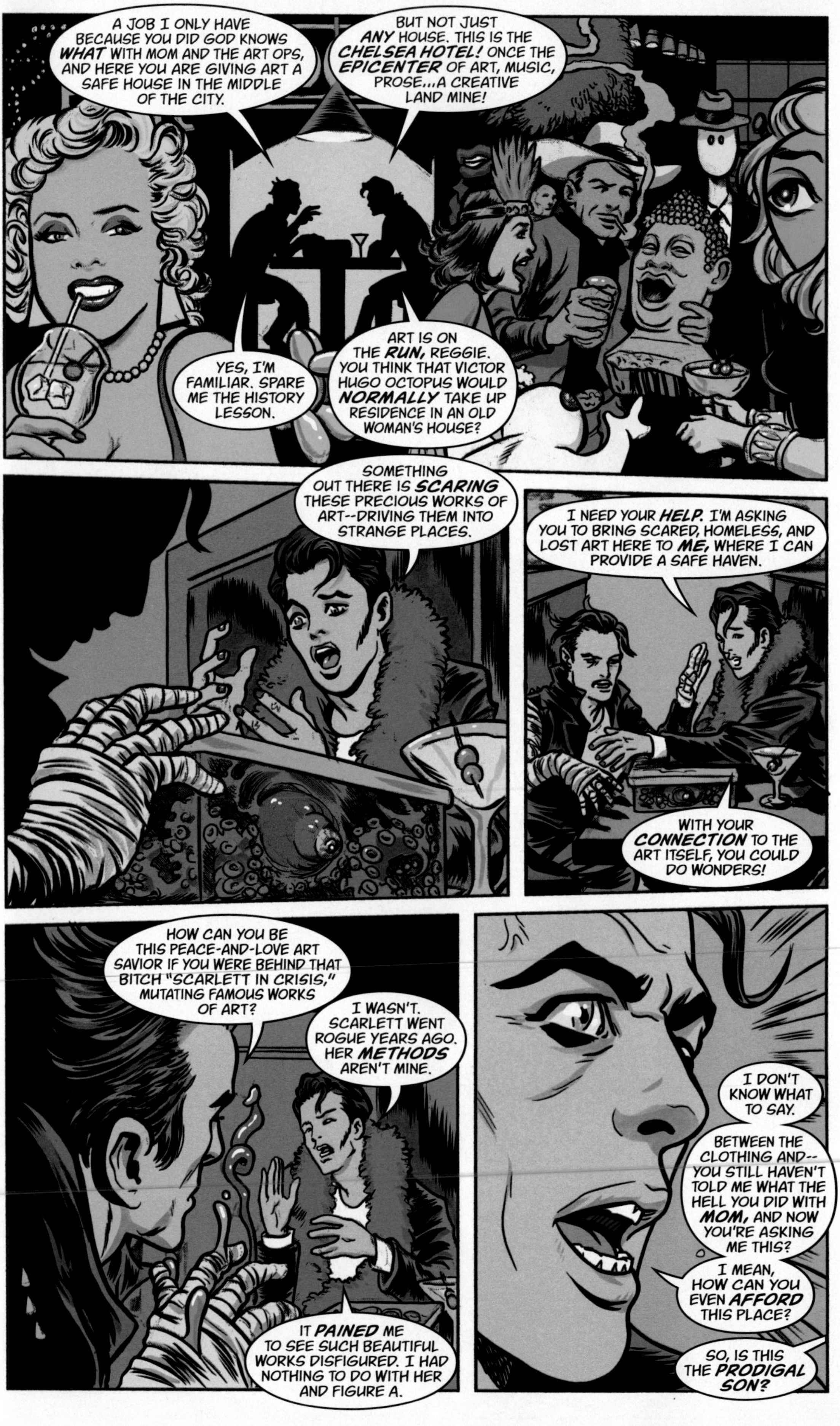
A JOB I ONLY HAVE BECAUSE YOU DID GOD KNOWS WHAT WITH MOM AND THE ART OPS, AND HERE YOU ARE GIVING ART A SAFE HOUSE IN THE MIDDLE OF THE CITY.
BUT NOT JUST ANY HOUSE. THIS IS THE CHELSEA HOTEL! ONCE THE EPICENTER OF ART, MUSIC, PROSE...A CREATIVE LAND MINE!
YES, I'M FAMILIAR. SPARE ME THE HISTORY LESSON.
ART IS ON THE RUN, REGGIE. YOU THINK THAT VICTOR HUGO OCTOPUS WOULD NORMALLY TAKE UP RESIDENCE IN AN OLD WOMAN'S HOUSE?
SOMETHING OUT THERE IS SCARING THESE PRECIOUS WORKS OF ART--DRIVING THEM INTO STRANGE PLACES.
I NEED YOUR HELP. I'M ASKING YOU TO BRING SCARED, HOMELESS, AND LOST ART HERE TO ME, WHERE I CAN PROVIDE A SAFE HAVEN.
WITH YOUR CONNECTION TO THE ART ITSELF, YOU COULD DO WONDERS!
HOW CAN YOU BE THIS PEACE-AND-LOVE ART SAVIOR IF YOU WERE BEHIND THAT BITCH "SCARLETT IN CRISIS," MUTATING FAMOUS WORKS OF ART?
I WASN'T. SCARLETT WENT ROGUE YEARS AGO. HER METHODS AREN'T MINE.
IT PAINED ME TO SEE SUCH BEAUTIFUL WORKS DISFIGURED. I HAD NOTHING TO DO WITH HER AND FIGURE A.
I DON'T KNOW WHAT TO SAY.
BETWEEN THE CLOTHING AND-- YOU STILL HAVEN'T TOLD ME WHAT THE HELL YOU DID WITH MOM, AND NOW YOU'RE ASKING ME THIS?
I MEAN, HOW CAN YOU EVEN AFFORD THIS PLACE?
SO, IS THIS THE PRODIGAL SON?

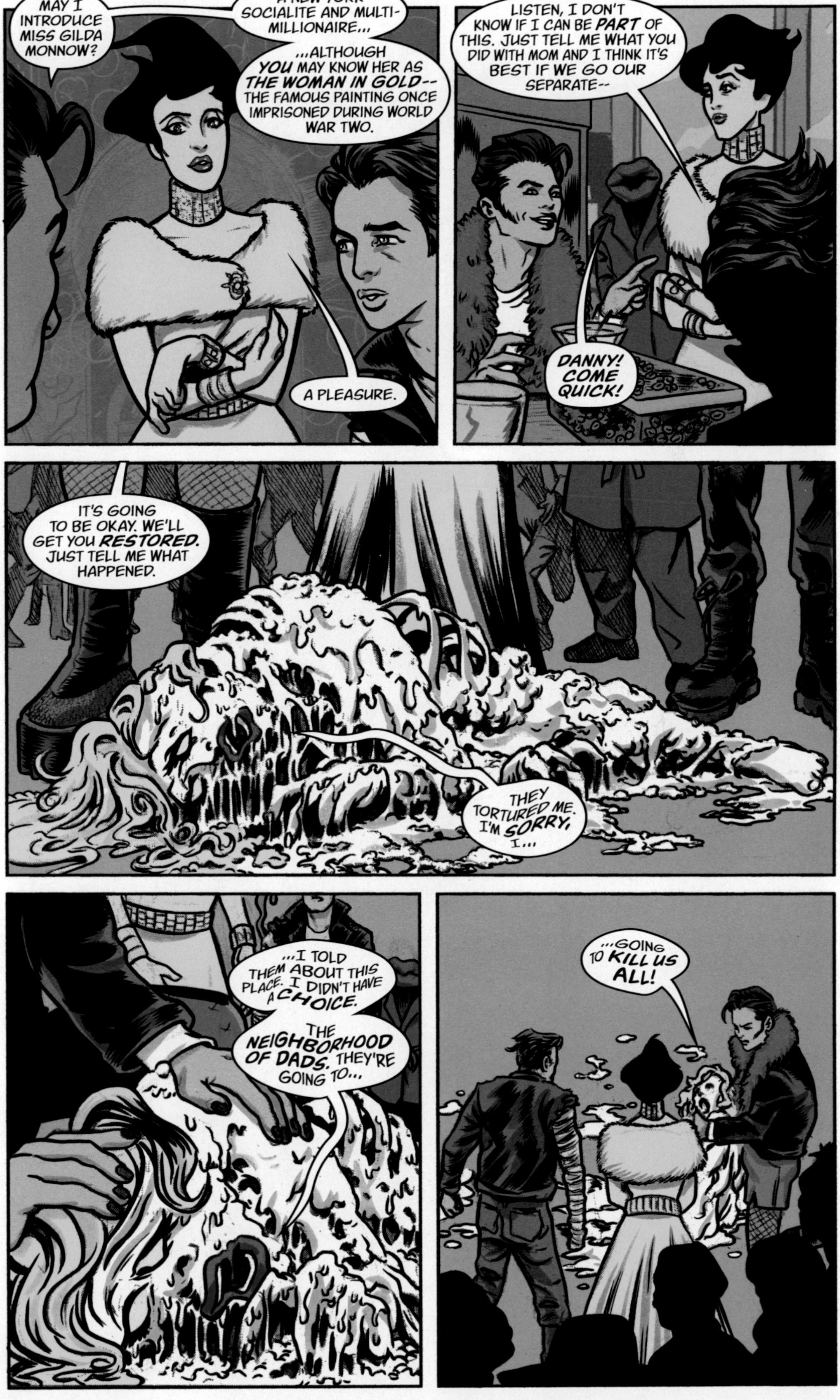
MAY I INTRODUCE MISS GILDA MONNOW?
A NEW YORK SOCIALITE AND MULTI-MILLIONAIRE...
...ALTHOUGH YOU MAY KNOW HER AS THE WOMAN IN GOLD-- THE FAMOUS PAINTING ONCE IMPRISONED DURING WORLD WAR TWO.
A PLEASURE.
LISTEN, I DON'T KNOW IF I CAN BE PART OF THIS. JUST TELL ME WHAT YOU DID WITH MOM AND I THINK IT'S BEST IF WE GO OUR SEPARATE--
DANNY! COME QUICK!
IT'S GOING TO BE OKAY. WE'LL GET YOU RESTORED. JUST TELL ME WHAT HAPPENED.
THEY TORTURED ME. I'M SORRY, I...
...I TOLD THEM ABOUT THIS PLACE. I DIDN'T HAVE A CHOICE.
THE NEIGHBORHOOD OF DADS. THEY'RE GOING TO...
...GOING TO KILL US ALL!

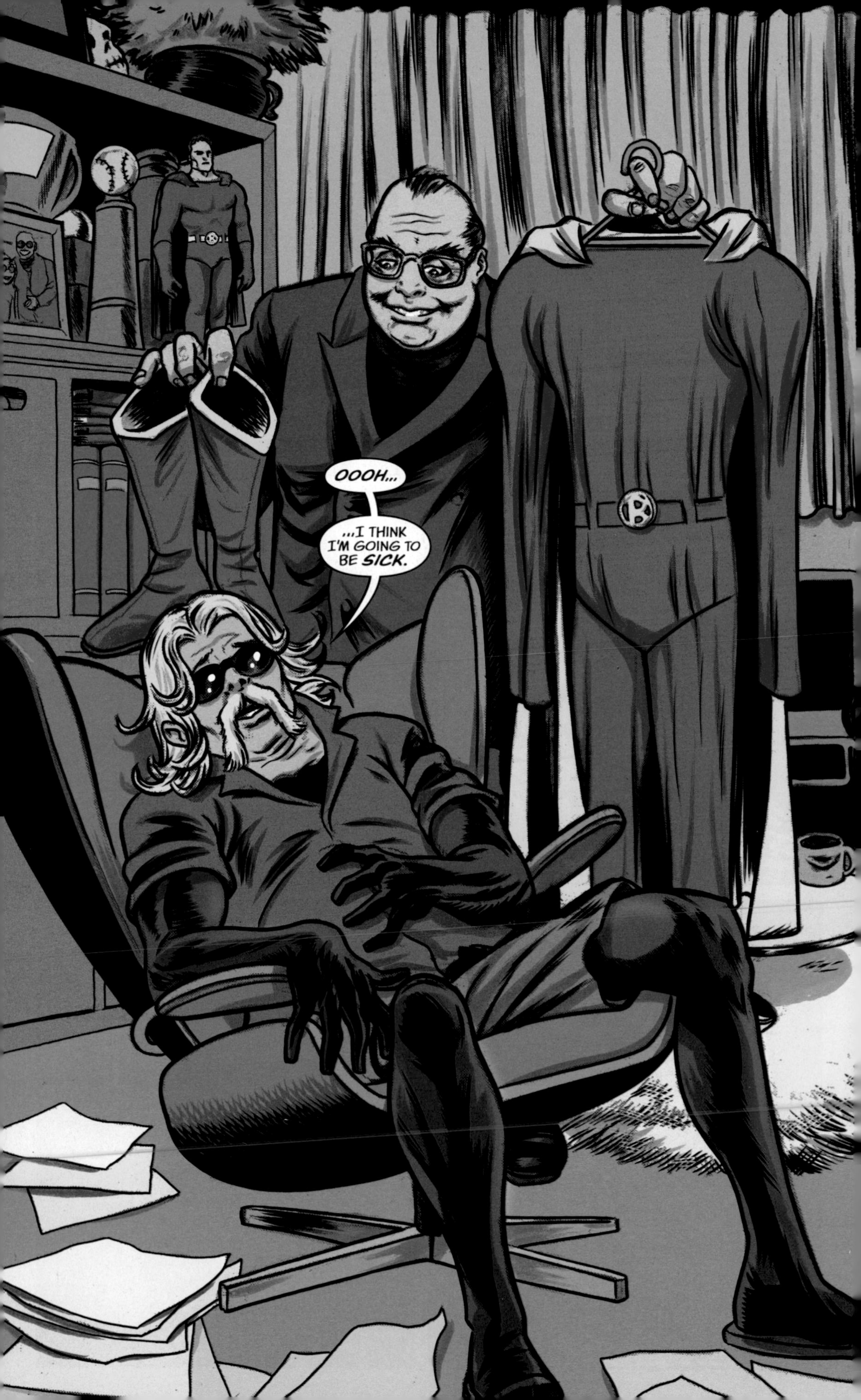
OOOH...
...I THINK I'M GOING TO BE SICK.

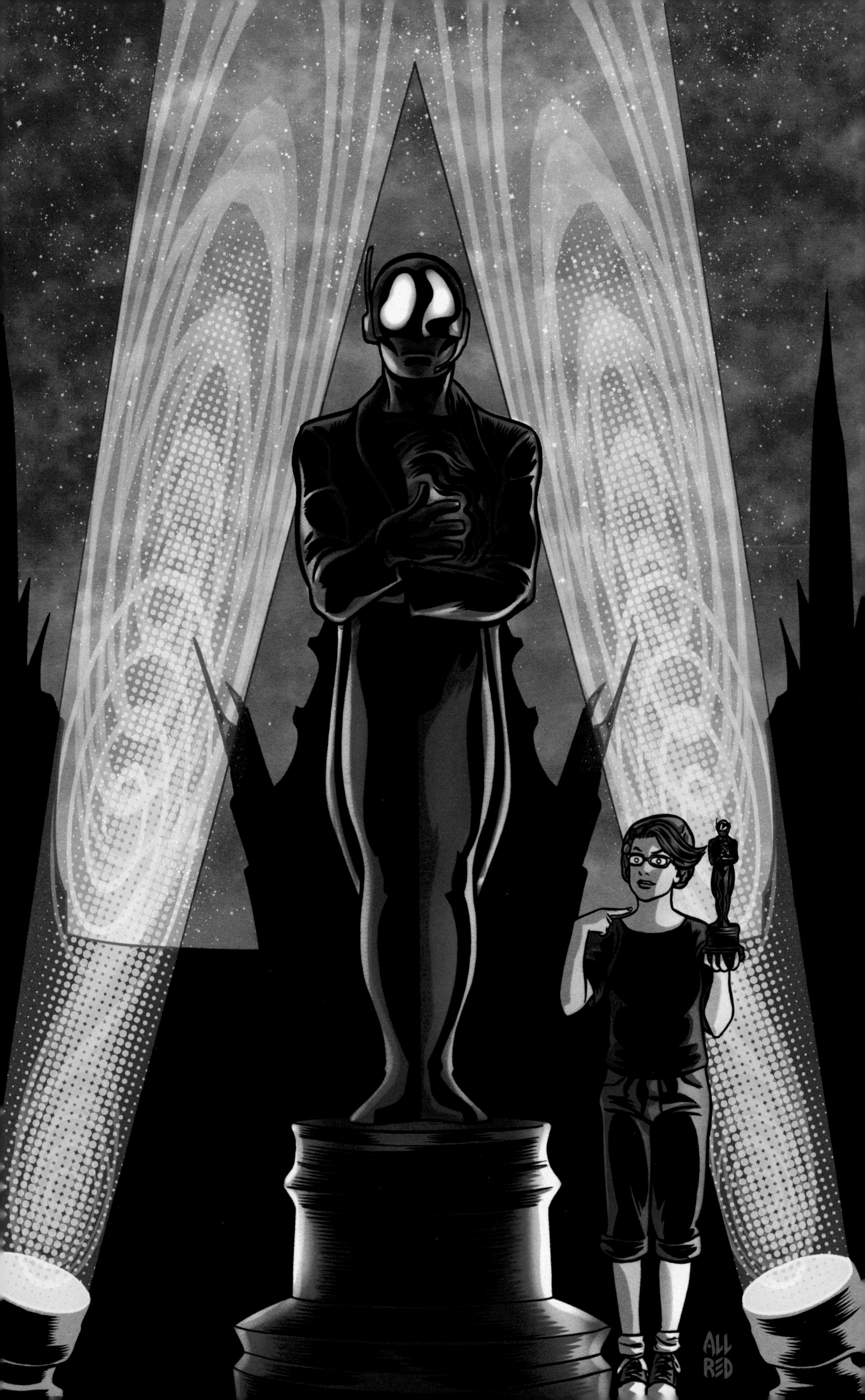
ALL
RED

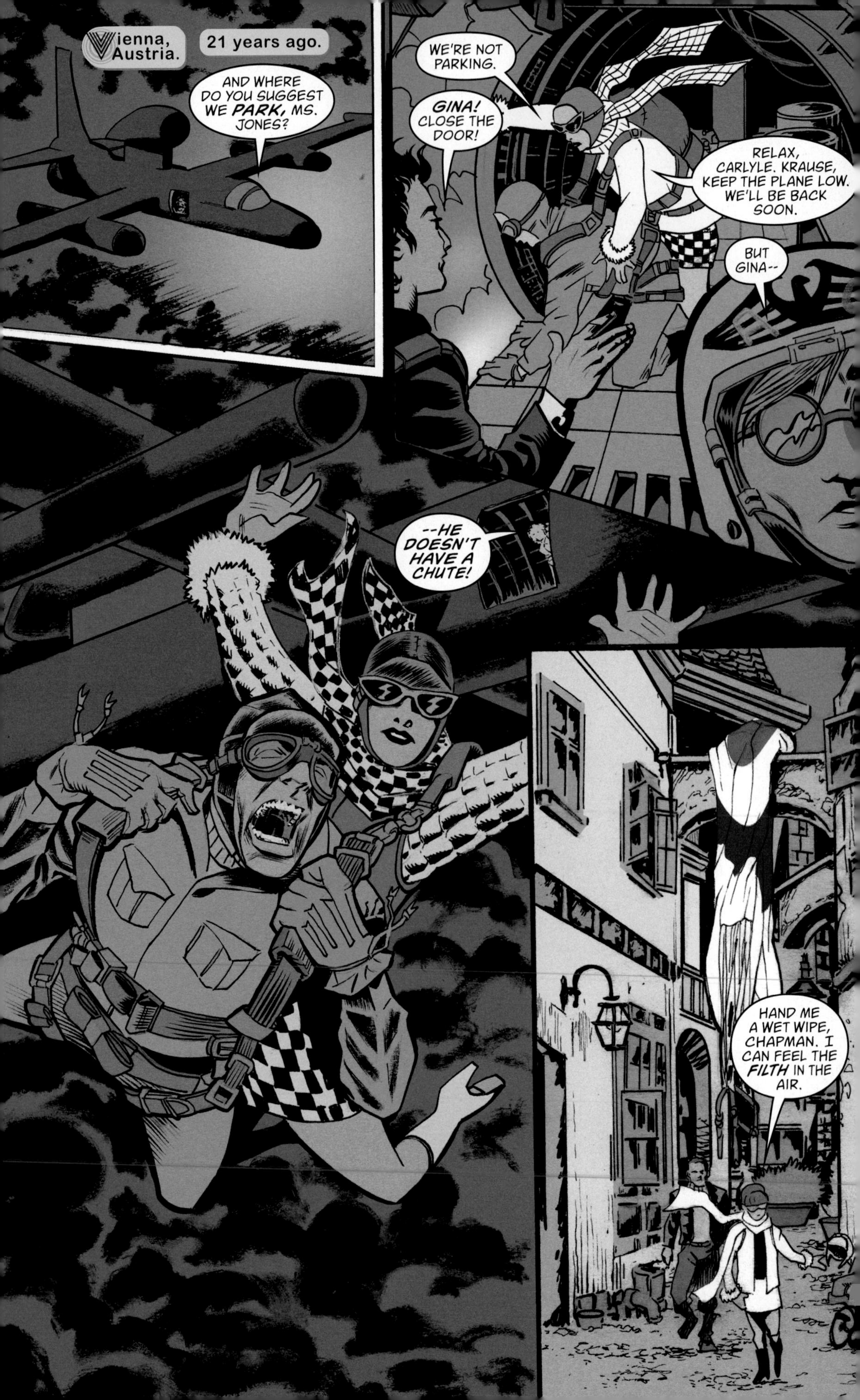

Vienna, Austria.
21 years ago.
AND WHERE DO YOU SUGGEST WE PARK, MS. JONES?
WE'RE NOT PARKING.
GINA! CLOSE THE DOOR!
RELAX, CARLYLE. KRAUSE, KEEP THE PLANE LOW. WE'LL BE BACK SOON.
BUT GINA--
--HE DOESN'T HAVE A CHUTE!
HAND ME A WET WIPE, CHAPMAN. I CAN FEEL THE FILTH IN THE AIR.

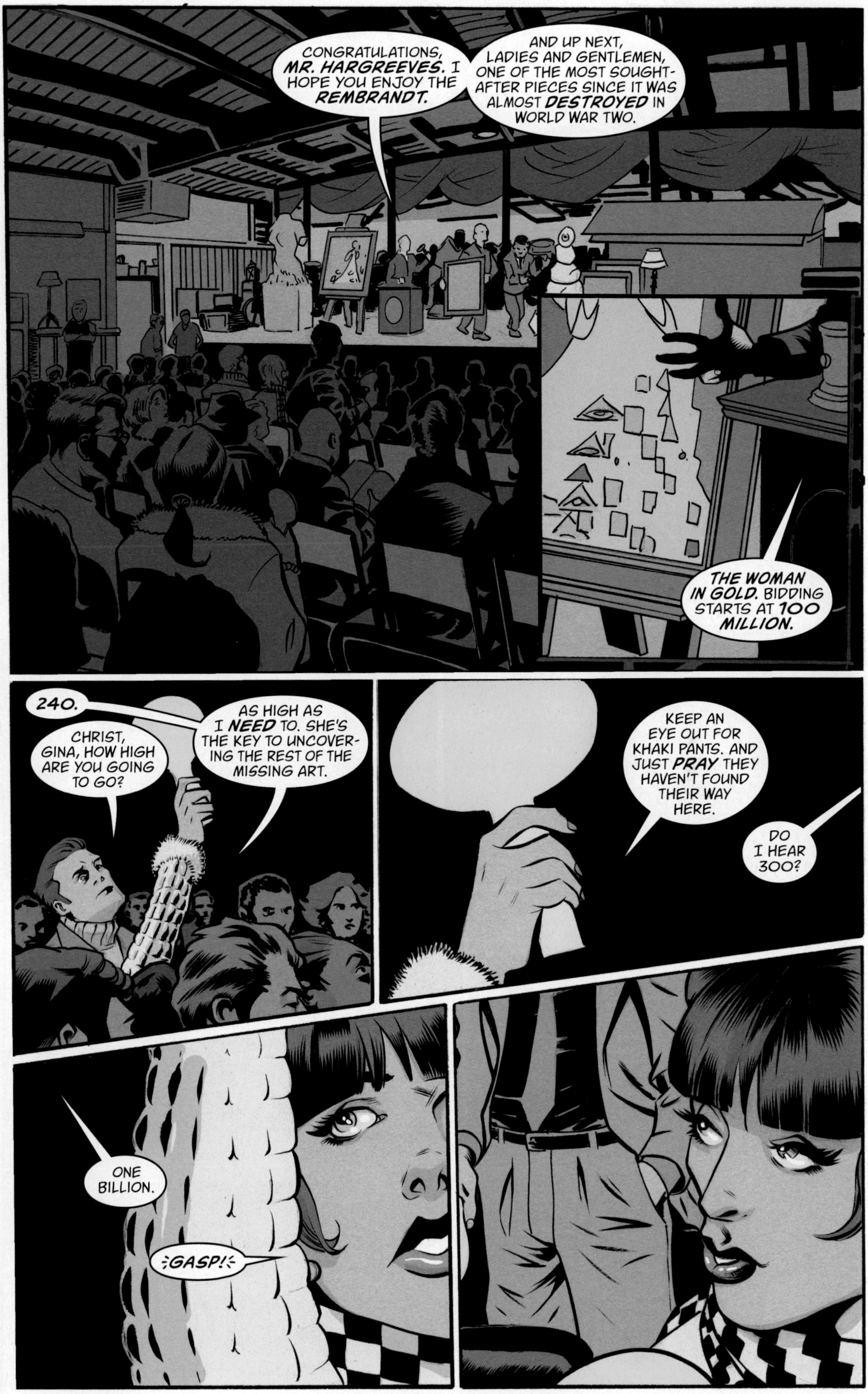
CONGRATULATIONS, MR. HARGREEVES. I HOPE YOU ENJOY THE REMBRANDT.
AND UP NEXT, LADIES AND GENTLEMEN, ONE OF THE MOST SOUGHT-AFTER PIECES SINCE IT WAS ALMOST DESTROYED IN WORLD WAR TWO.
THE WOMAN IN GOLD. BIDDING STARTS AT 100 MILLION.
240.
CHRIST, GINA, HOW HIGH ARE YOU GOING TO GO?
AS HIGH AS I NEED TO. SHE'S THE KEY TO UNCOVERING THE REST OF THE MISSING ART.
KEEP AN EYE OUT FOR KHAKI PANTS. AND JUST PRAY THEY HAVEN'T FOUND THEIR WAY HERE.
DO I HEAR 300?
ONE BILLION.
GASP!

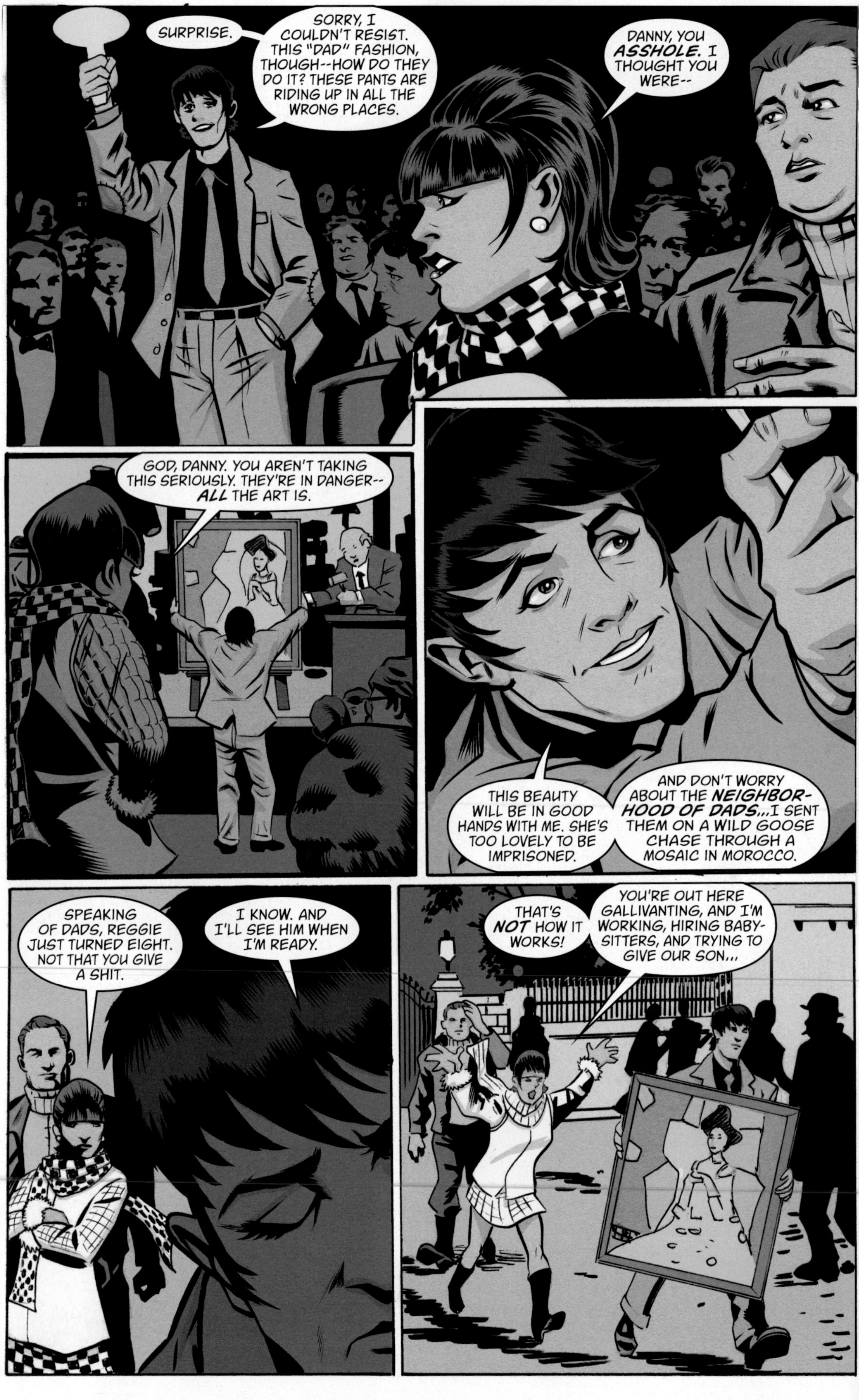
SURPRISE.
SORRY, I COULDN'T RESIST. THIS "DAD" FASHION, THOUGH--HOW DO THEY DO IT? THESE PANTS ARE RIDING UP IN ALL THE WRONG PLACES.
DANNY, YOU ASSHOLE. I THOUGHT YOU WERE--
GOD, DANNY. YOU AREN'T TAKING THIS SERIOUSLY. THEY'RE IN DANGER--ALL THE ART IS.
THIS BEAUTY WILL BE IN GOOD HANDS WITH ME. SHE'S TOO LOVELY TO BE IMPRISONED.
AND DON'T WORRY ABOUT THE NEIGHBORHOOD OF DADS... I SENT THEM ON A WILD GOOSE CHASE THROUGH A MOSAIC IN MOROCCO.
SPEAKING OF DADS, REGGIE JUST TURNED EIGHT. NOT THAT YOU GIVE A SHIT.
I KNOW. AND I'LL SEE HIM WHEN I'M READY.
THAT'S NOT HOW IT WORKS!
YOU'RE OUT HERE GALLIVANTING, AND I'M WORKING, HIRING BABY-SITTERS, AND TRYING TO GIVE OUR SON...

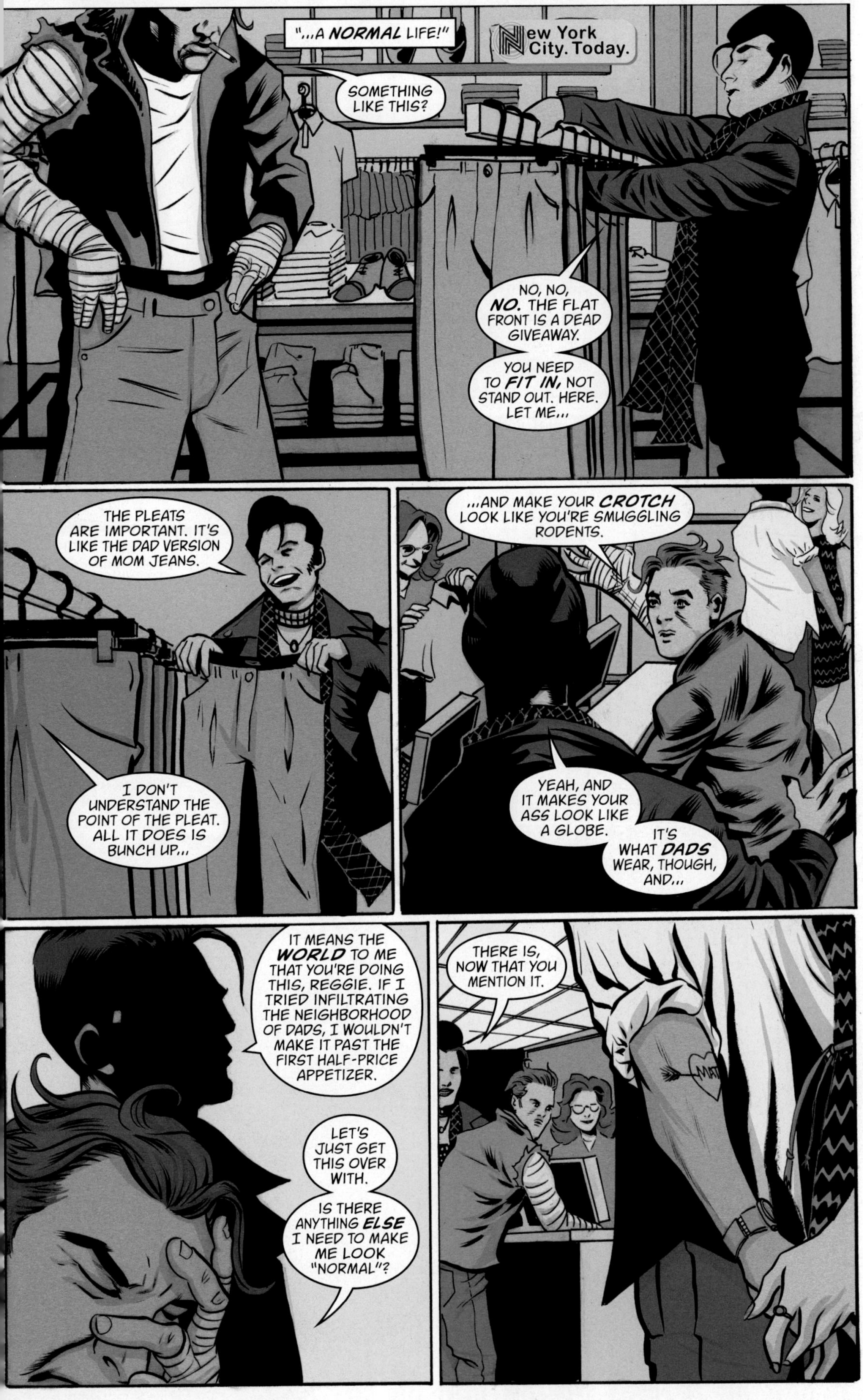

"...A NORMAL LIFE!"
New York City. Today.
SOMETHING LIKE THIS?
NO, NO, NO. THE FLAT FRONT IS A DEAD GIVEAWAY.
YOU NEED TO FIT IN, NOT STAND OUT. HERE. LET ME...
THE PLEATS ARE IMPORTANT. IT'S LIKE THE DAD VERSION OF MOM JEANS.
I DON'T UNDERSTAND THE POINT OF THE PLEAT. ALL IT DOES IS BUNCH UP...
...AND MAKE YOUR CROTCH LOOK LIKE YOU'RE SMUGGLING RODENTS.
YEAH, AND IT MAKES YOUR ASS LOOK LIKE A GLOBE.
IT'S WHAT DADS WEAR, THOUGH, AND...
IT MEANS THE WORLD TO ME THAT YOU'RE DOING THIS, REGGIE. IF I TRIED INFILTRATING THE NEIGHBORHOOD OF DADS, I WOULDN'T MAKE IT PAST THE FIRST HALF-PRICE APPETIZER.
LET'S JUST GET THIS OVER WITH.
IS THERE ANYTHING ELSE I NEED TO MAKE ME LOOK "NORMAL"?
THERE IS, NOW THAT YOU MENTION IT.

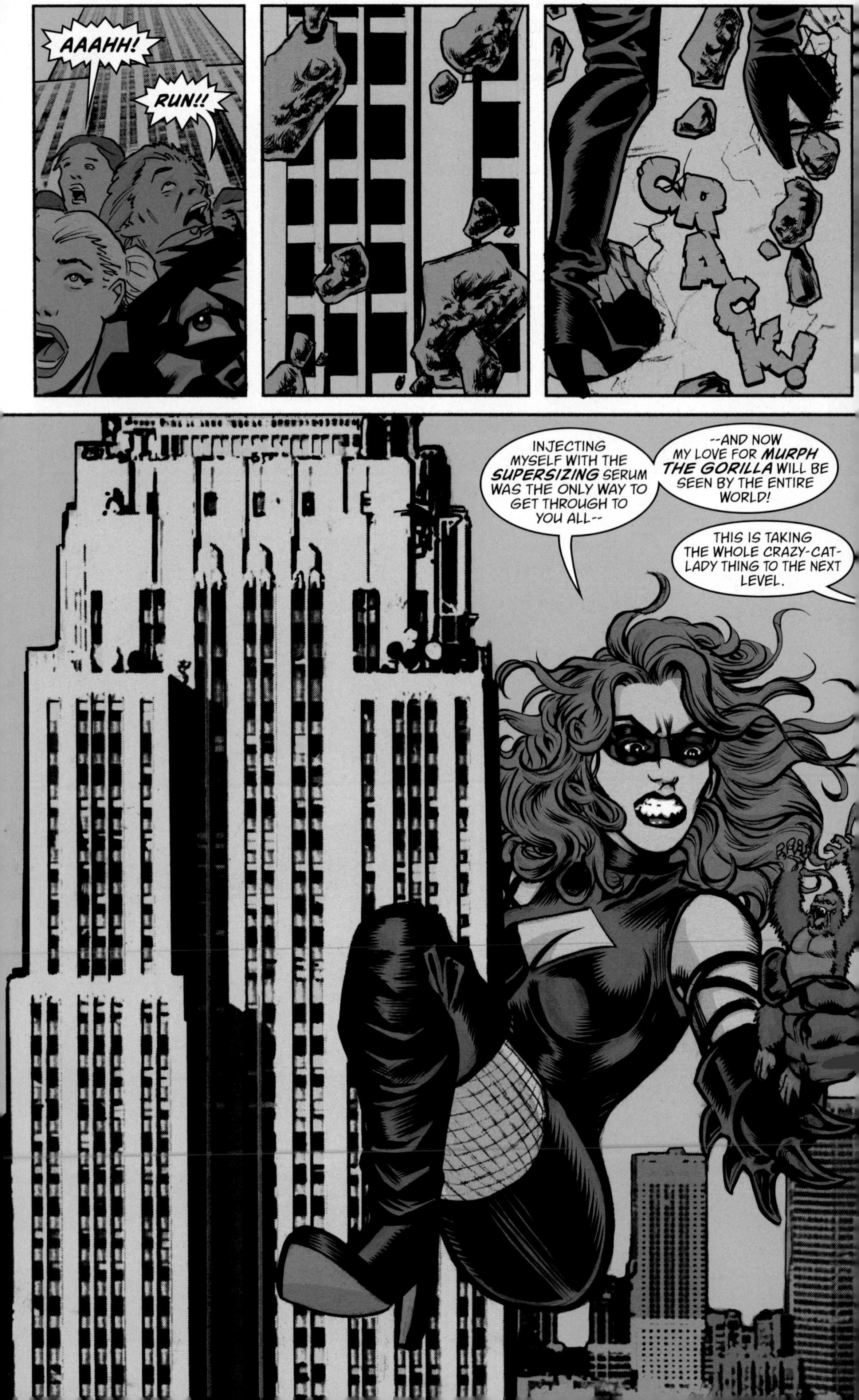
AAAHH!
RUN!!
CRACK!
INJECTING MYSELF WITH THE SUPERSIZING SERUM WAS THE ONLY WAY TO GET THROUGH TO YOU ALL--
--AND NOW MY LOVE FOR MURPH THE GORILLA WILL BE SEEN BY THE ENTIRE WORLD!
THIS IS TAKING THE WHOLE CRAZY-CAT-LADY THING TO THE NEXT LEVEL.

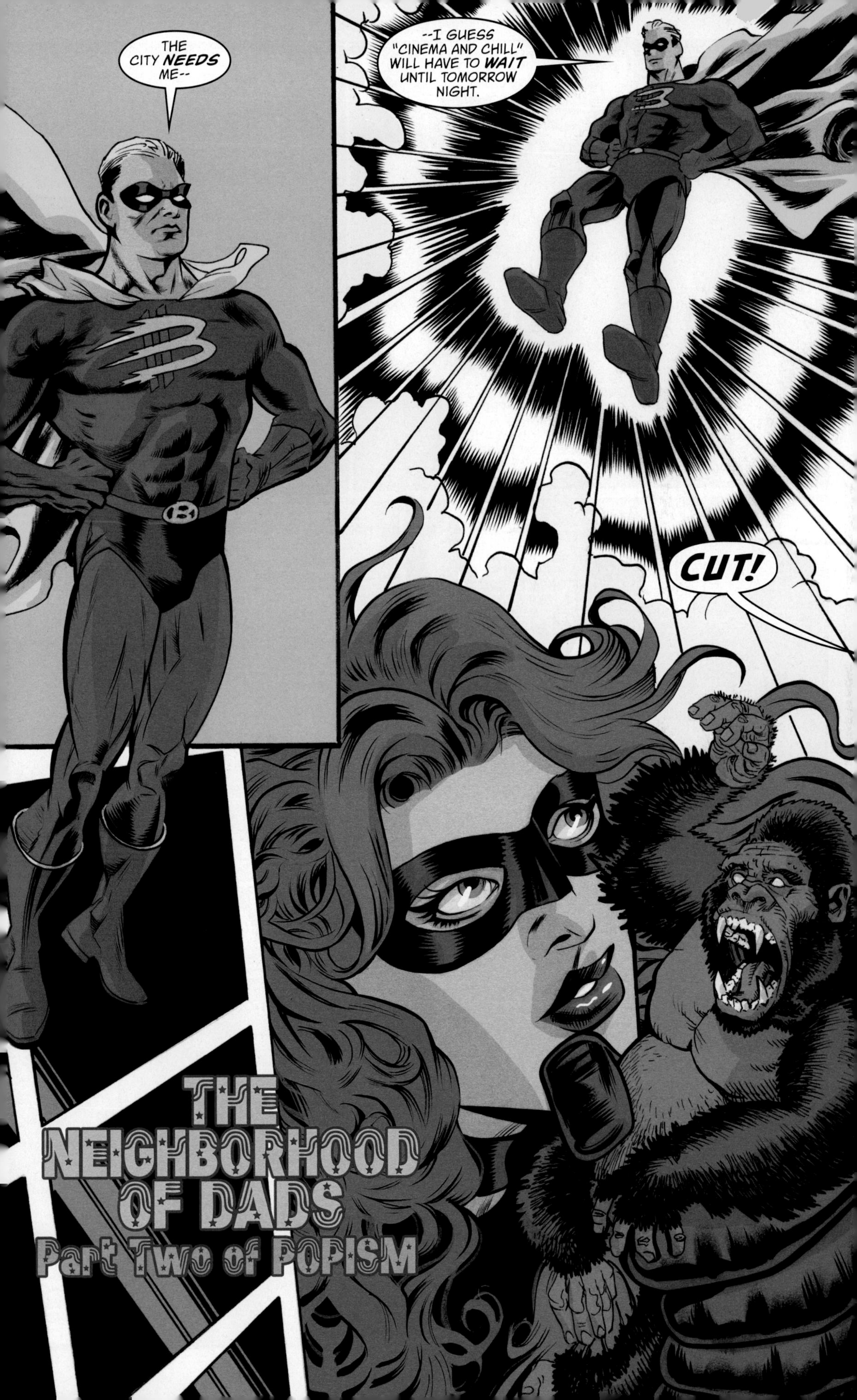
THE CITY NEEDS ME--
--I GUESS "CINEMA AND CHILL" WILL HAVE TO WAIT UNTIL TOMORROW NIGHT.
CUT!
THE NEIGHBORHOOD OF DADS
Part Two of POPISM

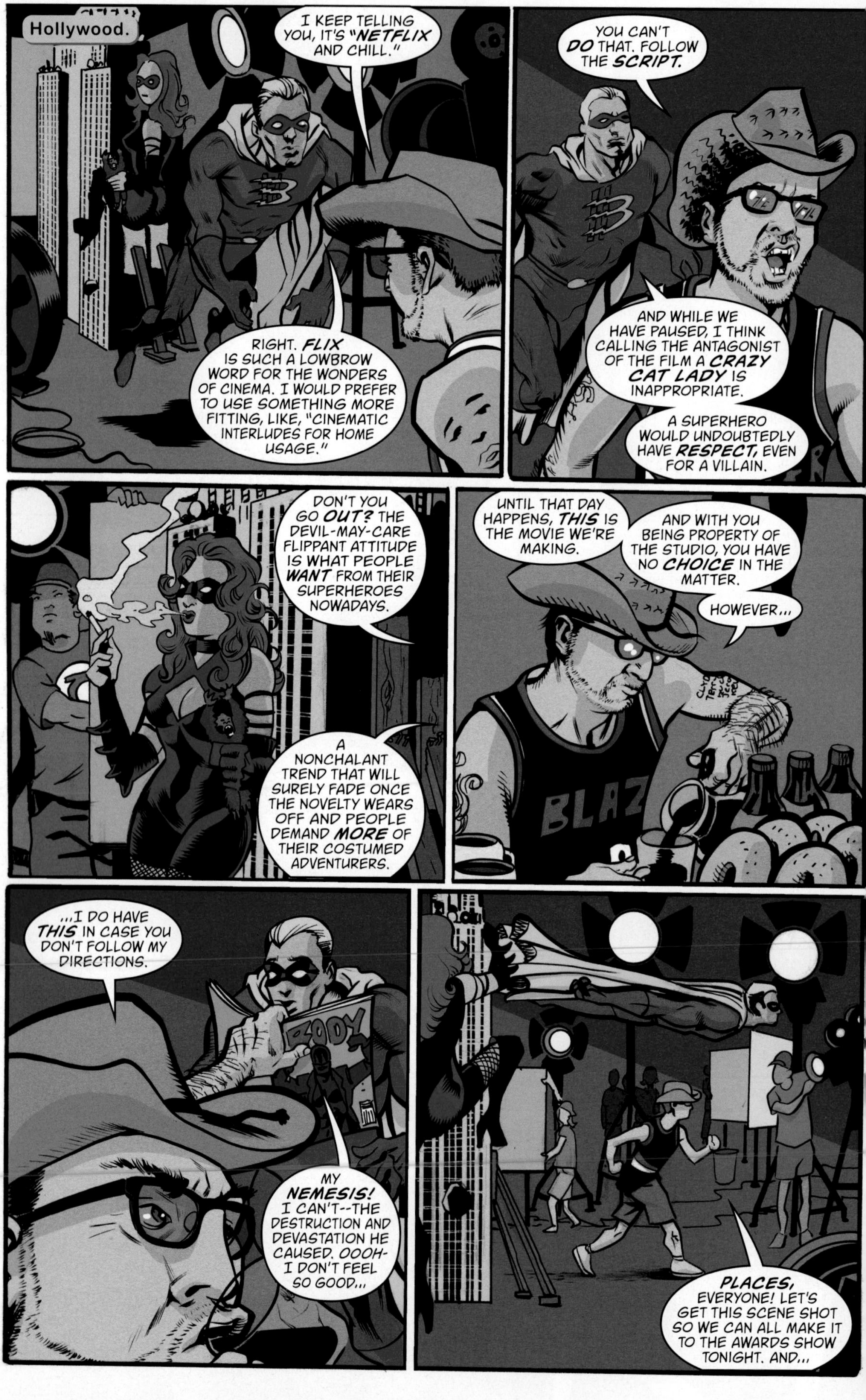
Hollywood.
I KEEP TELLING YOU, IT'S "NETFLIX AND CHILL."
RIGHT. FLIX IS SUCH A LOWBROW WORD FOR THE WONDERS OF CINEMA. I WOULD PREFER TO USE SOMETHING MORE FITTING, LIKE, "CINEMATIC INTERLUDES FOR HOME USAGE."
YOU CAN'T DO THAT. FOLLOW THE SCRIPT.
AND WHILE WE HAVE PAUSED, I THINK CALLING THE ANTAGONIST OF THE FILM A CRAZY CAT LADY IS INAPPROPRIATE.
A SUPERHERO WOULD UNDOUBTEDLY HAVE RESPECT, EVEN FOR A VILLAIN.
DON'T YOU GO OUT? THE DEVIL-MAY-CARE FLIPPANT ATTITUDE IS WHAT PEOPLE WANT FROM THEIR SUPERHEROES NOWADAYS.
A NONCHALANT TREND THAT WILL SURELY FADE ONCE THE NOVELTY WEARS OFF AND PEOPLE DEMAND MORE OF THEIR COSTUMED ADVENTURERS.
UNTIL THAT DAY HAPPENS, THIS IS THE MOVIE WE'RE MAKING.
AND WITH YOU BEING PROPERTY OF THE STUDIO, YOU HAVE NO CHOICE IN THE MATTER.
HOWEVER...
BLAZ
...I DO HAVE THIS IN CASE YOU DON'T FOLLOW MY DIRECTIONS.
MY NEMESIS! I CAN'T--THE DESTRUCTION AND DEVASTATION HE CAUSED. OOOH-I DON'T FEEL SO GOOD...
PLACES, EVERYONE! LET'S GET THIS SCENE SHOT SO WE CAN ALL MAKE IT TO THE AWARDS SHOW TONIGHT. AND...

"...ACTION!"

Upstate New York.

I GOT THE SAME MUG FROM MY SON!

World's BEST DAD

I GUESS WE'RE ALL THE WORLD'S BEST DAD!

BILL, DID YOU FIND THE BOOK?

THE LAST PIECE OF THE PUZZLE FROM ONE OF OUR ORGANIZATION'S FINEST MEMBERS-- MAY GOD REST HIS SOUL.

SEDUCTION OF THE INNOCENT

Fredric Wertham, M.D.

GREAT, SET IT DOWN NEXT TO THE OTHERS AND LET'S BEGIN.

WHEN THE SUMMONING STARTS, WE MUST BE COMPLETELY CALM OR THE NUMBERS WILL NOTICE OUR PRESENCE.

I WISH WE COULD COMMUTE THIS WAY EVERY DAY. BETWEEN THE PEOPLE ON THE BUS AND THE ADS OUT THE WINDOW,...

I KNOW. IT'S VERY DISTURBING. NOW, LET'S BEGIN.

UMMMMM. UMMMMM.

World's BEST DAD

MISSING

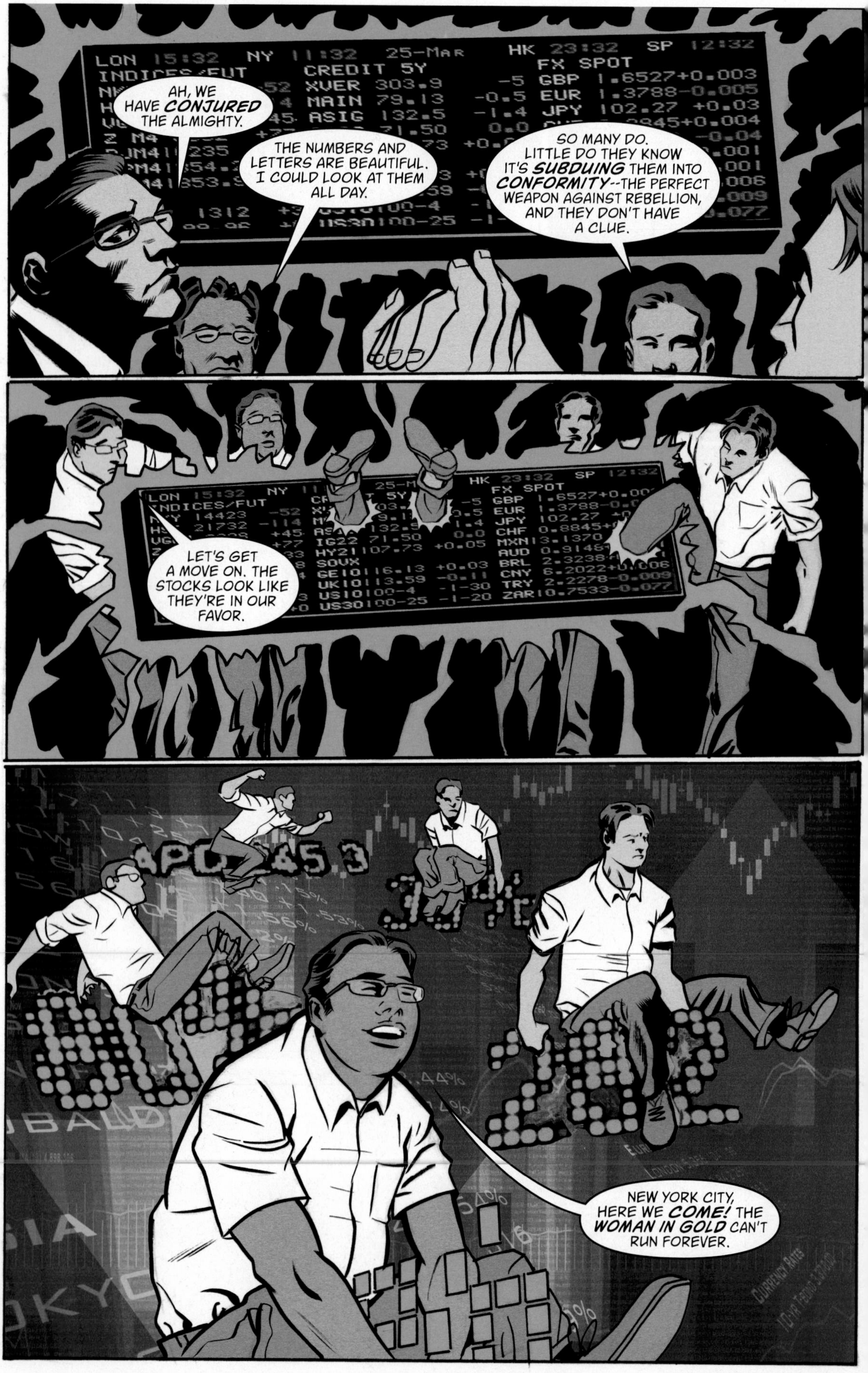
LON 15:32 NY 11:32 25-MAR HK 23:32 SP 12:32
INDICES/FUT
CREDIT 5Y
FX SPOT
AH, WE HAVE CONJURED THE ALMIGHTY.
THE NUMBERS AND LETTERS ARE BEAUTIFUL. I COULD LOOK AT THEM ALL DAY.
SO MANY DO. LITTLE DO THEY KNOW IT'S SUBDUING THEM INTO CONFORMITY--THE PERFECT WEAPON AGAINST REBELLION, AND THEY DON'T HAVE A CLUE.
LET'S GET A MOVE ON. THE STOCKS LOOK LIKE THEY'RE IN OUR FAVOR.
NEW YORK CITY, HERE WE COME! THE WOMAN IN GOLD CAN'T RUN FOREVER.

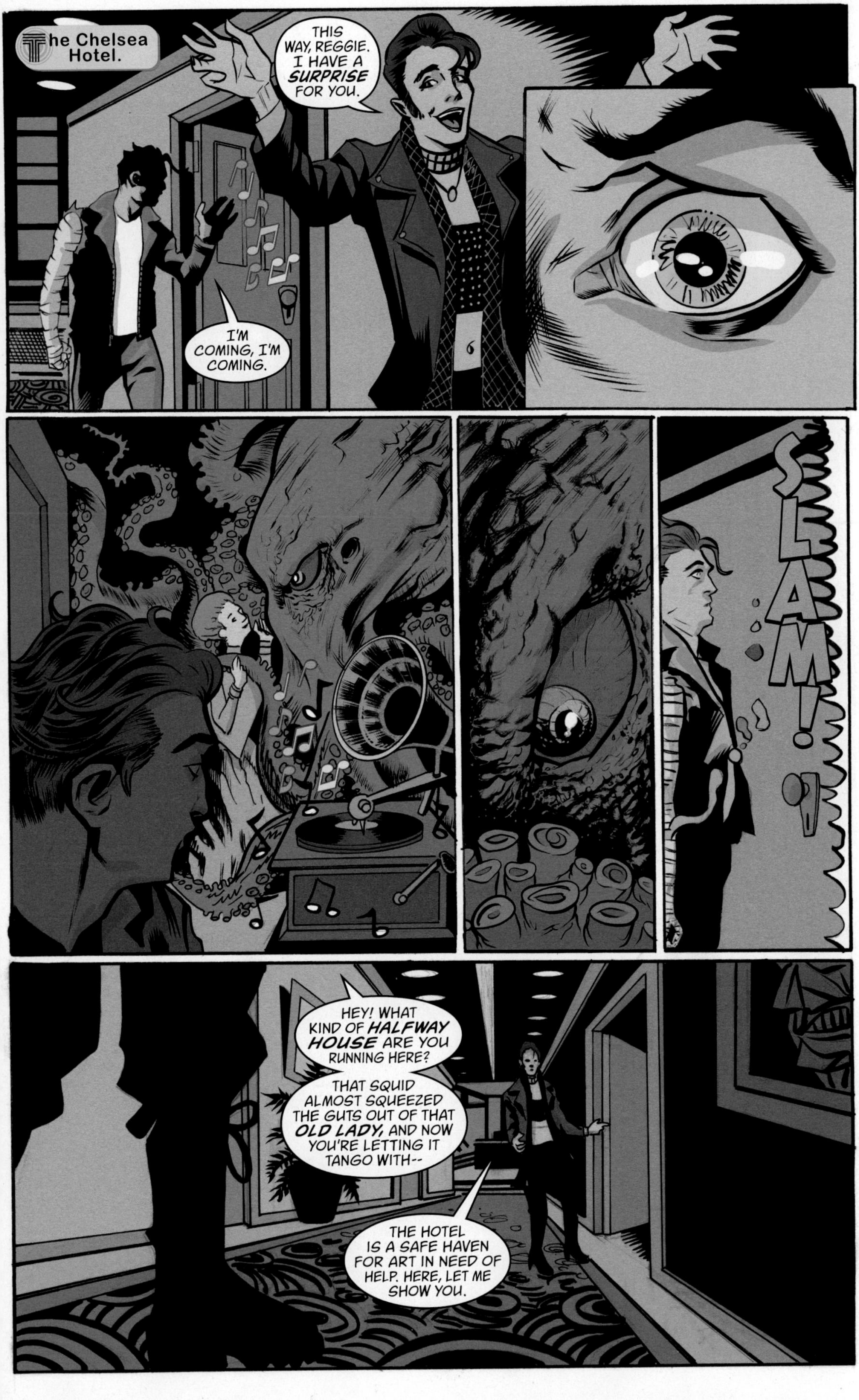
The Chelsea Hotel.
THIS WAY, REGGIE. I HAVE A SURPRISE FOR YOU.
I'M COMING, I'M COMING.
SLAM!
HEY! WHAT KIND OF HALFWAY HOUSE ARE YOU RUNNING HERE?
THAT SQUID ALMOST SQUEEZED THE GUTS OUT OF THAT OLD LADY, AND NOW YOU'RE LETTING IT TANGO WITH--
THE HOTEL IS A SAFE HAVEN FOR ART IN NEED OF HELP. HERE, LET ME SHOW YOU.

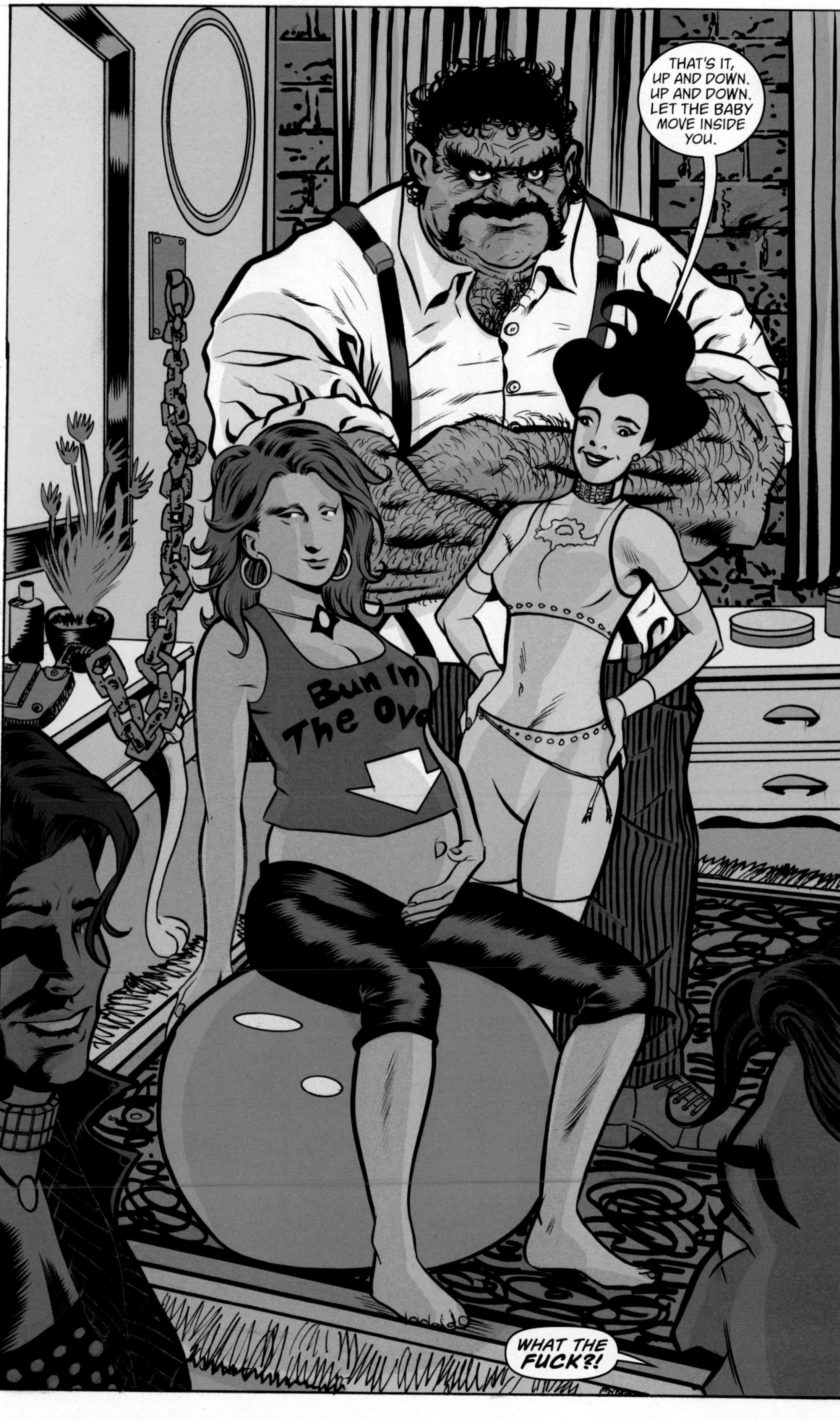
THAT'S IT, UP AND DOWN. UP AND DOWN. LET THE BABY MOVE INSIDE YOU.
Bun In The Ov
WHAT THE FUCK?!

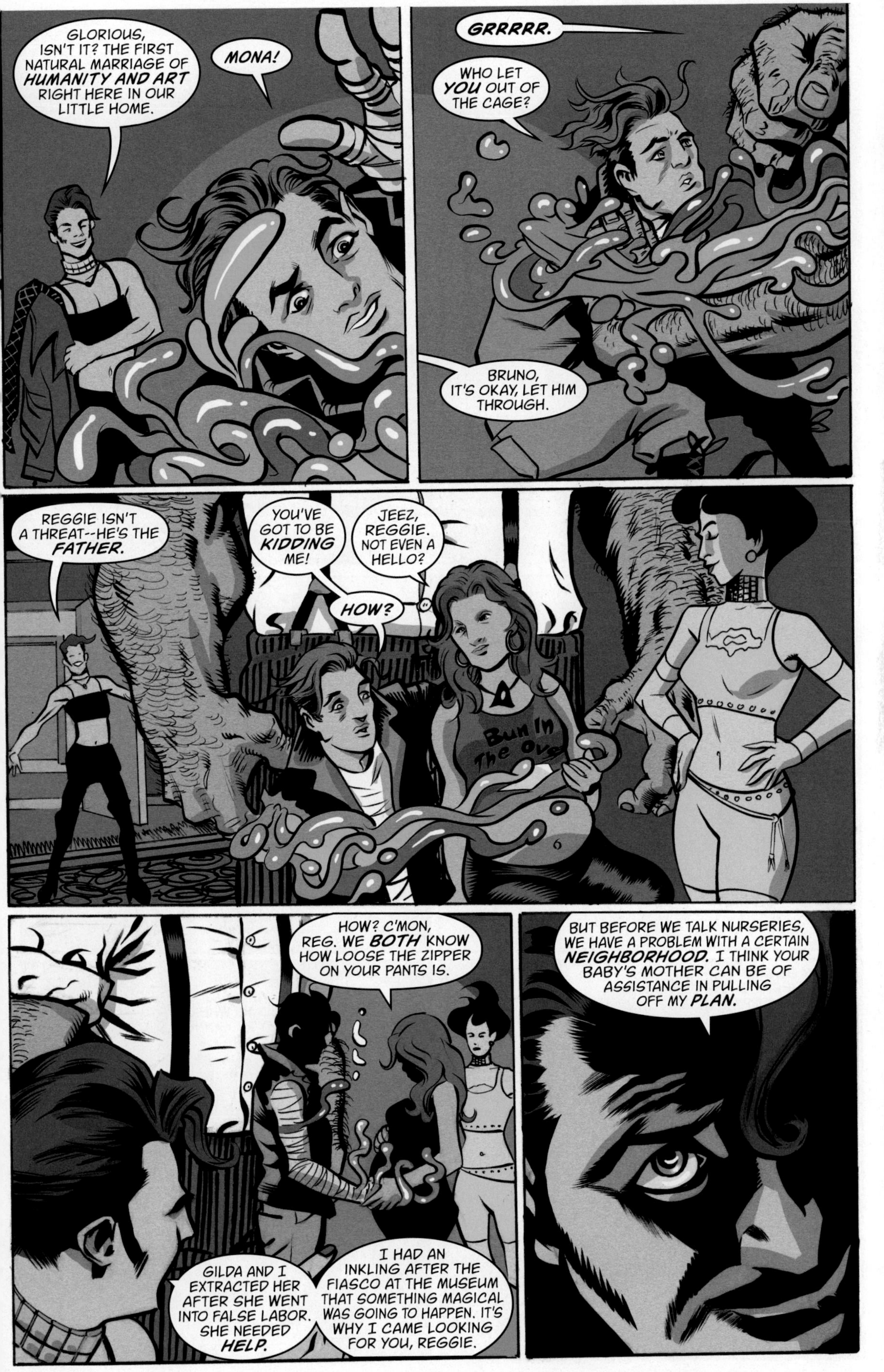

GLORIOUS, ISN'T IT? THE FIRST NATURAL MARRIAGE OF **HUMANITY AND ART** RIGHT HERE IN OUR LITTLE HOME.
MONA!
GRRRRR.
WHO LET **YOU** OUT OF THE CAGE?
BRUNO, IT'S OKAY, LET HIM THROUGH.
REGGIE ISN'T A THREAT--HE'S THE **FATHER.**
YOU'VE GOT TO BE **KIDDING** ME!
HOW?
JEEZ, REGGIE. NOT EVEN A HELLO?
Bun In The Ove
HOW? C'MON, REG. WE **BOTH** KNOW HOW LOOSE THE ZIPPER ON YOUR PANTS IS.
GILDA AND I EXTRACTED HER AFTER SHE WENT INTO FALSE LABOR. SHE NEEDED **HELP.**
I HAD AN INKLING AFTER THE FIASCO AT THE MUSEUM THAT SOMETHING MAGICAL WAS GOING TO HAPPEN. IT'S WHY I CAME LOOKING FOR YOU, REGGIE.
BUT BEFORE WE TALK NURSERIES, WE HAVE A PROBLEM WITH A CERTAIN **NEIGHBORHOOD.** I THINK YOUR BABY'S MOTHER CAN BE OF ASSISTANCE IN PULLING OFF MY **PLAN.**

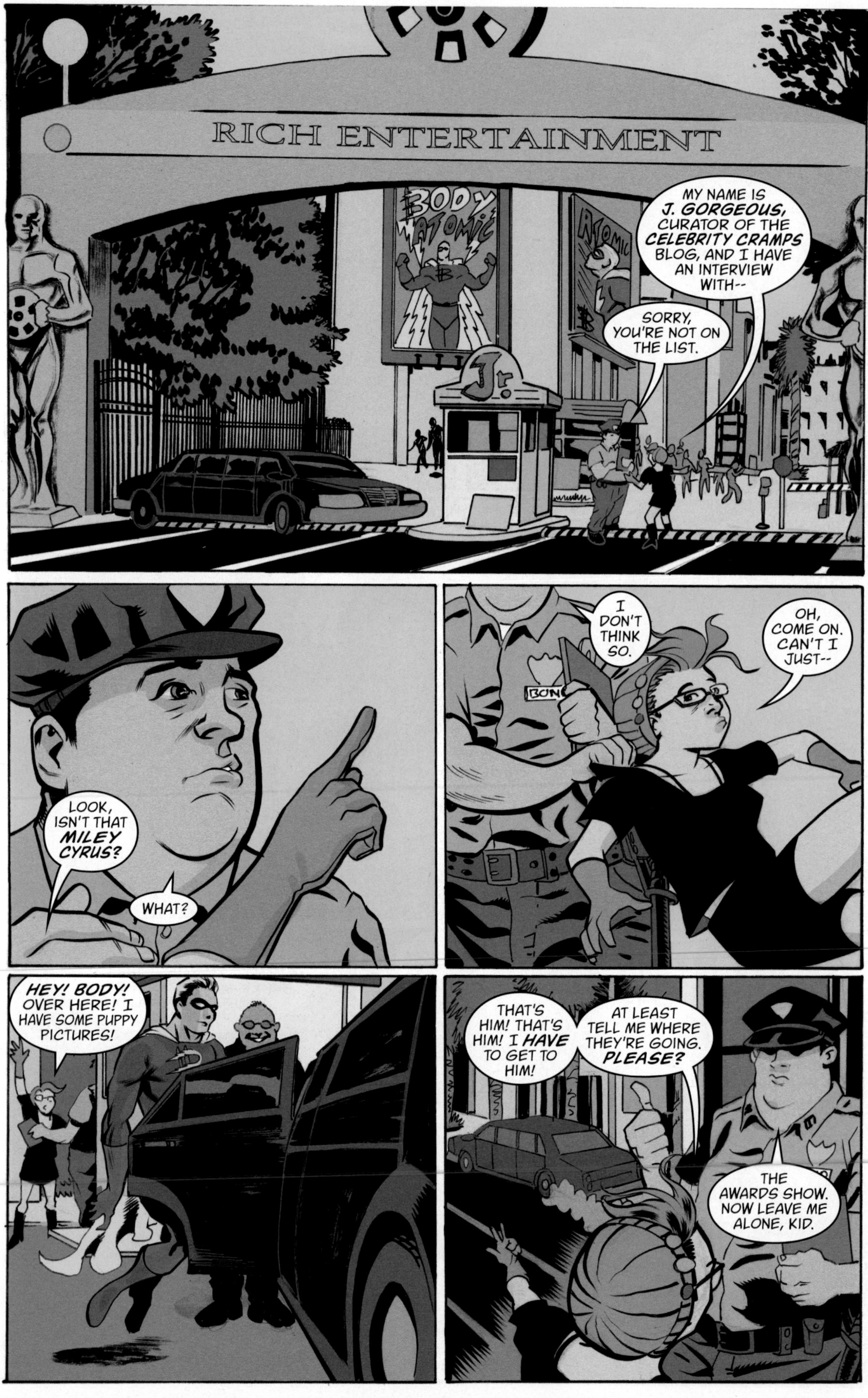
RICH ENTERTAINMENT
BODY ATOMIC
MY NAME IS J. GORGEOUS, CURATOR OF THE CELEBRITY CRAMPS BLOG, AND I HAVE AN INTERVIEW WITH--
SORRY, YOU'RE NOT ON THE LIST.
LOOK, ISN'T THAT MILEY CYRUS?
WHAT?
I DON'T THINK SO.
OH, COME ON. CAN'T I JUST--
HEY! BODY! OVER HERE! I HAVE SOME PUPPY PICTURES!
THAT'S HIM! THAT'S HIM! I HAVE TO GET TO HIM!
AT LEAST TELL ME WHERE THEY'RE GOING. PLEASE?
THE AWARDS SHOW. NOW LEAVE ME ALONE, KID.

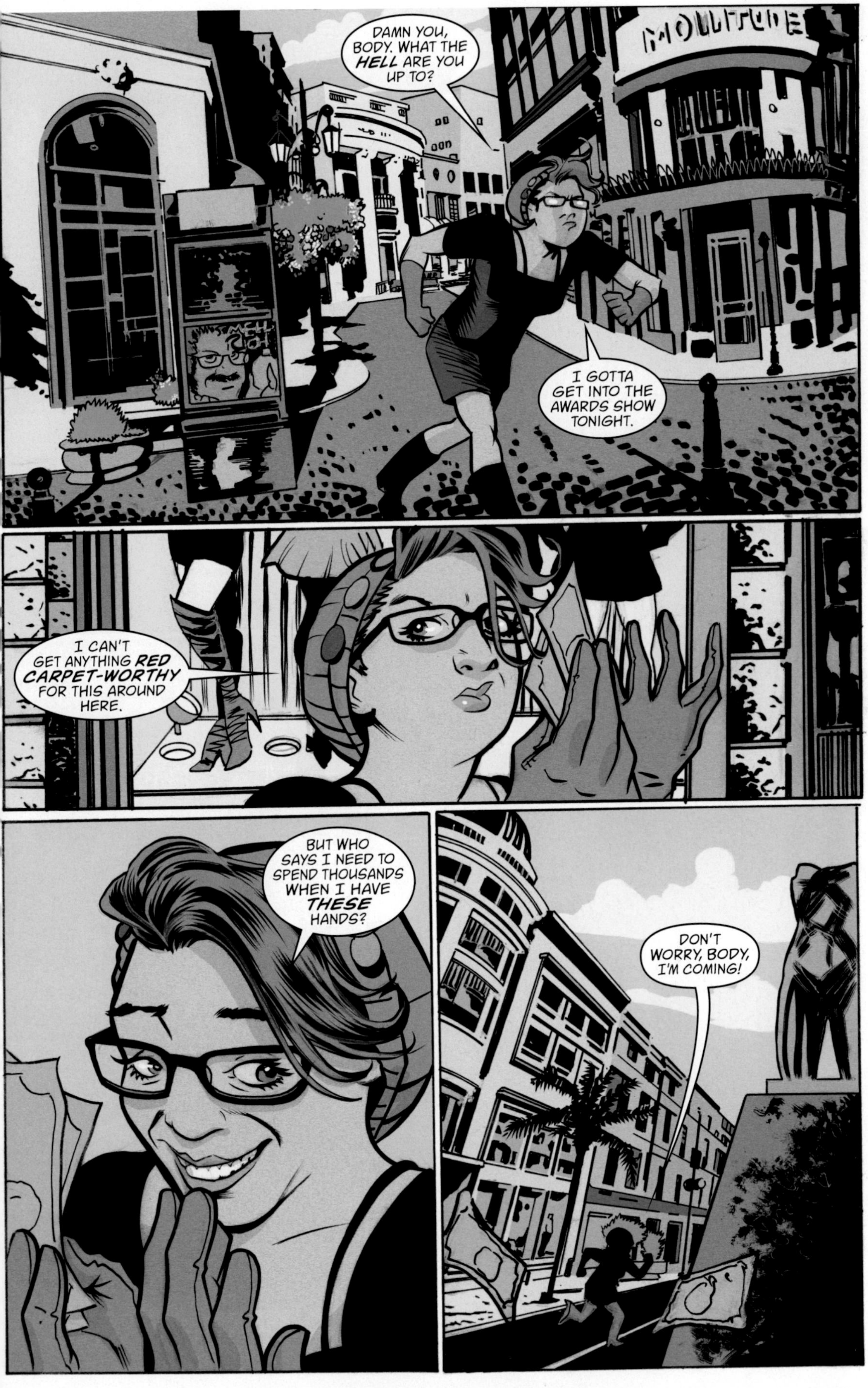
DAMN YOU, BODY. WHAT THE HELL ARE YOU UP TO?
I GOTTA GET INTO THE AWARDS SHOW TONIGHT.
I CAN'T GET ANYTHING RED CARPET-WORTHY FOR THIS AROUND HERE.
BUT WHO SAYS I NEED TO SPEND THOUSANDS WHEN I HAVE THESE HANDS?
DON'T WORRY, BODY, I'M COMING!

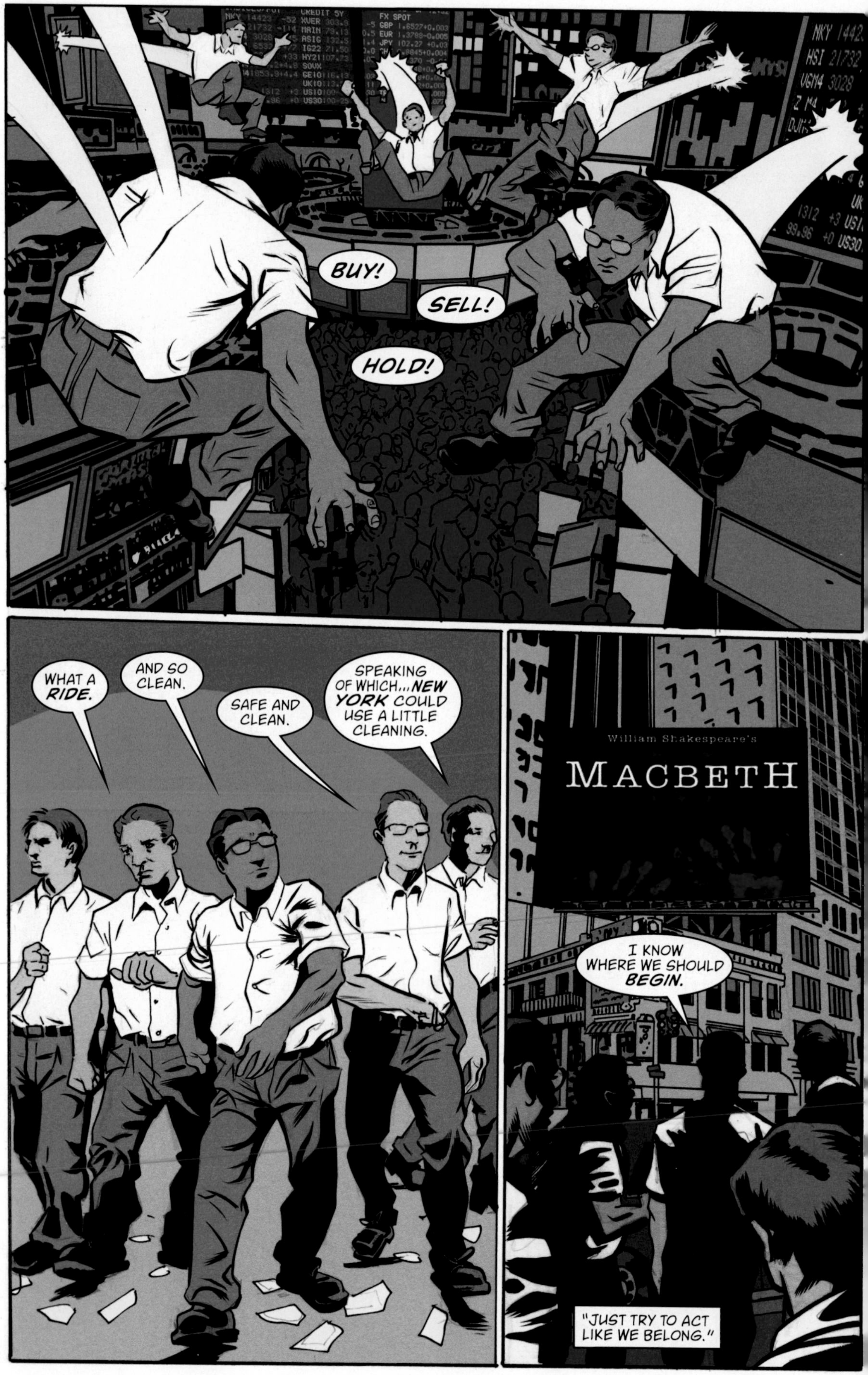
BUY!
SELL!
HOLD!
WHAT A RIDE.
AND SO CLEAN.
SAFE AND CLEAN.
SPEAKING OF WHICH... NEW YORK COULD USE A LITTLE CLEANING.
William Shakespeare's
MACBETH
I KNOW WHERE WE SHOULD BEGIN.
"JUST TRY TO ACT LIKE WE BELONG."

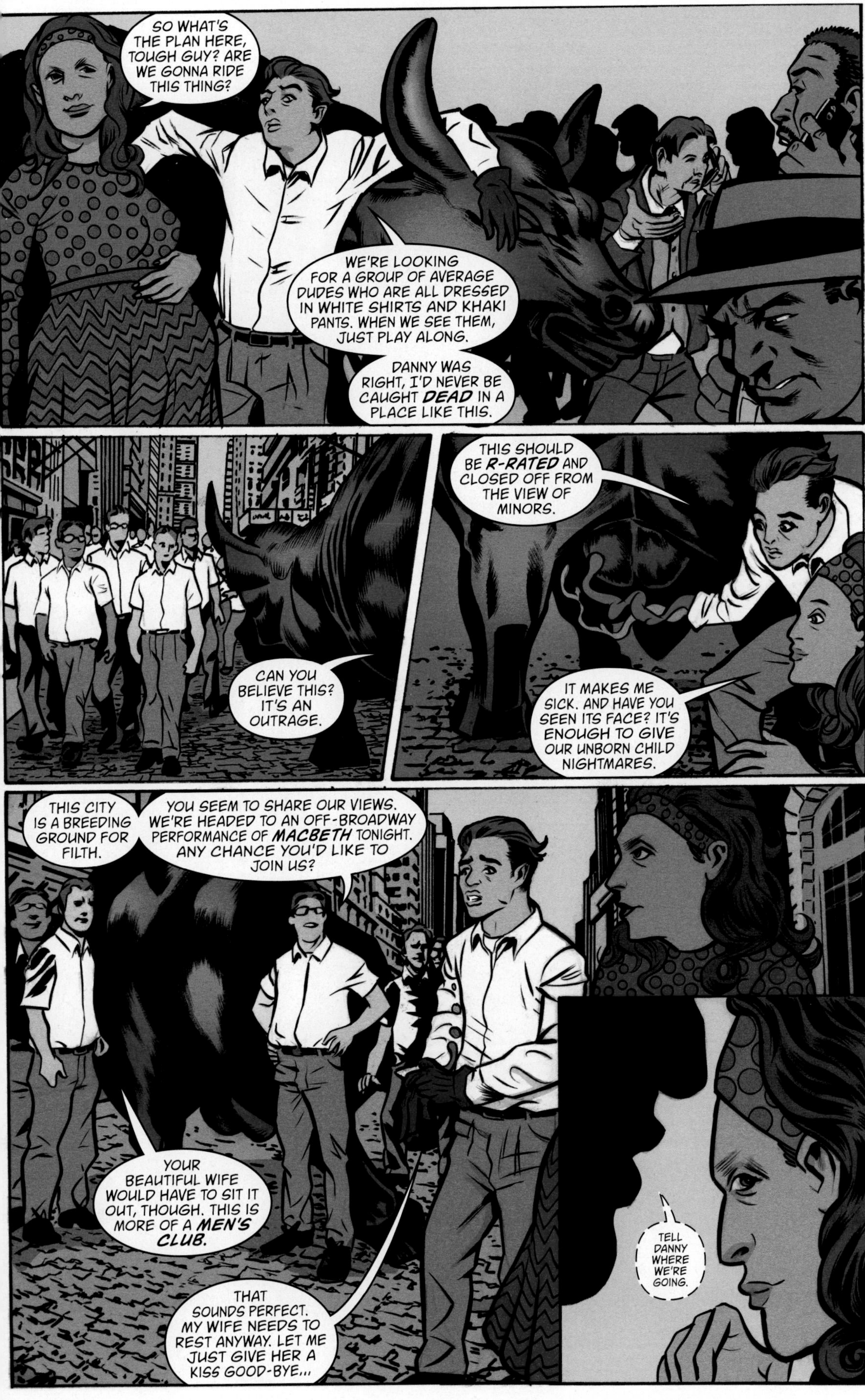
SO WHAT'S THE PLAN HERE, TOUGH GUY? ARE WE GONNA RIDE THIS THING?
WE'RE LOOKING FOR A GROUP OF AVERAGE DUDES WHO ARE ALL DRESSED IN WHITE SHIRTS AND KHAKI PANTS. WHEN WE SEE THEM, JUST PLAY ALONG.
DANNY WAS RIGHT, I'D NEVER BE CAUGHT DEAD IN A PLACE LIKE THIS.
CAN YOU BELIEVE THIS? IT'S AN OUTRAGE.
THIS SHOULD BE R-RATED AND CLOSED OFF FROM THE VIEW OF MINORS.
IT MAKES ME SICK. AND HAVE YOU SEEN ITS FACE? IT'S ENOUGH TO GIVE OUR UNBORN CHILD NIGHTMARES.
THIS CITY IS A BREEDING GROUND FOR FILTH.
YOU SEEM TO SHARE OUR VIEWS. WE'RE HEADED TO AN OFF-BROADWAY PERFORMANCE OF MACBETH TONIGHT. ANY CHANCE YOU'D LIKE TO JOIN US?
YOUR BEAUTIFUL WIFE WOULD HAVE TO SIT IT OUT, THOUGH. THIS IS MORE OF A MEN'S CLUB.
THAT SOUNDS PERFECT. MY WIFE NEEDS TO REST ANYWAY. LET ME JUST GIVE HER A KISS GOOD-BYE...
TELL DANNY WHERE WE'RE GOING.

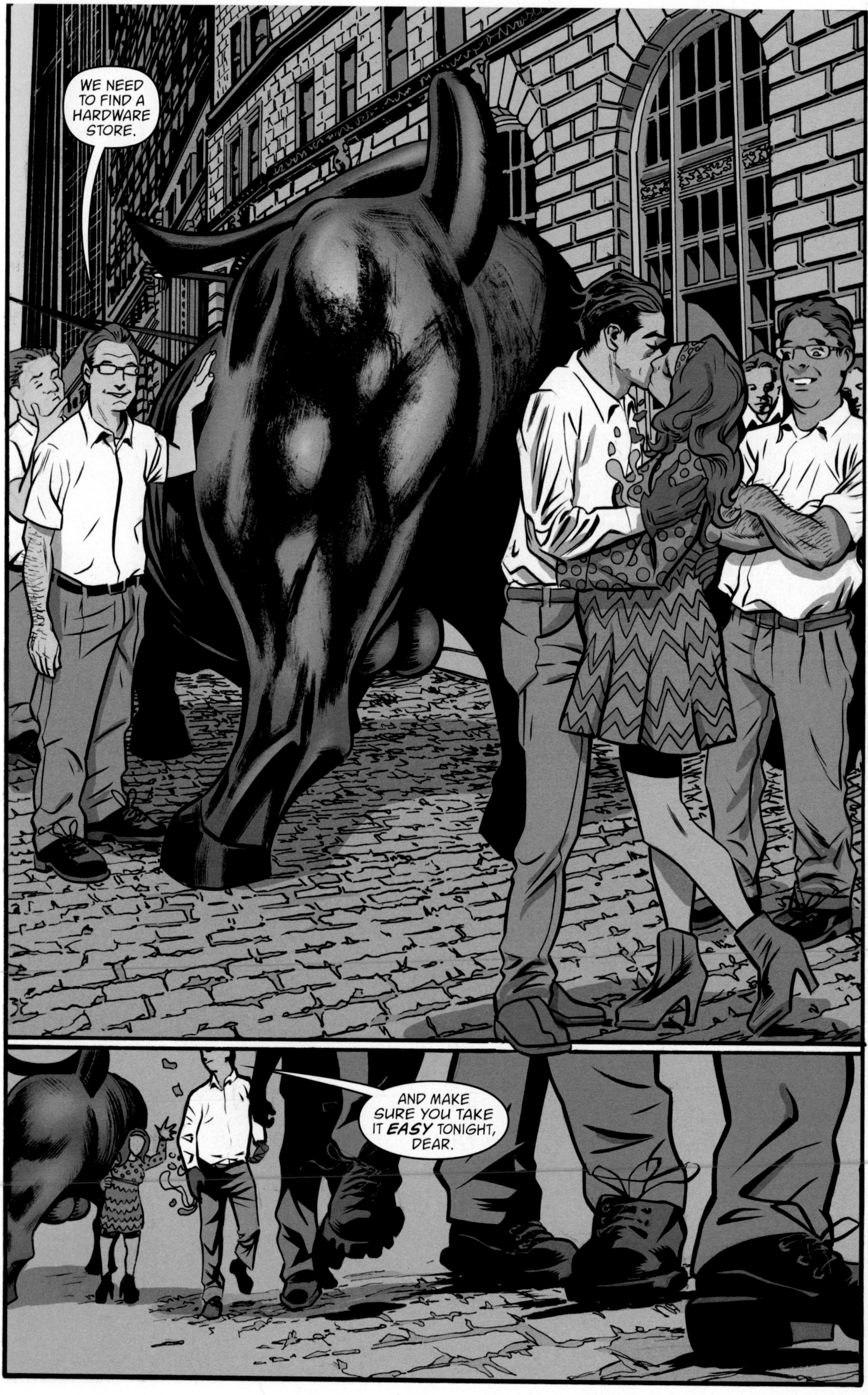
WE NEED TO FIND A HARDWARE STORE.
AND MAKE SURE YOU TAKE IT EASY TONIGHT, DEAR.

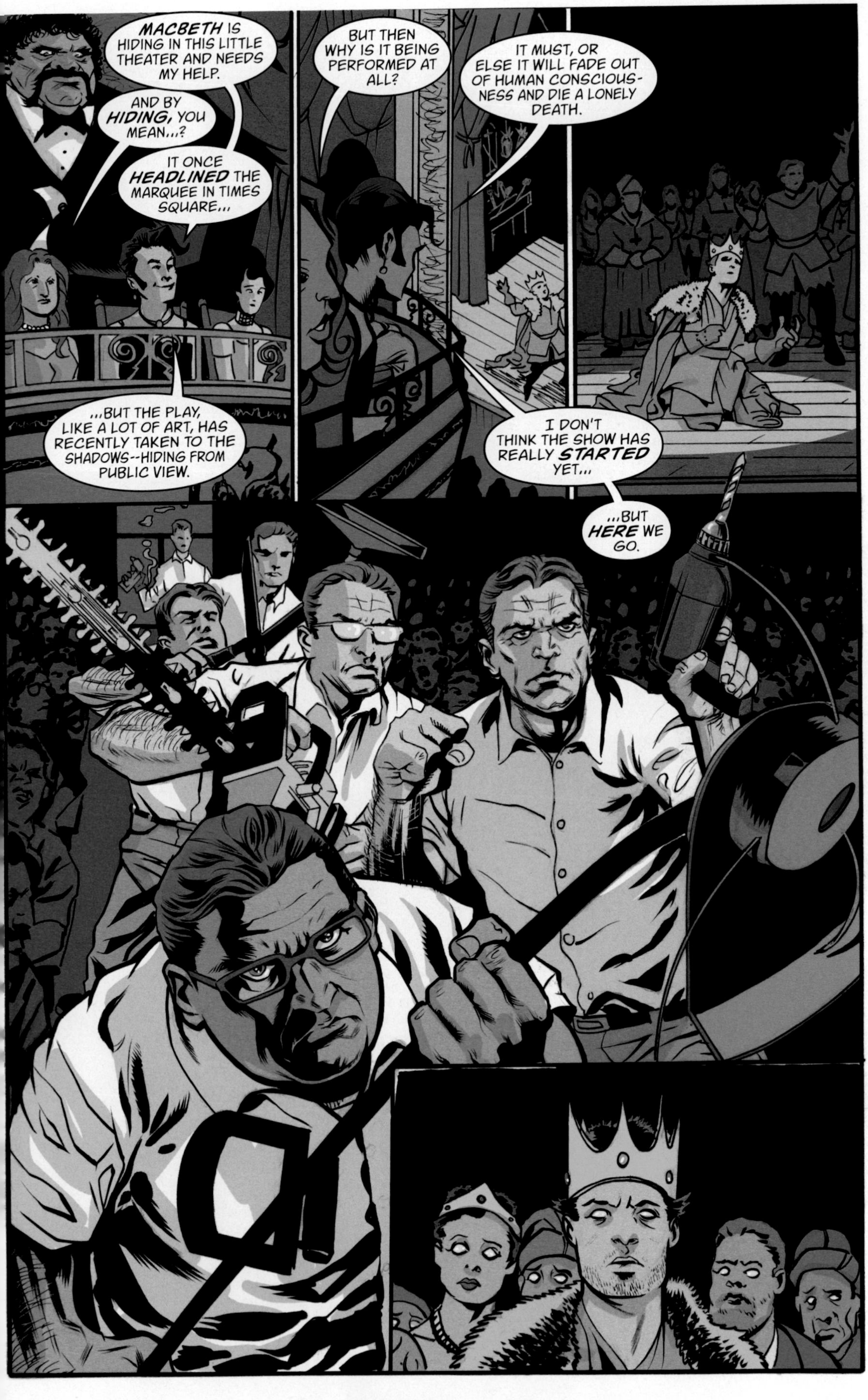

MACBETH IS HIDING IN THIS LITTLE THEATER AND NEEDS MY HELP.
AND BY HIDING, YOU MEAN...?
IT ONCE HEADLINED THE MARQUEE IN TIMES SQUARE...
...BUT THE PLAY, LIKE A LOT OF ART, HAS RECENTLY TAKEN TO THE SHADOWS--HIDING FROM PUBLIC VIEW.
BUT THEN WHY IS IT BEING PERFORMED AT ALL?
IT MUST, OR ELSE IT WILL FADE OUT OF HUMAN CONSCIOUSNESS AND DIE A LONELY DEATH.
I DON'T THINK THE SHOW HAS REALLY STARTED YET...
...BUT HERE WE GO.

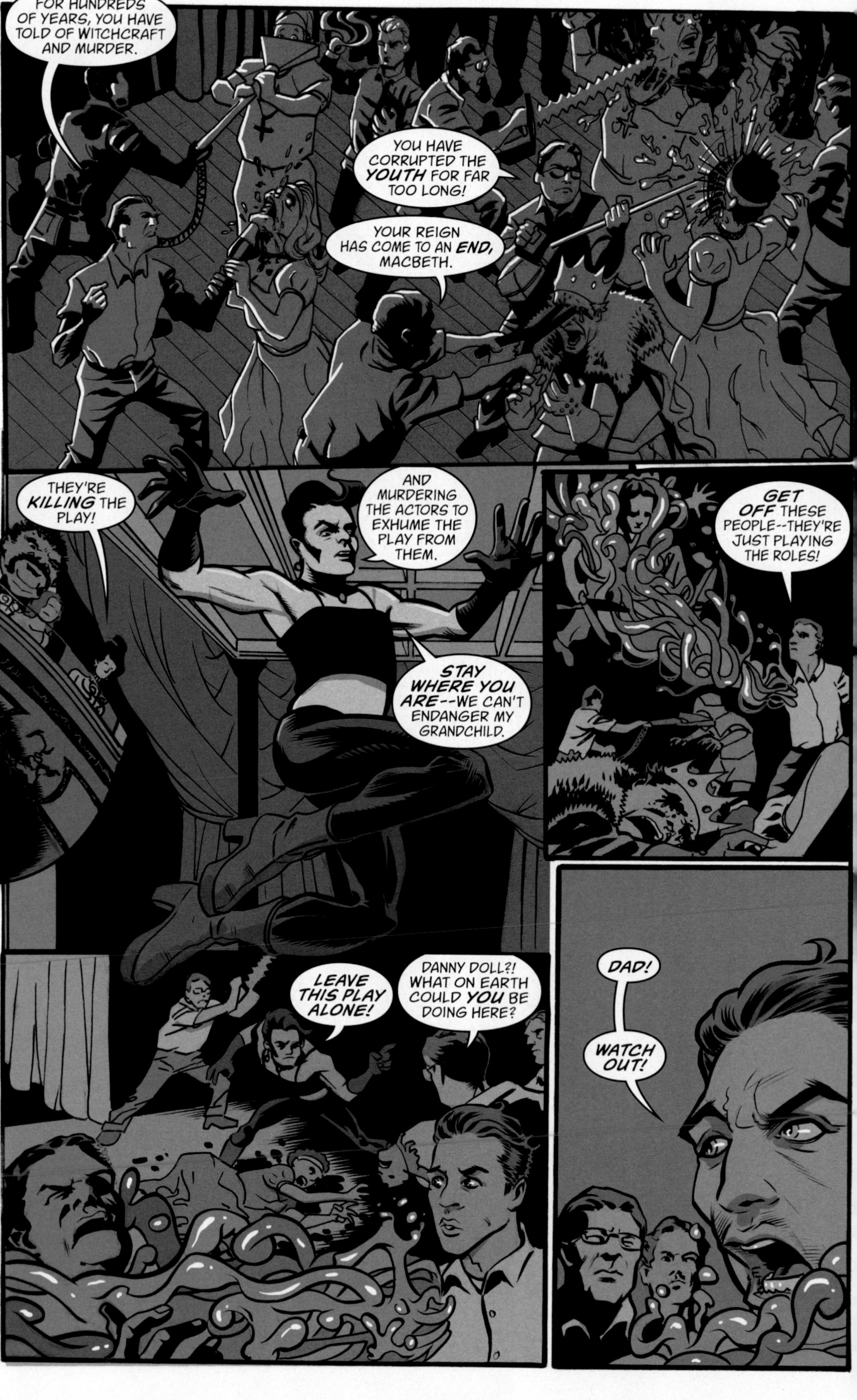
FOR HUNDREDS OF YEARS, YOU HAVE TOLD OF WITCHCRAFT AND MURDER.
YOU HAVE CORRUPTED THE YOUTH FOR FAR TOO LONG!
YOUR REIGN HAS COME TO AN END, MACBETH.
THEY'RE KILLING THE PLAY!
AND MURDERING THE ACTORS TO EXHUME THE PLAY FROM THEM.
STAY WHERE YOU ARE--WE CAN'T ENDANGER MY GRANDCHILD.
GET OFF THESE PEOPLE--THEY'RE JUST PLAYING THE ROLES!
LEAVE THIS PLAY ALONE!
DANNY DOLL?! WHAT ON EARTH COULD YOU BE DOING HERE?
DAD!
WATCH OUT!

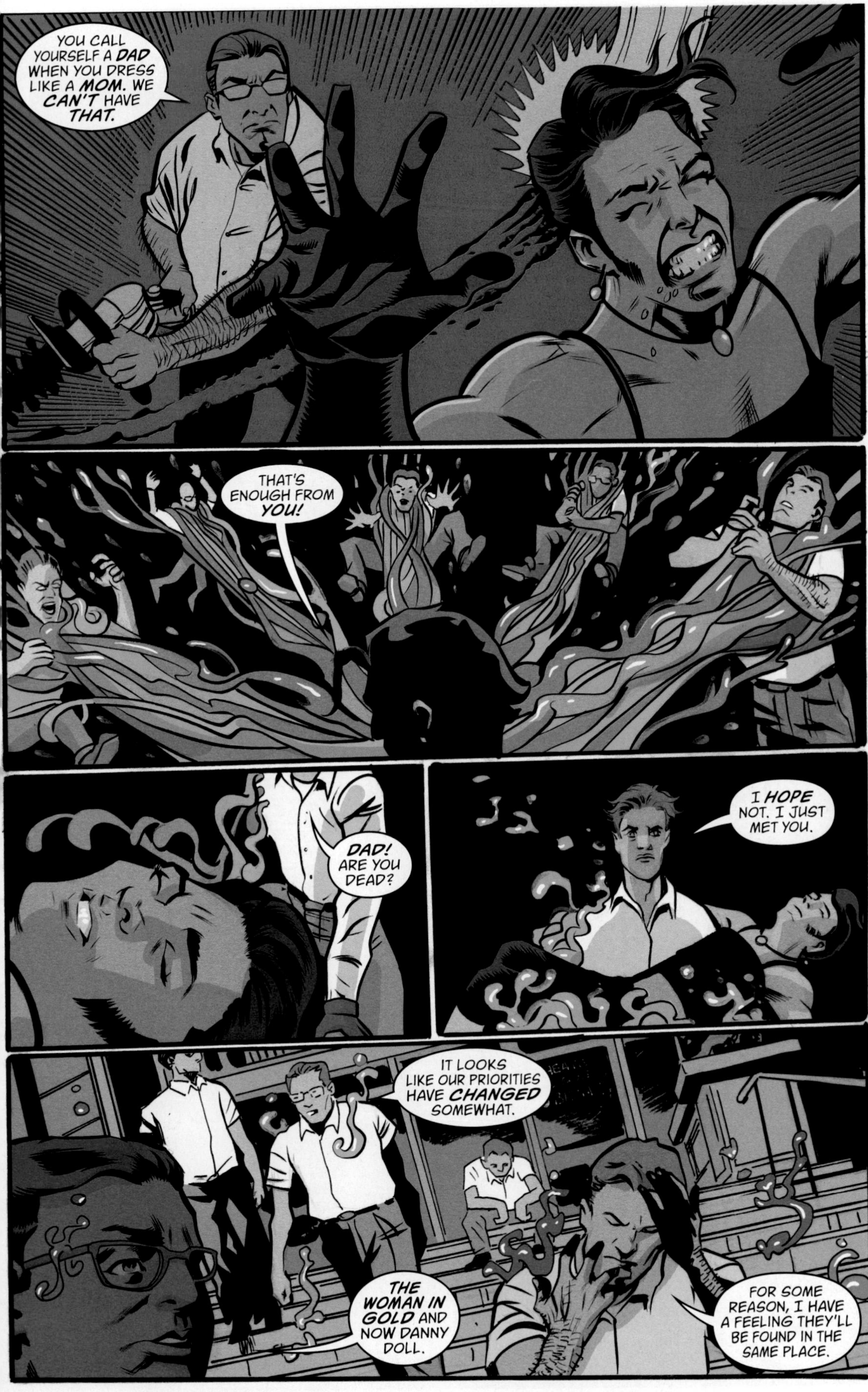
YOU CALL YOURSELF A DAD WHEN YOU DRESS LIKE A MOM. WE CAN'T HAVE THAT.
THAT'S ENOUGH FROM YOU!
DAD! ARE YOU DEAD?
I HOPE NOT. I JUST MET YOU.
IT LOOKS LIKE OUR PRIORITIES HAVE CHANGED SOMEWHAT.
THE WOMAN IN GOLD AND NOW DANNY DOLL.
FOR SOME REASON, I HAVE A FEELING THEY'LL BE FOUND IN THE SAME PLACE.

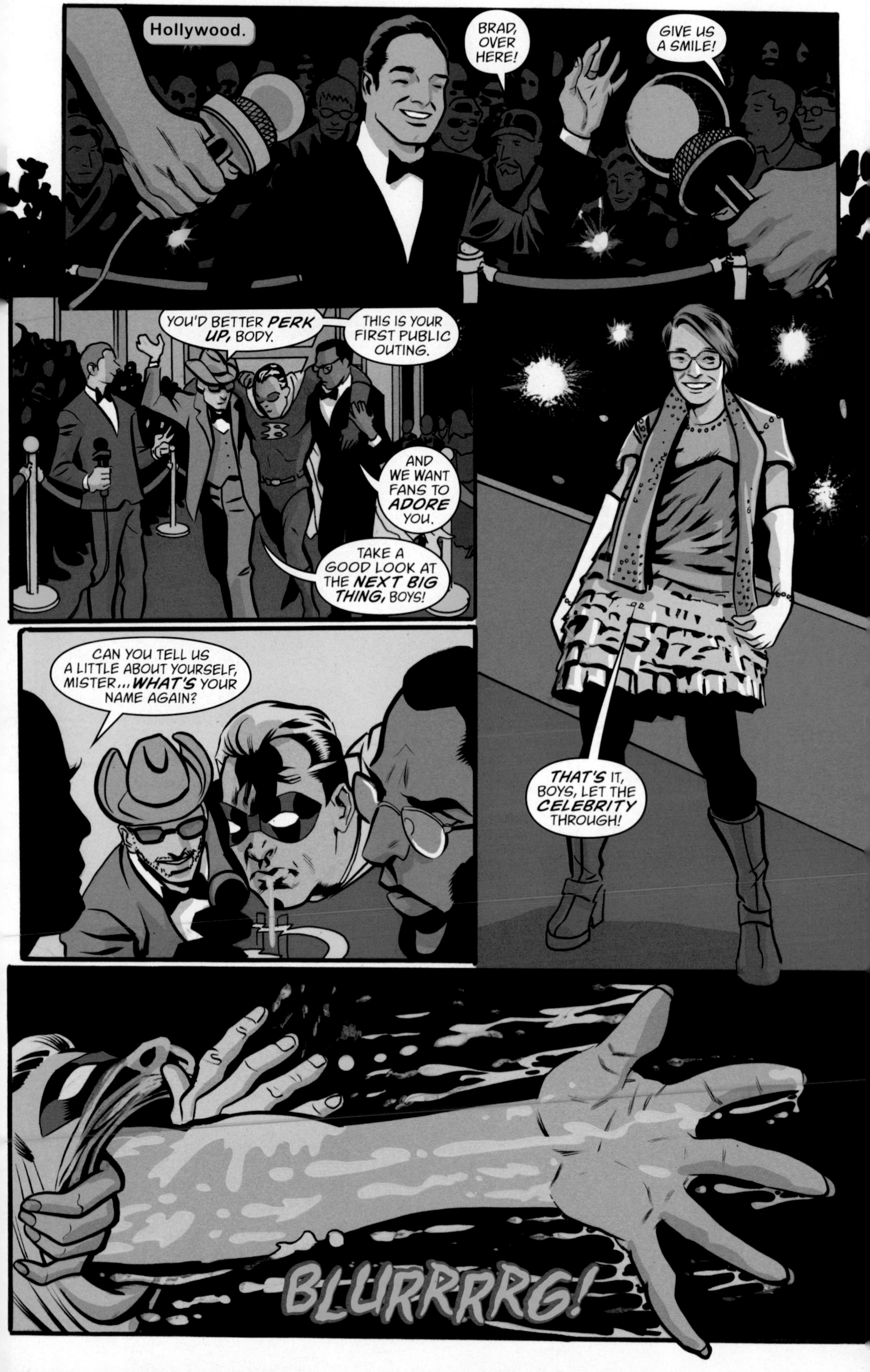
Hollywood.
BRAD, OVER HERE!
GIVE US A SMILE!
YOU'D BETTER PERK UP, BODY.
THIS IS YOUR FIRST PUBLIC OUTING.
AND WE WANT FANS TO ADORE YOU.
TAKE A GOOD LOOK AT THE NEXT BIG THING, BOYS!
THAT'S IT, BOYS, LET THE CELEBRITY THROUGH!
CAN YOU TELL US A LITTLE ABOUT YOURSELF, MISTER... WHAT'S YOUR NAME AGAIN?
BLURRRRG!

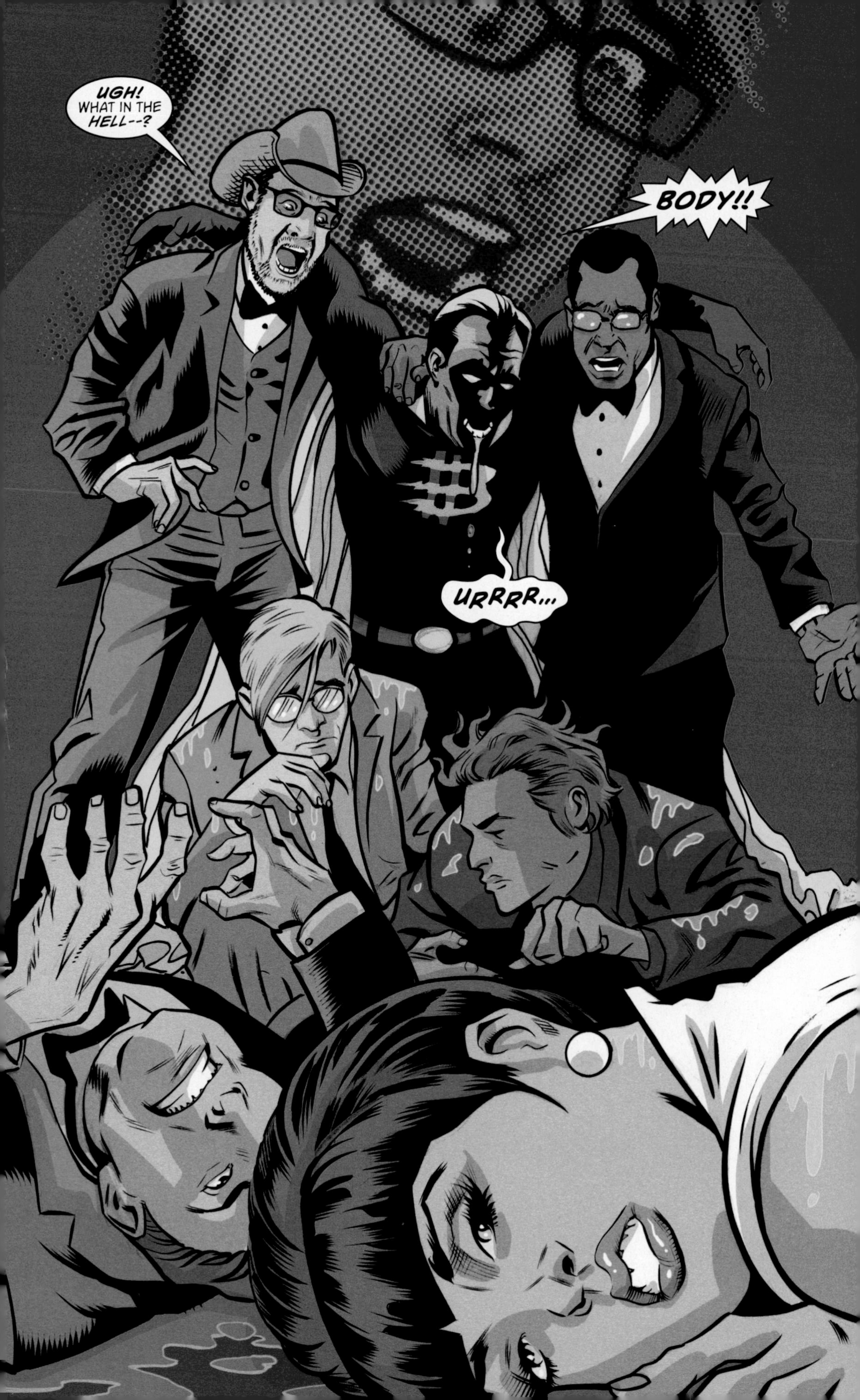
UGH! WHAT IN THE HELL--?
BODY!!
URRRR...

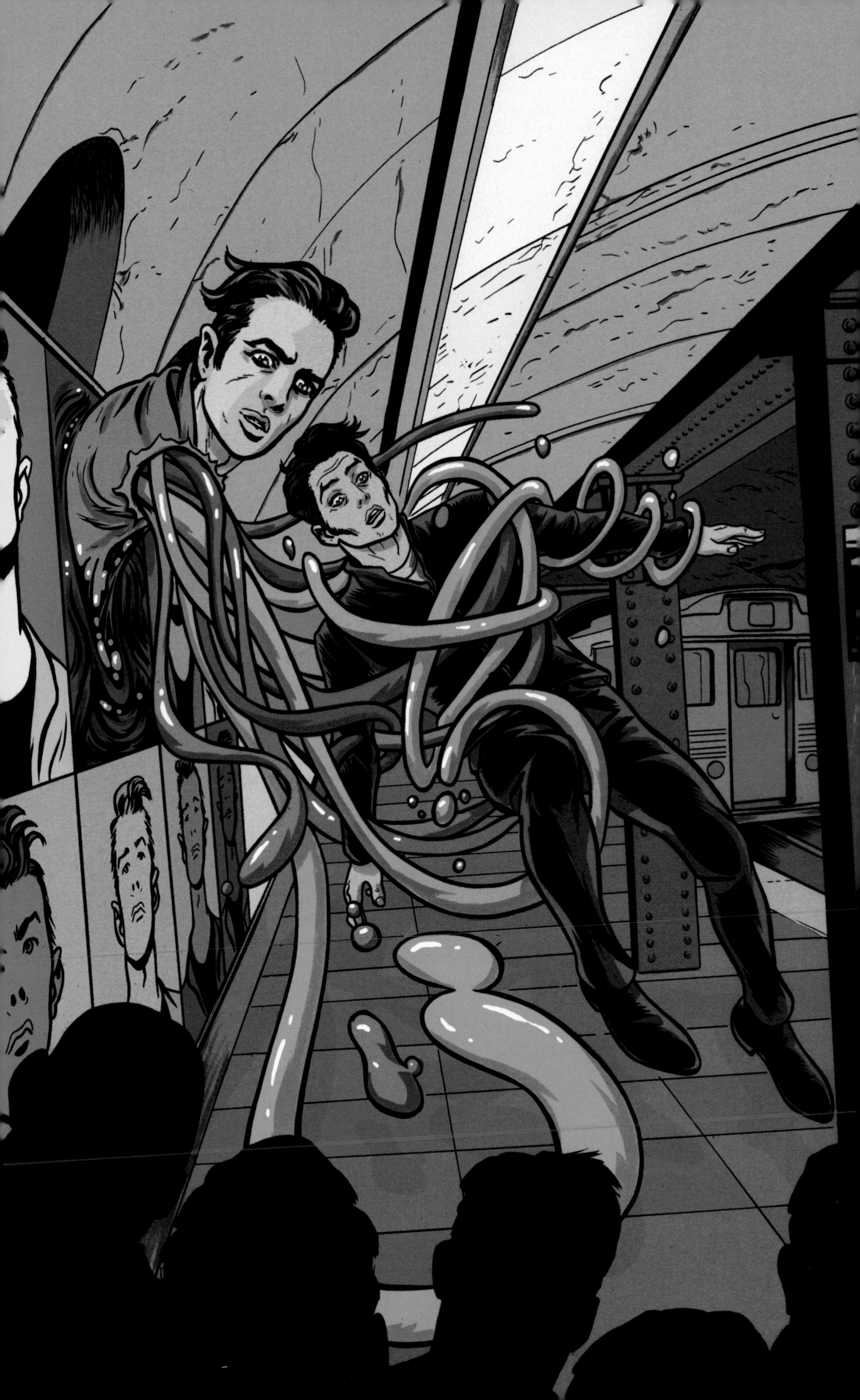

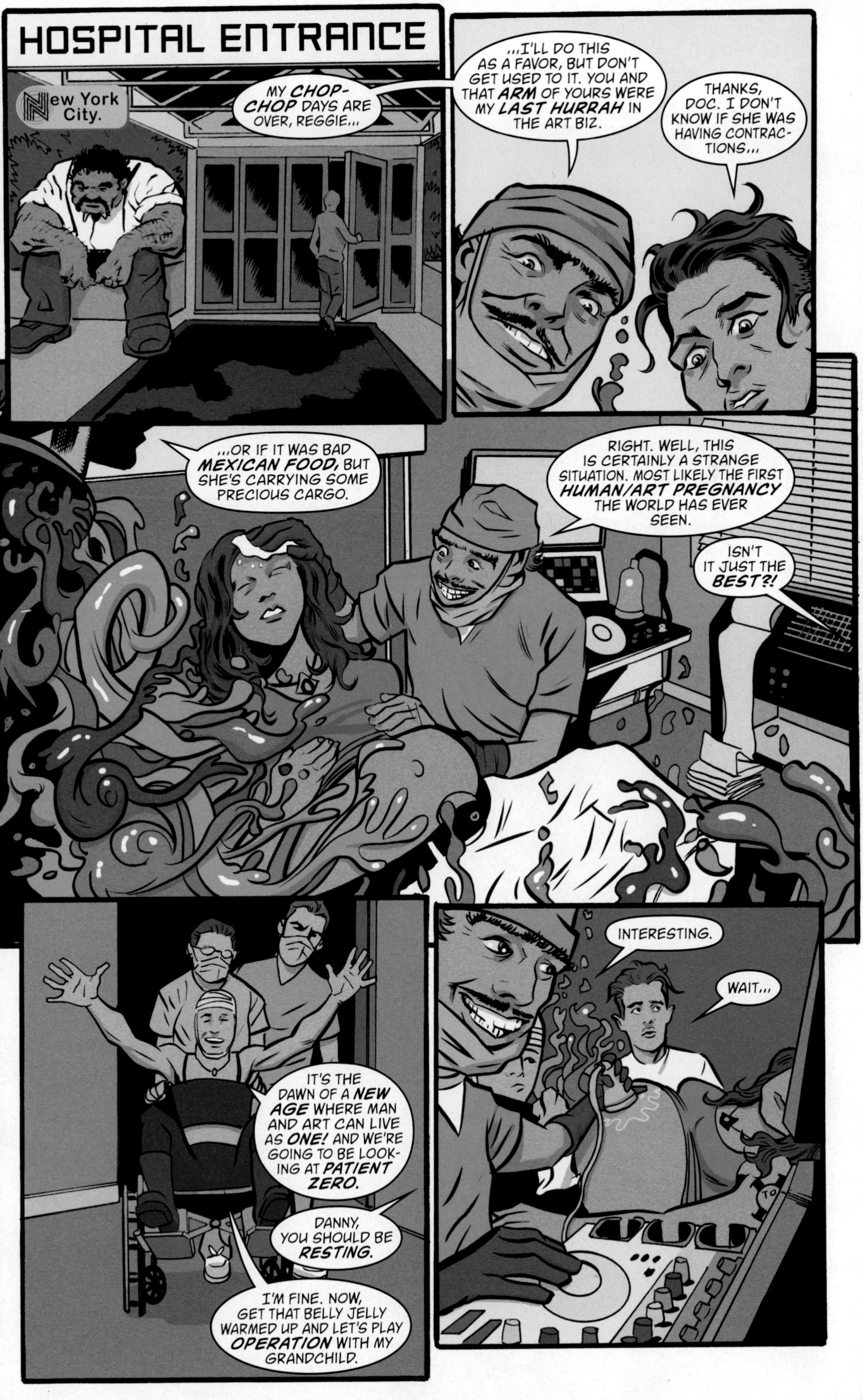
HOSPITAL ENTRANCE
New York City.
MY CHOP-CHOP DAYS ARE OVER, REGGIE...
...I'LL DO THIS AS A FAVOR, BUT DON'T GET USED TO IT. YOU AND THAT ARM OF YOURS WERE MY LAST HURRAH IN THE ART BIZ.
THANKS, DOC. I DON'T KNOW IF SHE WAS HAVING CONTRACTIONS...
...OR IF IT WAS BAD MEXICAN FOOD, BUT SHE'S CARRYING SOME PRECIOUS CARGO.
RIGHT. WELL, THIS IS CERTAINLY A STRANGE SITUATION. MOST LIKELY THE FIRST HUMAN/ART PREGNANCY THE WORLD HAS EVER SEEN.
ISN'T IT JUST THE BEST?!
IT'S THE DAWN OF A NEW AGE WHERE MAN AND ART CAN LIVE AS ONE! AND WE'RE GOING TO BE LOOKING AT PATIENT ZERO.
DANNY, YOU SHOULD BE RESTING.
I'M FINE. NOW, GET THAT BELLY JELLY WARMED UP AND LET'S PLAY OPERATION WITH MY GRANDCHILD.
INTERESTING.
WAIT...

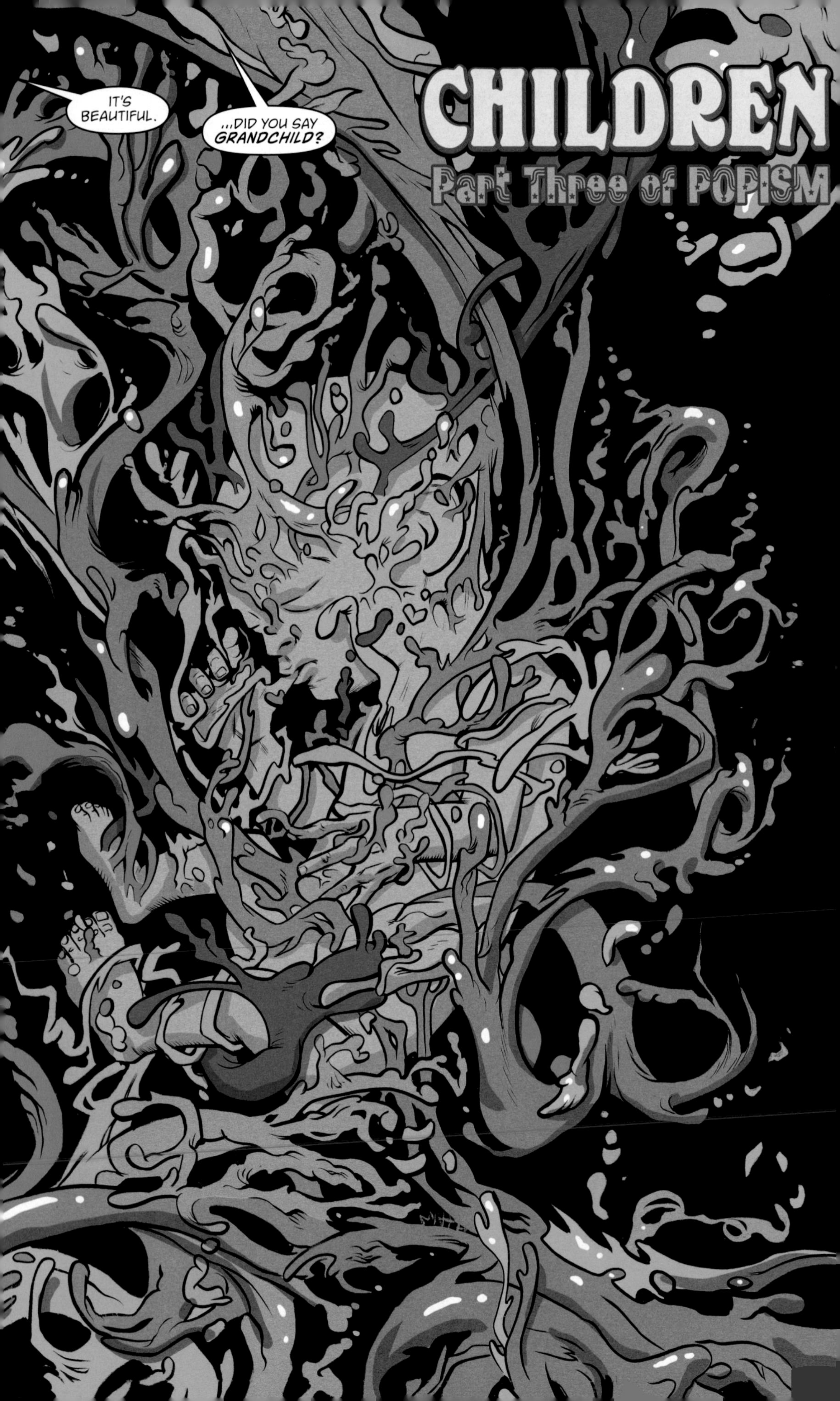
IT'S BEAUTIFUL.
...DID YOU SAY GRANDCHILD?
CHILDREN
Part Three of POPISM

BECAUSE THE LAST TIME I CHECKED, YOU WEREN'T EVEN A REGULAR *DAD.* GRANDDAD IS A TITLE YOU HAVE TO *EARN.*

I'M BACK NOW, REGGIE. I WANT TO MAKE THINGS *RIGHT.*

NO! YOU DON'T GET TO *DO* THAT! YOU DON'T GET TO JUST *SHOW UP* AND MAGICALLY BE PART OF MY LIFE!

LISTEN, SON, IF IT WEREN'T FOR ME, YOU WOULD HAVE *DIED* THAT NIGHT IN THE ALLEY. WHERE DO YOU THINK THAT PROCEDURE CAME FROM? WHO DO YOU THINK *PIONEERED* IT?

SON? YOU DON'T GET THAT LUXURY. AND FOR ALL I KNOW, YOU SET ME UP IN THAT ALLEY. HOW DO I KNOW *YOU* DIDN'T HAVE THAT GRAFFITI *ATTACK* ME AND KILL JESS?

PLEASE...

LISTEN, YOU GUYS WILL HAVE TO GET OUT OF THE ROOM IF YOU'RE GOING TO CONTINUE THIS...

...HER BLOOD PRESSURE IS *THROUGH THE ROOF.*

NOT TO MENTION YOU *STILL* HAVEN'T TOLD ME WHAT THE HELL YOU DID WITH *MOM!*

THEY'RE GONE.

NURSES...

...TRY TO CALM HER DOWN AND RUN A *STRESS TEST.*

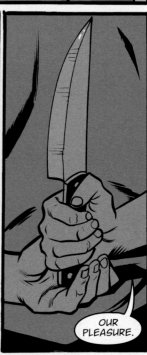

OUR PLEASURE.

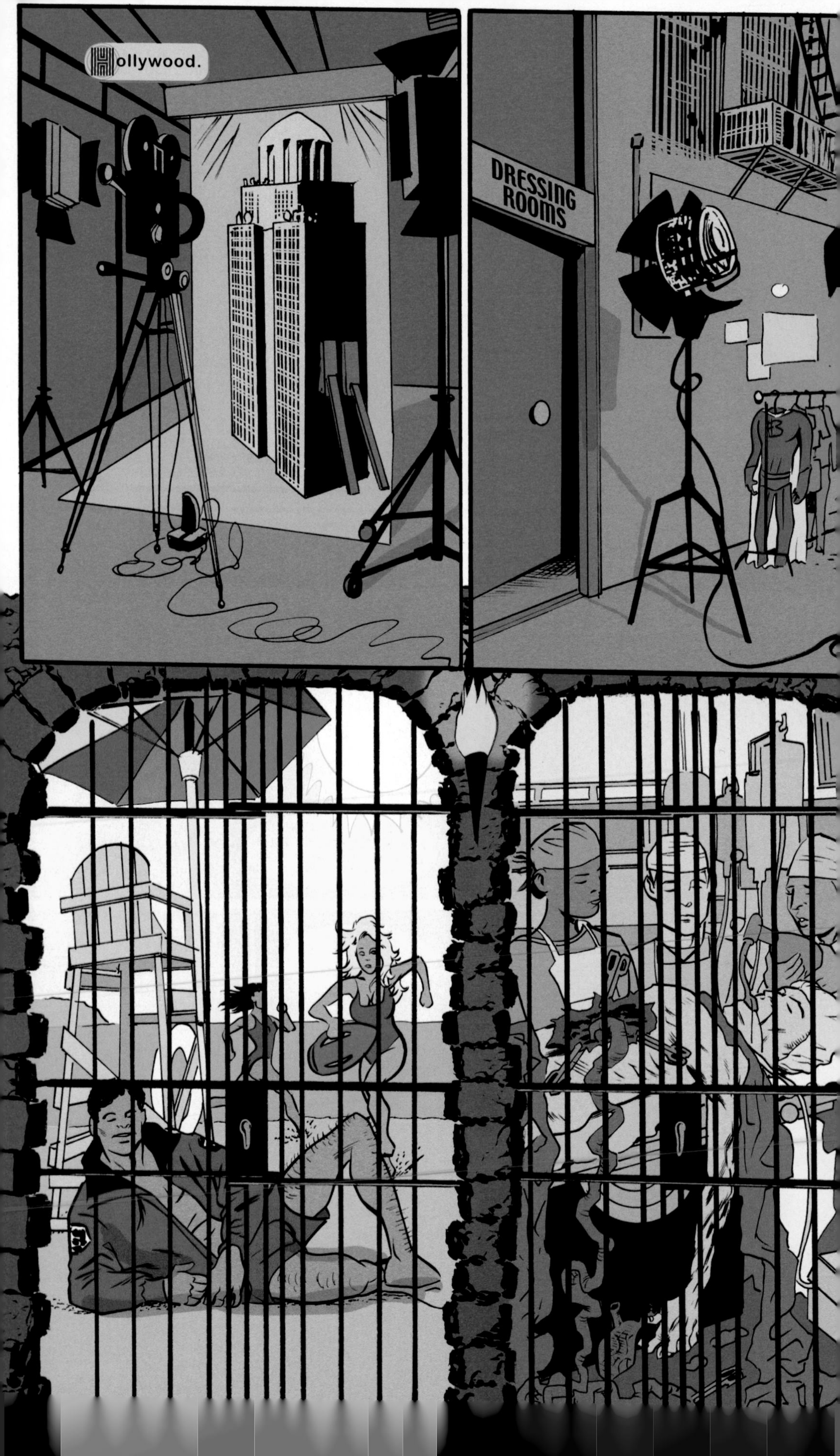
Hollywood.
DRESSING ROOMS

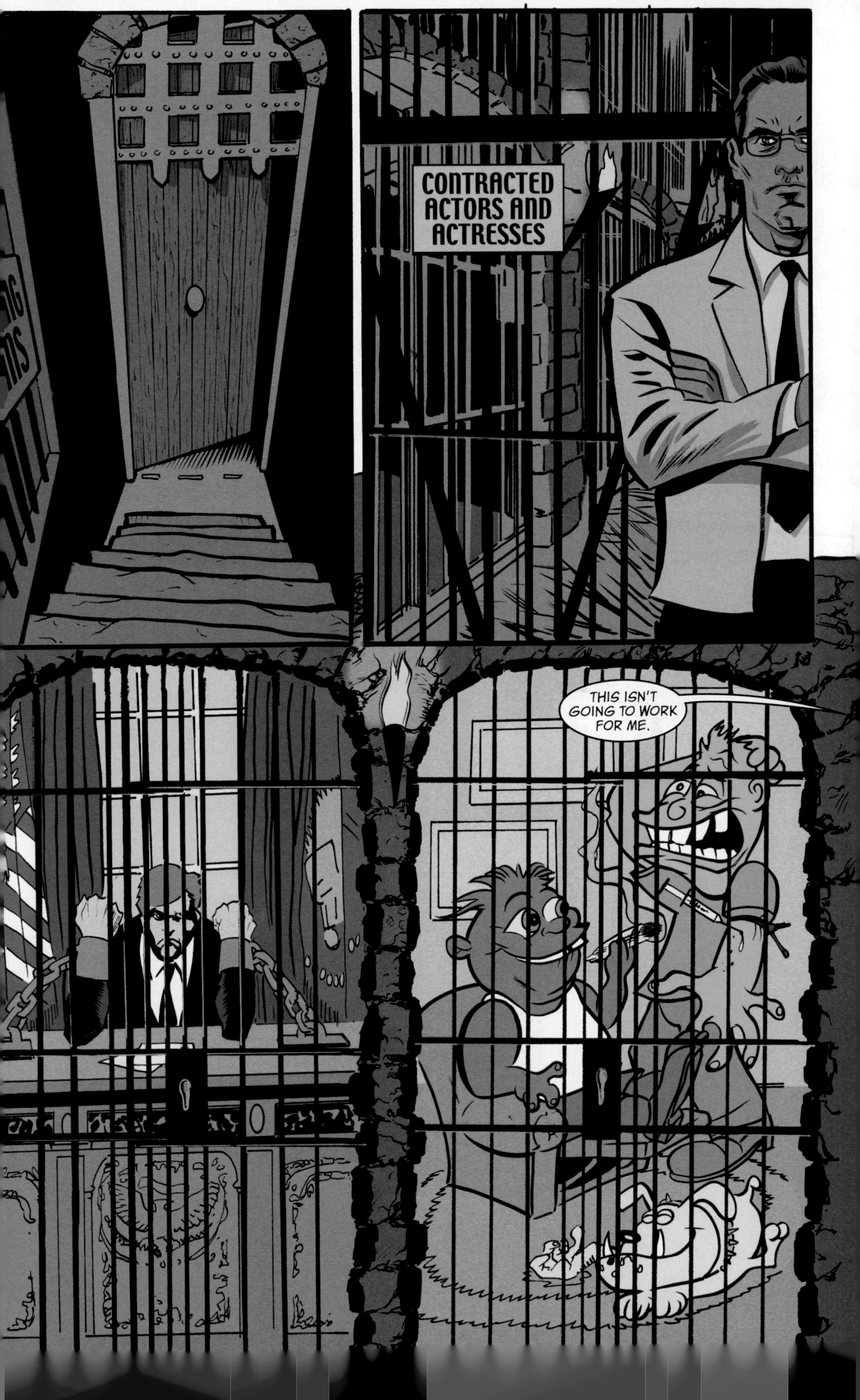
CONTRACTED
ACTORS AND
ACTRESSES
THIS ISN'T
GOING TO WORK
FOR ME.

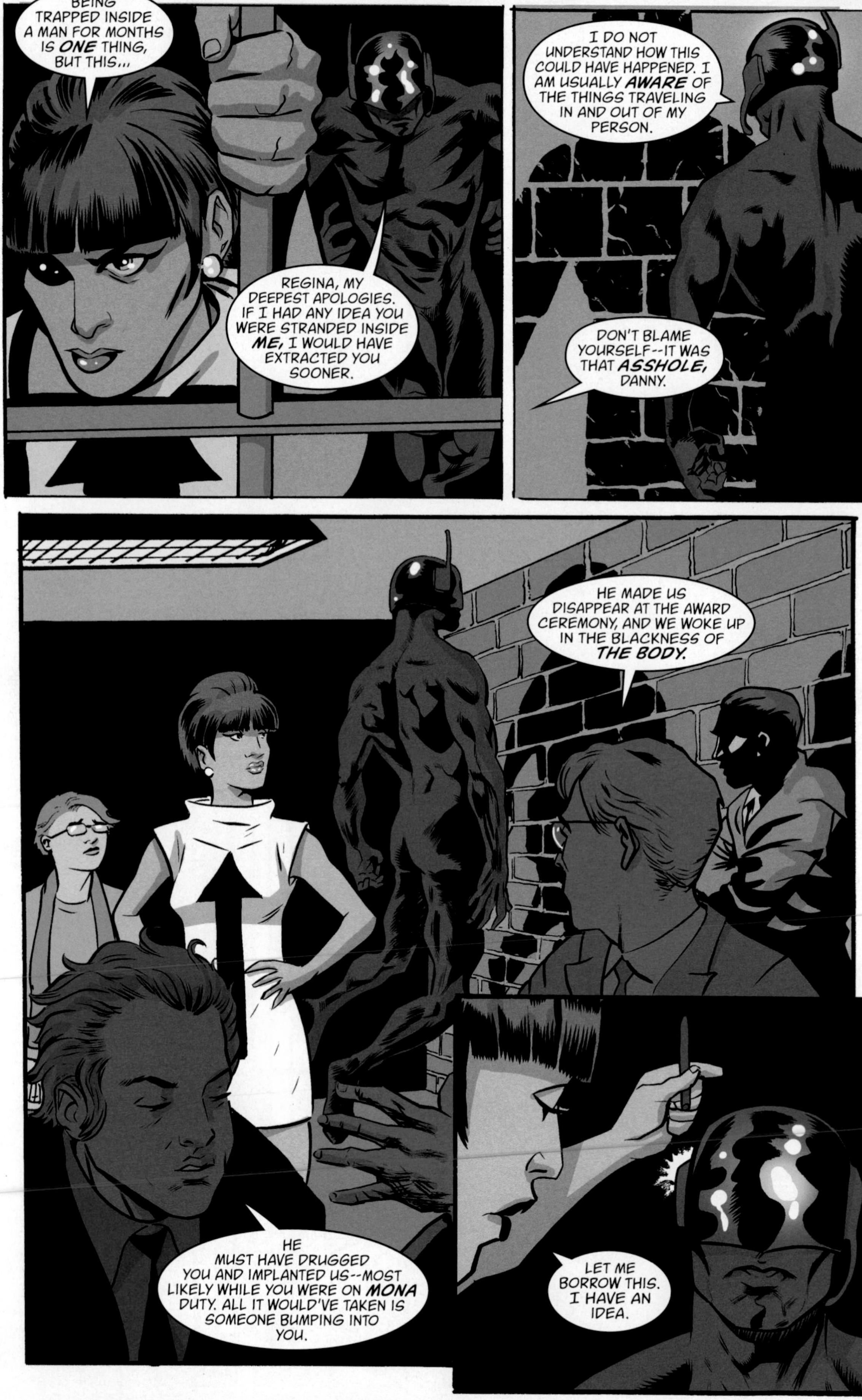

BEING TRAPPED INSIDE A MAN FOR MONTHS IS ONE THING, BUT THIS...
REGINA, MY DEEPEST APOLOGIES. IF I HAD ANY IDEA YOU WERE STRANDED INSIDE ME, I WOULD HAVE EXTRACTED YOU SOONER.
I DO NOT UNDERSTAND HOW THIS COULD HAVE HAPPENED. I AM USUALLY AWARE OF THE THINGS TRAVELING IN AND OUT OF MY PERSON.
DON'T BLAME YOURSELF--IT WAS THAT ASSHOLE, DANNY.
HE MADE US DISAPPEAR AT THE AWARD CEREMONY, AND WE WOKE UP IN THE BLACKNESS OF THE BODY.
HE MUST HAVE DRUGGED YOU AND IMPLANTED US--MOST LIKELY WHILE YOU WERE ON MONA DUTY. ALL IT WOULD'VE TAKEN IS SOMEONE BUMPING INTO YOU.
LET ME BORROW THIS. I HAVE AN IDEA.

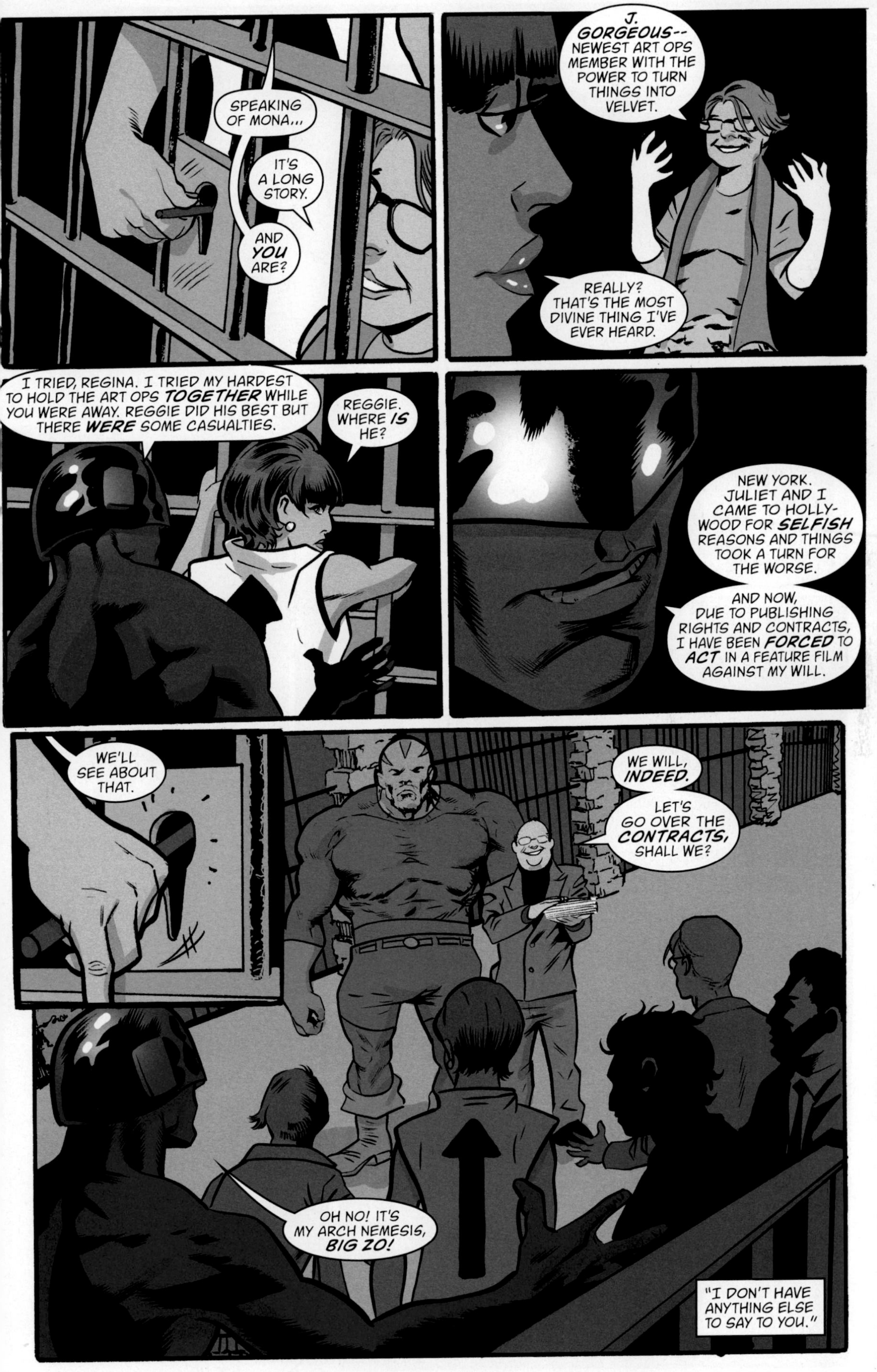
SPEAKING OF MONA...
IT'S A LONG STORY.
AND YOU ARE?
J. GORGEOUS-- NEWEST ART OPS MEMBER WITH THE POWER TO TURN THINGS INTO VELVET.
REALLY? THAT'S THE MOST DIVINE THING I'VE EVER HEARD.
I TRIED, REGINA. I TRIED MY HARDEST TO HOLD THE ART OPS TOGETHER WHILE YOU WERE AWAY. REGGIE DID HIS BEST BUT THERE WERE SOME CASUALTIES.
REGGIE. WHERE IS HE?
NEW YORK. JULIET AND I CAME TO HOLLY-WOOD FOR SELFISH REASONS AND THINGS TOOK A TURN FOR THE WORSE.
AND NOW, DUE TO PUBLISHING RIGHTS AND CONTRACTS, I HAVE BEEN FORCED TO ACT IN A FEATURE FILM AGAINST MY WILL.
WE'LL SEE ABOUT THAT.
WE WILL, INDEED.
LET'S GO OVER THE CONTRACTS, SHALL WE?
OH NO! IT'S MY ARCH NEMESIS, BIG ZO!
"I DON'T HAVE ANYTHING ELSE TO SAY TO YOU."

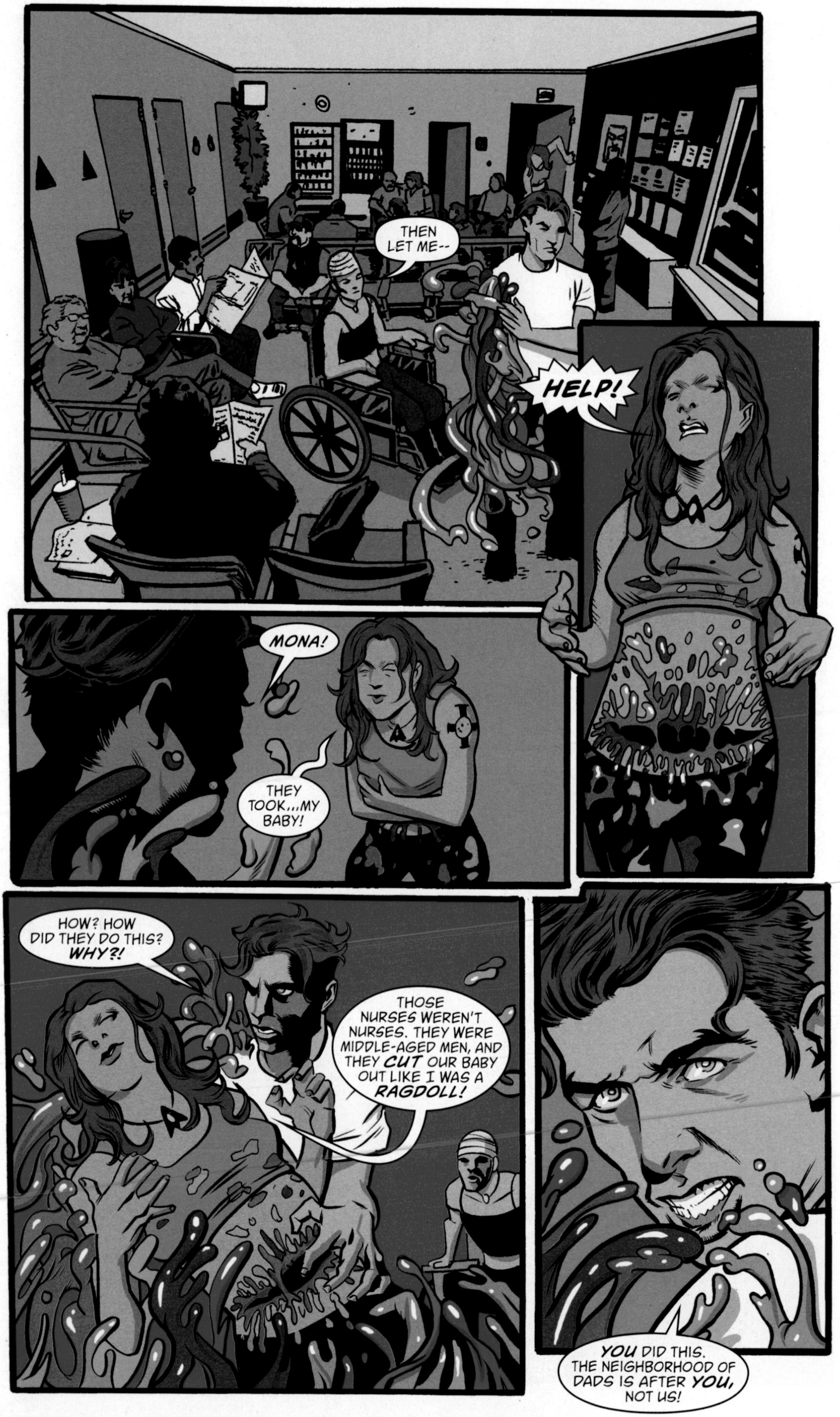
THEN LET ME--
HELP!
MONA!
THEY TOOK...MY BABY!
HOW? HOW DID THEY DO THIS? WHY?!
THOSE NURSES WEREN'T NURSES. THEY WERE MIDDLE-AGED MEN, AND THEY CUT OUR BABY OUT LIKE I WAS A RAGDOLL!
YOU DID THIS. THE NEIGHBORHOOD OF DADS IS AFTER YOU, NOT US!

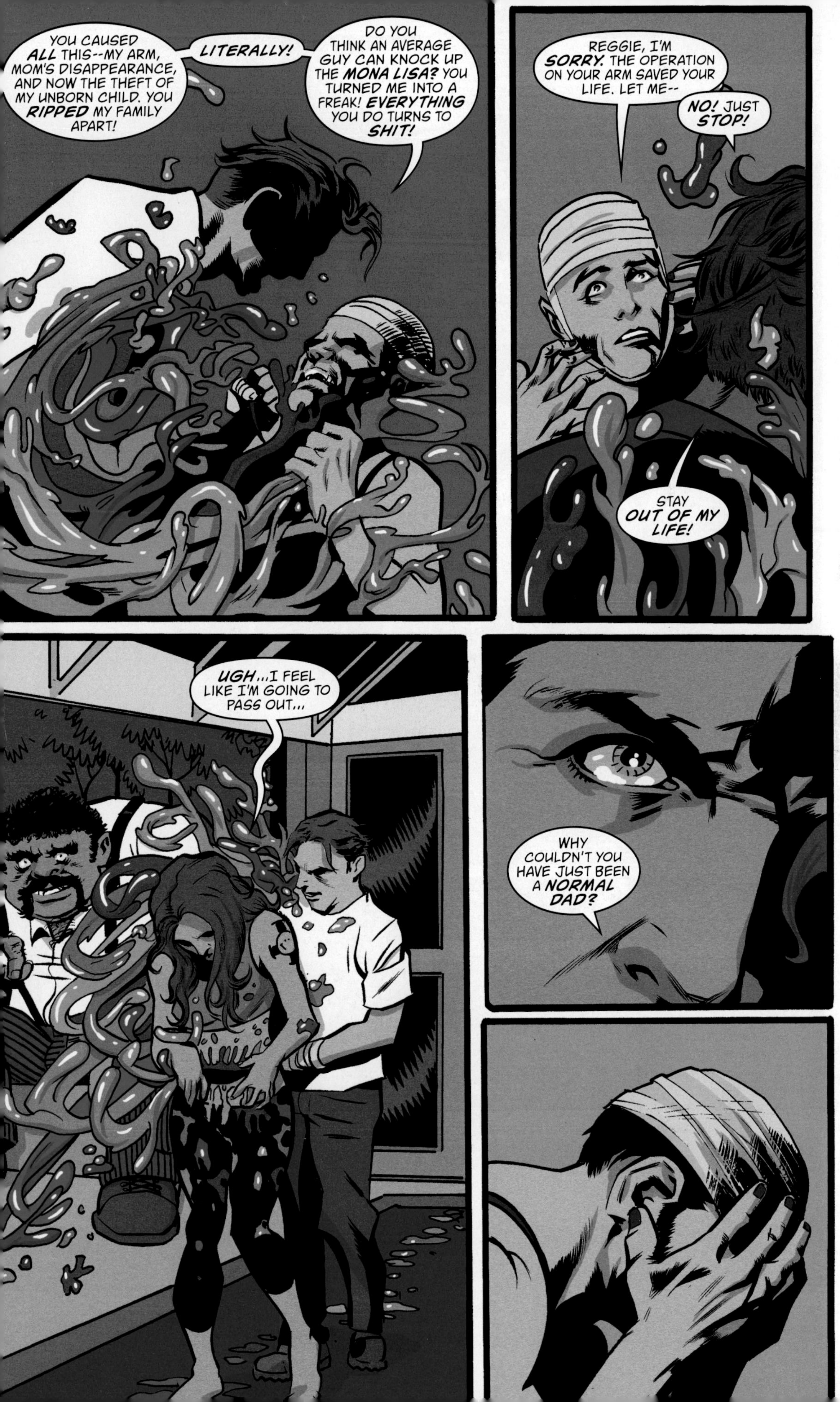
YOU CAUSED ALL THIS--MY ARM, MOM'S DISAPPEARANCE, AND NOW THE THEFT OF MY UNBORN CHILD. YOU RIPPED MY FAMILY APART!
LITERALLY!
DO YOU THINK AN AVERAGE GUY CAN KNOCK UP THE MONA LISA? YOU TURNED ME INTO A FREAK! EVERYTHING YOU DO TURNS TO SHIT!
REGGIE, I'M SORRY. THE OPERATION ON YOUR ARM SAVED YOUR LIFE. LET ME--
NO! JUST STOP!
STAY OUT OF MY LIFE!
UGH...I FEEL LIKE I'M GOING TO PASS OUT...
WHY COULDN'T YOU HAVE JUST BEEN A NORMAL DAD?

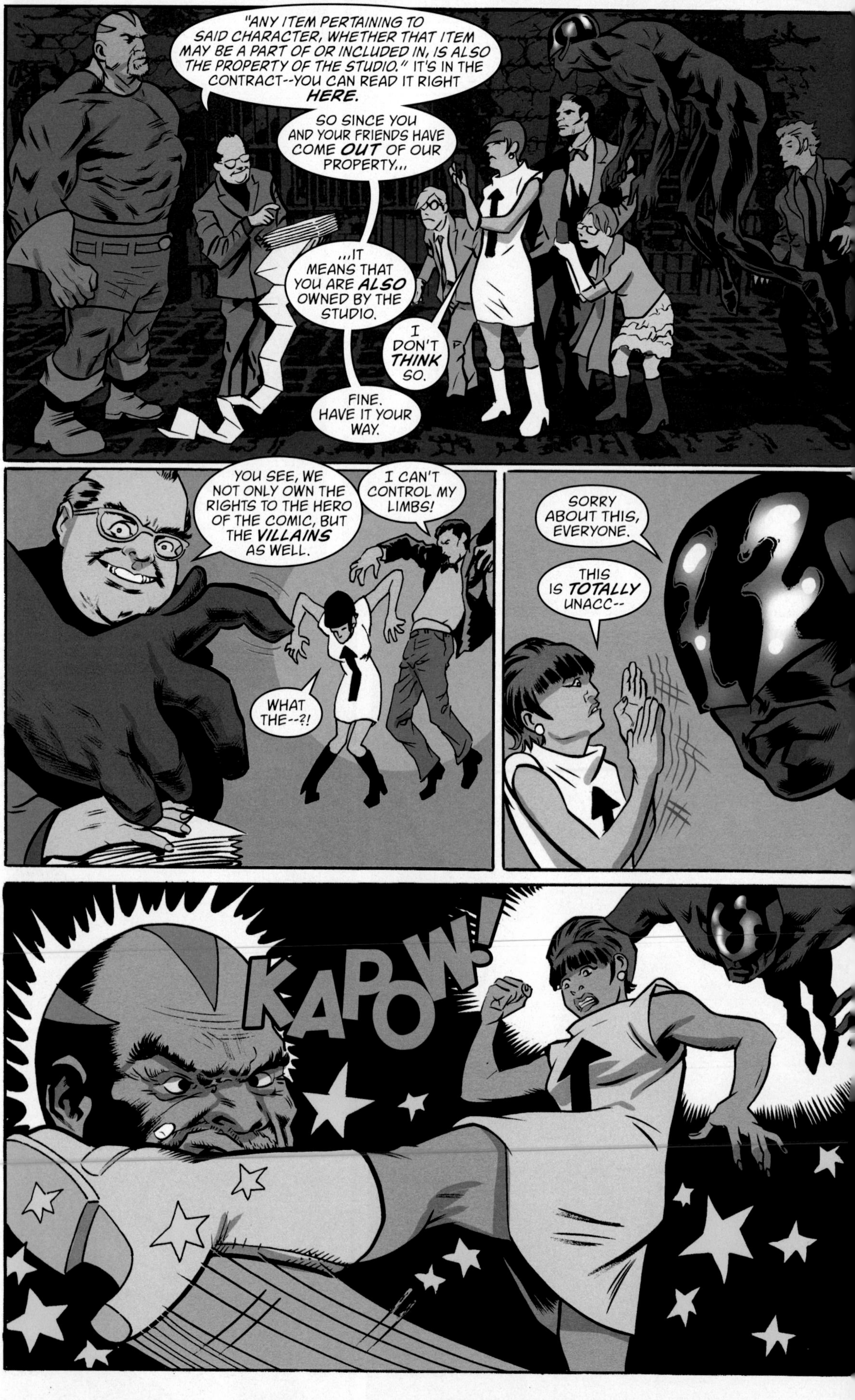
"ANY ITEM PERTAINING TO SAID CHARACTER, WHETHER THAT ITEM MAY BE A PART OF OR INCLUDED IN, IS ALSO THE PROPERTY OF THE STUDIO." IT'S IN THE CONTRACT--YOU CAN READ IT RIGHT HERE.
SO SINCE YOU AND YOUR FRIENDS HAVE COME OUT OF OUR PROPERTY...
...IT MEANS THAT YOU ARE ALSO OWNED BY THE STUDIO.
I DON'T THINK SO.
FINE. HAVE IT YOUR WAY.
YOU SEE, WE NOT ONLY OWN THE RIGHTS TO THE HERO OF THE COMIC, BUT THE VILLAINS AS WELL.
I CAN'T CONTROL MY LIMBS!
WHAT THE--?!
SORRY ABOUT THIS, EVERYONE.
THIS IS TOTALLY UNACC--
KAPOW!

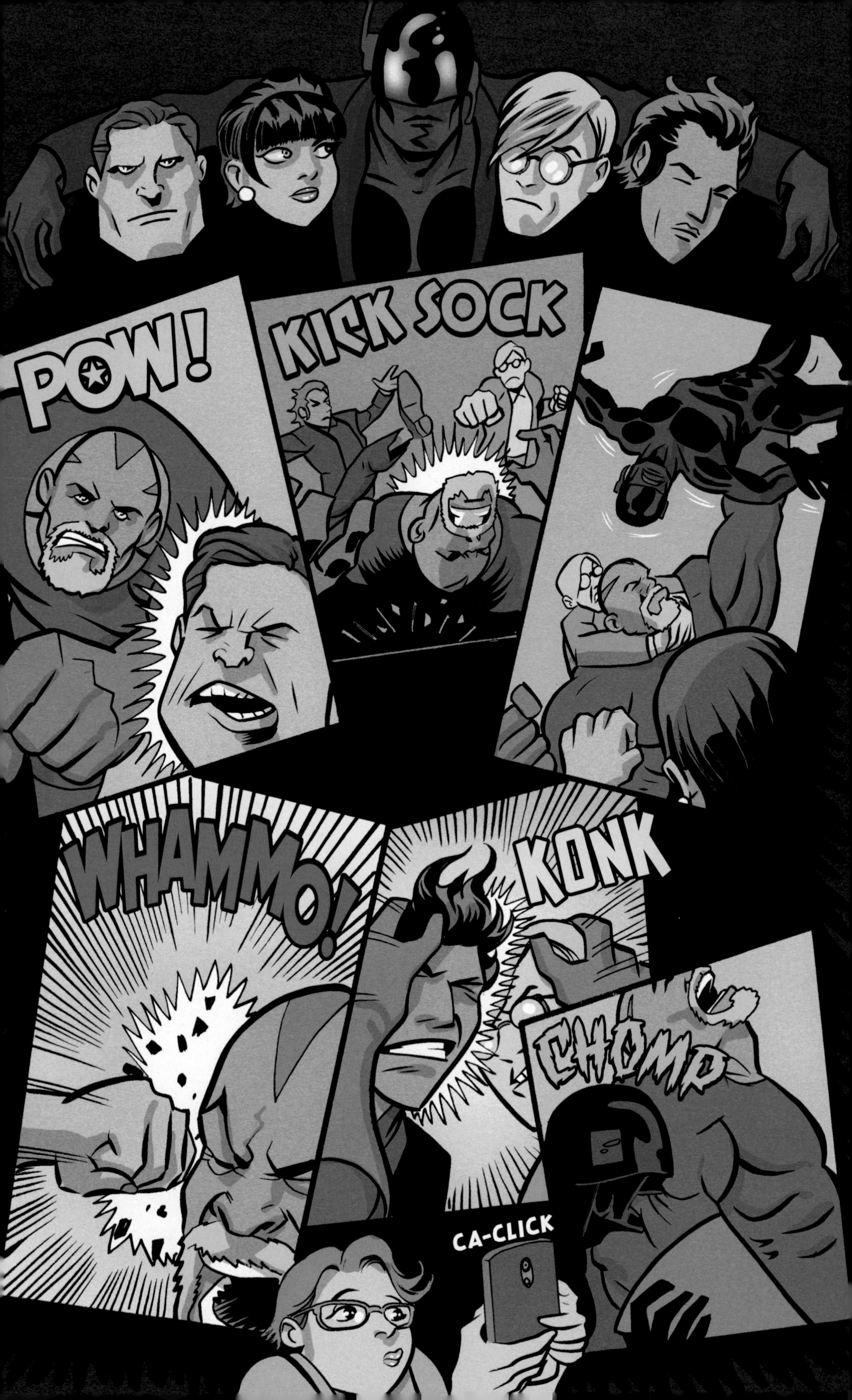
POW!
KICK SOCK
WHAMMO!
KONK
CHOMP
CA-CLICK

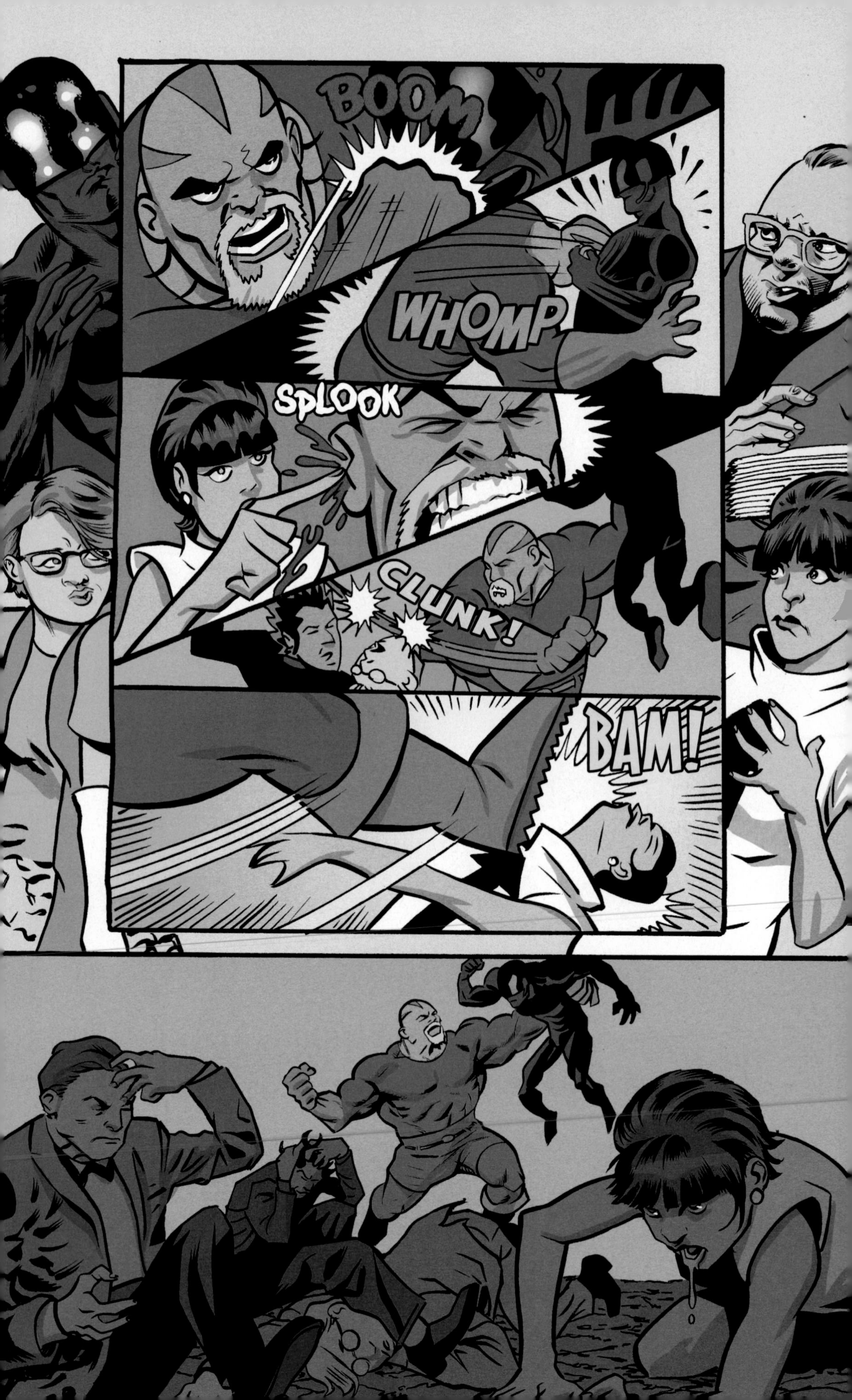
BOOM
WHOMP
SPLOOK
CLUNK!
BAM!

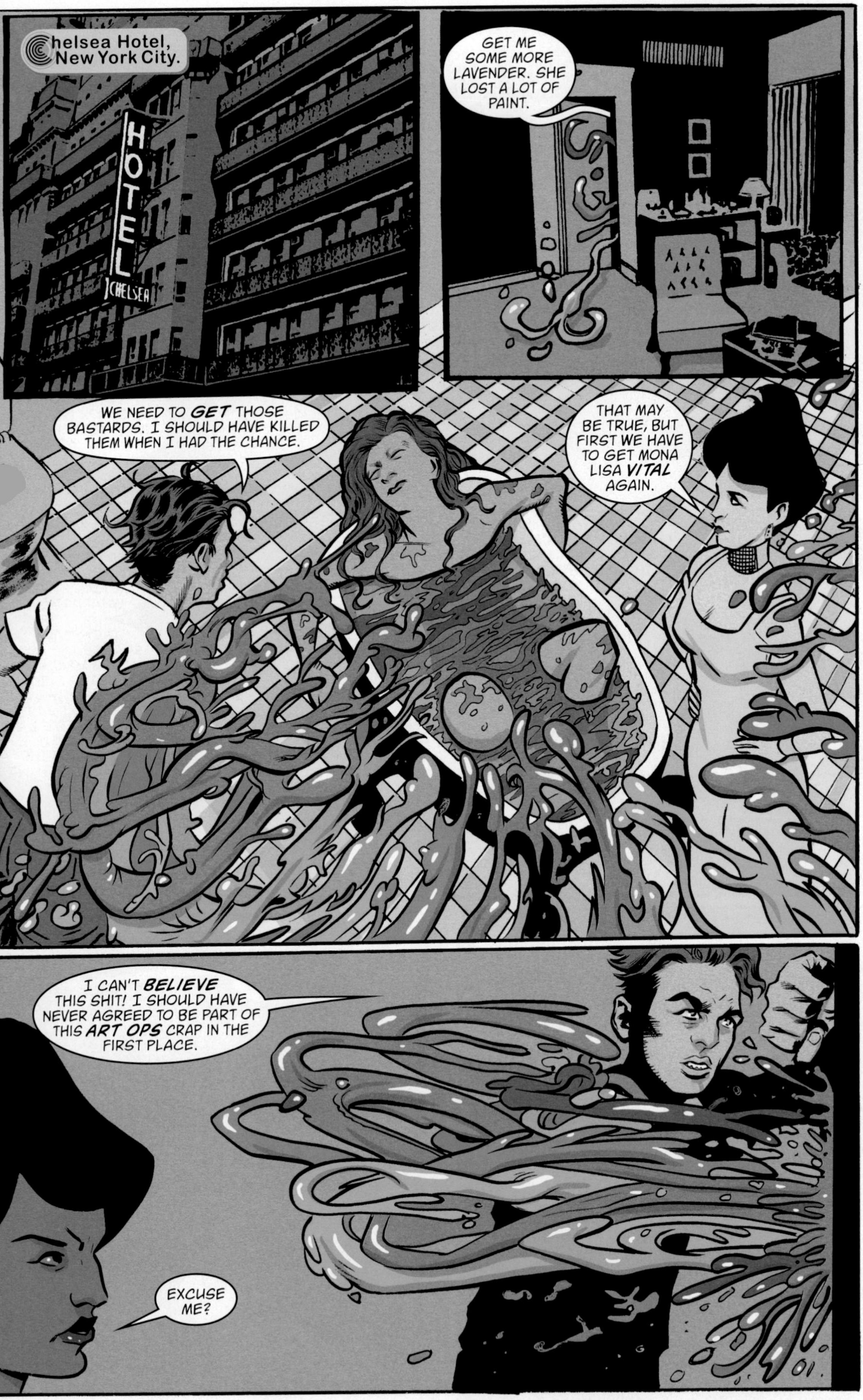
Chelsea Hotel, New York City.
HOTEL
CHELSEA
GET ME SOME MORE LAVENDER. SHE LOST A LOT OF PAINT.
WE NEED TO GET THOSE BASTARDS. I SHOULD HAVE KILLED THEM WHEN I HAD THE CHANCE.
THAT MAY BE TRUE, BUT FIRST WE HAVE TO GET MONA LISA VITAL AGAIN.
I CAN'T BELIEVE THIS SHIT! I SHOULD HAVE NEVER AGREED TO BE PART OF THIS ART OPS CRAP IN THE FIRST PLACE.
EXCUSE ME?

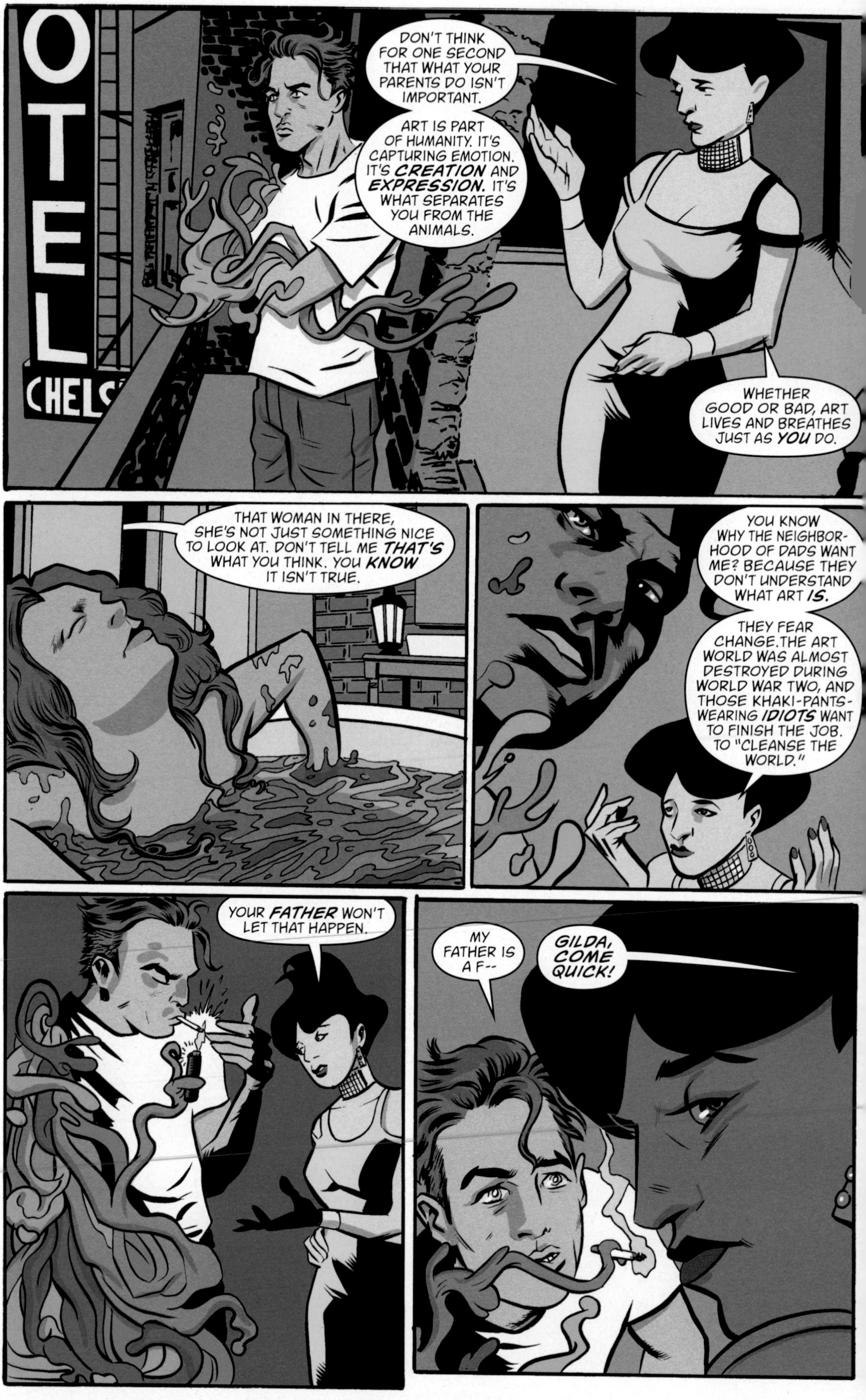
OTEL
CHELS
DON'T THINK FOR ONE SECOND THAT WHAT YOUR PARENTS DO ISN'T IMPORTANT.
ART IS PART OF HUMANITY. IT'S CAPTURING EMOTION. IT'S *CREATION* AND *EXPRESSION.* IT'S WHAT SEPARATES YOU FROM THE ANIMALS.
WHETHER GOOD OR BAD, ART LIVES AND BREATHES JUST AS *YOU* DO.
THAT WOMAN IN THERE, SHE'S NOT JUST SOMETHING NICE TO LOOK AT. DON'T TELL ME *THAT'S* WHAT YOU THINK. YOU *KNOW* IT ISN'T TRUE.
YOU KNOW WHY THE NEIGHBORHOOD OF DADS WANT ME? BECAUSE THEY DON'T UNDERSTAND WHAT ART *IS.*
THEY FEAR CHANGE. THE ART WORLD WAS ALMOST DESTROYED DURING WORLD WAR TWO, AND THOSE KHAKI-PANTS-WEARING *IDIOTS* WANT TO FINISH THE JOB. TO "CLEANSE THE WORLD."
YOUR *FATHER* WON'T LET THAT HAPPEN.
MY FATHER IS A F--
GILDA, COME QUICK!

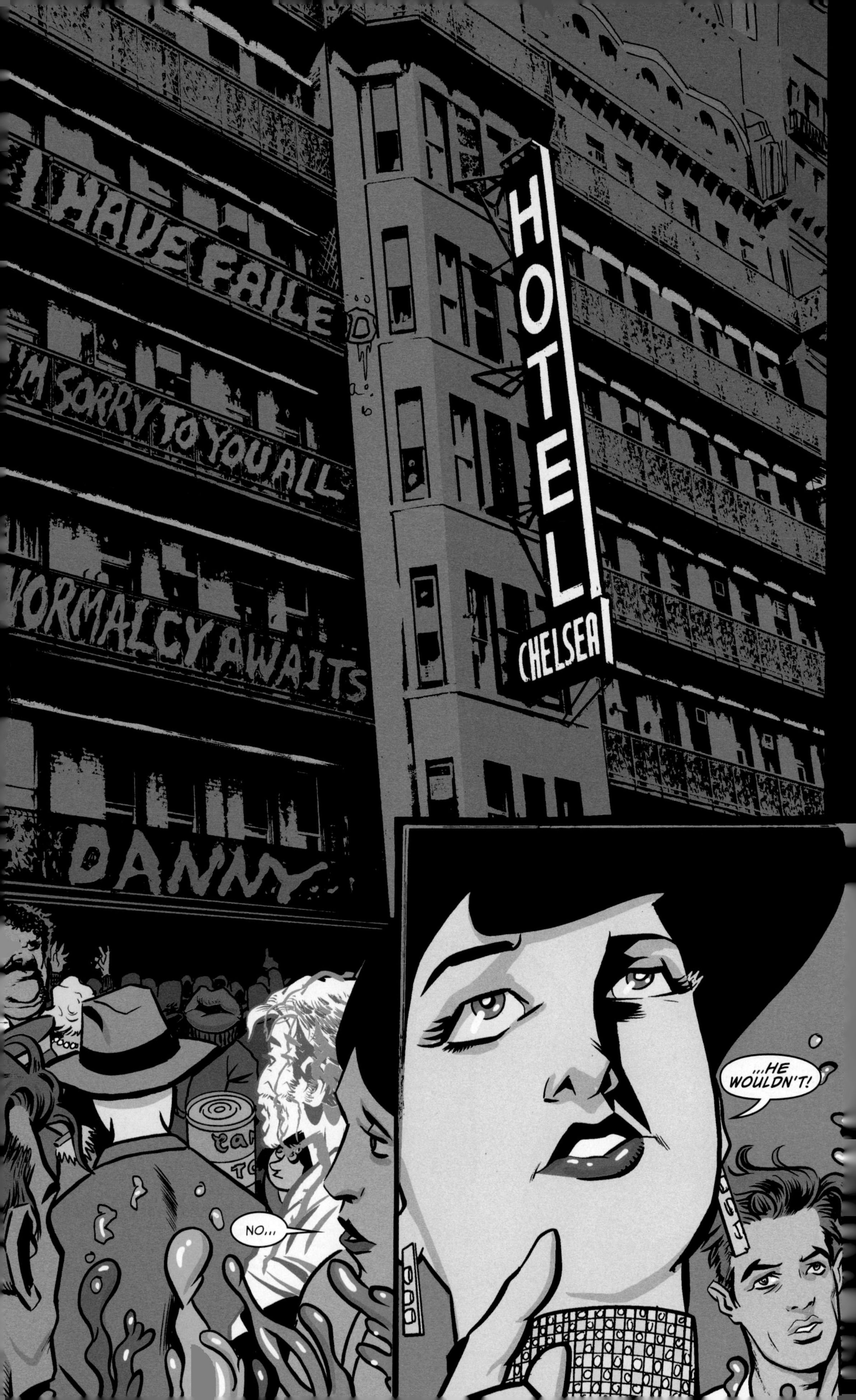
I HAVE FAILED
I'M SORRY TO YOU ALL
NORMALCY AWAITS
DANNY
HOTEL
CHELSEA
NO...
...HE WOULDN'T!

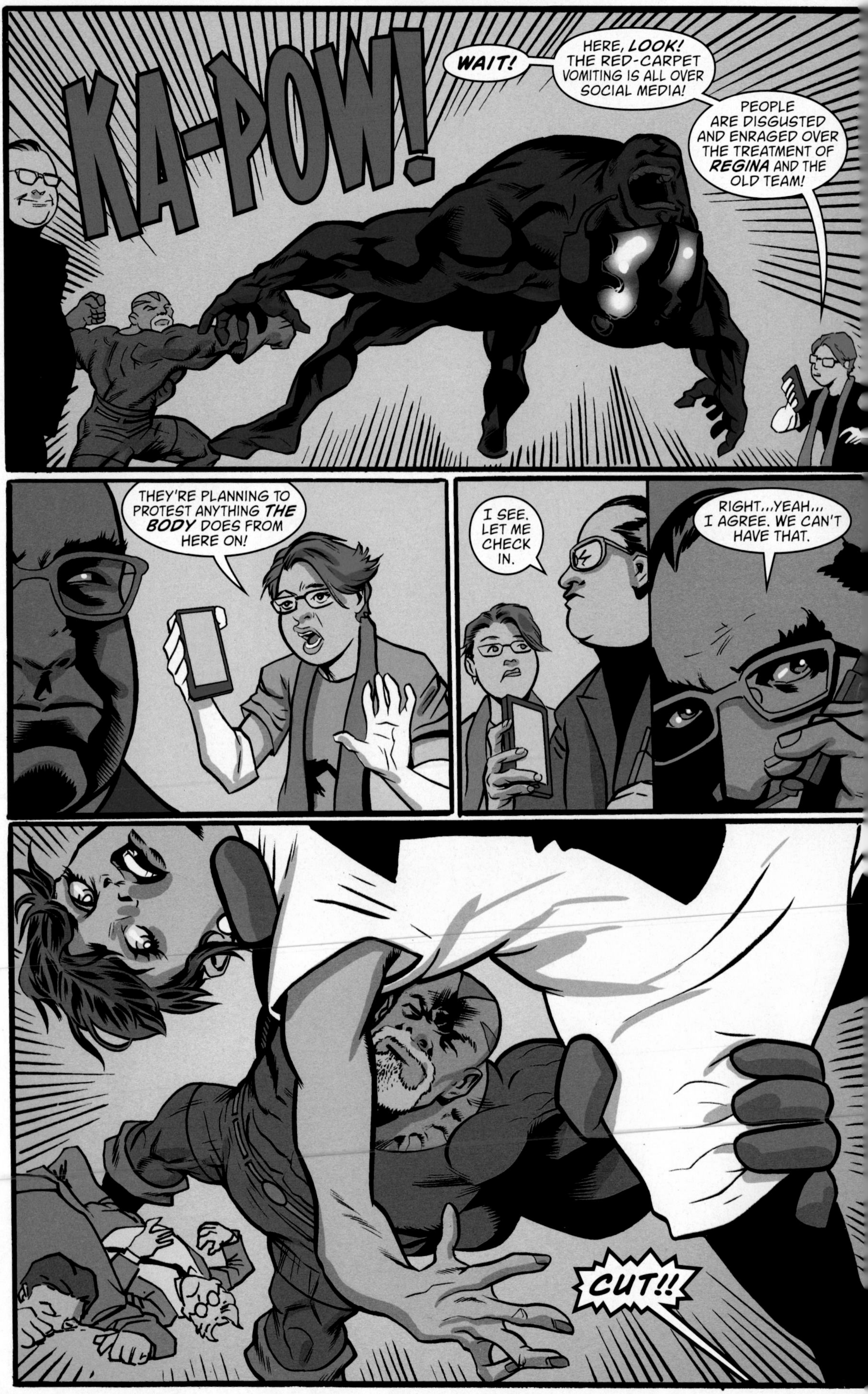
KA-POW!
WAIT!
HERE, LOOK! THE RED-CARPET VOMITING IS ALL OVER SOCIAL MEDIA!
PEOPLE ARE DISGUSTED AND ENRAGED OVER THE TREATMENT OF REGINA AND THE OLD TEAM!
THEY'RE PLANNING TO PROTEST ANYTHING THE BODY DOES FROM HERE ON!
I SEE. LET ME CHECK IN.
RIGHT...YEAH... I AGREE. WE CAN'T HAVE THAT.
CUT!!

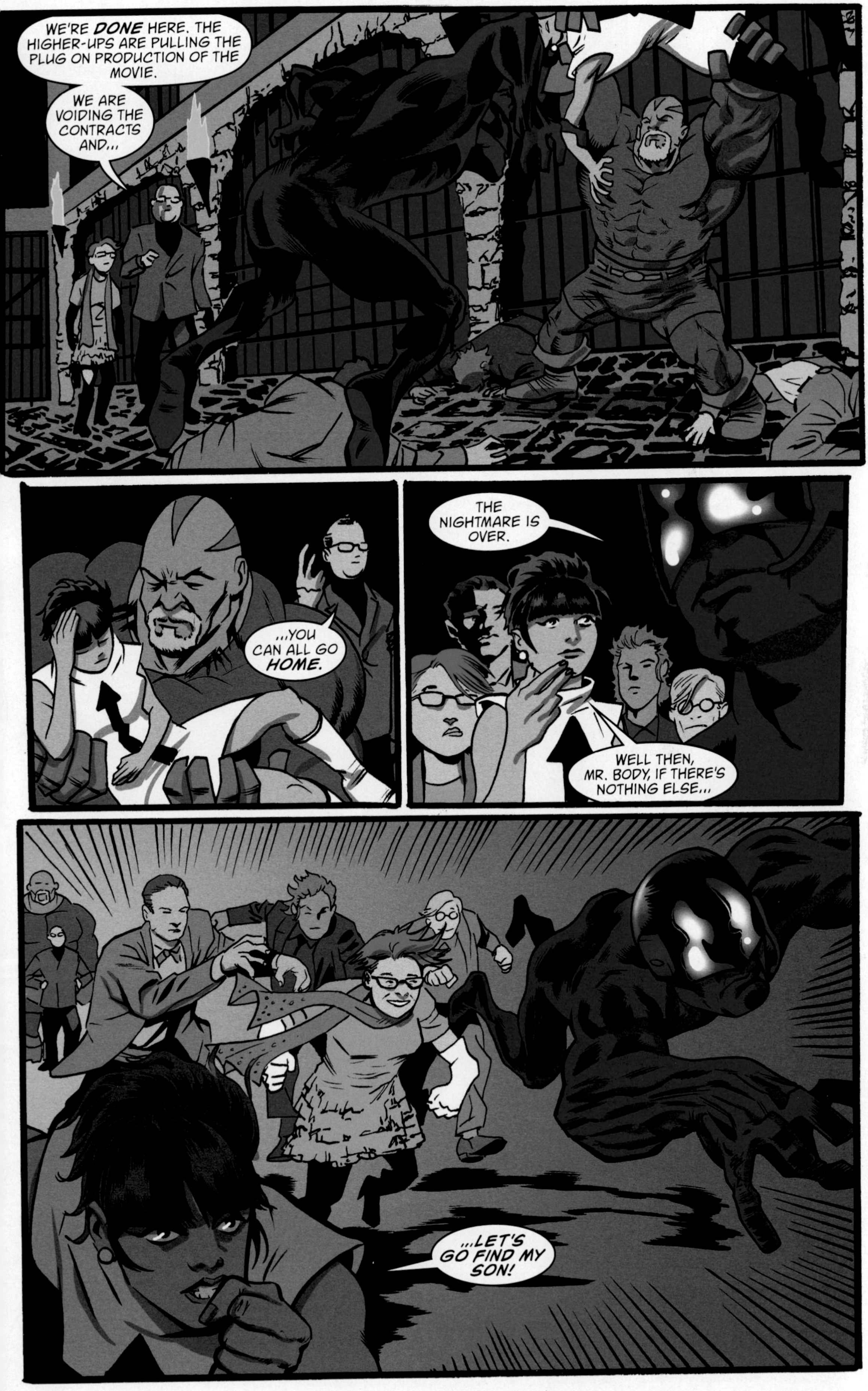
WE'RE DONE HERE. THE HIGHER-UPS ARE PULLING THE PLUG ON PRODUCTION OF THE MOVIE.
WE ARE VOIDING THE CONTRACTS AND...
...YOU CAN ALL GO HOME.
THE NIGHTMARE IS OVER.
WELL THEN, MR. BODY, IF THERE'S NOTHING ELSE...
...LET'S GO FIND MY SON!

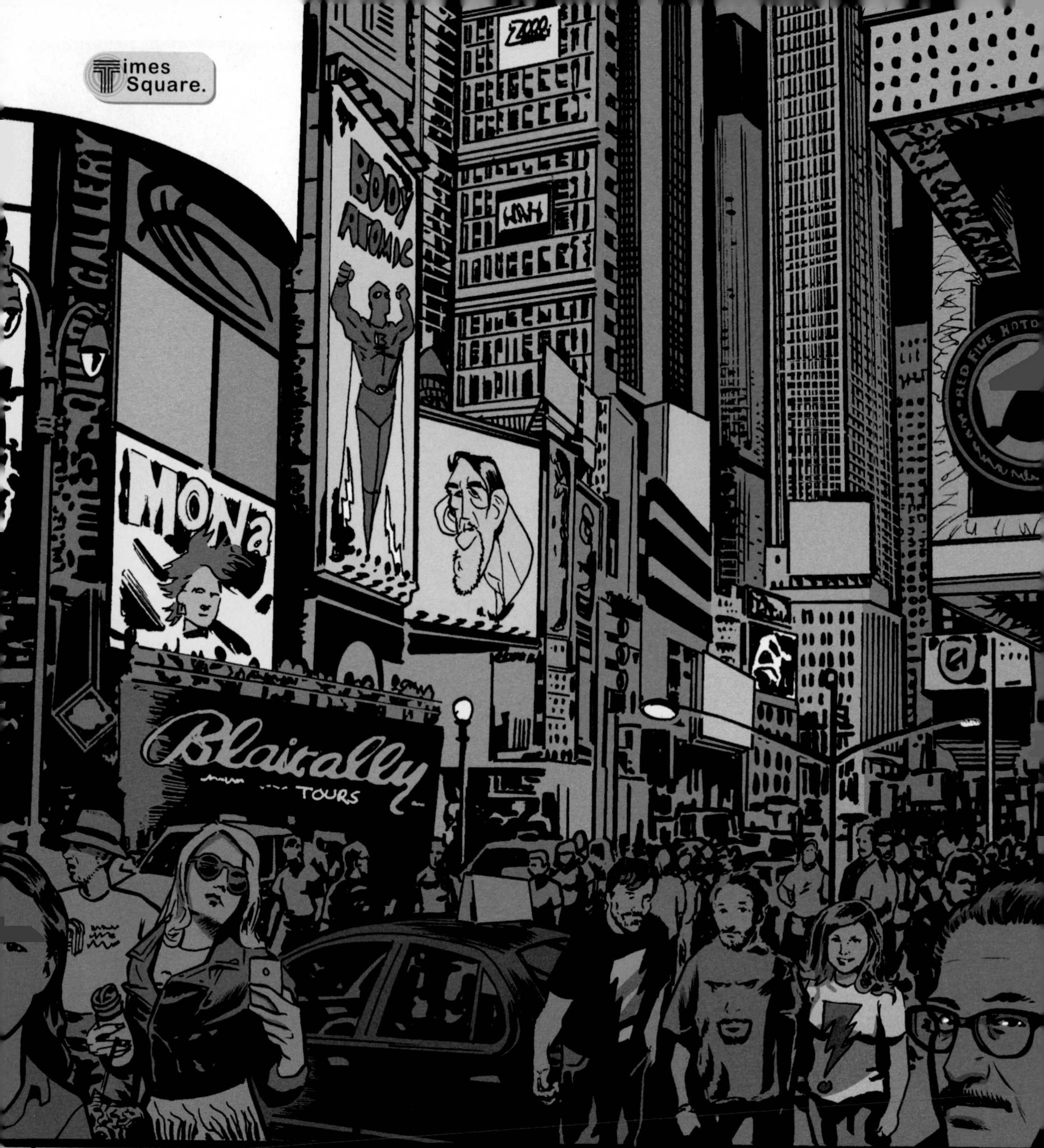
Times Square.
GALLERY
MONA
BODY ATOMIC
TOURS

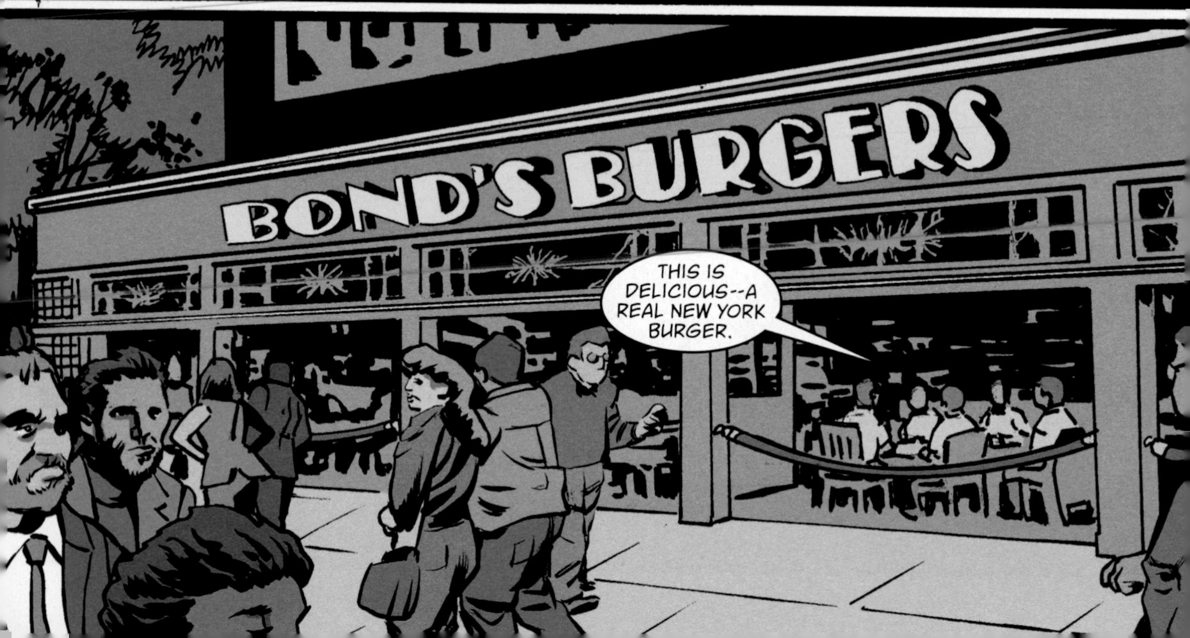
BOND'S BURGERS
THIS IS DELICIOUS--A REAL NEW YORK BURGER.

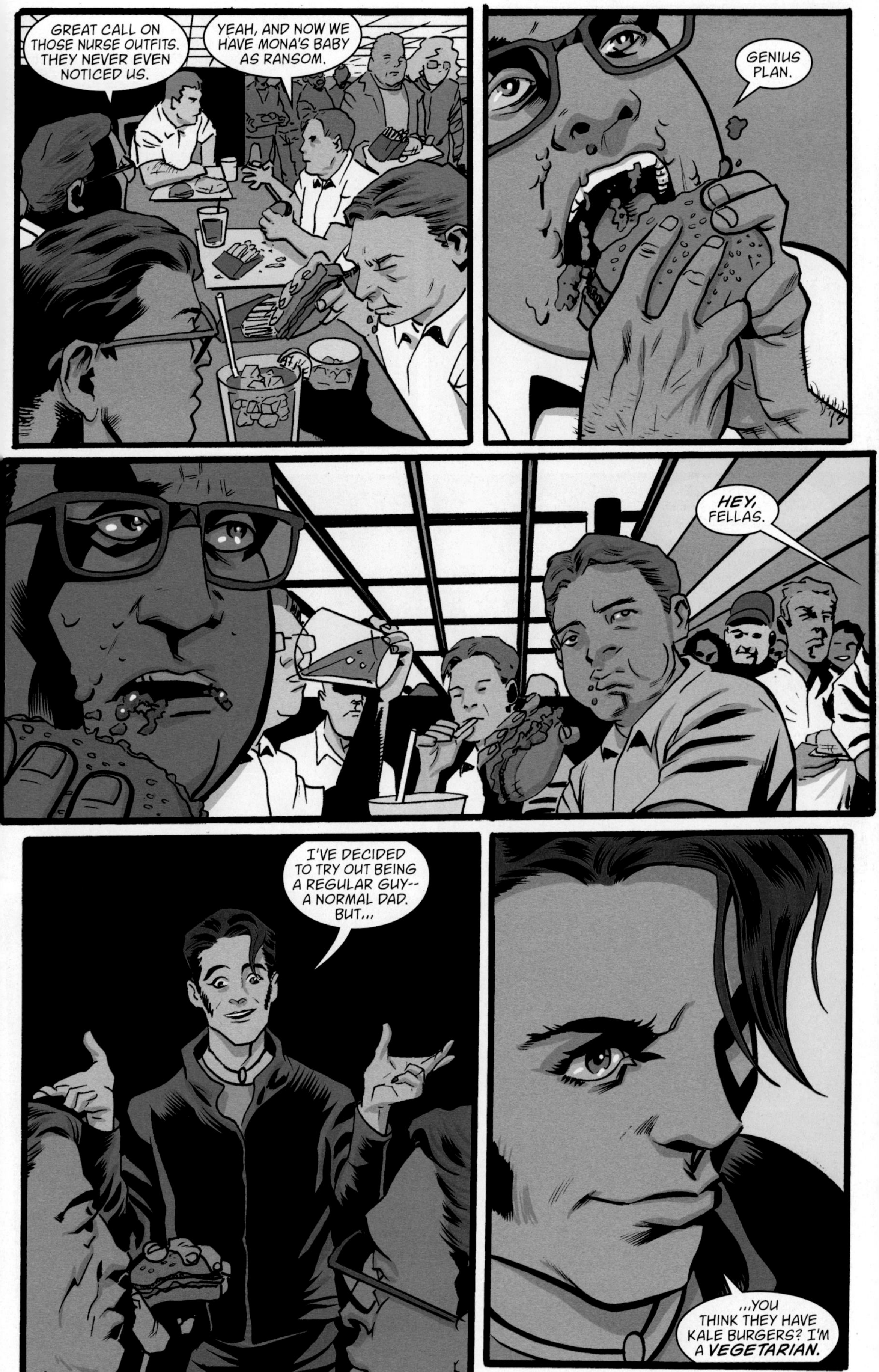
GREAT CALL ON THOSE NURSE OUTFITS. THEY NEVER EVEN NOTICED US.
YEAH, AND NOW WE HAVE MONA'S BABY AS RANSOM.
GENIUS PLAN.
HEY, FELLAS.
I'VE DECIDED TO TRY OUT BEING A REGULAR GUY-- A NORMAL DAD. BUT...
...YOU THINK THEY HAVE KALE BURGERS? I'M A VEGETARIAN.

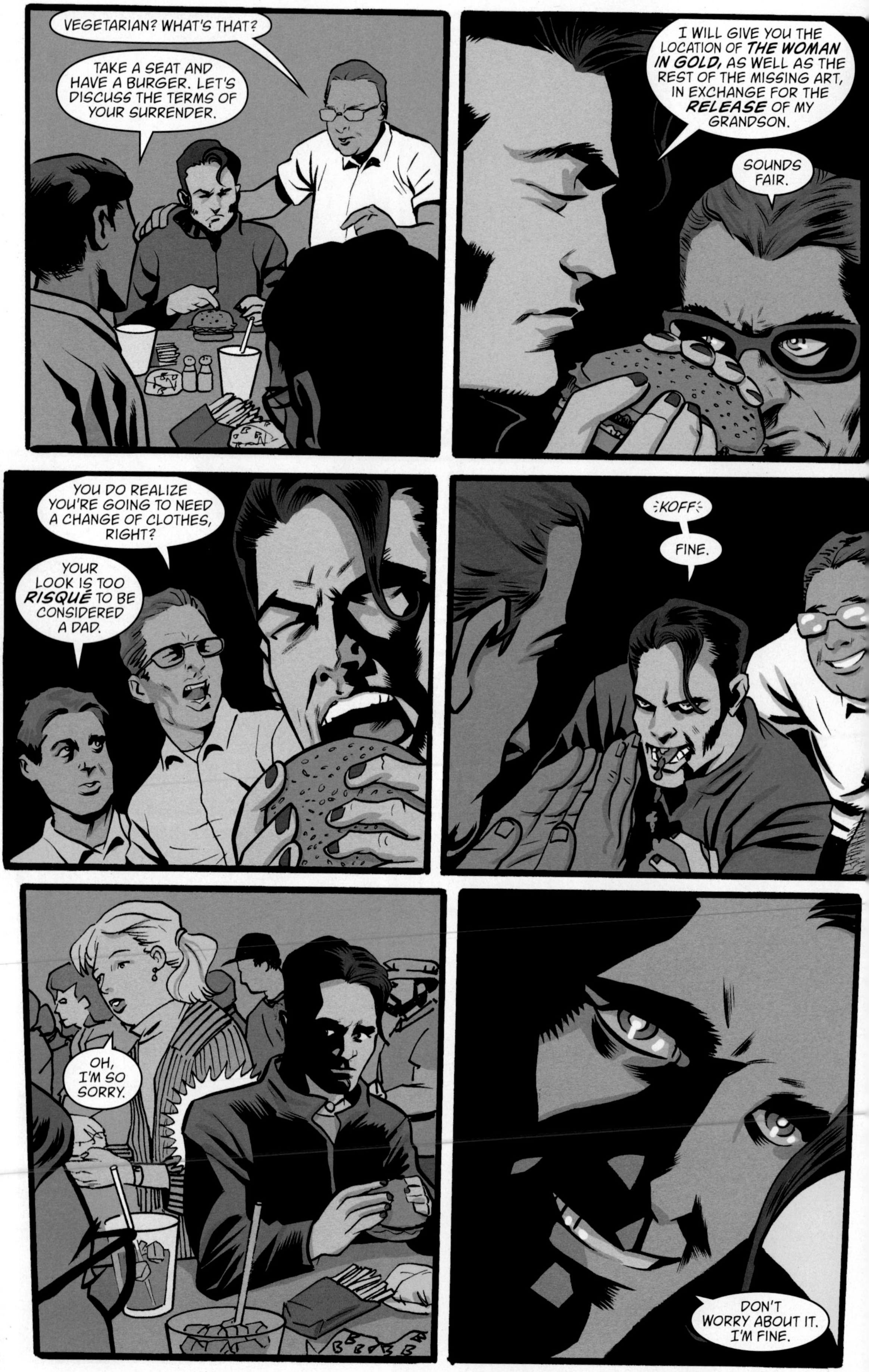
VEGETARIAN? WHAT'S THAT?
TAKE A SEAT AND HAVE A BURGER. LET'S DISCUSS THE TERMS OF YOUR SURRENDER.
I WILL GIVE YOU THE LOCATION OF THE WOMAN IN GOLD, AS WELL AS THE REST OF THE MISSING ART, IN EXCHANGE FOR THE RELEASE OF MY GRANDSON.
SOUNDS FAIR.
YOU DO REALIZE YOU'RE GOING TO NEED A CHANGE OF CLOTHES, RIGHT?
YOUR LOOK IS TOO RISQUÉ TO BE CONSIDERED A DAD.
KOFF
FINE.
OH, I'M SO SORRY.
DON'T WORRY ABOUT IT. I'M FINE.

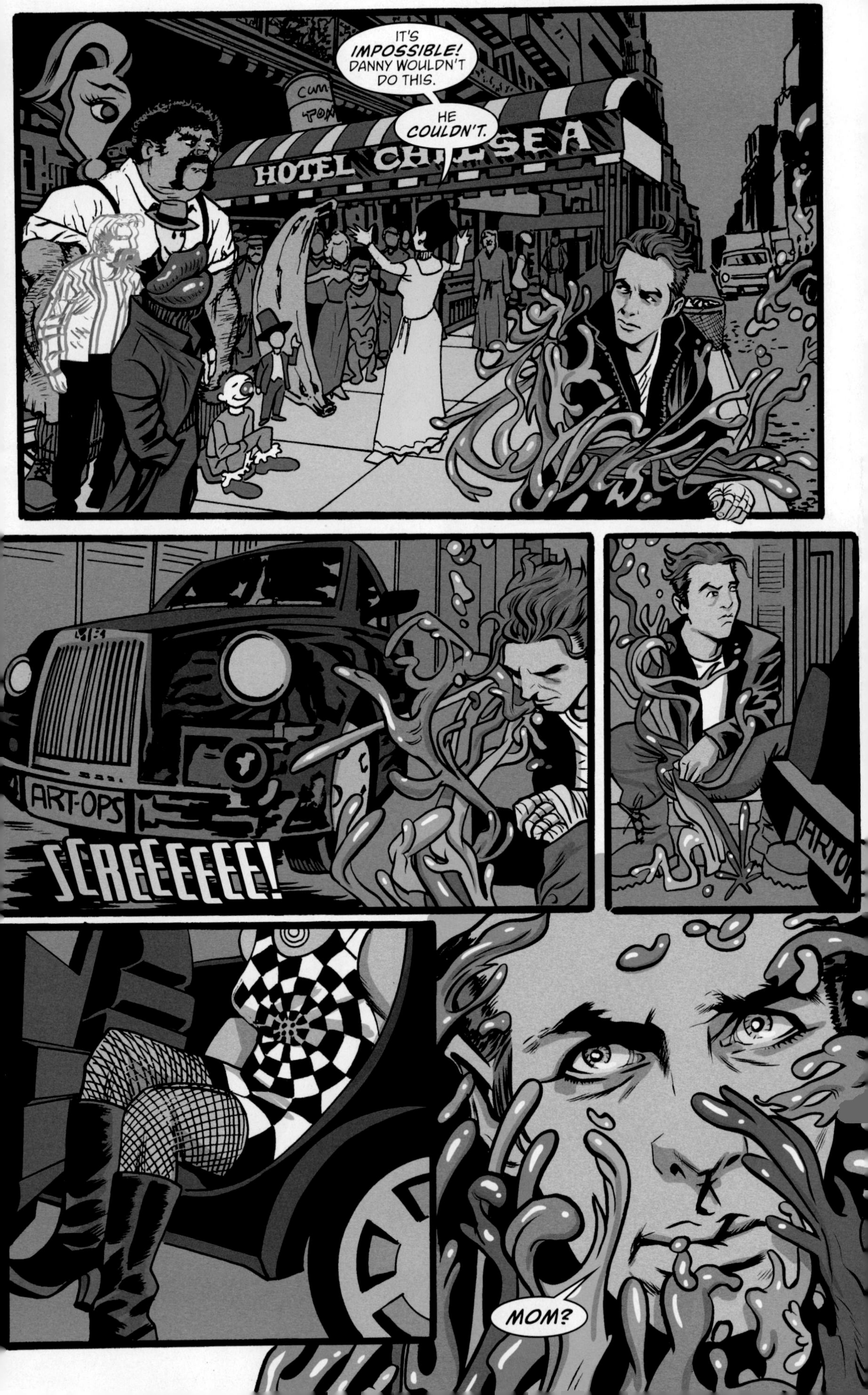
IT'S *IMPOSSIBLE!* DANNY WOULDN'T DO THIS.
HE *COULDN'T.*
HOTEL CHELSEA
ART-OPS
SCREEEEEEE!
ARTO
MOM?

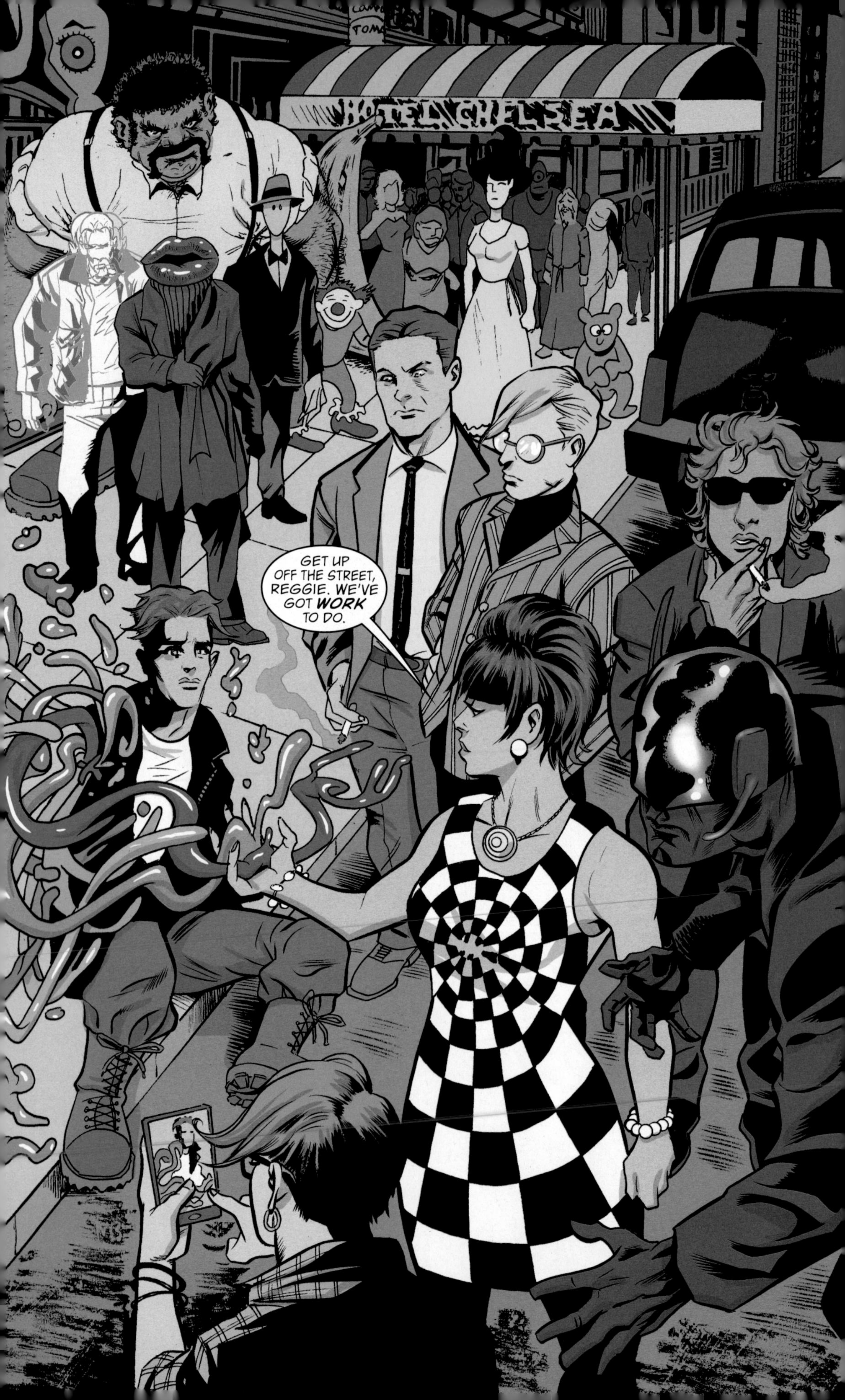
HOTEL CHELSEA
GET UP OFF THE STREET, REGGIE. WE'VE GOT **WORK** TO DO.

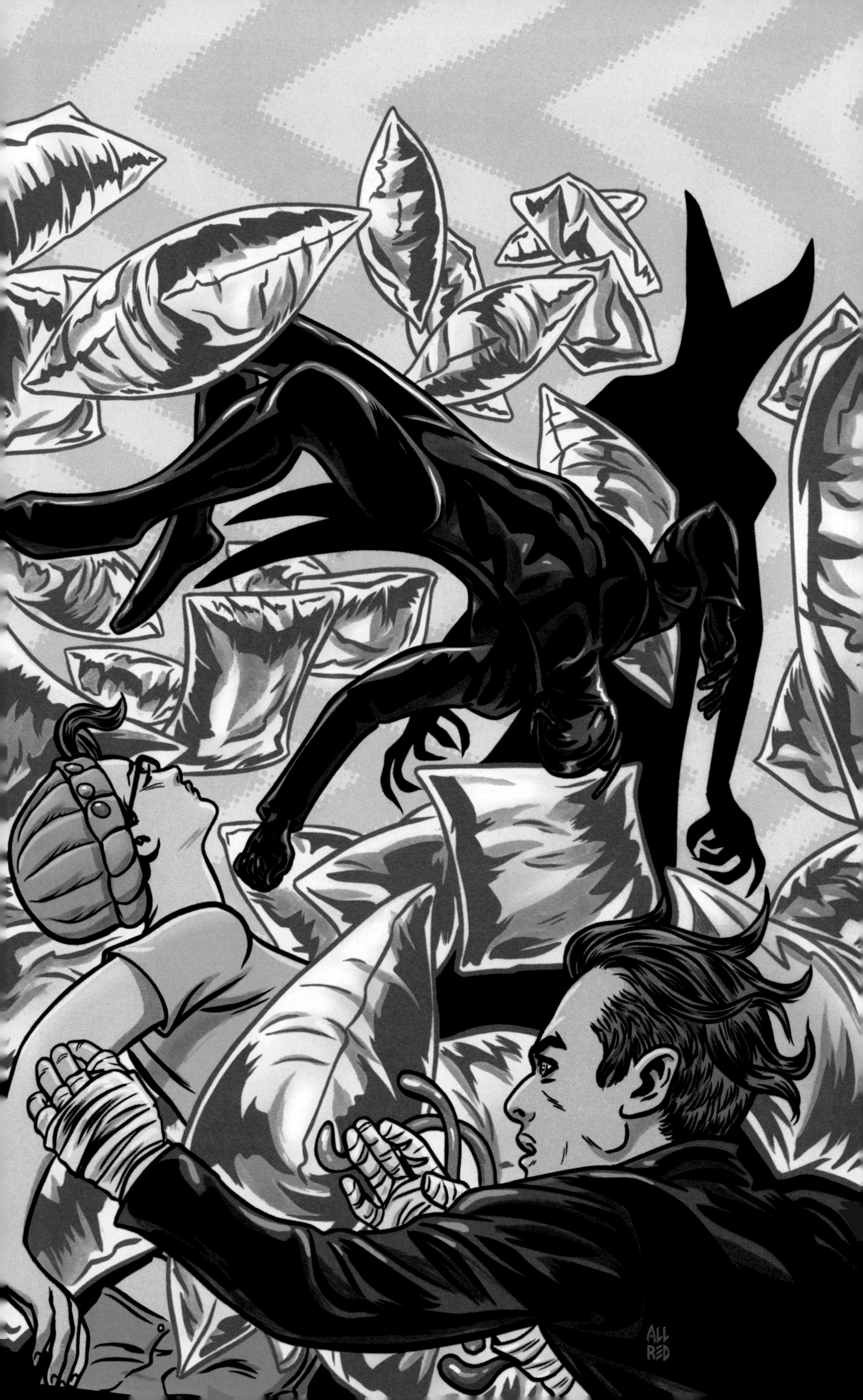
ALL
RED

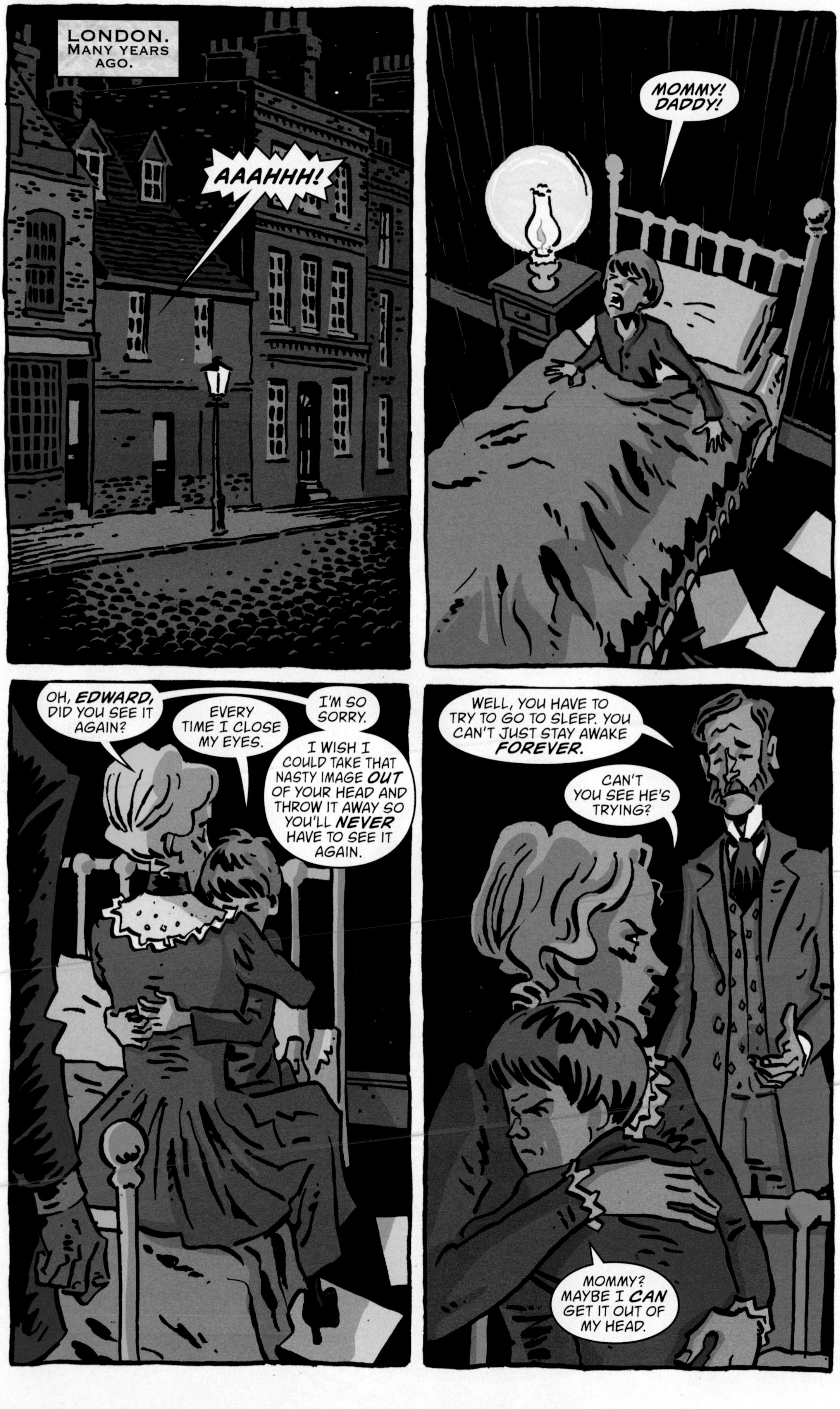
LONDON. MANY YEARS AGO.
AAAHHH!
MOMMY! DADDY!
OH, EDWARD, DID YOU SEE IT AGAIN?
EVERY TIME I CLOSE MY EYES.
I'M SO SORRY.
I WISH I COULD TAKE THAT NASTY IMAGE OUT OF YOUR HEAD AND THROW IT AWAY SO YOU'LL NEVER HAVE TO SEE IT AGAIN.
WELL, YOU HAVE TO TRY TO GO TO SLEEP. YOU CAN'T JUST STAY AWAKE FOREVER.
CAN'T YOU SEE HE'S TRYING?
MOMMY? MAYBE I CAN GET IT OUT OF MY HEAD.

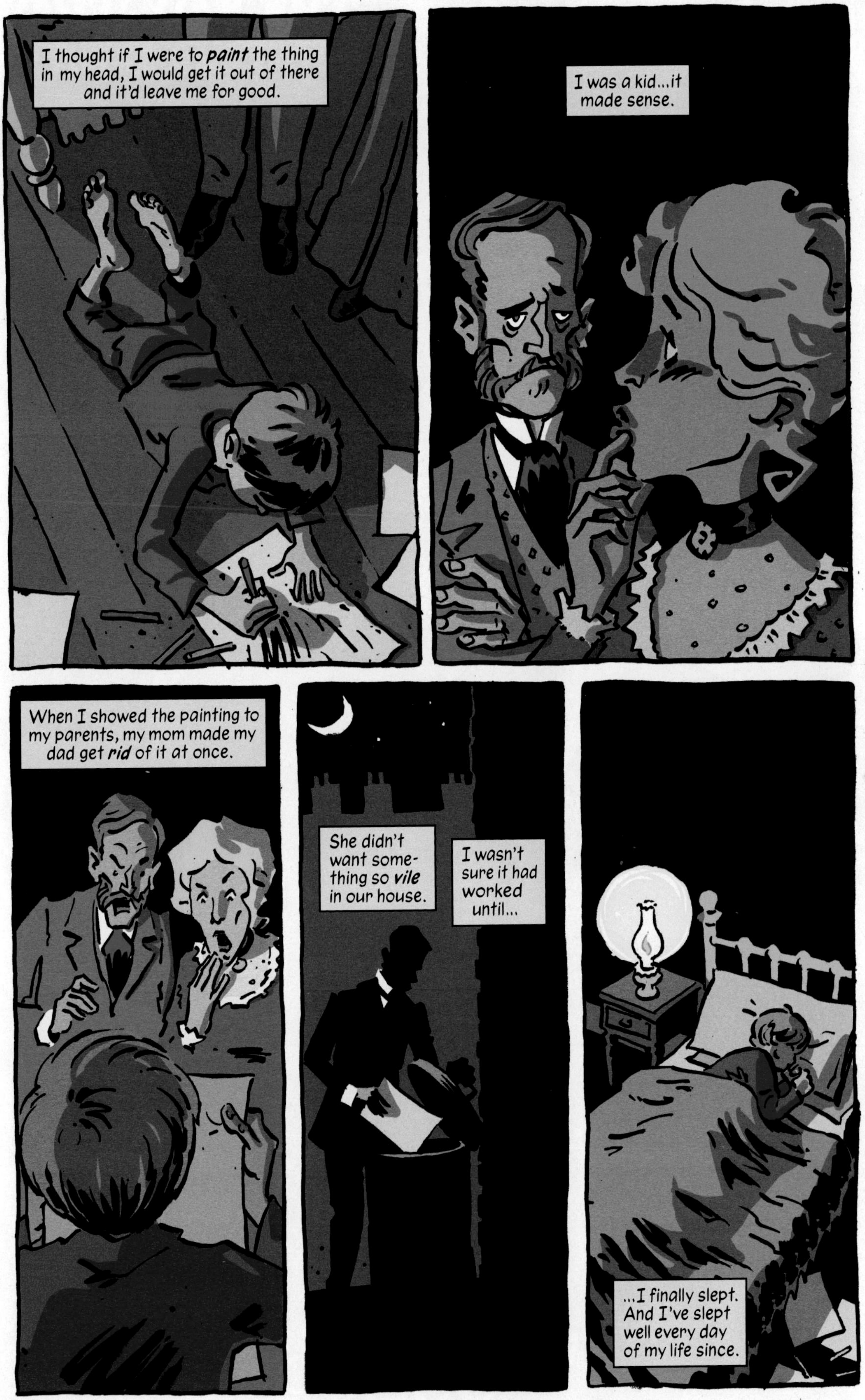
I thought if I were to *paint* the thing in my head, I would get it out of there and it'd leave me for good.
I was a kid...it made sense.
When I showed the painting to my parents, my mom made my dad get *rid* of it at once.
She didn't want something so *vile* in our house.
I wasn't sure it had worked until...
...I finally slept. And I've slept well every day of my life since.

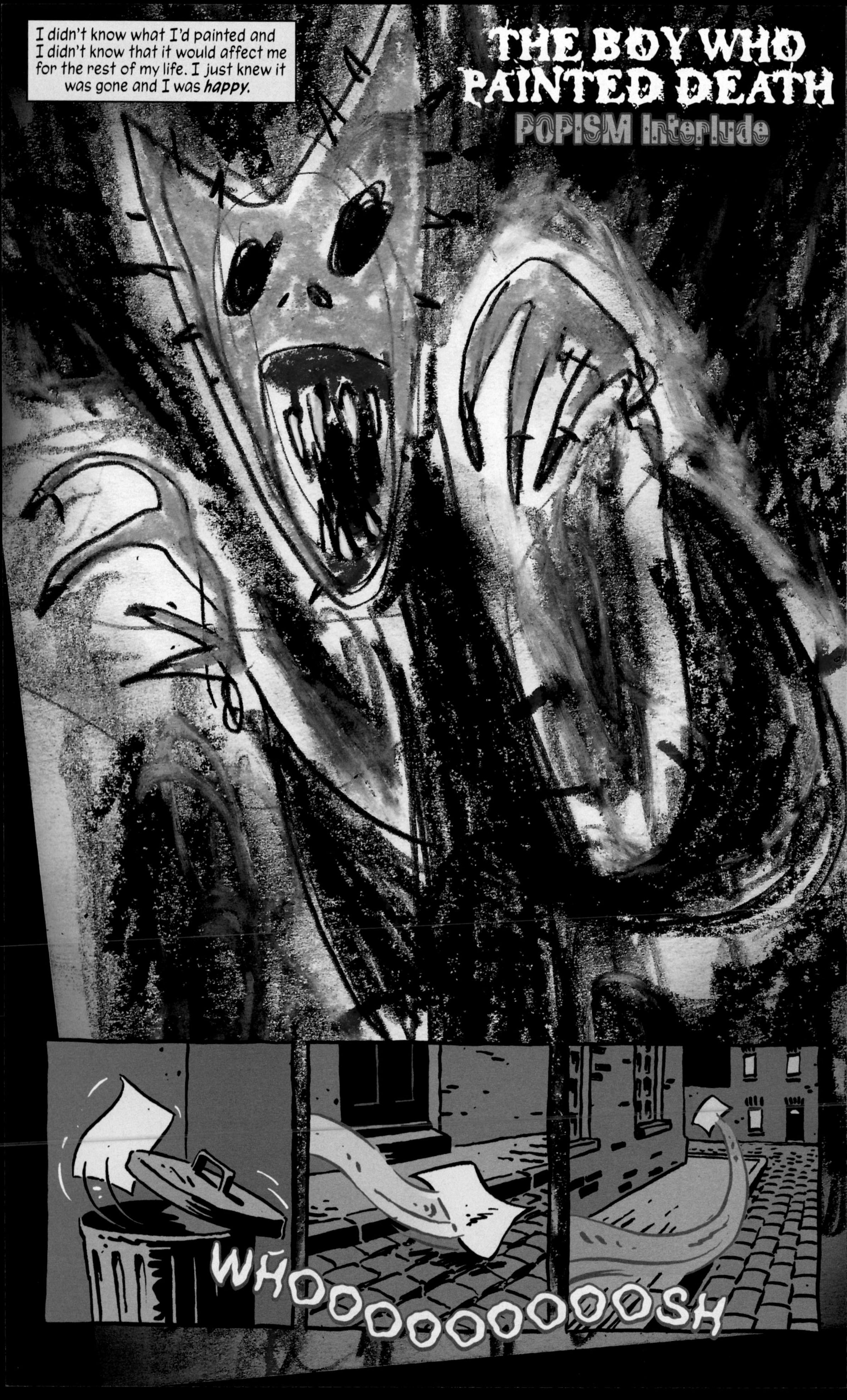

I didn't know what I'd painted and I didn't know that it would affect me for the rest of my life. I just knew it was gone and I was *happy.*
THE BOY WHO PAINTED DEATH
POPISM Interlude
WHOOOOOOOOOOOSH

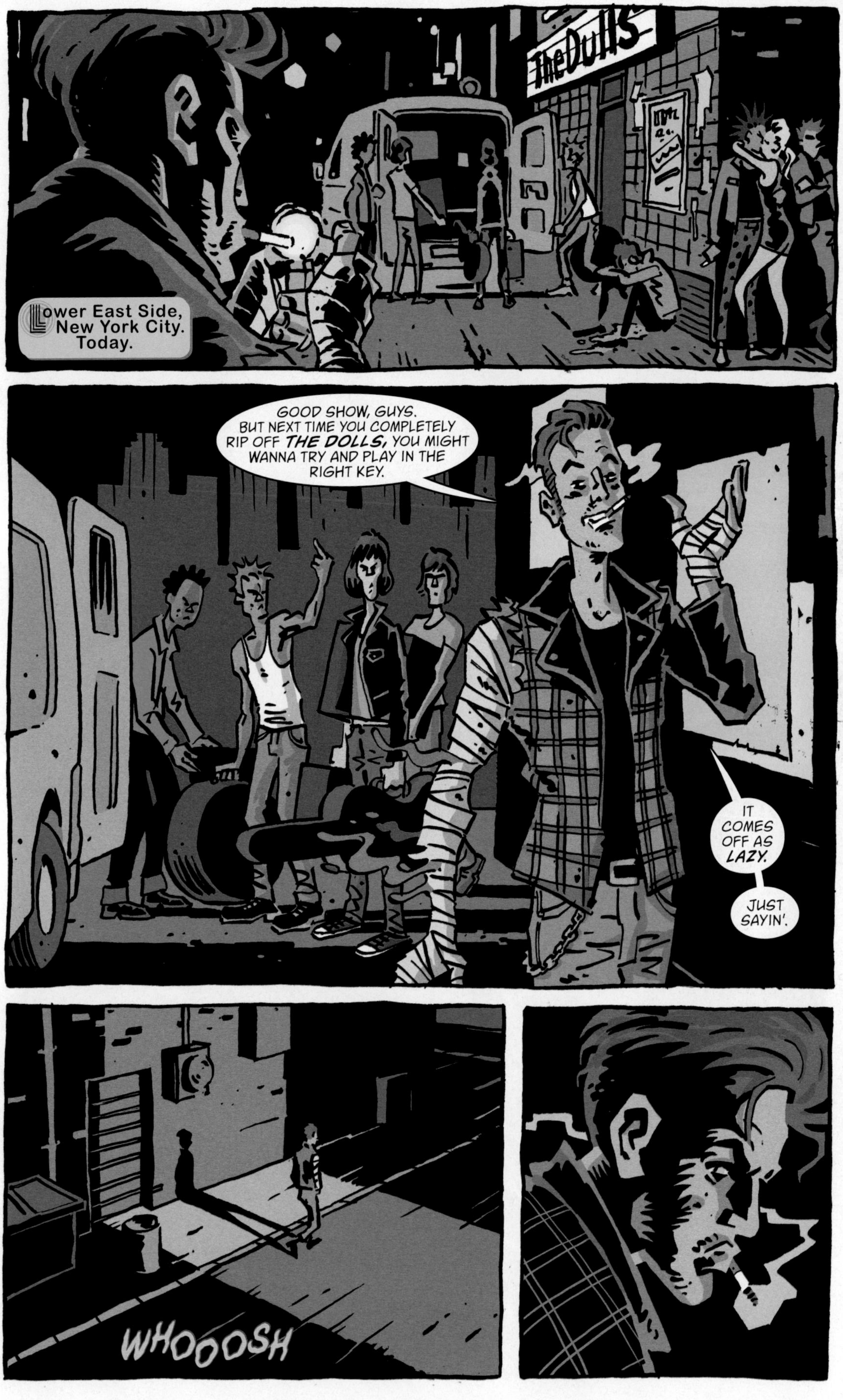

The Dolls
Lower East Side, New York City. Today.
GOOD SHOW, GUYS. BUT NEXT TIME YOU COMPLETELY RIP OFF *THE DOLLS,* YOU MIGHT WANNA TRY AND PLAY IN THE RIGHT KEY.
IT COMES OFF AS *LAZY.*
JUST SAYIN'.
WHOOOSH

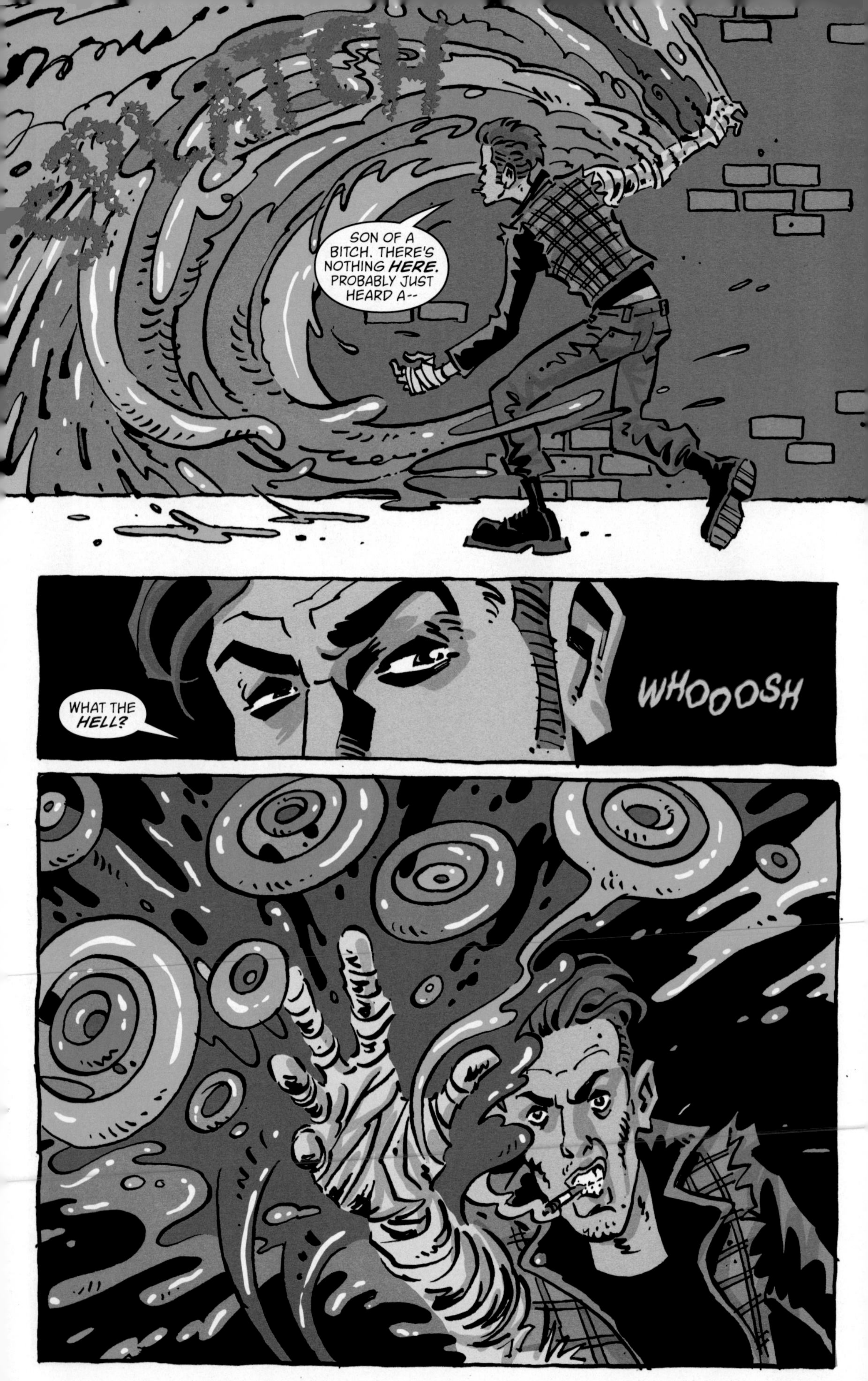
SON OF A BITCH. THERE'S NOTHING *HERE.* PROBABLY JUST HEARD A--
WHAT THE *HELL?*
WHOOOSH

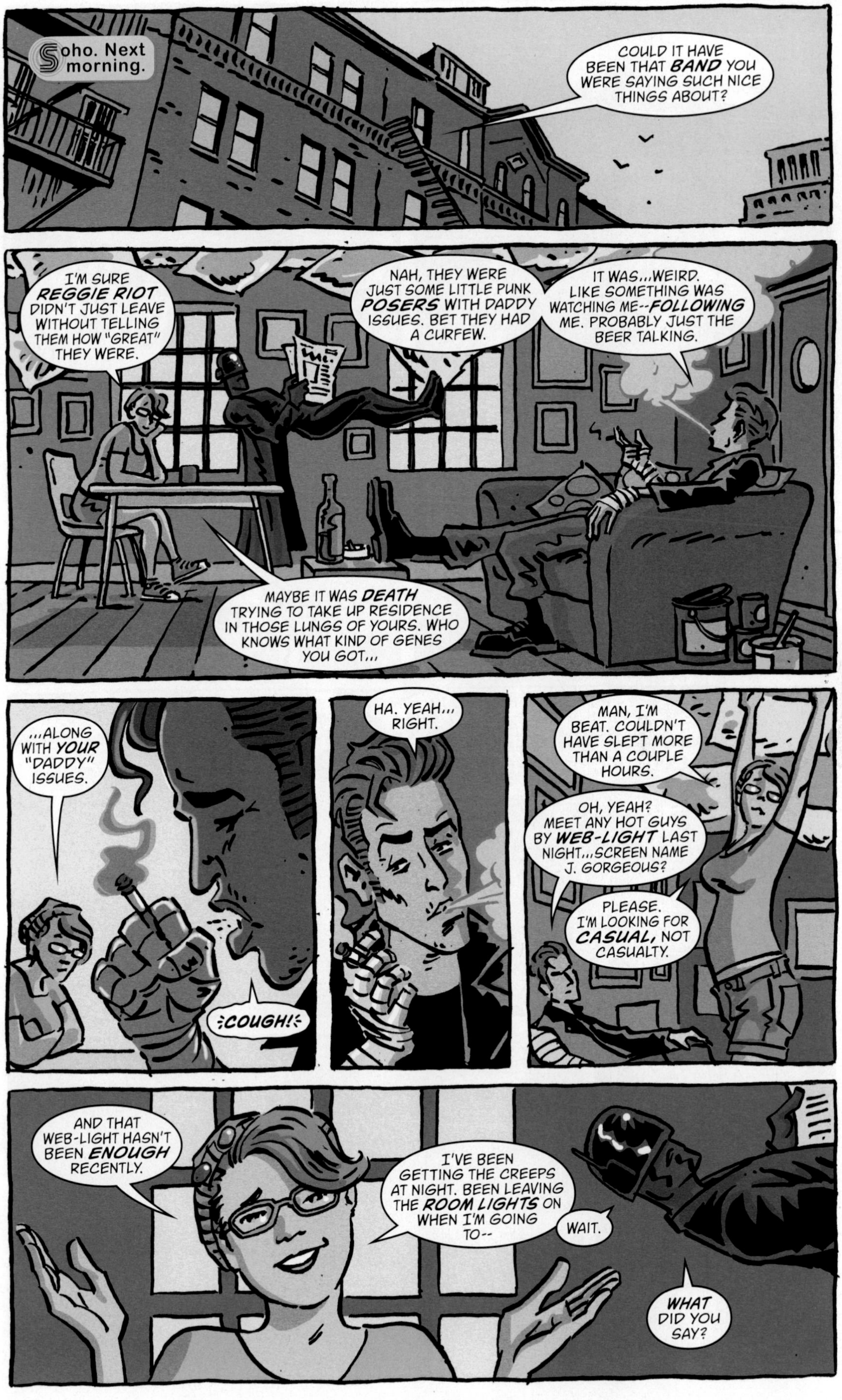
Soho. Next morning.
COULD IT HAVE BEEN THAT BAND YOU WERE SAYING SUCH NICE THINGS ABOUT?
I'M SURE REGGIE RIOT DIDN'T JUST LEAVE WITHOUT TELLING THEM HOW "GREAT" THEY WERE.
NAH, THEY WERE JUST SOME LITTLE PUNK POSERS WITH DADDY ISSUES. BET THEY HAD A CURFEW.
IT WAS...WEIRD. LIKE SOMETHING WAS WATCHING ME--FOLLOWING ME. PROBABLY JUST THE BEER TALKING.
MAYBE IT WAS DEATH TRYING TO TAKE UP RESIDENCE IN THOSE LUNGS OF YOURS. WHO KNOWS WHAT KIND OF GENES YOU GOT...
...ALONG WITH YOUR "DADDY" ISSUES.
COUGH!
HA. YEAH... RIGHT.
MAN, I'M BEAT. COULDN'T HAVE SLEPT MORE THAN A COUPLE HOURS.
OH, YEAH? MEET ANY HOT GUYS BY WEB-LIGHT LAST NIGHT...SCREEN NAME J. GORGEOUS?
PLEASE. I'M LOOKING FOR CASUAL, NOT CASUALTY.
AND THAT WEB-LIGHT HASN'T BEEN ENOUGH RECENTLY.
I'VE BEEN GETTING THE CREEPS AT NIGHT. BEEN LEAVING THE ROOM LIGHTS ON WHEN I'M GOING TO--
WAIT.
WHAT DID YOU SAY?

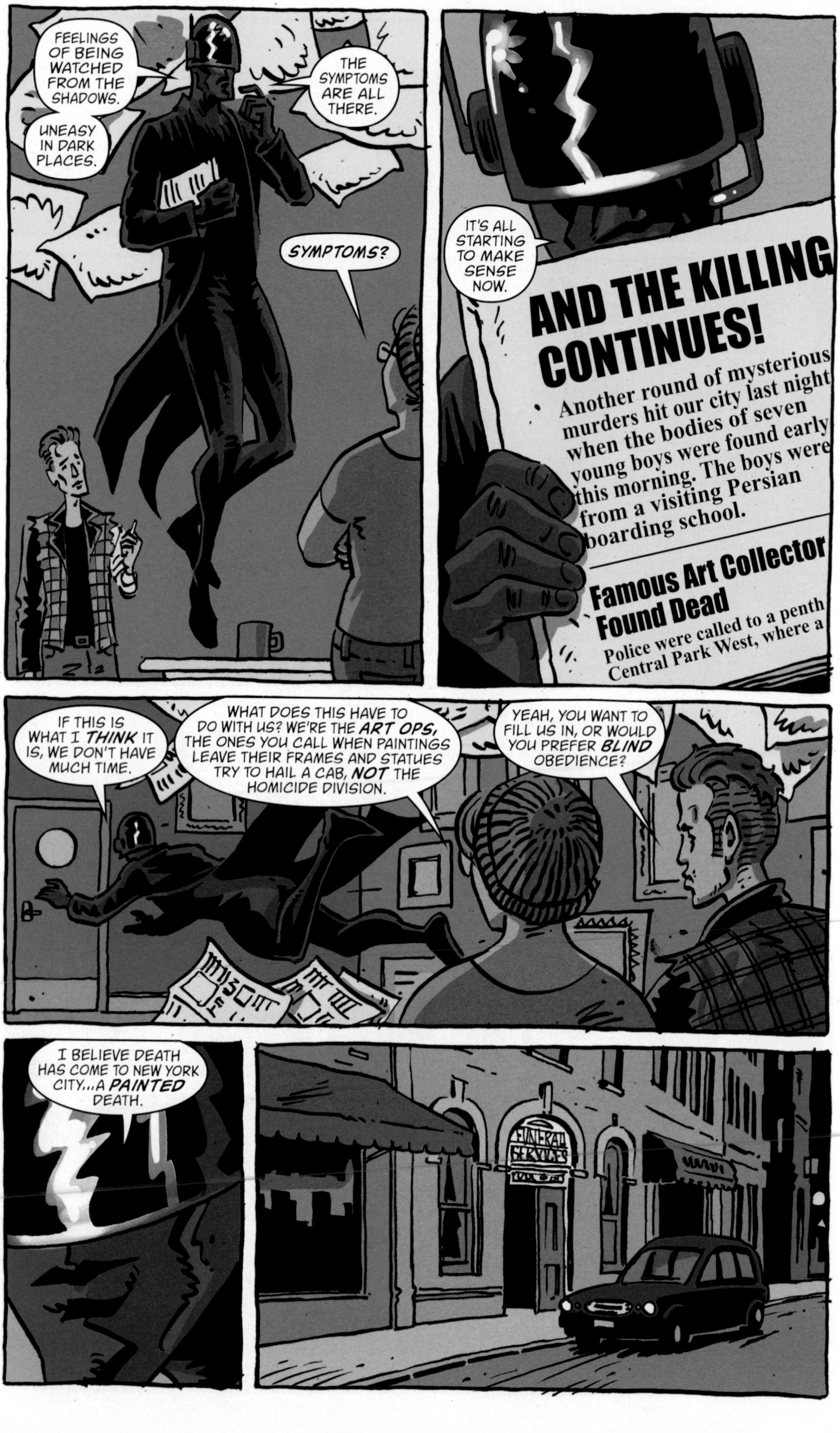
FEELINGS OF BEING WATCHED FROM THE SHADOWS.
UNEASY IN DARK PLACES.
THE SYMPTOMS ARE ALL THERE.
SYMPTOMS?
IT'S ALL STARTING TO MAKE SENSE NOW.
AND THE KILLING CONTINUES!
Another round of mysterious murders hit our city last night when the bodies of seven young boys were found early this morning. The boys were from a visiting Persian boarding school.
Famous Art Collector Found Dead
Police were called to a penth Central Park West, where a
IF THIS IS WHAT I THINK IT IS, WE DON'T HAVE MUCH TIME.
WHAT DOES THIS HAVE TO DO WITH US? WE'RE THE ART OPS, THE ONES YOU CALL WHEN PAINTINGS LEAVE THEIR FRAMES AND STATUES TRY TO HAIL A CAB, NOT THE HOMICIDE DIVISION.
YEAH, YOU WANT TO FILL US IN, OR WOULD YOU PREFER BLIND OBEDIENCE?
I BELIEVE DEATH HAS COME TO NEW YORK CITY...A PAINTED DEATH.
FUNERAL SERVICES

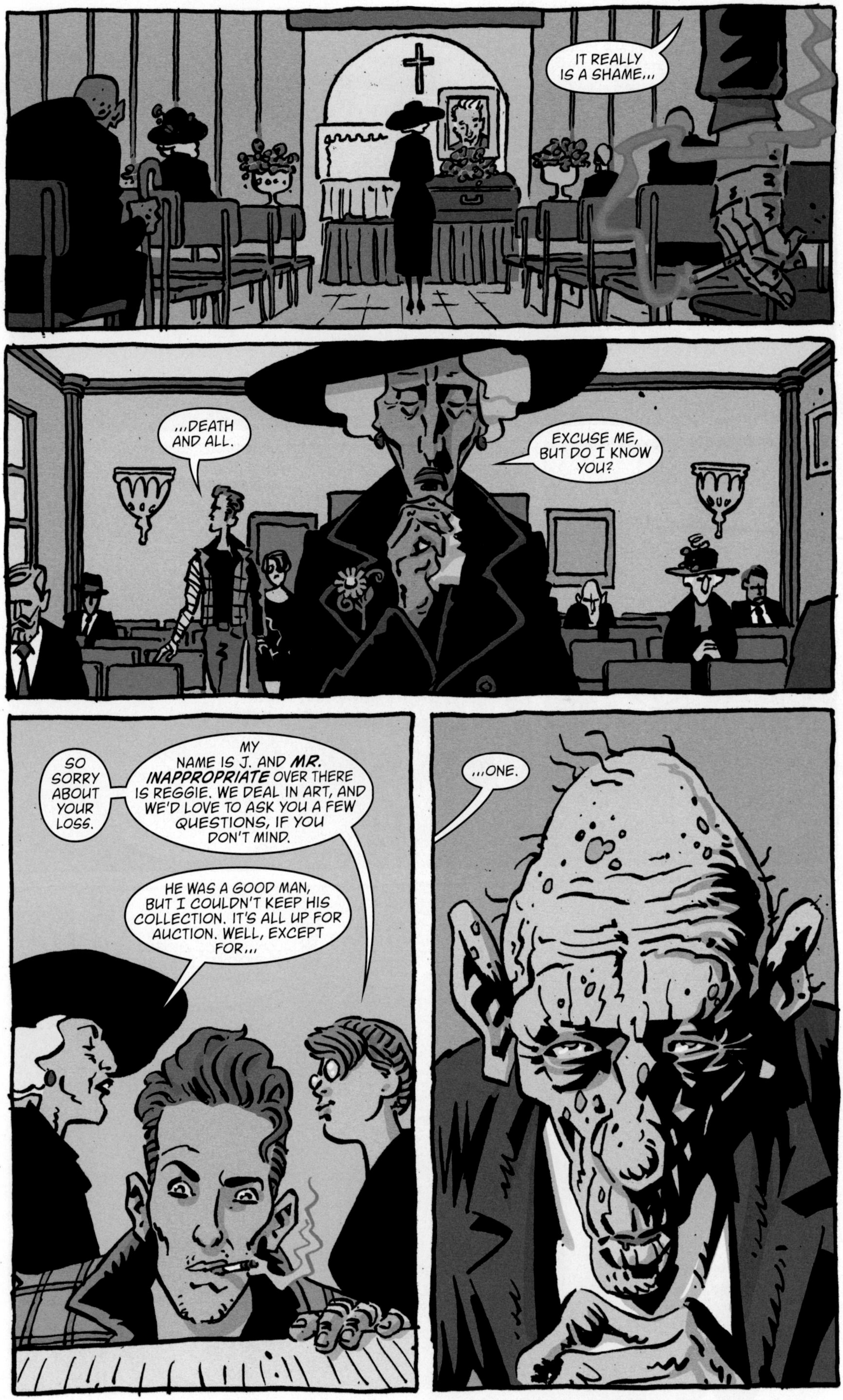
IT REALLY IS A SHAME...
...DEATH AND ALL.
EXCUSE ME, BUT DO I KNOW YOU?
SO SORRY ABOUT YOUR LOSS.
MY NAME IS J. AND **MR. INAPPROPRIATE** OVER THERE IS REGGIE. WE DEAL IN ART, AND WE'D LOVE TO ASK YOU A FEW QUESTIONS, IF YOU DON'T MIND.
HE WAS A GOOD MAN, BUT I COULDN'T KEEP HIS COLLECTION. IT'S ALL UP FOR AUCTION. WELL, EXCEPT FOR...
...ONE.

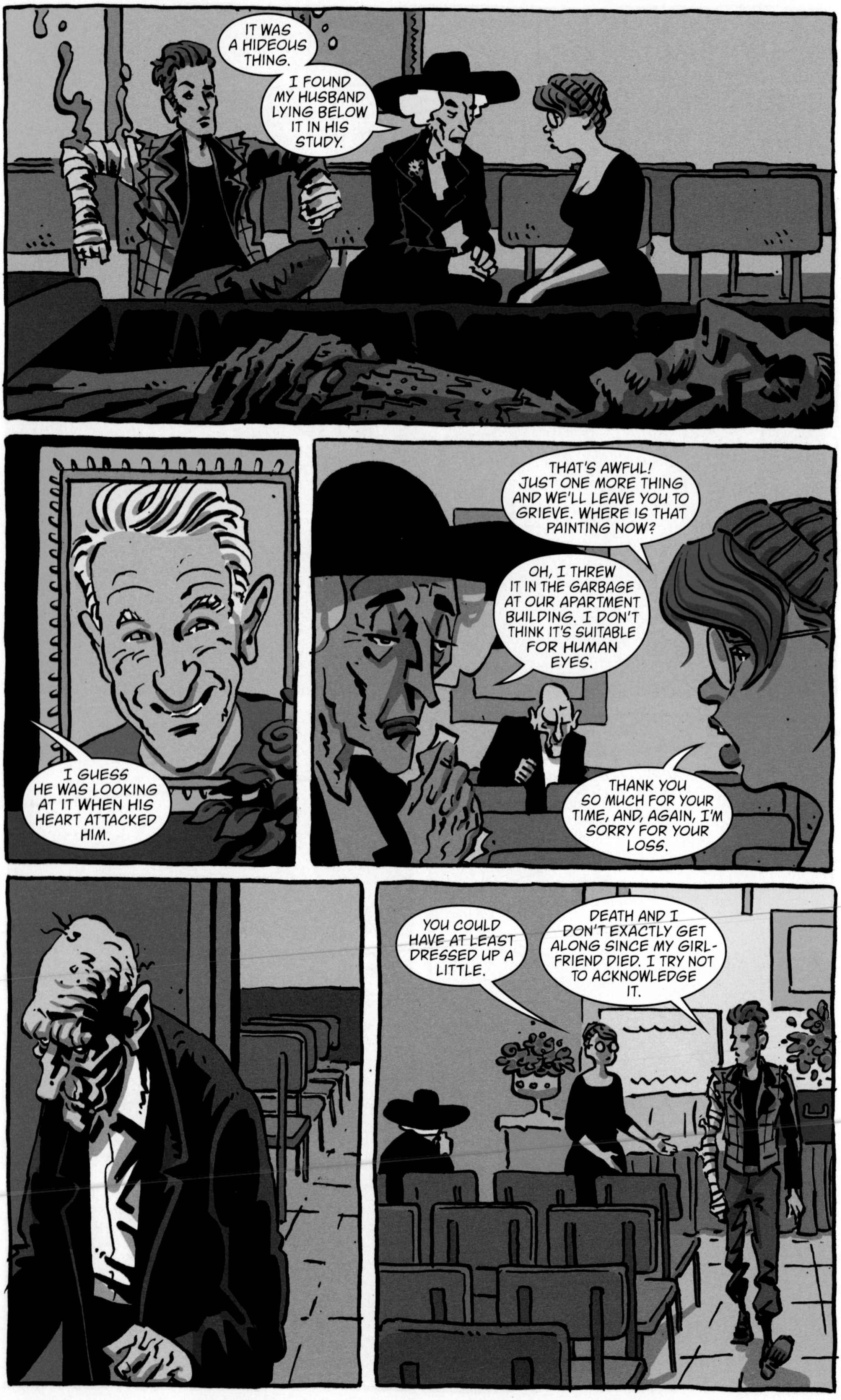
IT WAS A HIDEOUS THING.
I FOUND MY HUSBAND LYING BELOW IT IN HIS STUDY.
I GUESS HE WAS LOOKING AT IT WHEN HIS HEART ATTACKED HIM.
THAT'S AWFUL! JUST ONE MORE THING AND WE'LL LEAVE YOU TO GRIEVE. WHERE IS THAT PAINTING NOW?
OH, I THREW IT IN THE GARBAGE AT OUR APARTMENT BUILDING. I DON'T THINK IT'S SUITABLE FOR HUMAN EYES.
THANK YOU SO MUCH FOR YOUR TIME, AND, AGAIN, I'M SORRY FOR YOUR LOSS.
YOU COULD HAVE AT LEAST DRESSED UP A LITTLE.
DEATH AND I DON'T EXACTLY GET ALONG SINCE MY GIRL-FRIEND DIED. I TRY NOT TO ACKNOWLEDGE IT.

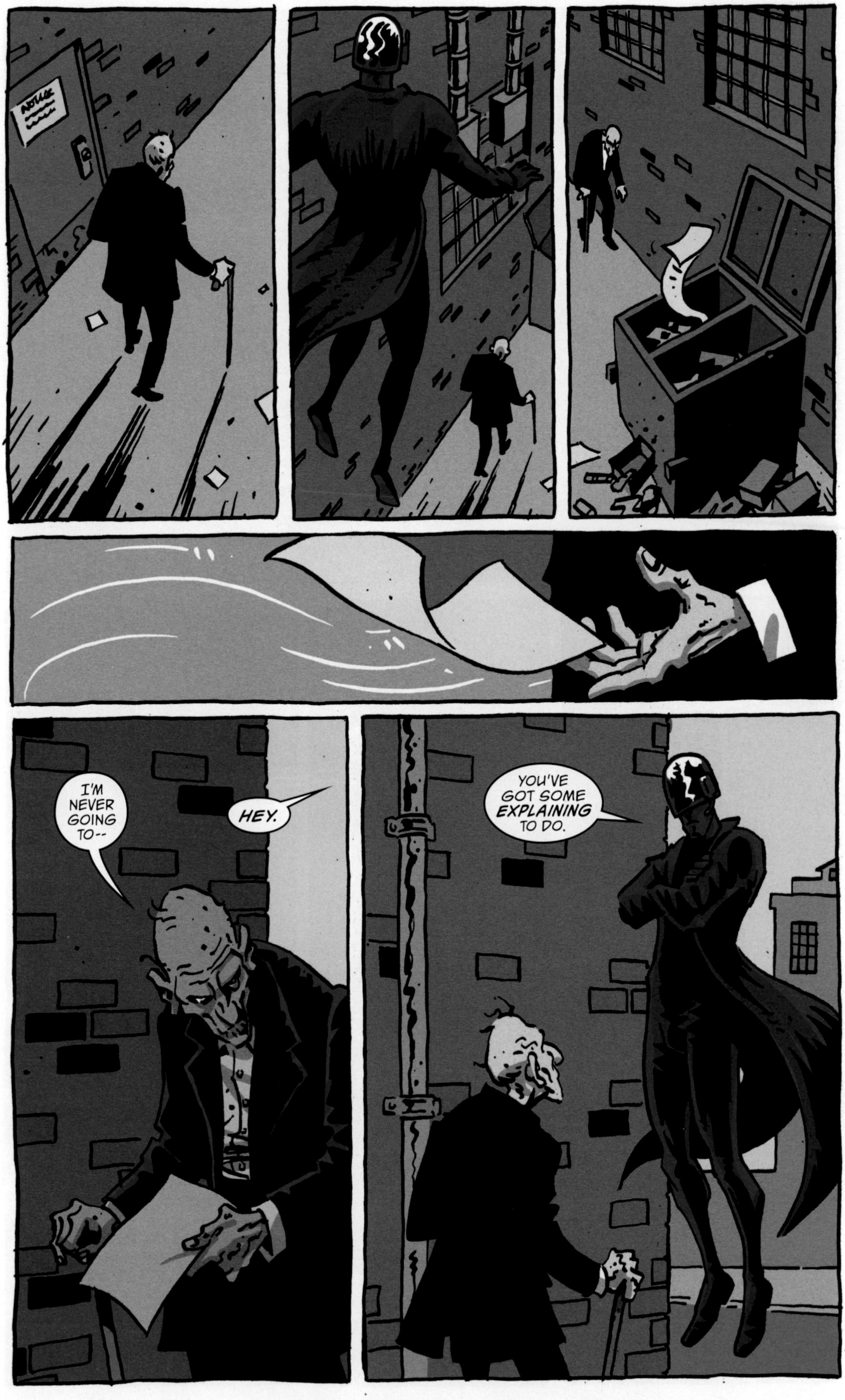
NOTICE
I'M NEVER GOING TO--
HEY.
YOU'VE GOT SOME EXPLAINING TO DO.

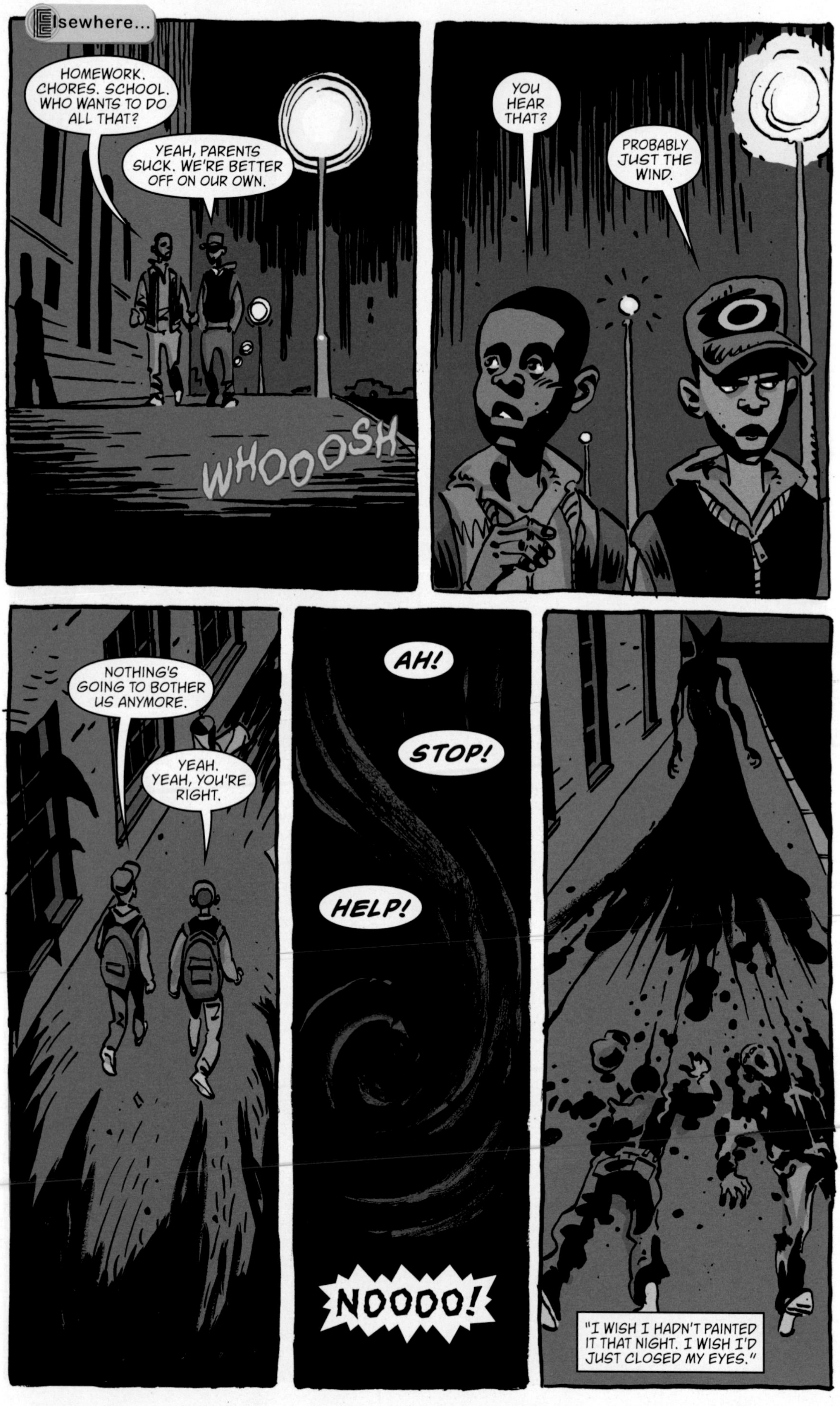
Elsewhere...
HOMEWORK. CHORES. SCHOOL. WHO WANTS TO DO ALL THAT?
YEAH, PARENTS SUCK. WE'RE BETTER OFF ON OUR OWN.
WHOOOOSH
YOU HEAR THAT?
PROBABLY JUST THE WIND.
NOTHING'S GOING TO BOTHER US ANYMORE.
YEAH. YEAH, YOU'RE RIGHT.
AH!
STOP!
HELP!
NOOOO!
"I WISH I HADN'T PAINTED IT THAT NIGHT. I WISH I'D JUST CLOSED MY EYES."

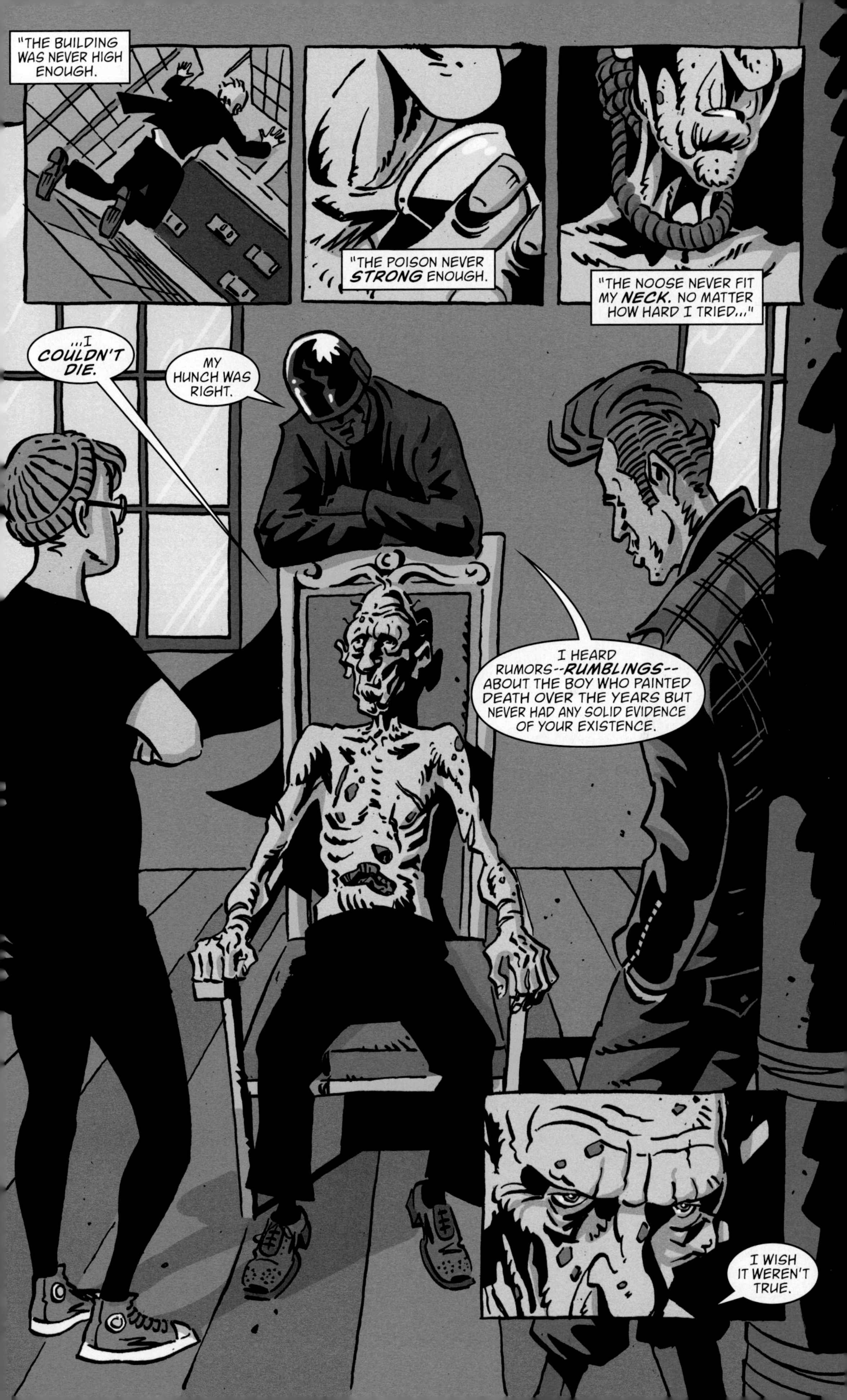
"THE BUILDING WAS NEVER HIGH ENOUGH.
"THE POISON NEVER STRONG ENOUGH.
"THE NOOSE NEVER FIT MY NECK. NO MATTER HOW HARD I TRIED..."
...I COULDN'T DIE.
MY HUNCH WAS RIGHT.
I HEARD RUMORS--RUMBLINGS--ABOUT THE BOY WHO PAINTED DEATH OVER THE YEARS BUT NEVER HAD ANY SOLID EVIDENCE OF YOUR EXISTENCE.
I WISH IT WEREN'T TRUE.

"IT'S NORMAL TO OUTLIVE YOUR PARENTS, BUT DO YOU KNOW WHAT IT'S LIKE TO SEE YOUR KIDS, GRANDKIDS, AND GREAT-GRANDKIDS *DIE?* TO SEE *EVERYONE* YOU EVER CARED ABOUT BECOME JUST A RIPPLE IN THE POND?

"*AGONY* ISN'T A POTENT ENOUGH WORD.

"I MADE A PROMISE TO MYSELF NEVER TO GET CLOSE TO ANYONE AGAIN. I COULDN'T BEAR THE HEARTBREAK.

"ETERNAL LIFE ISN'T A BLESSING...IT'S A *CURSE.*

"MY LIFE HAS BEEN SPENT TRACKING THE PAINTING--*CENTURIES* TRAVELING THE WORLD, FROM EVERY ECCENTRIC ART COLLECTOR TO EVERY BLACK-MARKET AUCTION HOUSE.

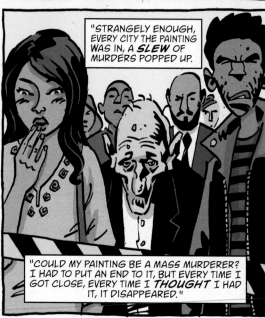

"STRANGELY ENOUGH, EVERY CITY THE PAINTING WAS IN, A *SLEW* OF MURDERS POPPED UP.

"COULD MY PAINTING BE A MASS MURDERER? I HAD TO PUT AN END TO IT, BUT EVERY TIME I GOT CLOSE, EVERY TIME I *THOUGHT* I HAD IT, IT DISAPPEARED."

WE WERE OPPOSING *MAGNETS*--LIGHT AND DARK. LIKE TRYING TO CAPTURE YOUR OWN SHADOW.

AH, EDWARD, YOU POOR THING.

POOR INDEED.

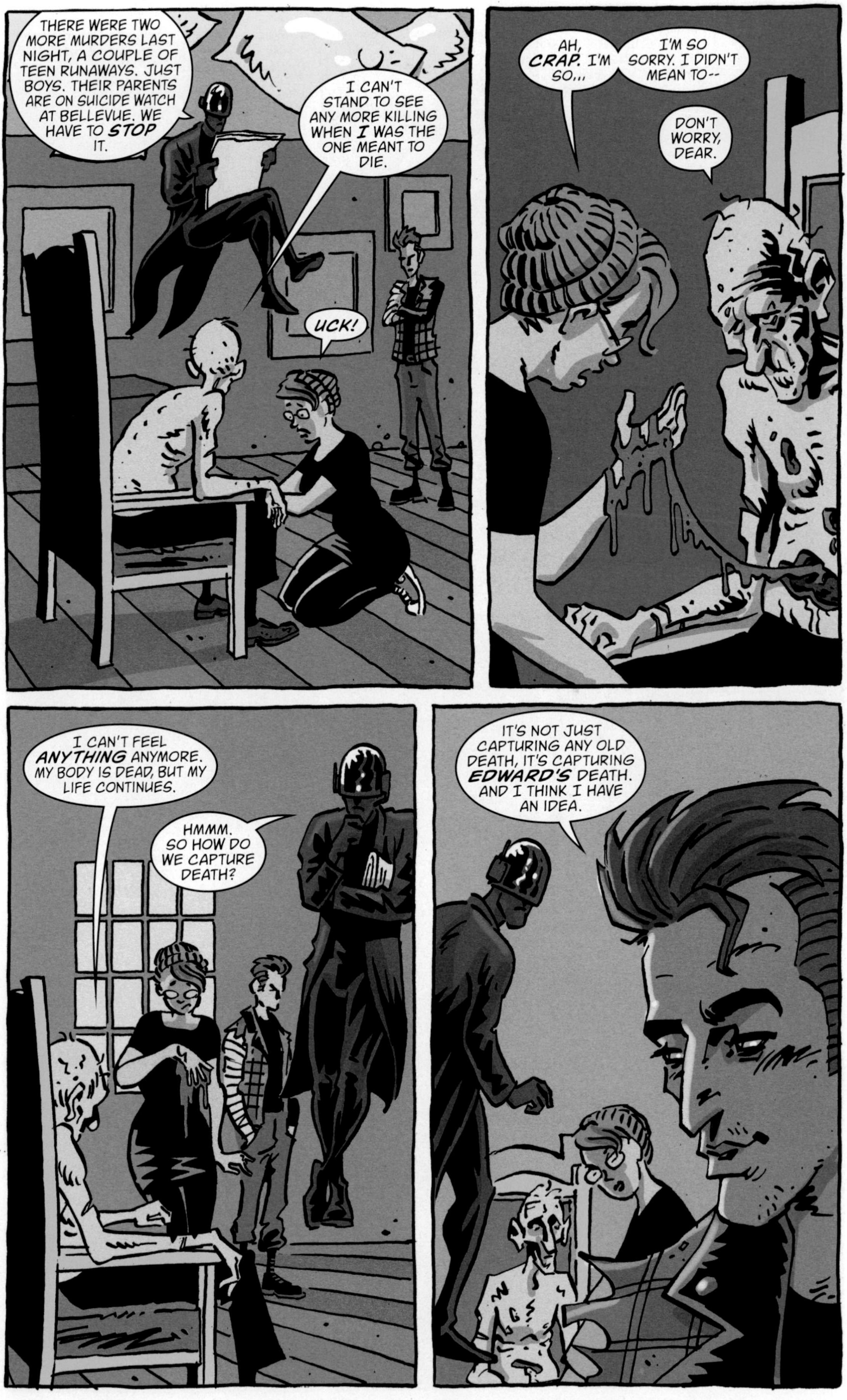
THERE WERE TWO MORE MURDERS LAST NIGHT, A COUPLE OF TEEN RUNAWAYS. JUST BOYS. THEIR PARENTS ARE ON SUICIDE WATCH AT BELLEVUE. WE HAVE TO STOP IT.
I CAN'T STAND TO SEE ANY MORE KILLING WHEN I WAS THE ONE MEANT TO DIE.
UCK!
AH, CRAP. I'M SO...
I'M SO SORRY. I DIDN'T MEAN TO--
DON'T WORRY, DEAR.
I CAN'T FEEL ANYTHING ANYMORE. MY BODY IS DEAD, BUT MY LIFE CONTINUES.
HMMM. SO HOW DO WE CAPTURE DEATH?
IT'S NOT JUST CAPTURING ANY OLD DEATH, IT'S CAPTURING EDWARD'S DEATH. AND I THINK I HAVE AN IDEA.

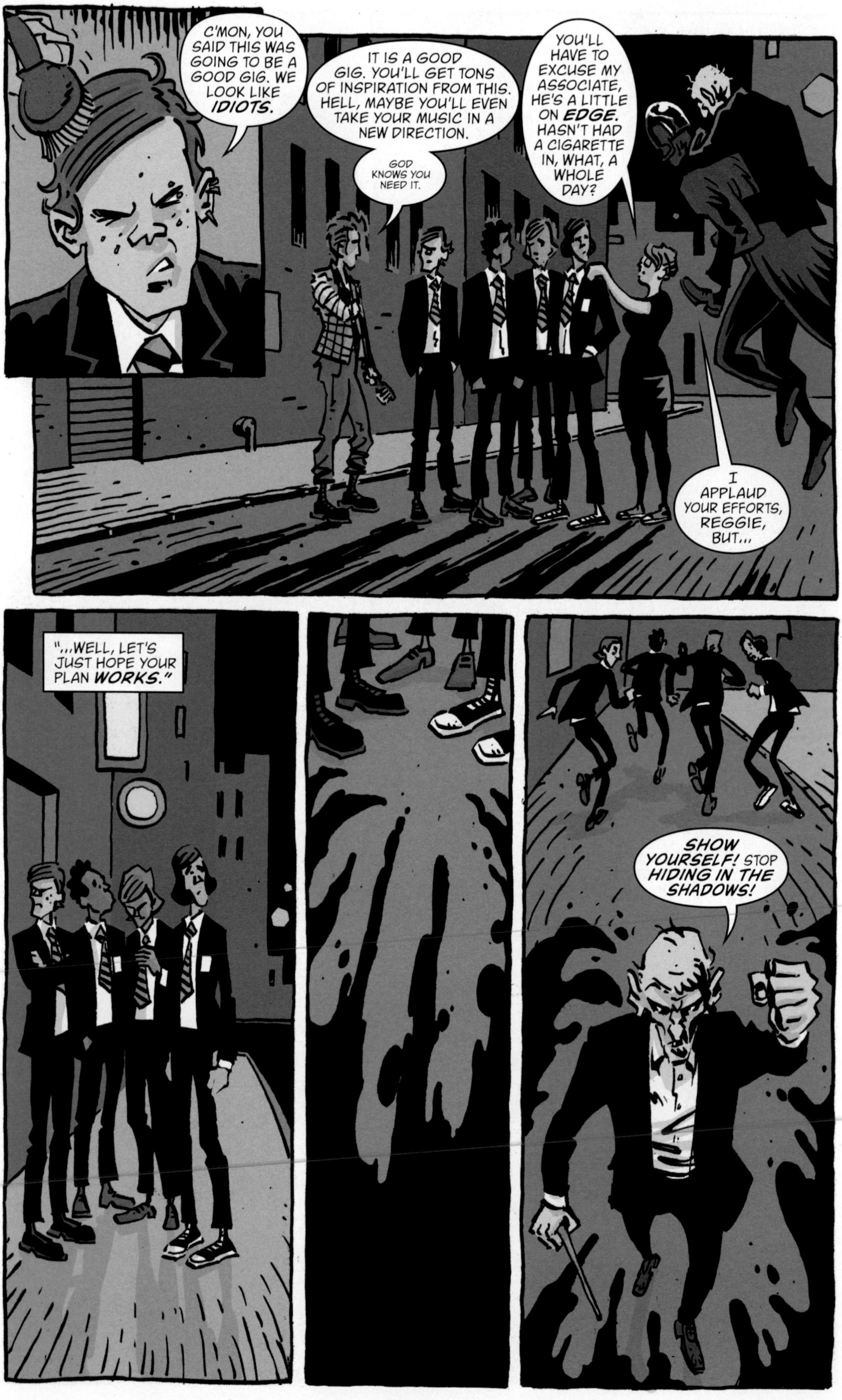
C'MON, YOU SAID THIS WAS GOING TO BE A GOOD GIG. WE LOOK LIKE *IDIOTS*.
IT IS A GOOD GIG. YOU'LL GET TONS OF INSPIRATION FROM THIS. HELL, MAYBE YOU'LL EVEN TAKE YOUR MUSIC IN A NEW DIRECTION.
GOD KNOWS YOU NEED IT.
YOU'LL HAVE TO EXCUSE MY ASSOCIATE, HE'S A LITTLE ON *EDGE.* HASN'T HAD A CIGARETTE IN, WHAT, A WHOLE DAY?
I APPLAUD YOUR EFFORTS, REGGIE, BUT...
"...WELL, LET'S JUST HOPE YOUR PLAN *WORKS.*"
SHOW YOURSELF! STOP *HIDING IN THE SHADOWS!*

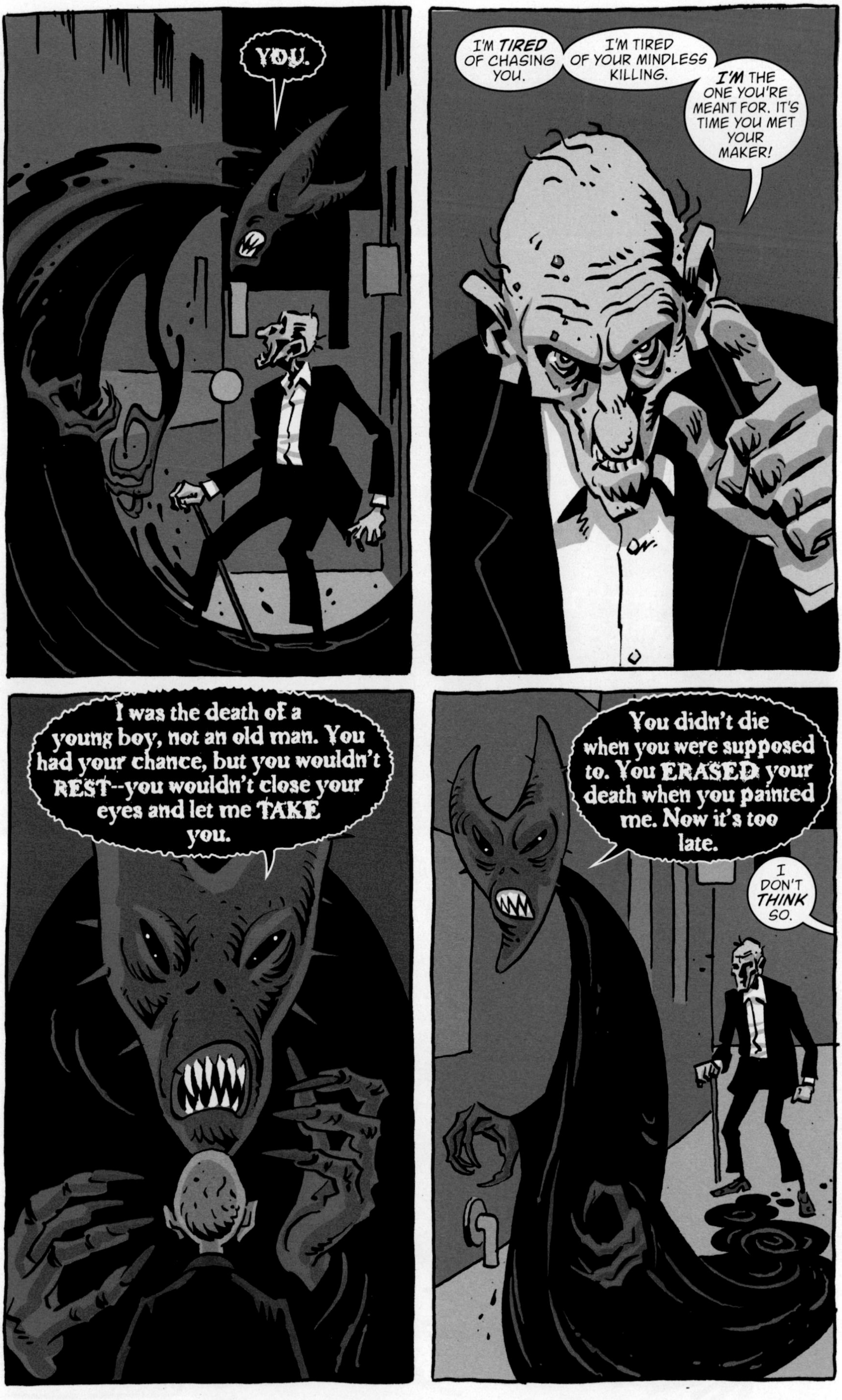
YOU.
I'M TIRED OF CHASING YOU.
I'M TIRED OF YOUR MINDLESS KILLING.
I'M THE ONE YOU'RE MEANT FOR. IT'S TIME YOU MET YOUR MAKER!
I was the death of a young boy, not an old man. You had your chance, but you wouldn't REST--you wouldn't close your eyes and let me TAKE you.
You didn't die when you were supposed to. You ERASED your death when you painted me. Now it's too late.
I DON'T THINK SO.

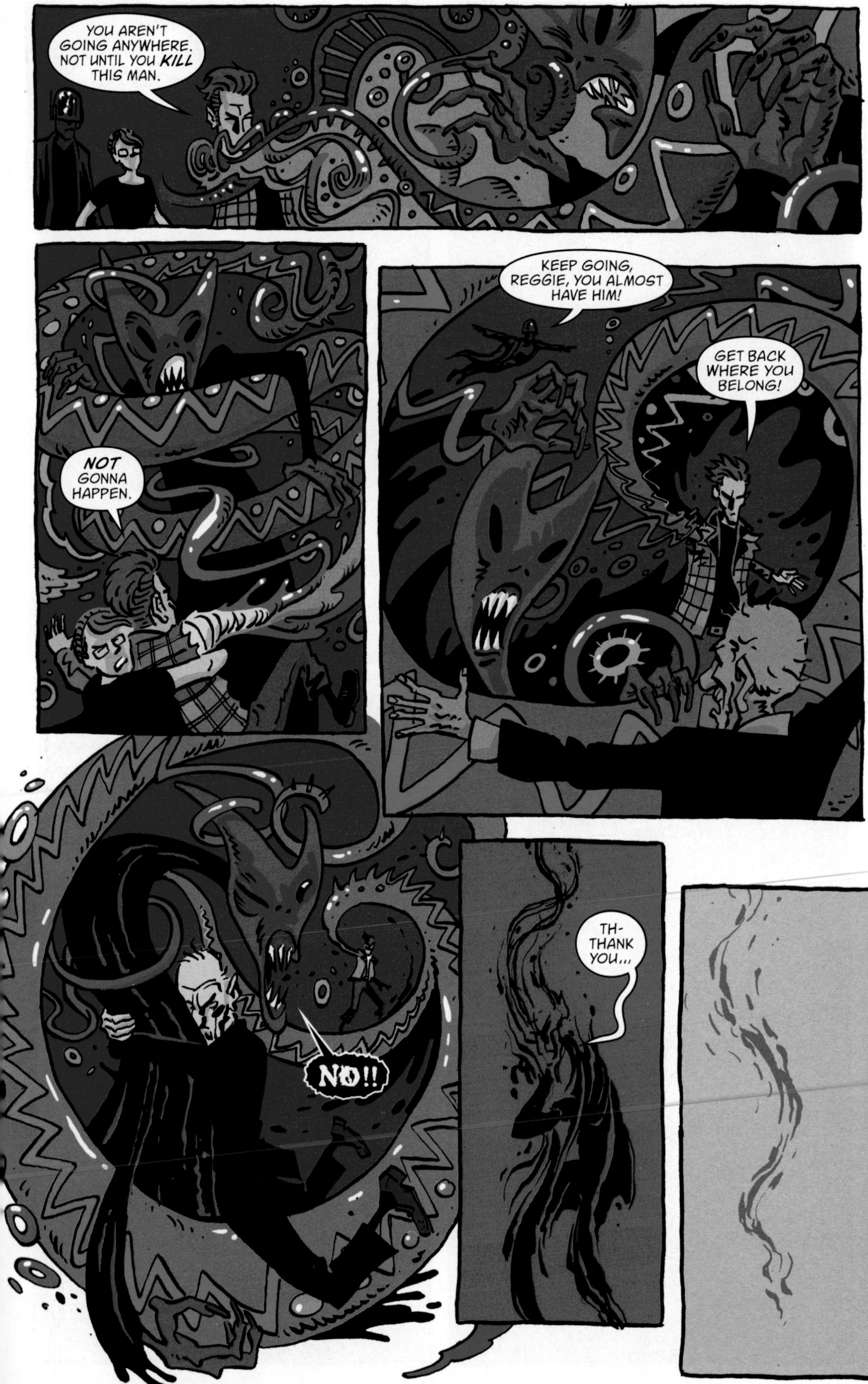
YOU AREN'T GOING ANYWHERE. NOT UNTIL YOU KILL THIS MAN.
NOT GONNA HAPPEN.
KEEP GOING, REGGIE, YOU ALMOST HAVE HIM!
GET BACK WHERE YOU BELONG!
NO!!
TH- THANK YOU...

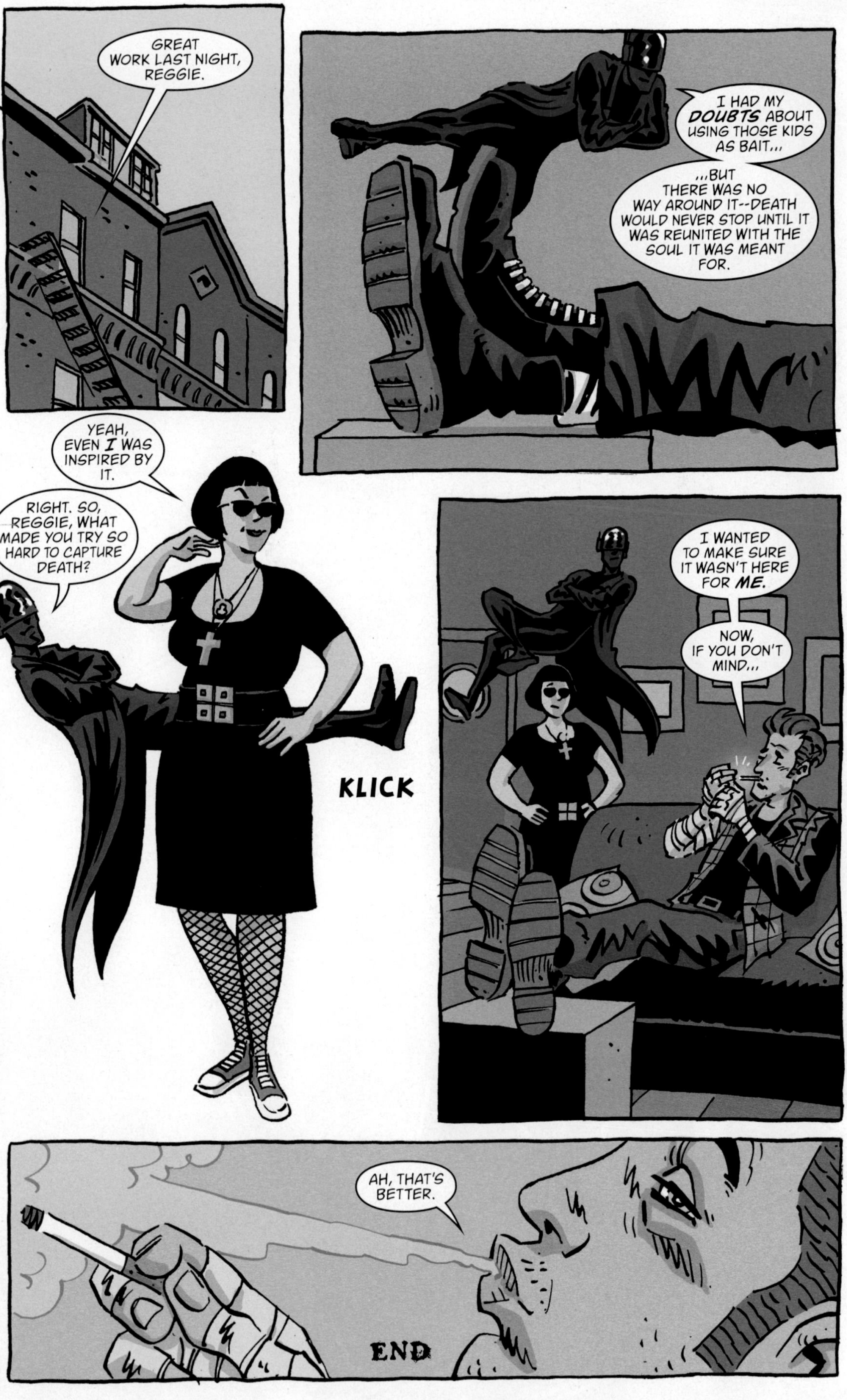

GREAT WORK LAST NIGHT, REGGIE.
I HAD MY DOUBTS ABOUT USING THOSE KIDS AS BAIT...
...BUT THERE WAS NO WAY AROUND IT--DEATH WOULD NEVER STOP UNTIL IT WAS REUNITED WITH THE SOUL IT WAS MEANT FOR.
YEAH, EVEN I WAS INSPIRED BY IT.
RIGHT. SO, REGGIE, WHAT MADE YOU TRY SO HARD TO CAPTURE DEATH?
KLICK
I WANTED TO MAKE SURE IT WASN'T HERE FOR ME.
NOW, IF YOU DON'T MIND...
AH, THAT'S BETTER.
END

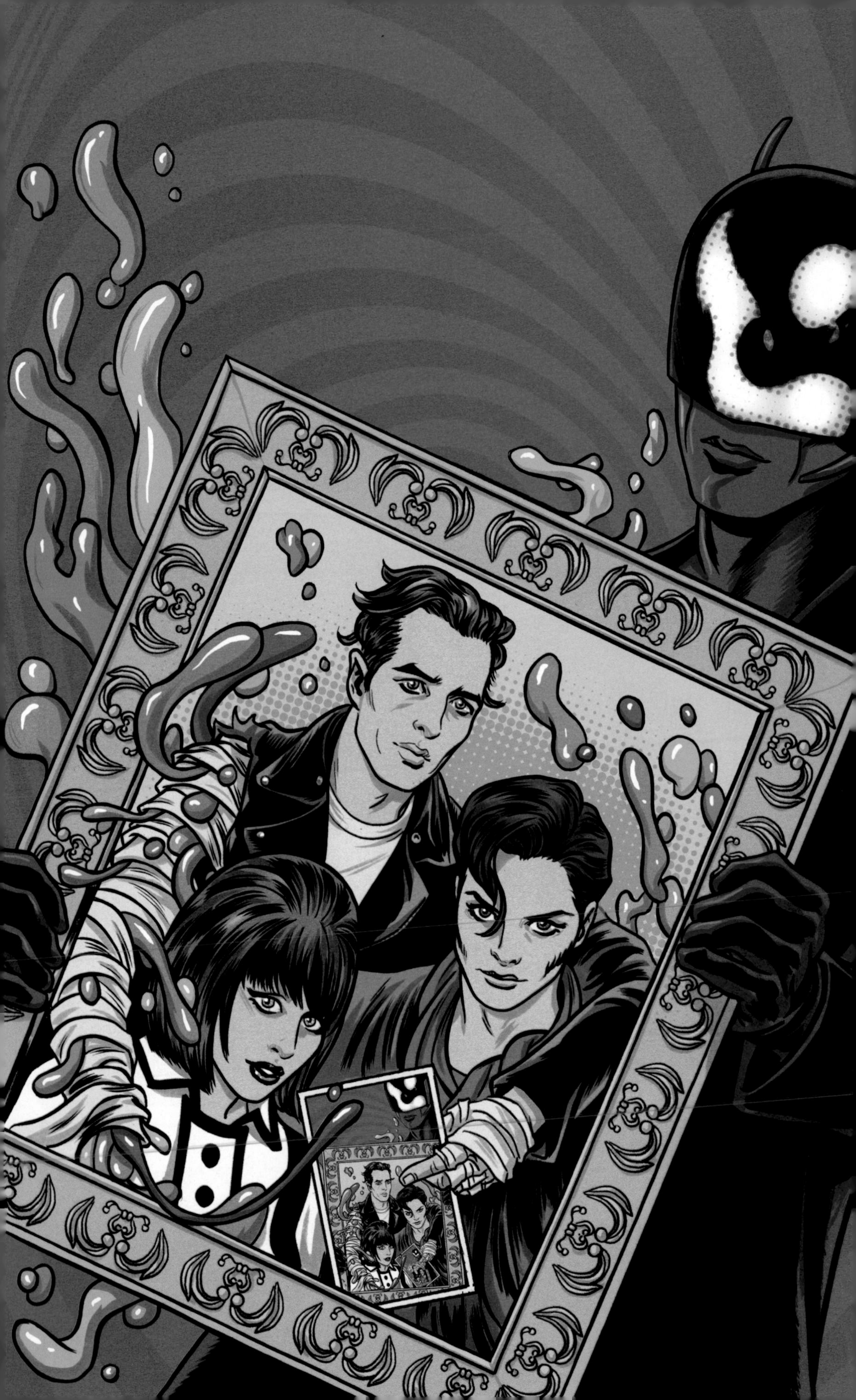

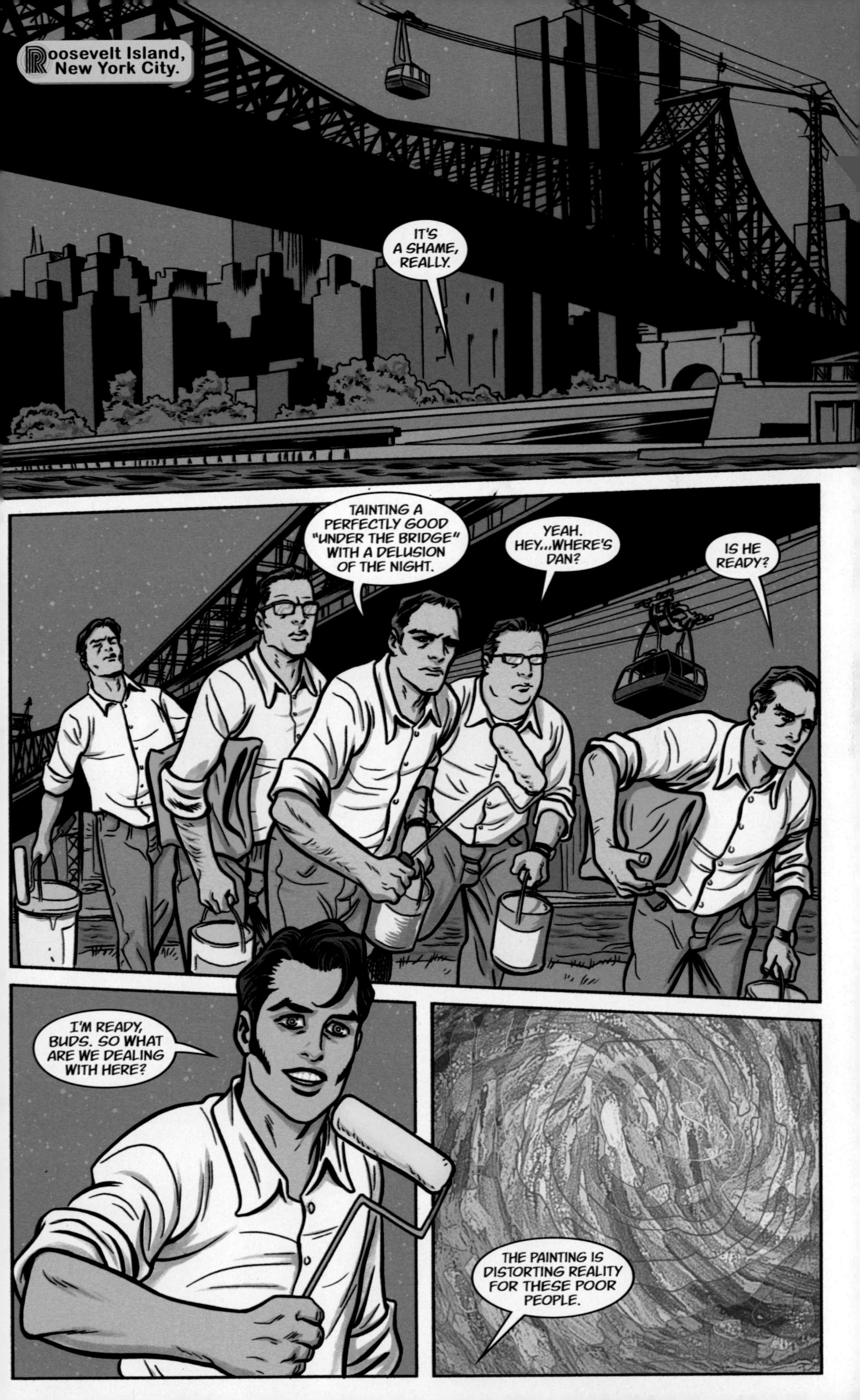
Roosevelt Island, New York City.
IT'S A SHAME, REALLY.
TAINTING A PERFECTLY GOOD "UNDER THE BRIDGE" WITH A DELUSION OF THE NIGHT.
YEAH. HEY...WHERE'S DAN?
IS HE READY?
I'M READY, BUDS. SO WHAT ARE WE DEALING WITH HERE?
THE PAINTING IS DISTORTING REALITY FOR THESE POOR PEOPLE.

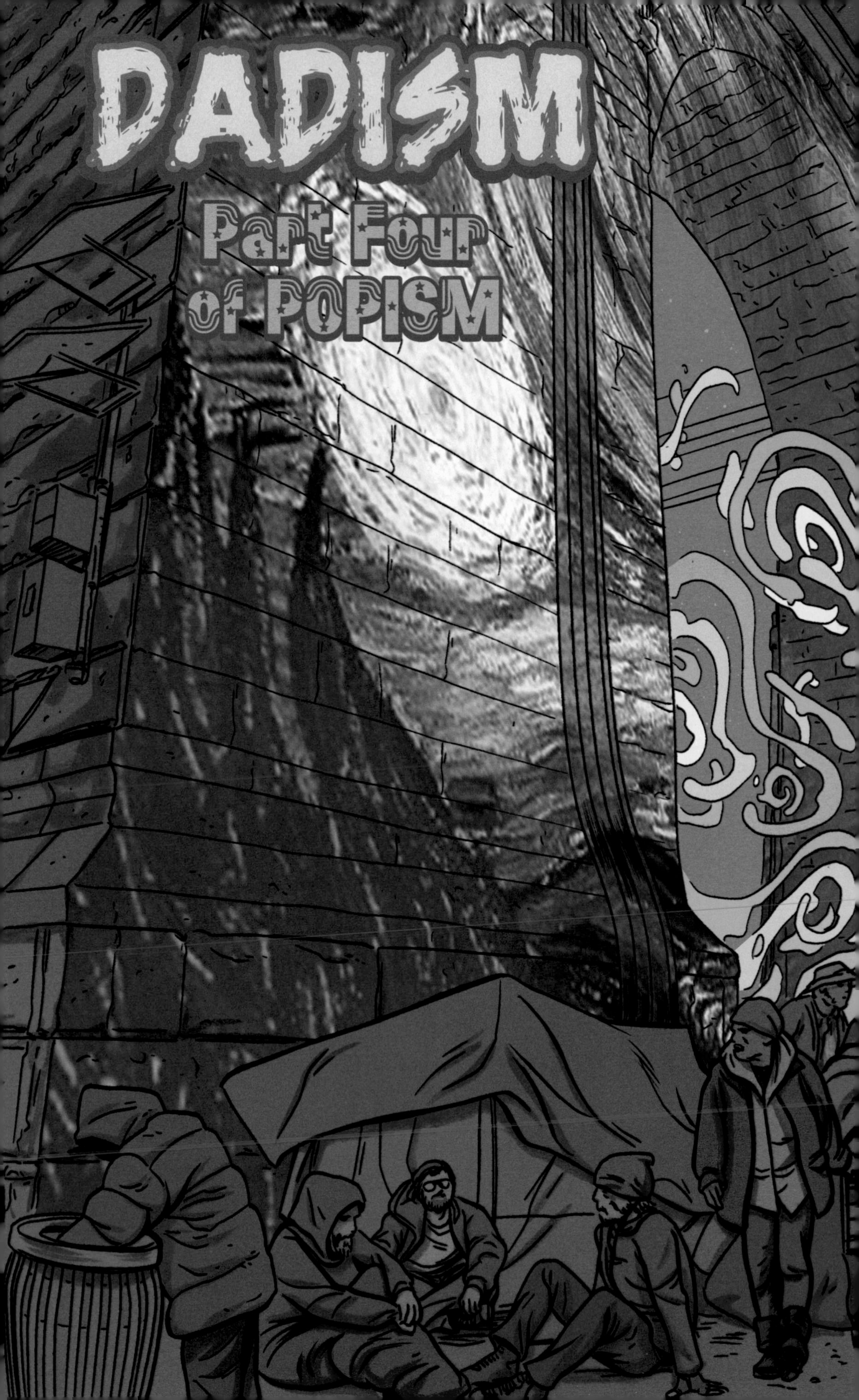
DADISM
Part Four
of POPISM

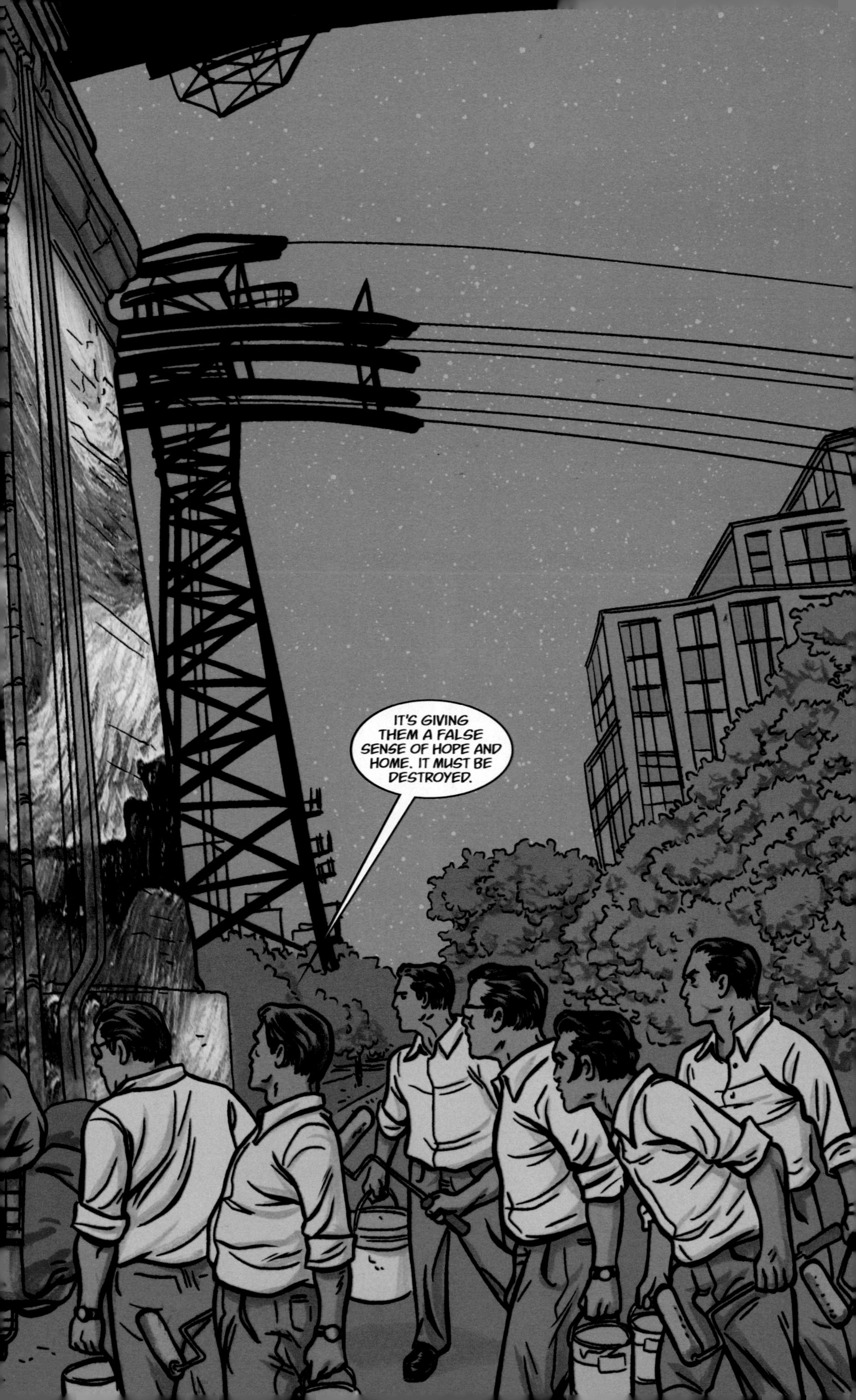
IT'S GIVING THEM A FALSE SENSE OF HOPE AND HOME. IT MUST BE DESTROYED.

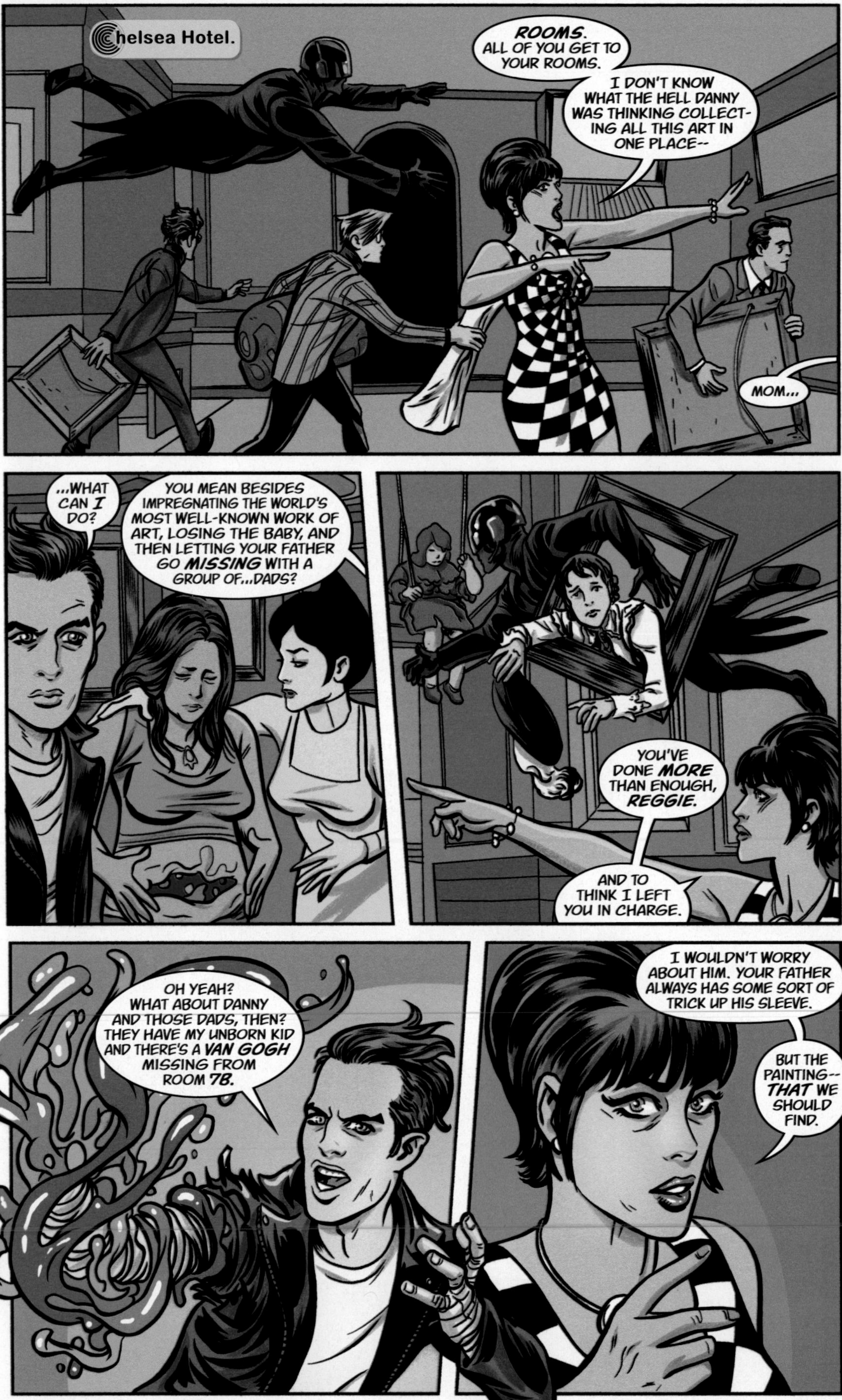
Chelsea Hotel.
ROOMS. ALL OF YOU GET TO YOUR ROOMS.
I DON'T KNOW WHAT THE HELL DANNY WAS THINKING COLLECTING ALL THIS ART IN ONE PLACE--
MOM...
...WHAT CAN I DO?
YOU MEAN BESIDES IMPREGNATING THE WORLD'S MOST WELL-KNOWN WORK OF ART, LOSING THE BABY, AND THEN LETTING YOUR FATHER GO MISSING WITH A GROUP OF...DADS?
YOU'VE DONE MORE THAN ENOUGH, REGGIE.
AND TO THINK I LEFT YOU IN CHARGE.
OH YEAH? WHAT ABOUT DANNY AND THOSE DADS, THEN? THEY HAVE MY UNBORN KID AND THERE'S A VAN GOGH MISSING FROM ROOM 7B.
I WOULDN'T WORRY ABOUT HIM. YOUR FATHER ALWAYS HAS SOME SORT OF TRICK UP HIS SLEEVE.
BUT THE PAINTING--THAT WE SHOULD FIND.

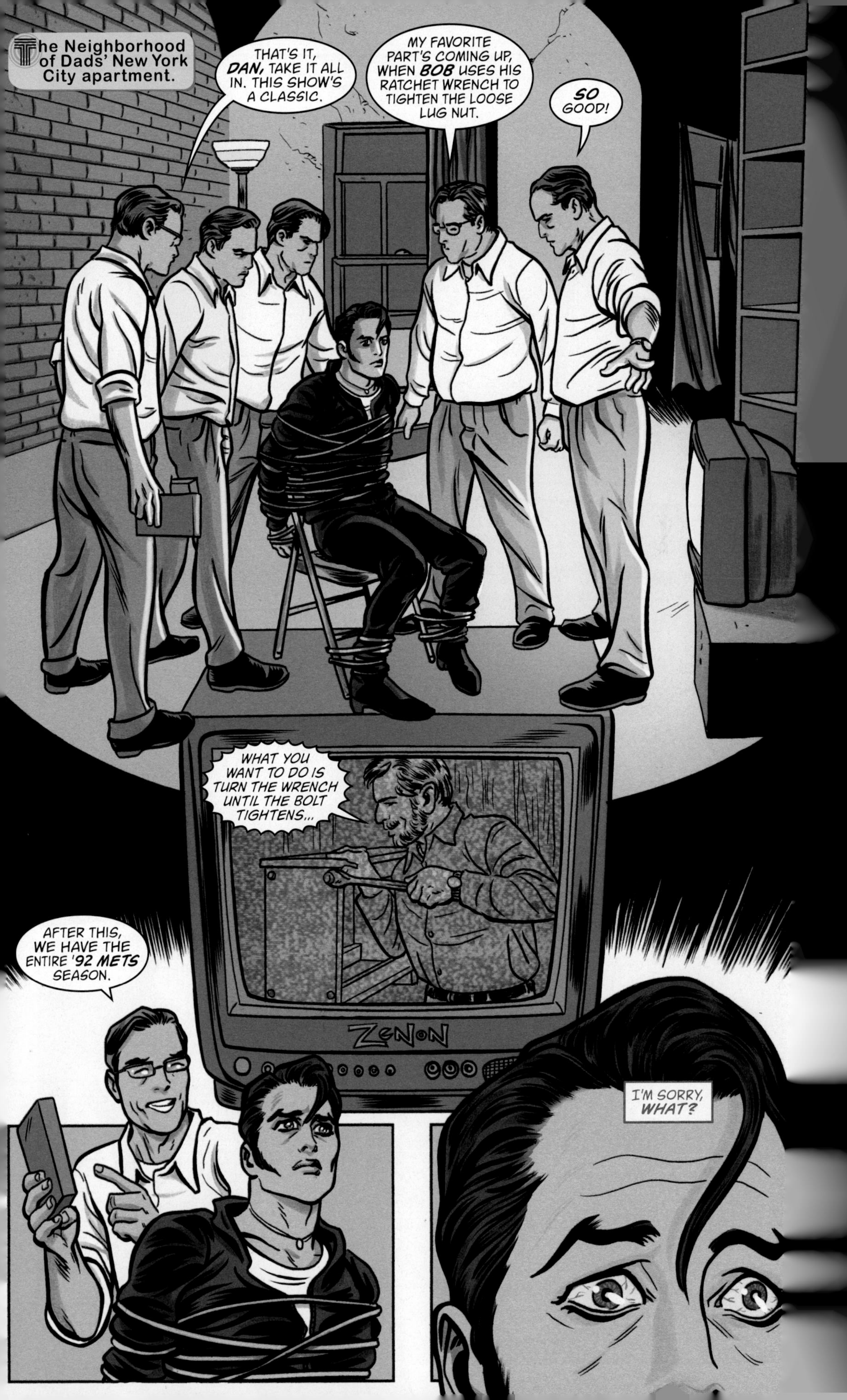
The Neighborhood of Dads' New York City apartment.
THAT'S IT, DAN, TAKE IT ALL IN. THIS SHOW'S A CLASSIC.
MY FAVORITE PART'S COMING UP, WHEN BOB USES HIS RATCHET WRENCH TO TIGHTEN THE LOOSE LUG NUT.
SO GOOD!
WHAT YOU WANT TO DO IS TURN THE WRENCH UNTIL THE BOLT TIGHTENS...
ZENON
AFTER THIS, WE HAVE THE ENTIRE '92 METS SEASON.
I'M SORRY, WHAT?

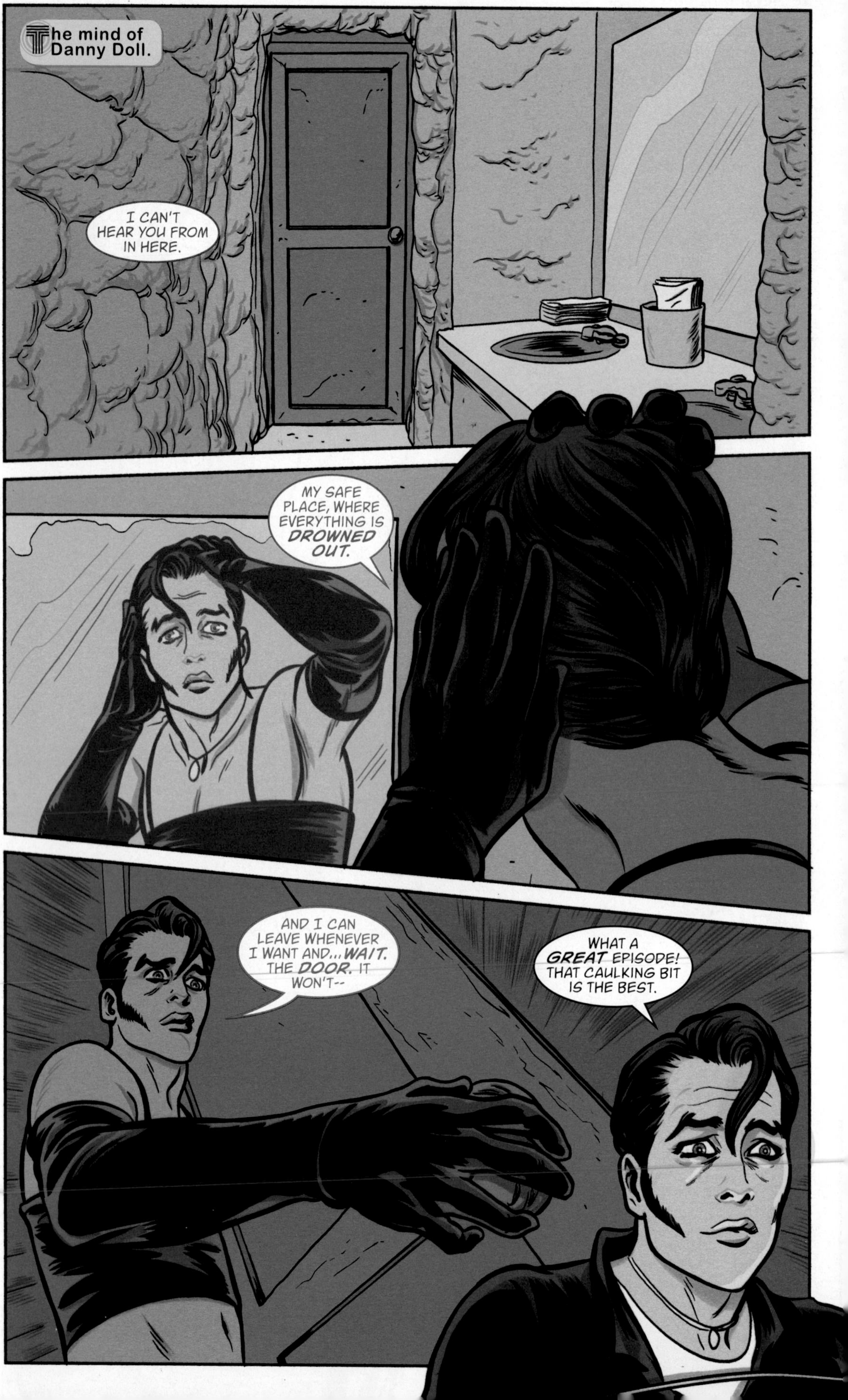
The mind of Danny Doll.
I CAN'T HEAR YOU FROM IN HERE.
MY SAFE PLACE, WHERE EVERYTHING IS DROWNED OUT.
AND I CAN LEAVE WHENEVER I WANT AND... WAIT. THE DOOR. IT WON'T--
WHAT A GREAT EPISODE! THAT CAULKING BIT IS THE BEST.

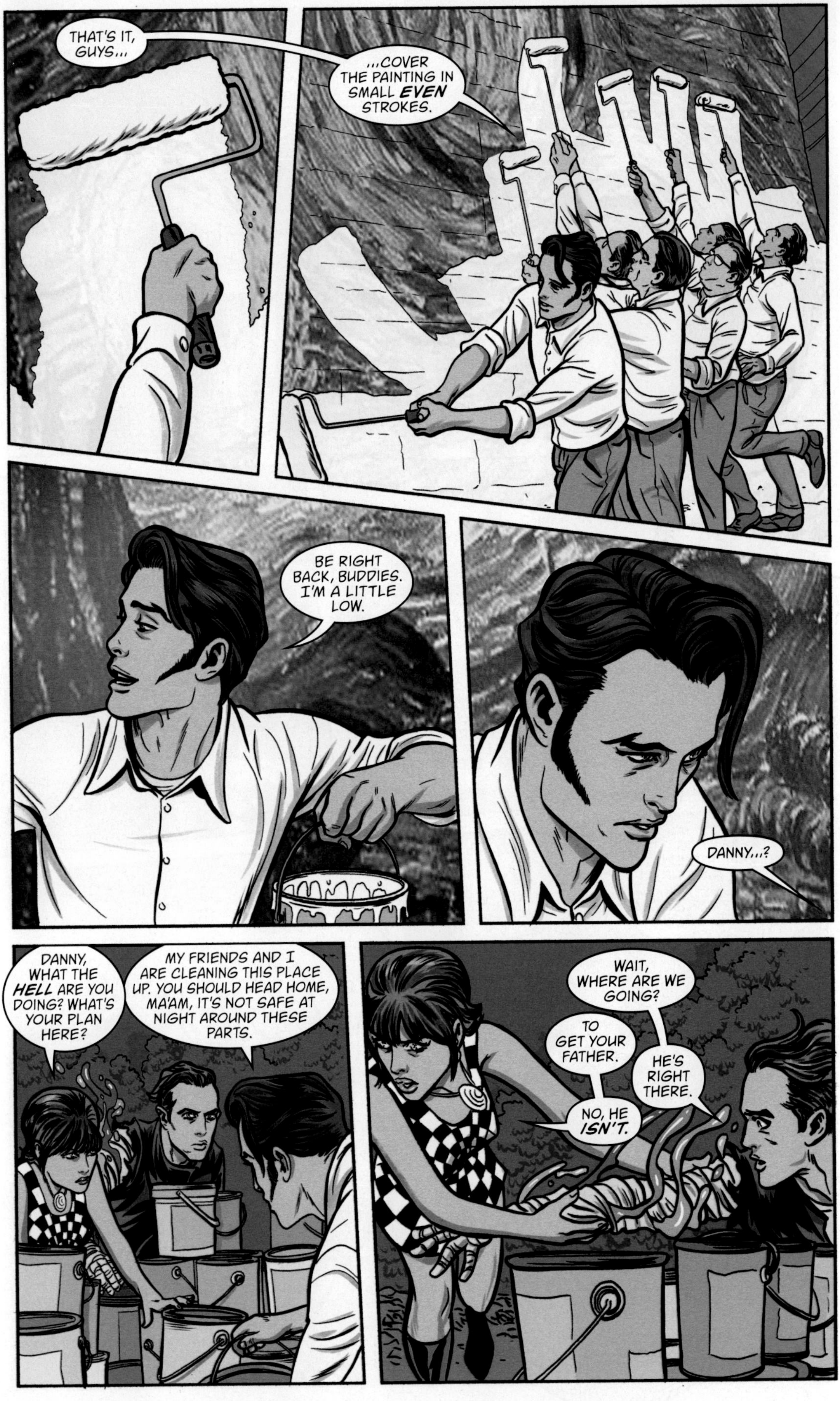
THAT'S IT, GUYS...
...COVER THE PAINTING IN SMALL EVEN STROKES.
BE RIGHT BACK, BUDDIES. I'M A LITTLE LOW.
DANNY...?
DANNY, WHAT THE HELL ARE YOU DOING? WHAT'S YOUR PLAN HERE?
MY FRIENDS AND I ARE CLEANING THIS PLACE UP. YOU SHOULD HEAD HOME, MA'AM, IT'S NOT SAFE AT NIGHT AROUND THESE PARTS.
WAIT, WHERE ARE WE GOING?
TO GET YOUR FATHER.
HE'S RIGHT THERE.
NO, HE ISN'T.

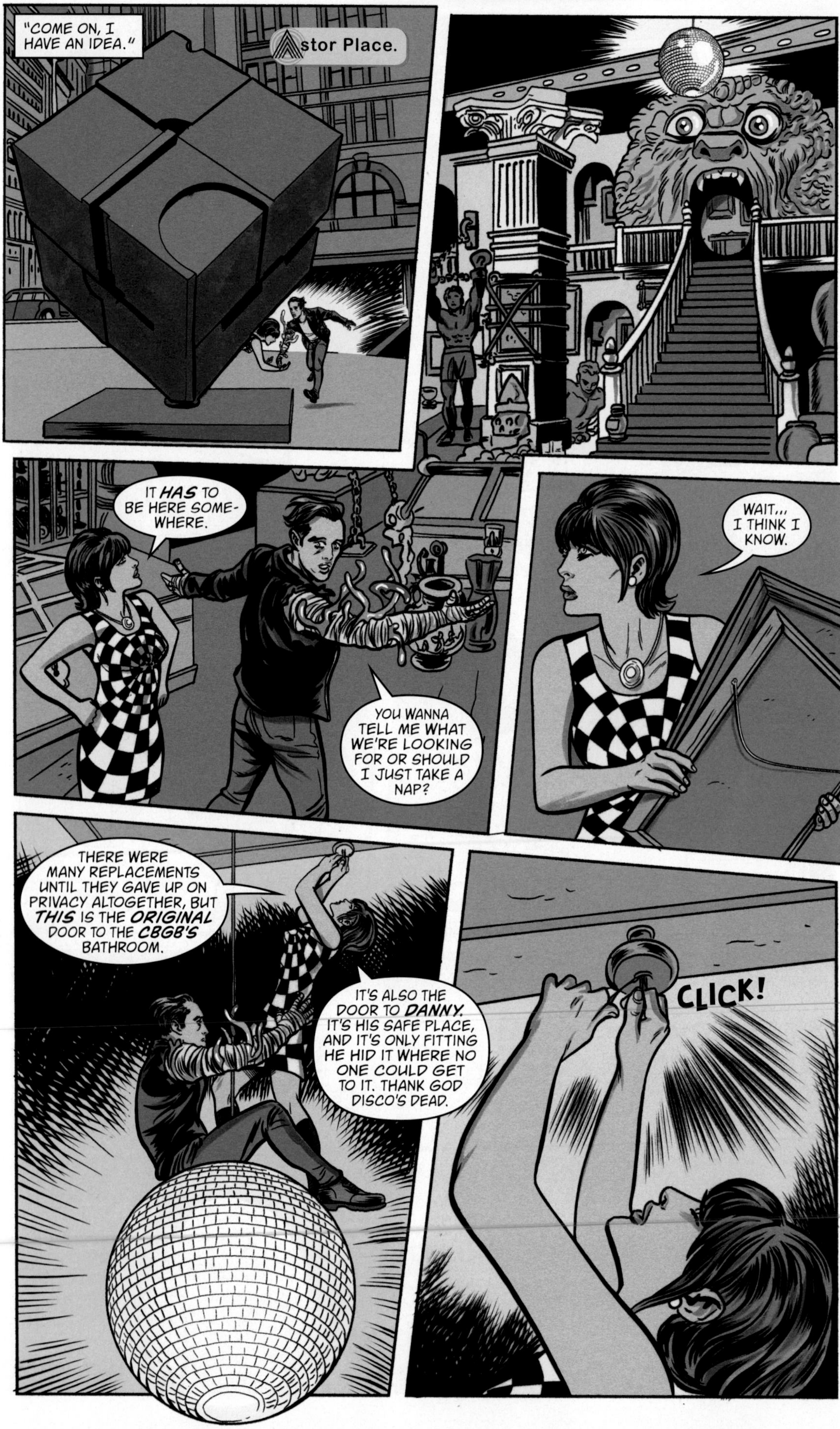
"COME ON, I HAVE AN IDEA."
Astor Place.
IT HAS TO BE HERE SOMEWHERE.
YOU WANNA TELL ME WHAT WE'RE LOOKING FOR OR SHOULD I JUST TAKE A NAP?
WAIT... I THINK I KNOW.
THERE WERE MANY REPLACEMENTS UNTIL THEY GAVE UP ON PRIVACY ALTOGETHER, BUT THIS IS THE ORIGINAL DOOR TO THE CBGB'S BATHROOM.
IT'S ALSO THE DOOR TO DANNY. IT'S HIS SAFE PLACE, AND IT'S ONLY FITTING HE HID IT WHERE NO ONE COULD GET TO IT. THANK GOD DISCO'S DEAD.
CLICK!

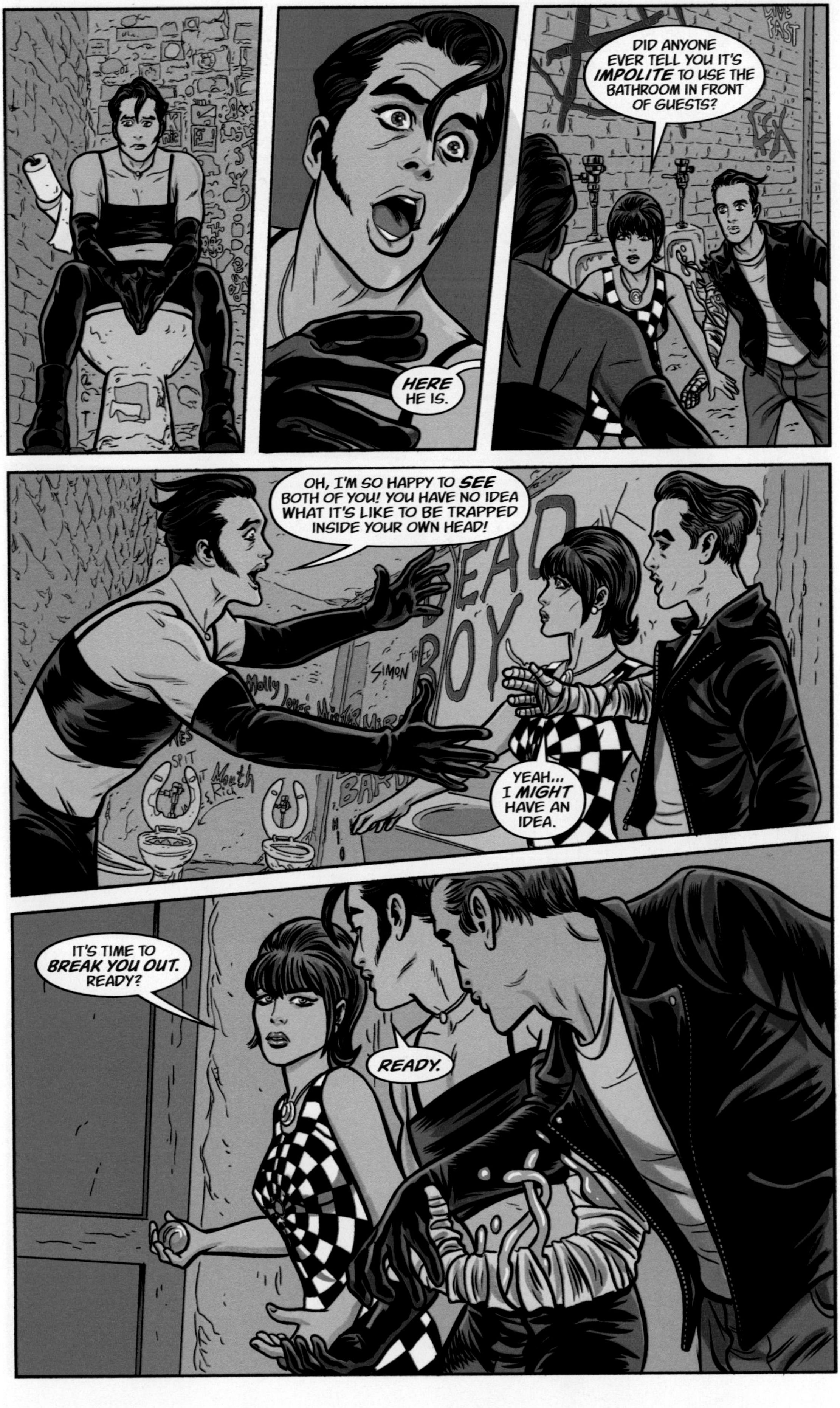
HERE HE IS.
DID ANYONE EVER TELL YOU IT'S IMPOLITE TO USE THE BATHROOM IN FRONT OF GUESTS?
OH, I'M SO HAPPY TO SEE BOTH OF YOU! YOU HAVE NO IDEA WHAT IT'S LIKE TO BE TRAPPED INSIDE YOUR OWN HEAD!
YEAH... I MIGHT HAVE AN IDEA.
IT'S TIME TO BREAK YOU OUT. READY?
READY.

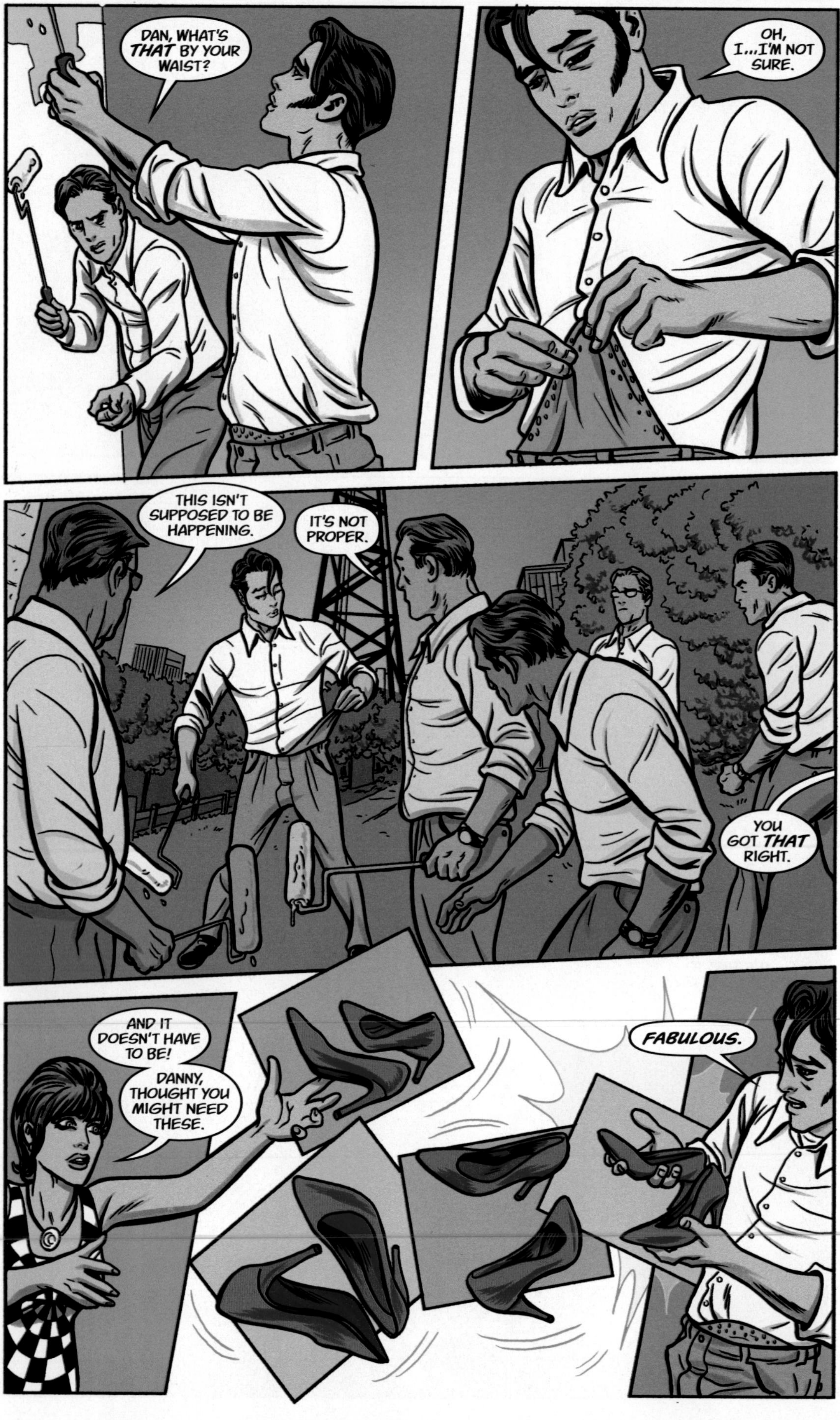
DAN, WHAT'S THAT BY YOUR WAIST?
OH, I...I'M NOT SURE.
THIS ISN'T SUPPOSED TO BE HAPPENING.
IT'S NOT PROPER.
YOU GOT THAT RIGHT.
AND IT DOESN'T HAVE TO BE!
DANNY, THOUGHT YOU MIGHT NEED THESE.
FABULOUS.

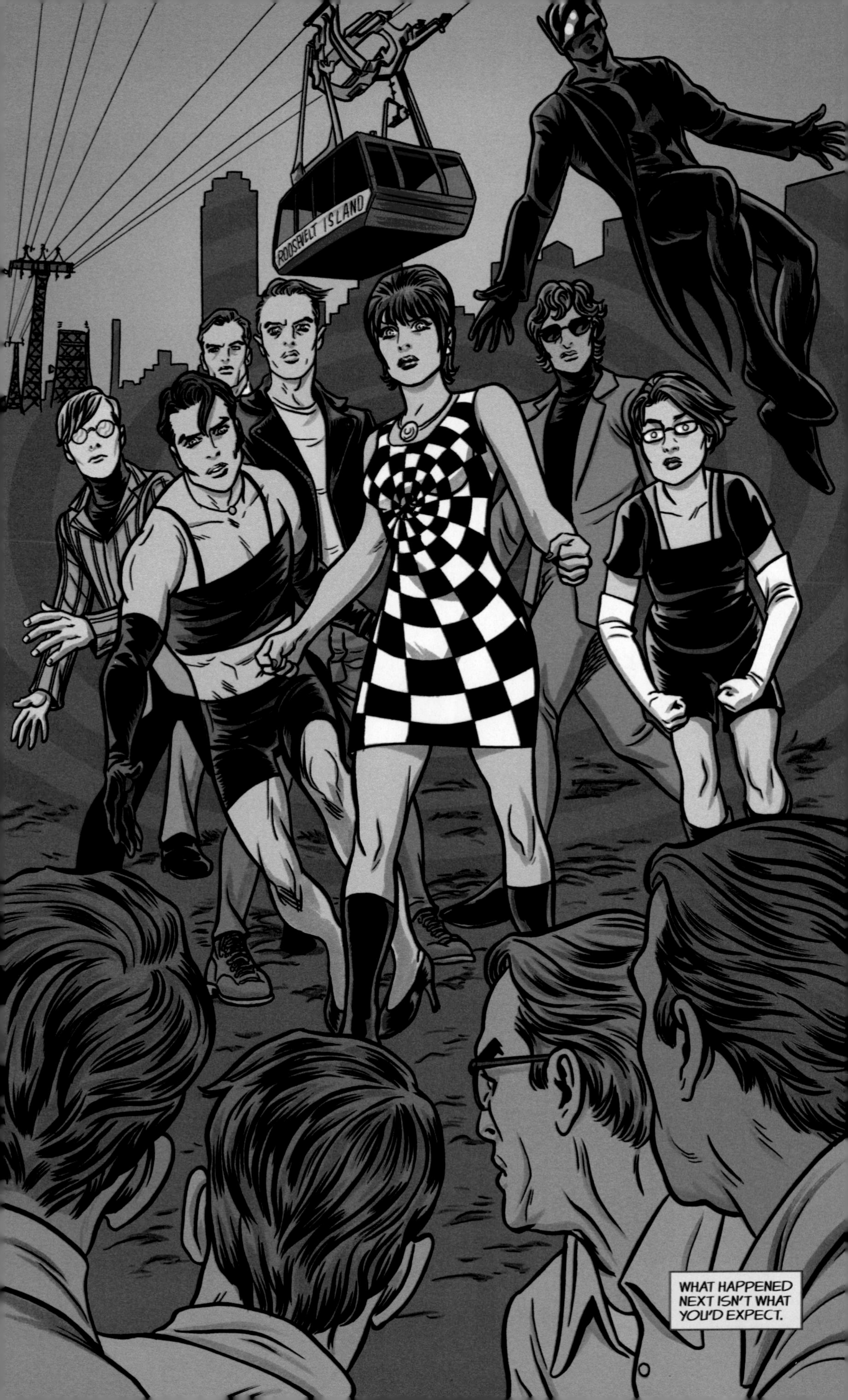
ROOSEVELT ISLAND
WHAT HAPPENED NEXT ISN'T WHAT YOU'D EXPECT.

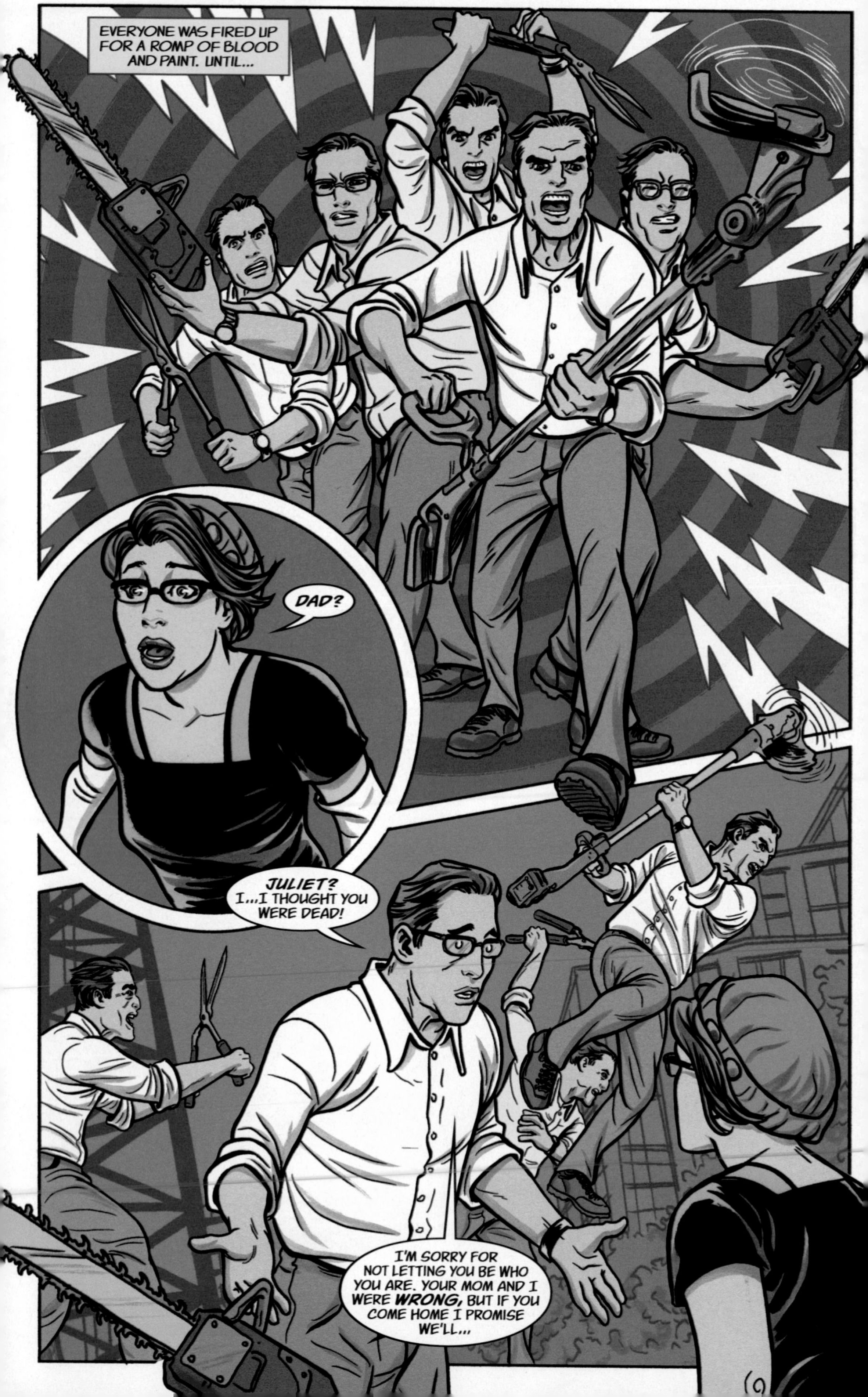

EVERYONE WAS FIRED UP FOR A ROMP OF BLOOD AND PAINT. UNTIL...
DAD?
JULIET? I...I THOUGHT YOU WERE DEAD!
I'M SORRY FOR NOT LETTING YOU BE WHO YOU ARE. YOUR MOM AND I WERE WRONG, BUT IF YOU COME HOME I PROMISE WE'LL...

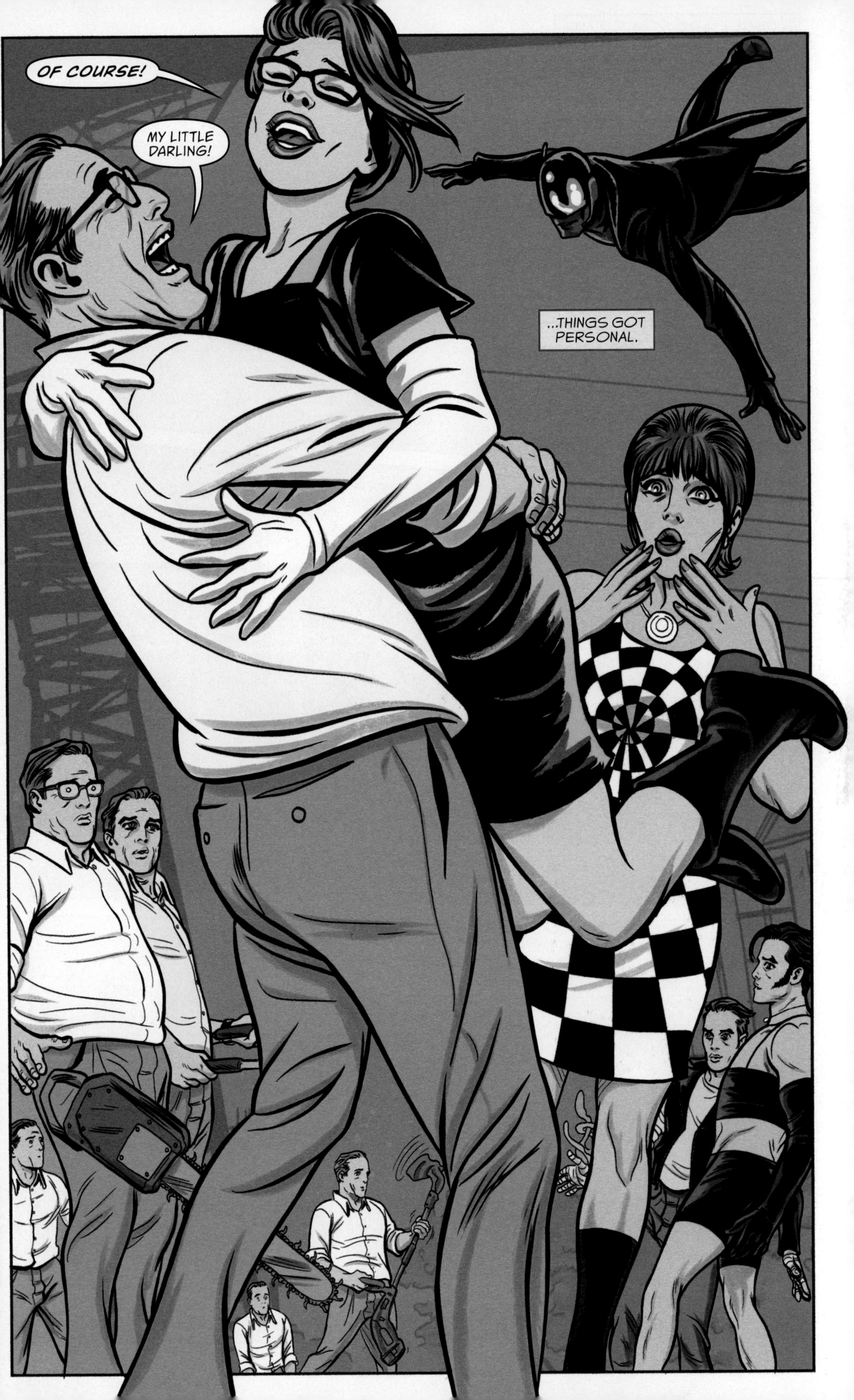
OF COURSE!
MY LITTLE DARLING!
...THINGS GOT PERSONAL.

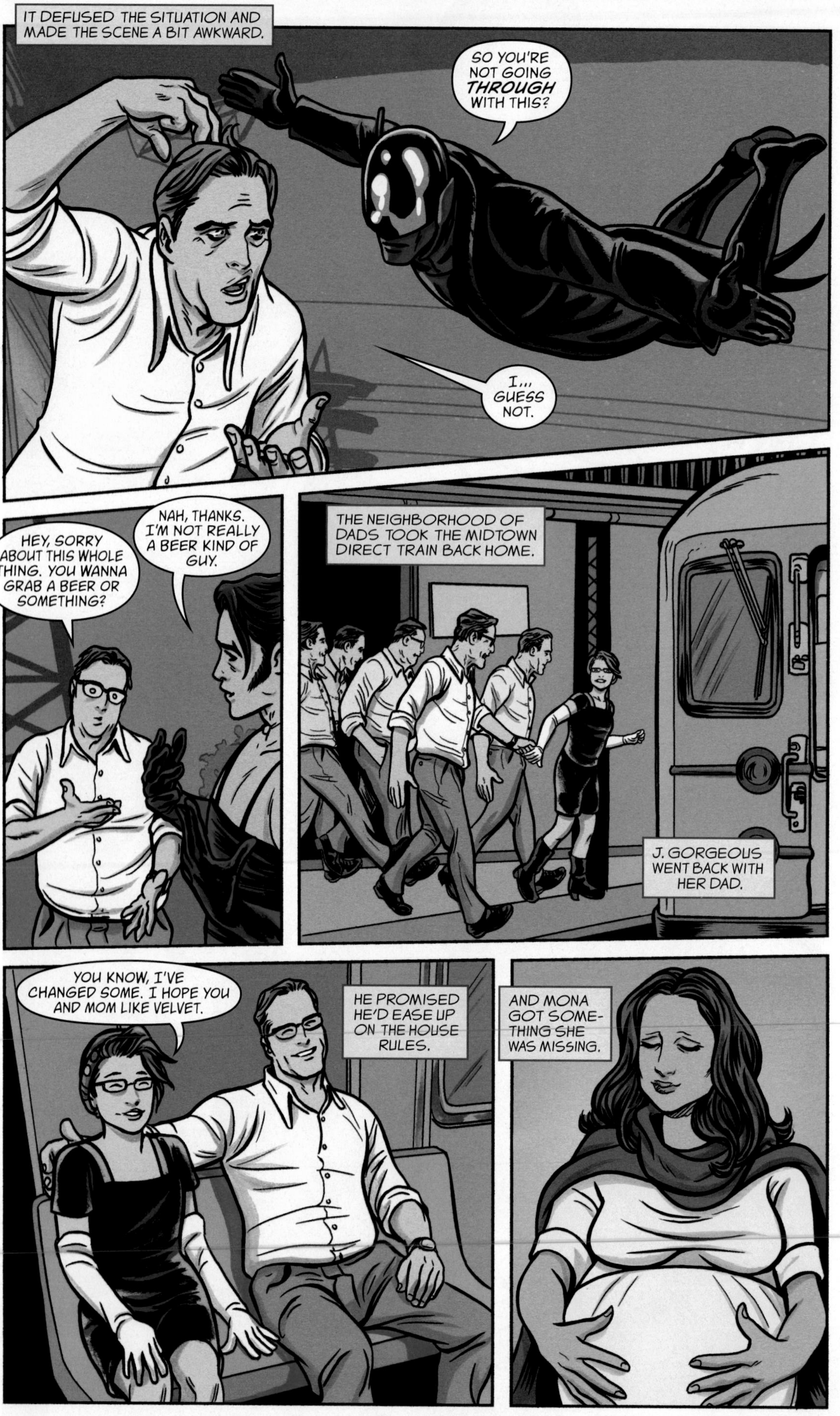
IT DEFUSED THE SITUATION AND MADE THE SCENE A BIT AWKWARD.
SO YOU'RE NOT GOING *THROUGH* WITH THIS?
I... GUESS NOT.
HEY, SORRY ABOUT THIS WHOLE THING. YOU WANNA GRAB A BEER OR SOMETHING?
NAH, THANKS. I'M NOT REALLY A BEER KIND OF GUY.
THE NEIGHBORHOOD OF DADS TOOK THE MIDTOWN DIRECT TRAIN BACK HOME.
J. GORGEOUS WENT BACK WITH HER DAD.
YOU KNOW, I'VE CHANGED SOME. I HOPE YOU AND MOM LIKE VELVET.
HE PROMISED HE'D EASE UP ON THE HOUSE RULES.
AND MONA GOT SOMETHING SHE WAS MISSING.

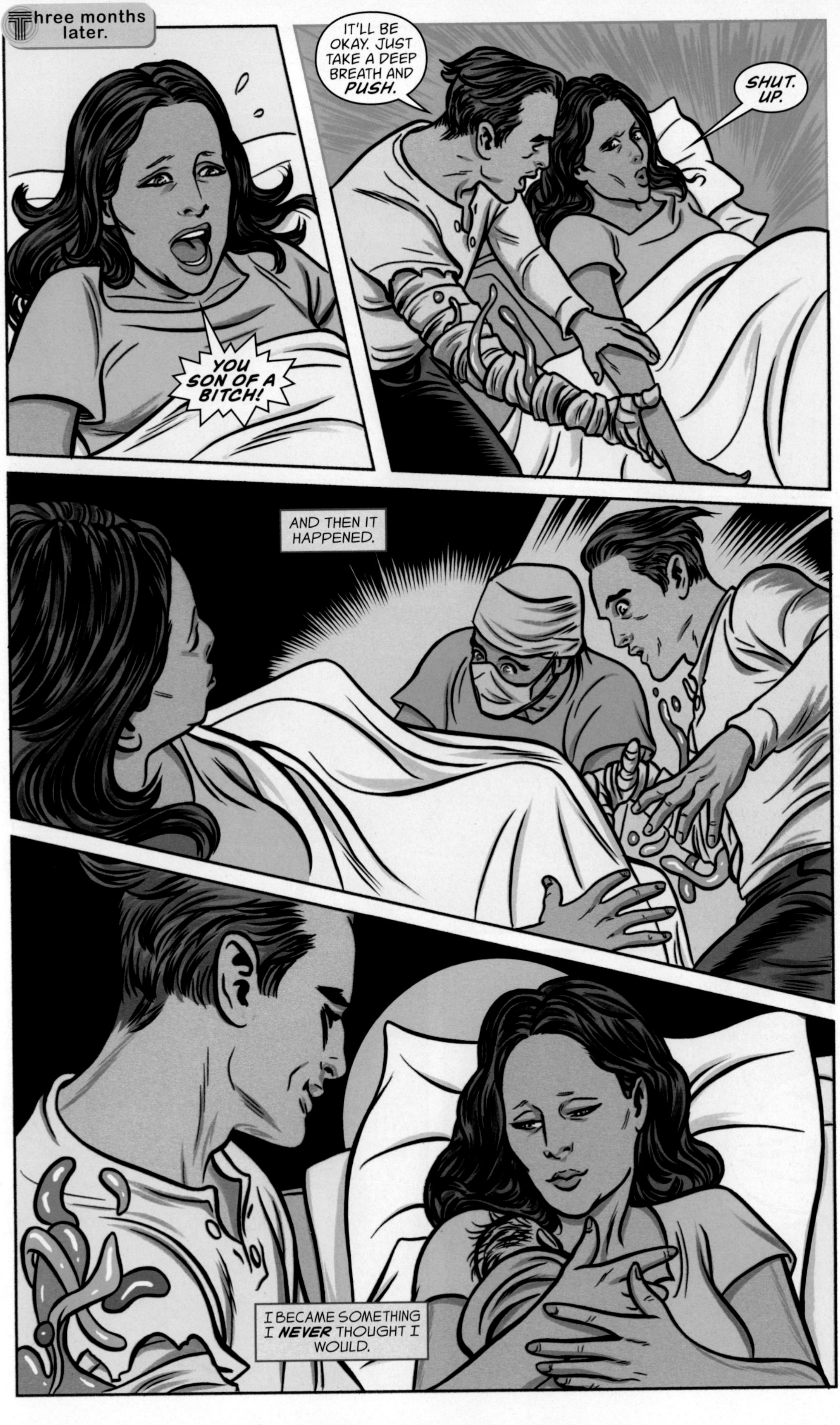
Three months later.
YOU SON OF A BITCH!
IT'LL BE OKAY. JUST TAKE A DEEP BREATH AND PUSH.
SHUT. UP.
AND THEN IT HAPPENED.
I BECAME SOMETHING I NEVER THOUGHT I WOULD.

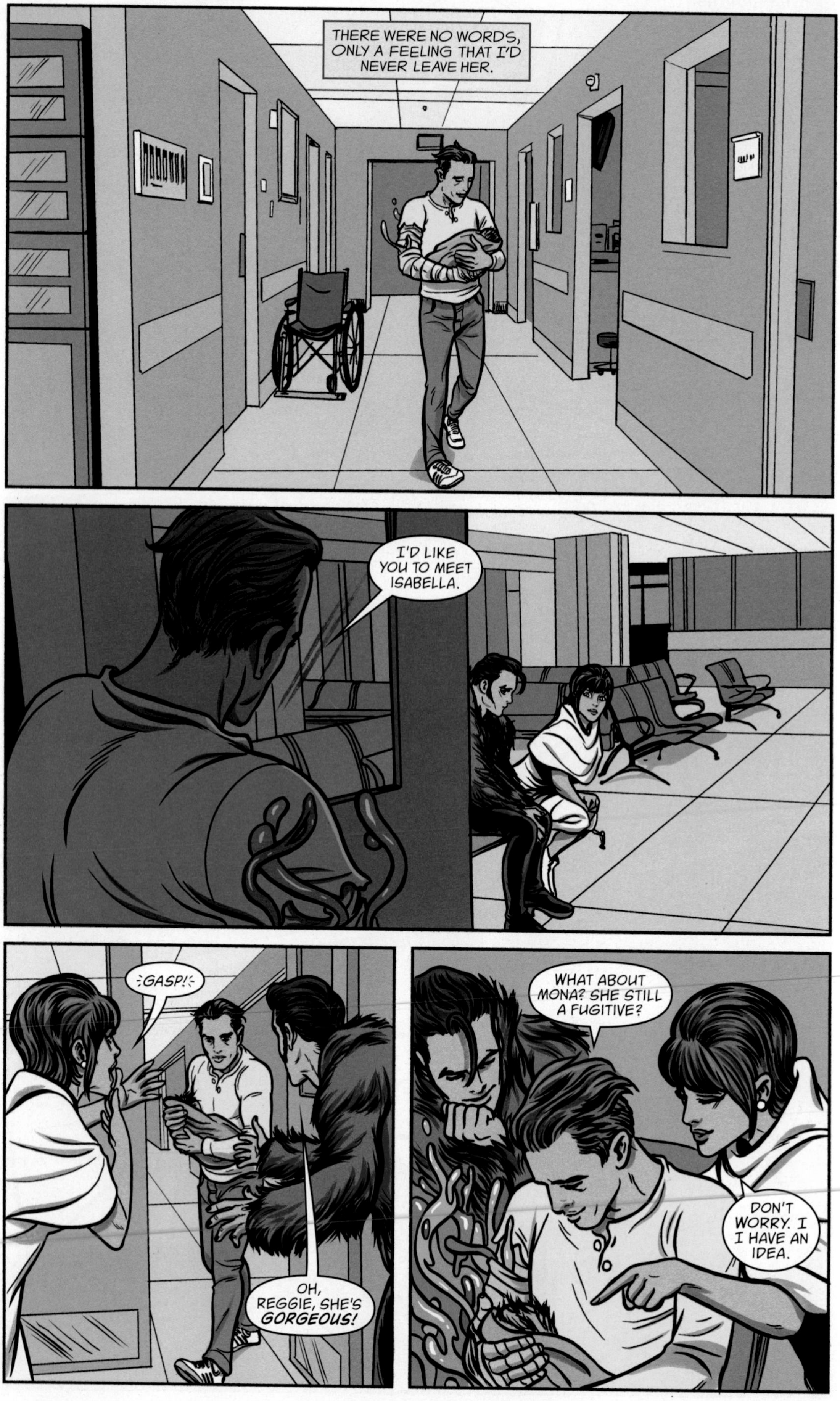
THERE WERE NO WORDS, ONLY A FEELING THAT I'D NEVER LEAVE HER.
I'D LIKE YOU TO MEET ISABELLA.
GASP!
OH, REGGIE, SHE'S GORGEOUS!
WHAT ABOUT MONA? SHE STILL A FUGITIVE?
DON'T WORRY. I I HAVE AN IDEA.

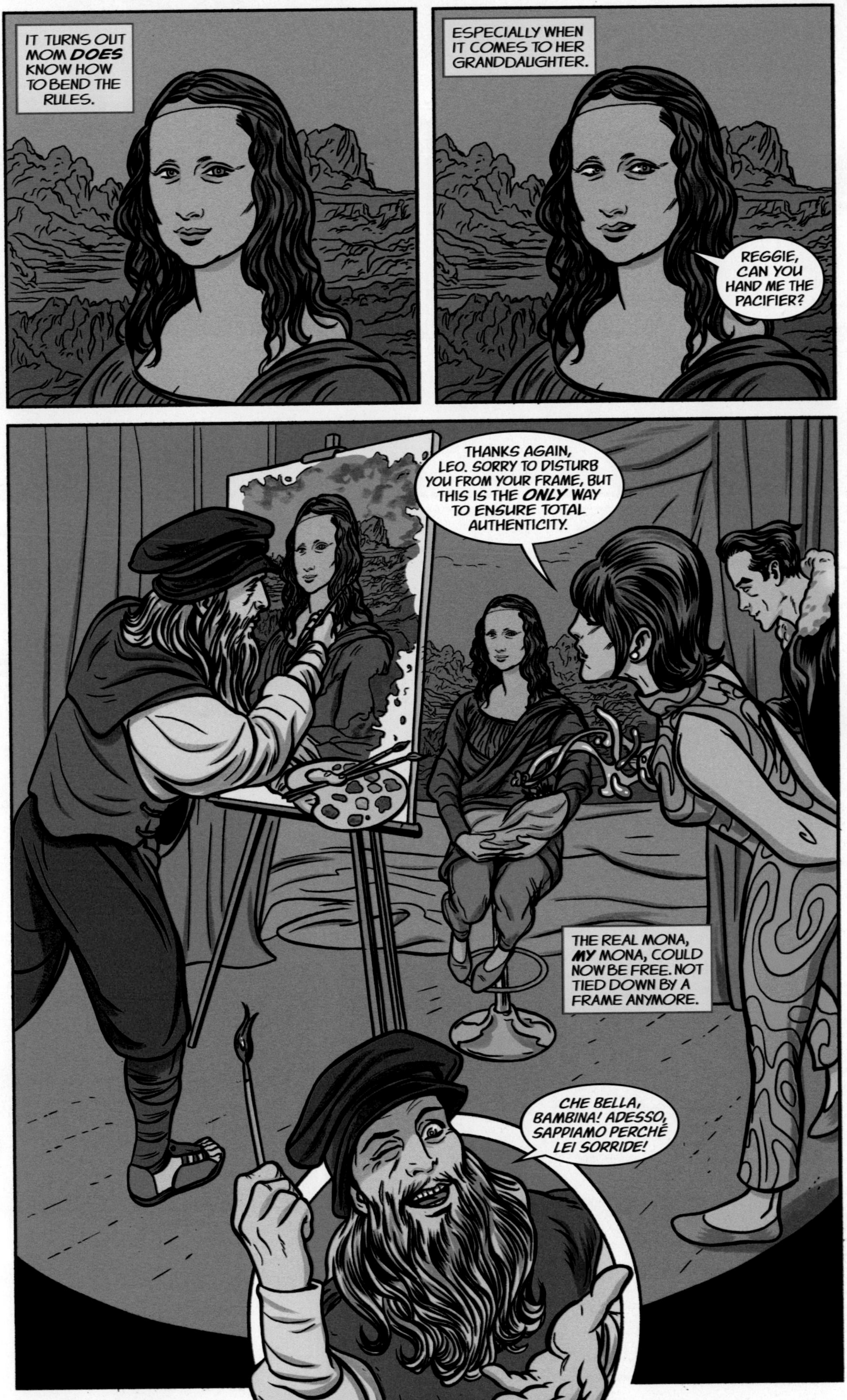
IT TURNS OUT MOM **DOES** KNOW HOW TO BEND THE RULES.
ESPECIALLY WHEN IT COMES TO HER GRANDDAUGHTER.
REGGIE, CAN YOU HAND ME THE PACIFIER?
THANKS AGAIN, LEO. SORRY TO DISTURB YOU FROM YOUR FRAME, BUT THIS IS THE **ONLY** WAY TO ENSURE TOTAL AUTHENTICITY.
THE REAL MONA, **MY** MONA, COULD NOW BE FREE. NOT TIED DOWN BY A FRAME ANYMORE.
CHE BELLA, BAMBINA! ADESSO, SAPPIAMO PERCHÉ LEI SORRIDE!

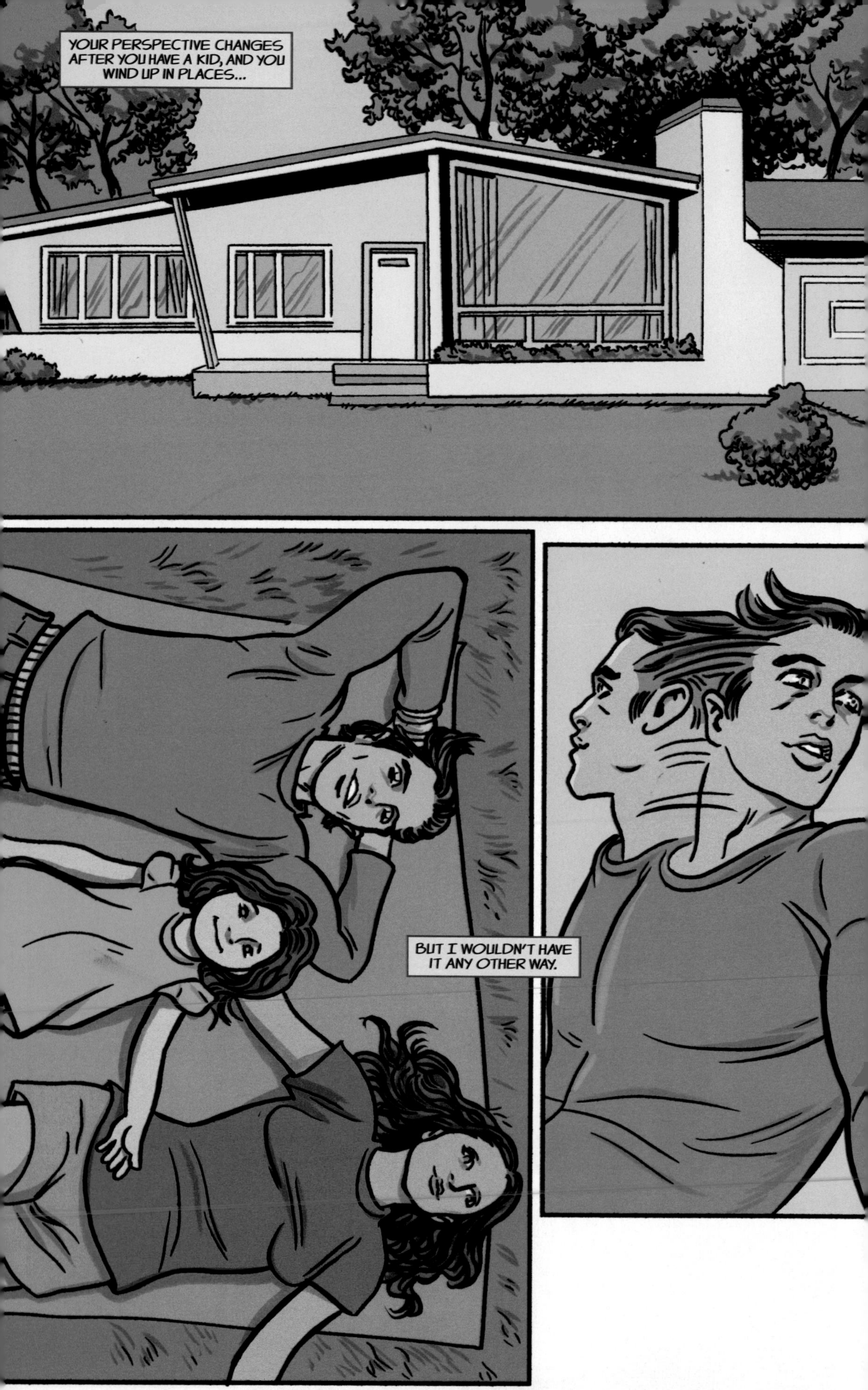
YOUR PERSPECTIVE CHANGES AFTER YOU HAVE A KID, AND YOU WIND UP IN PLACES...
BUT I WOULDN'T HAVE IT ANY OTHER WAY.

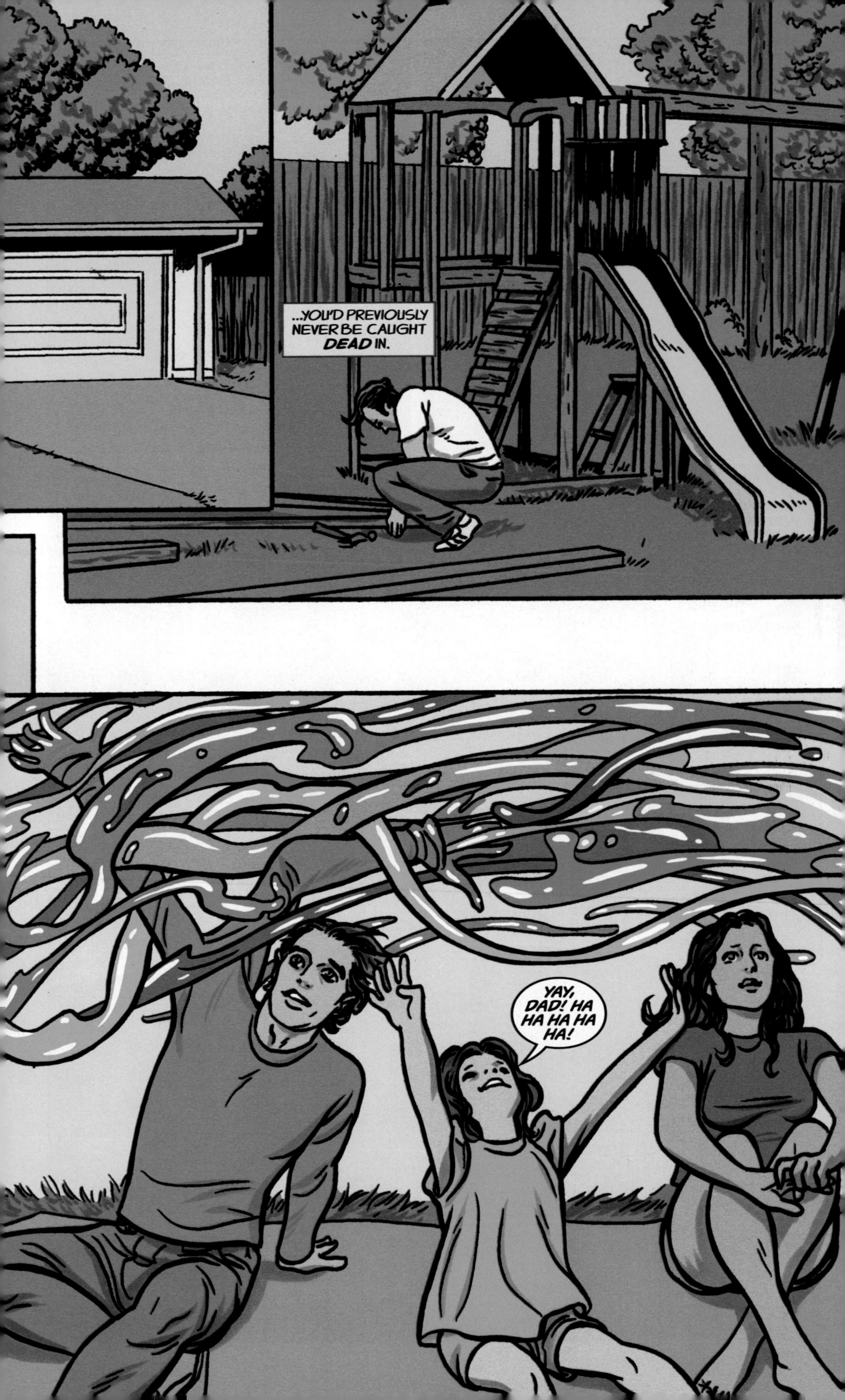
...YOU'D PREVIOUSLY NEVER BE CAUGHT DEAD IN.
YAY, DAD! HA HA HA HA HA!

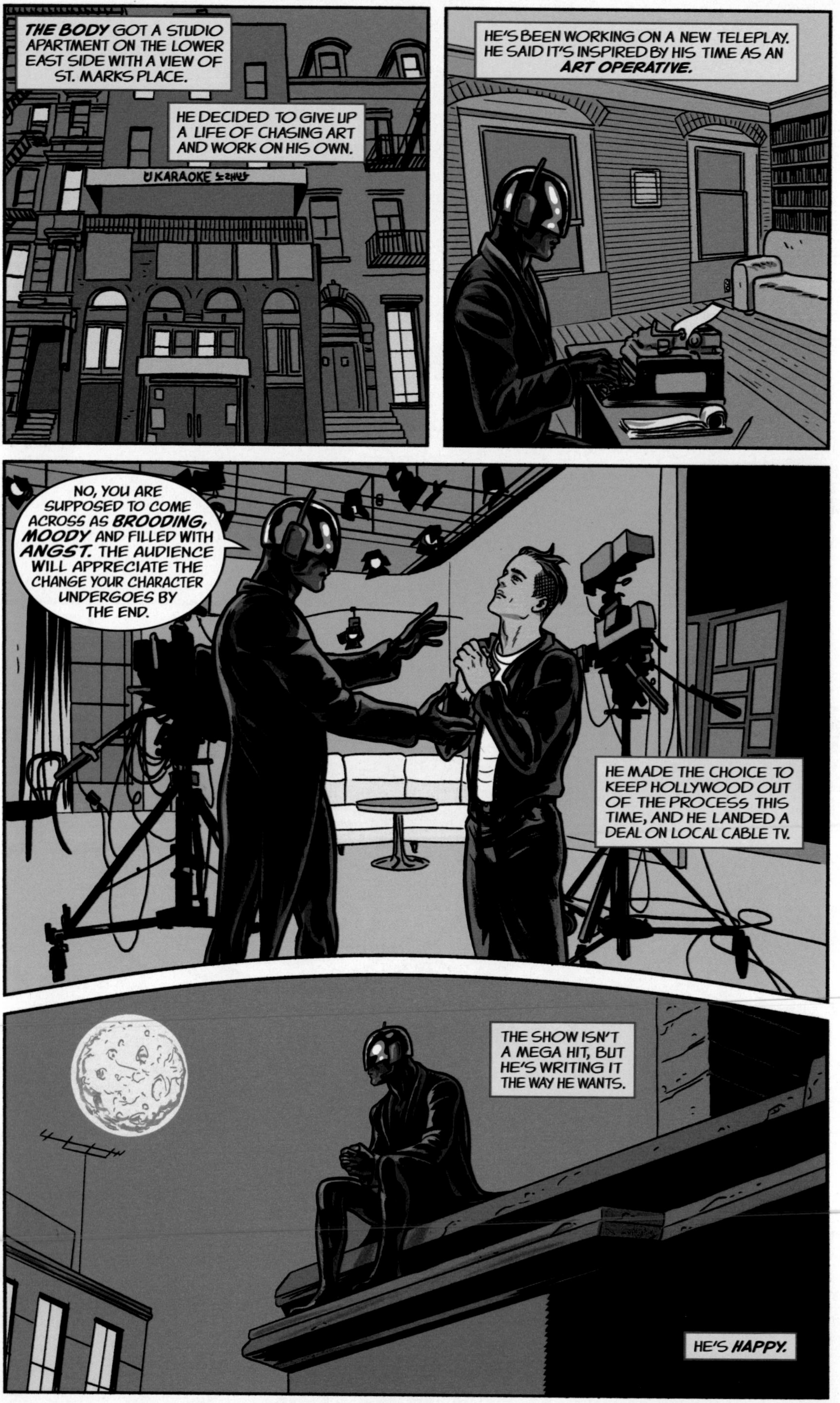
THE BODY GOT A STUDIO APARTMENT ON THE LOWER EAST SIDE WITH A VIEW OF ST. MARKS PLACE.
HE DECIDED TO GIVE UP A LIFE OF CHASING ART AND WORK ON HIS OWN.
KARAOKE 노래방
HE'S BEEN WORKING ON A NEW TELEPLAY. HE SAID IT'S INSPIRED BY HIS TIME AS AN ART OPERATIVE.
NO, YOU ARE SUPPOSED TO COME ACROSS AS BROODING, MOODY AND FILLED WITH ANGST. THE AUDIENCE WILL APPRECIATE THE CHANGE YOUR CHARACTER UNDERGOES BY THE END.
HE MADE THE CHOICE TO KEEP HOLLYWOOD OUT OF THE PROCESS THIS TIME, AND HE LANDED A DEAL ON LOCAL CABLE TV.
THE SHOW ISN'T A MEGA HIT, BUT HE'S WRITING IT THE WAY HE WANTS.
HE'S HAPPY.

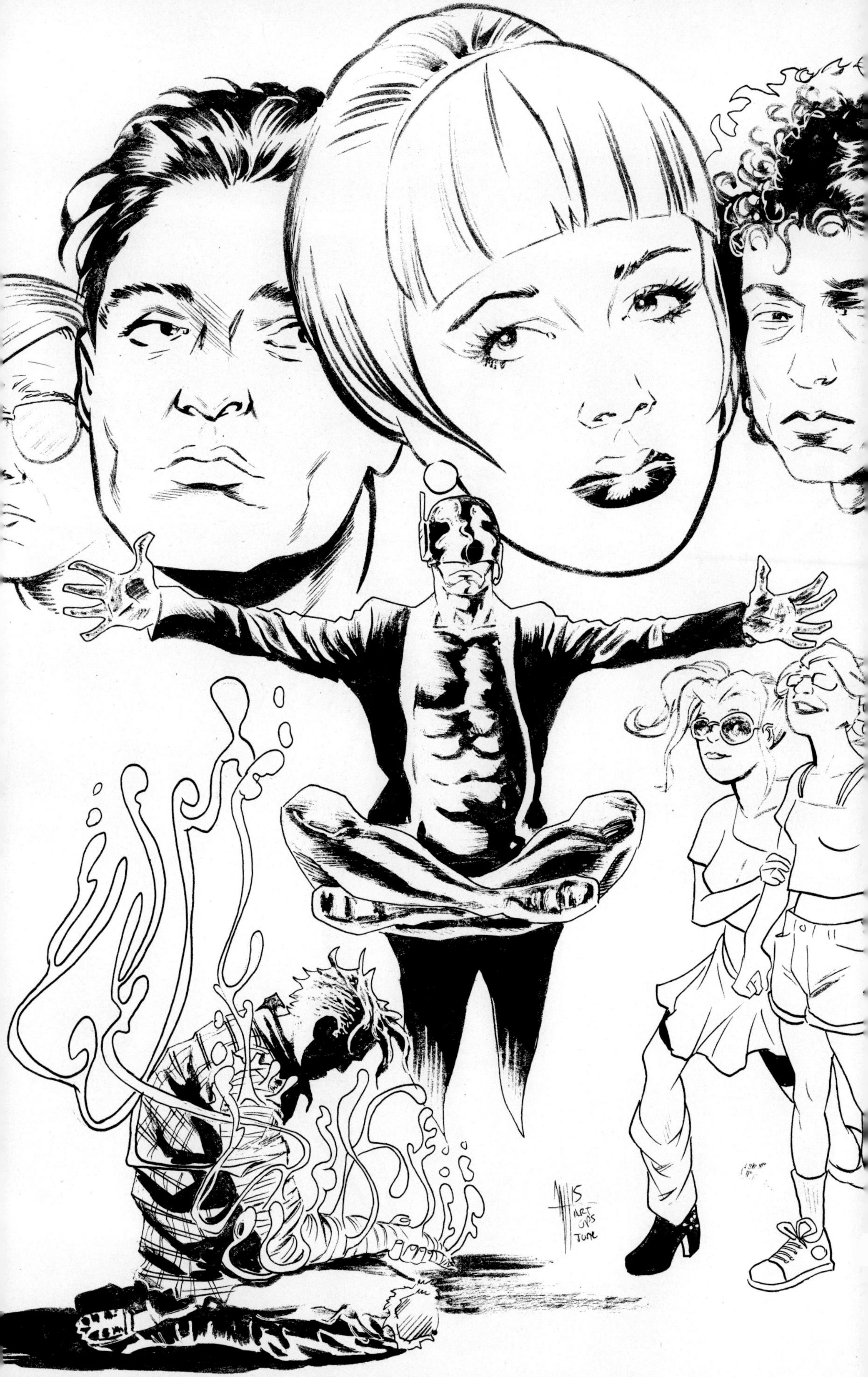

THE OPS FILES

SKETCHES AND PRELIMINARY ART BY **MATT BRUNDAGE**

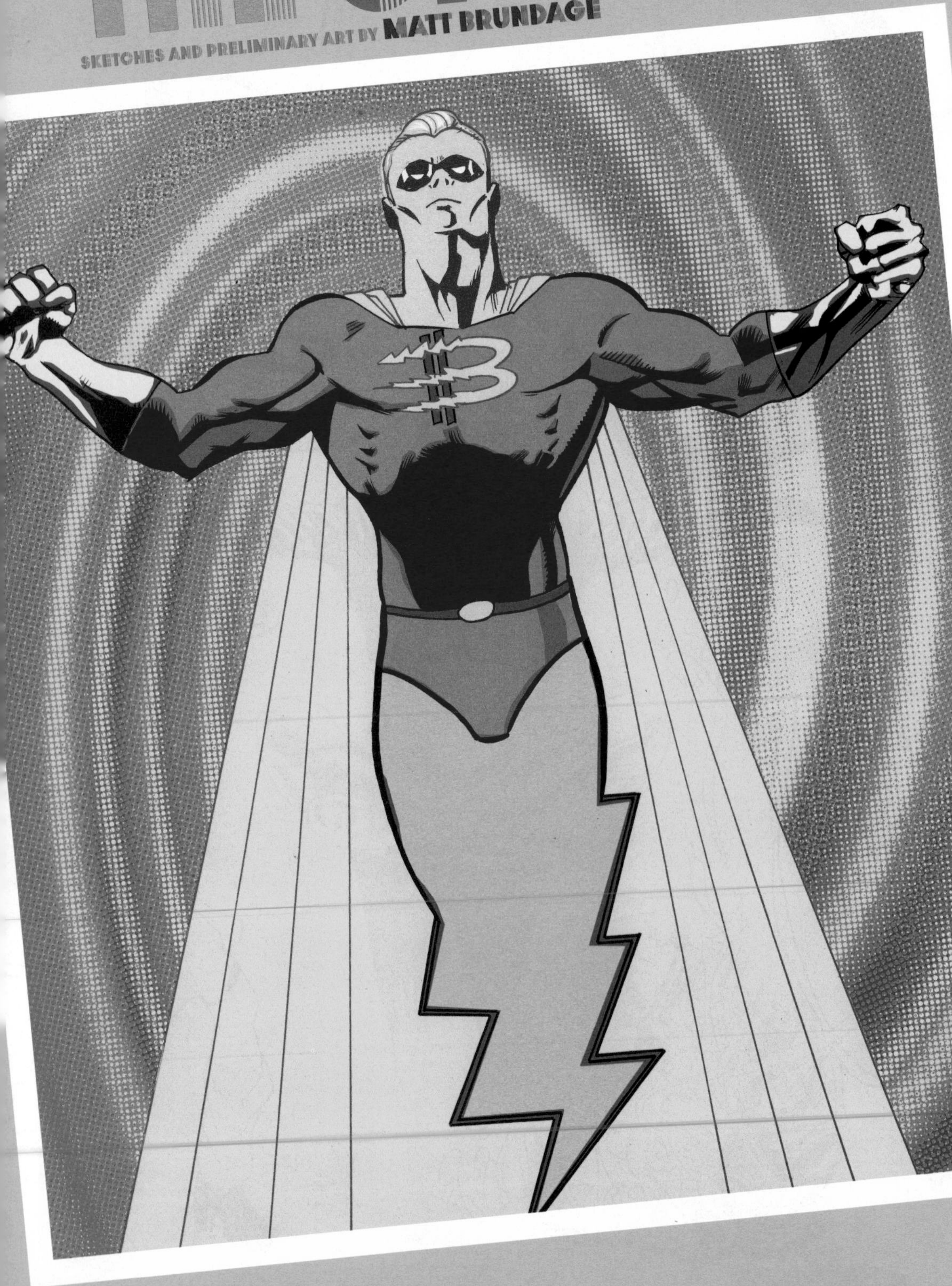

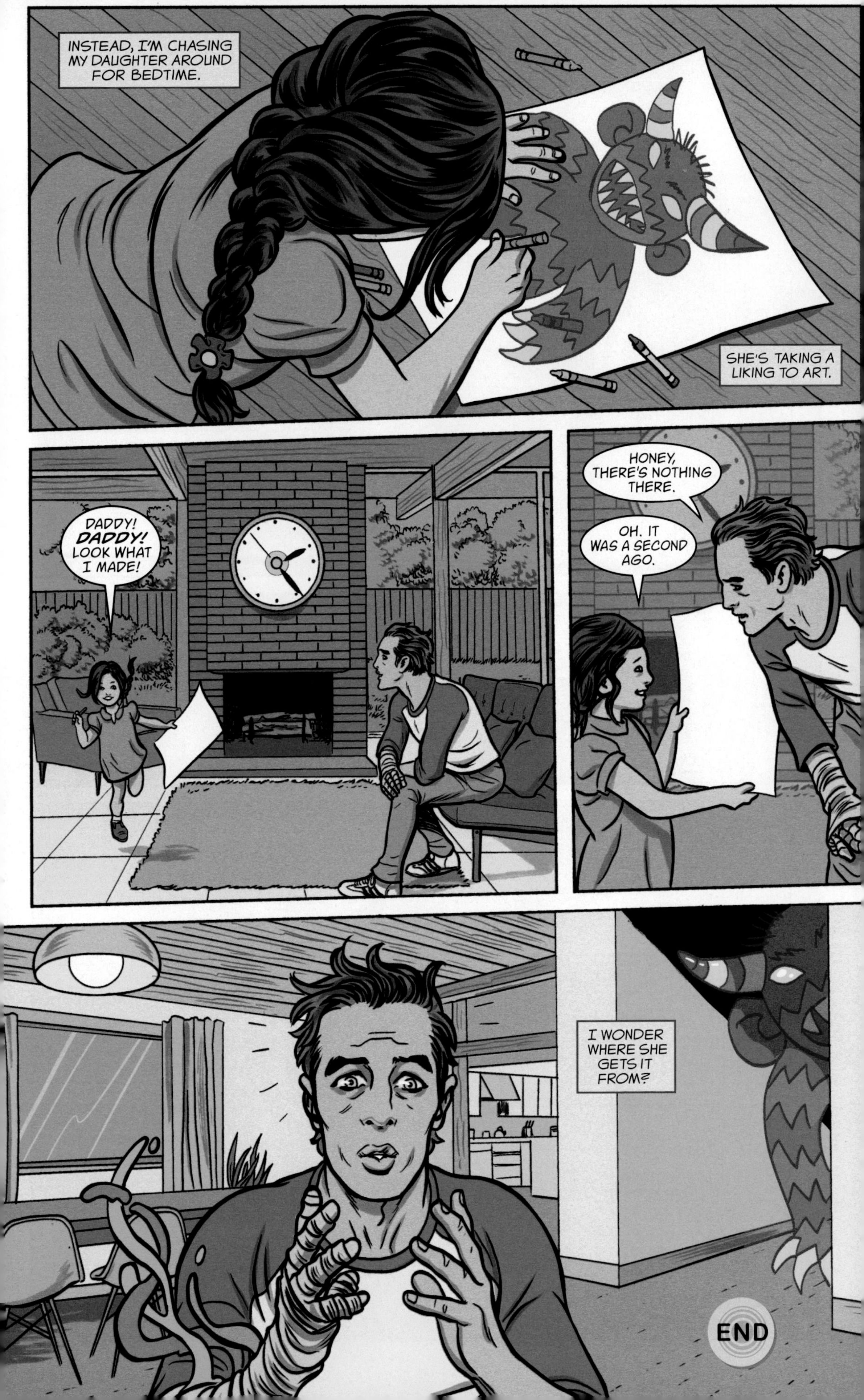
INSTEAD, I'M CHASING MY DAUGHTER AROUND FOR BEDTIME.
SHE'S TAKING A LIKING TO ART.
DADDY! **DADDY!** LOOK WHAT I MADE!
HONEY, THERE'S NOTHING THERE.
OH. IT WAS A SECOND AGO.
I WONDER WHERE SHE GETS IT FROM?
END

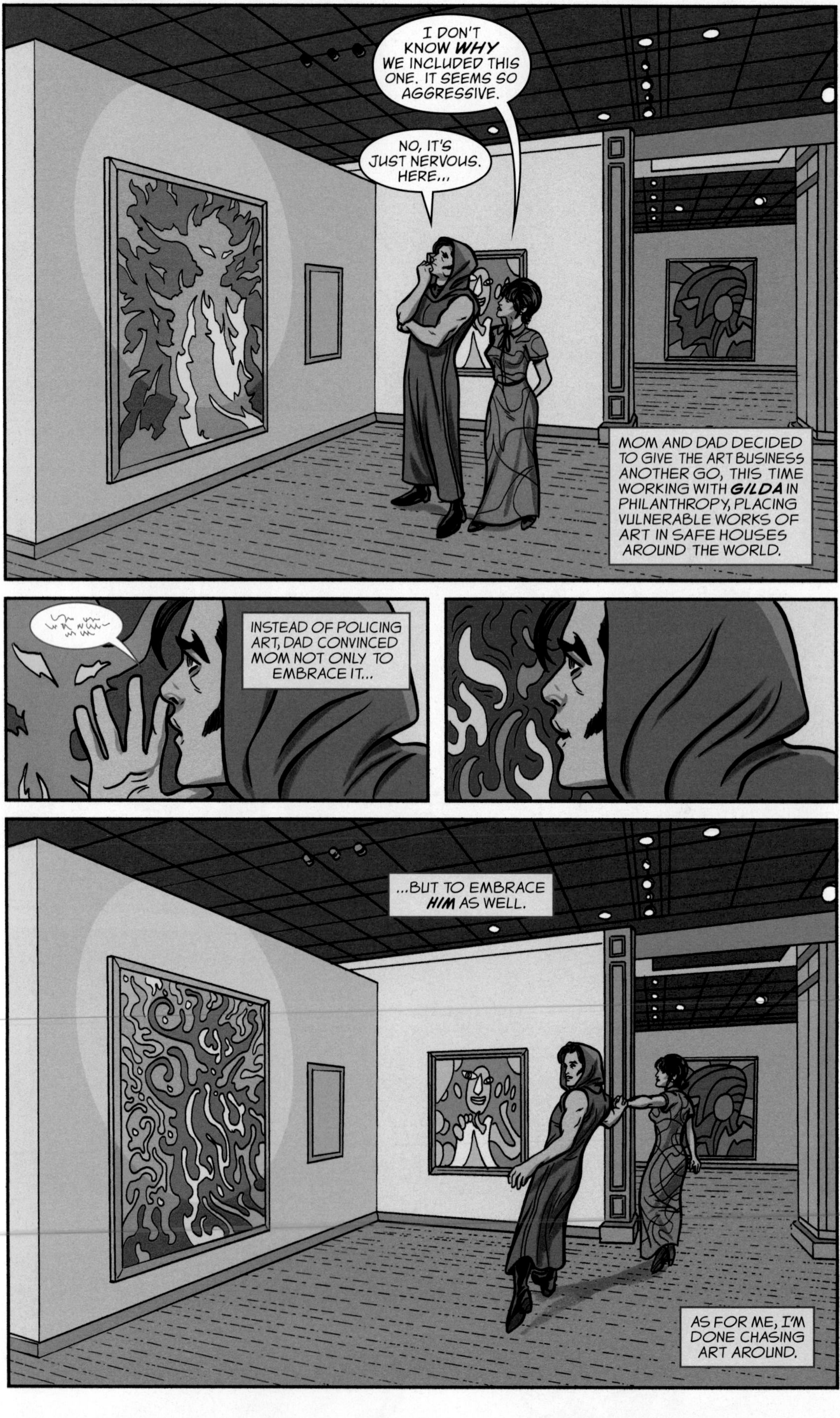
I DON'T KNOW **WHY** WE INCLUDED THIS ONE. IT SEEMS SO AGGRESSIVE.
NO, IT'S JUST NERVOUS. HERE...
MOM AND DAD DECIDED TO GIVE THE ART BUSINESS ANOTHER GO, THIS TIME WORKING WITH **GILDA** IN PHILANTHROPY, PLACING VULNERABLE WORKS OF ART IN SAFE HOUSES AROUND THE WORLD.
INSTEAD OF POLICING ART, DAD CONVINCED MOM NOT ONLY TO EMBRACE IT...
...BUT TO EMBRACE **HIM** AS WELL.
AS FOR ME, I'M DONE CHASING ART AROUND.

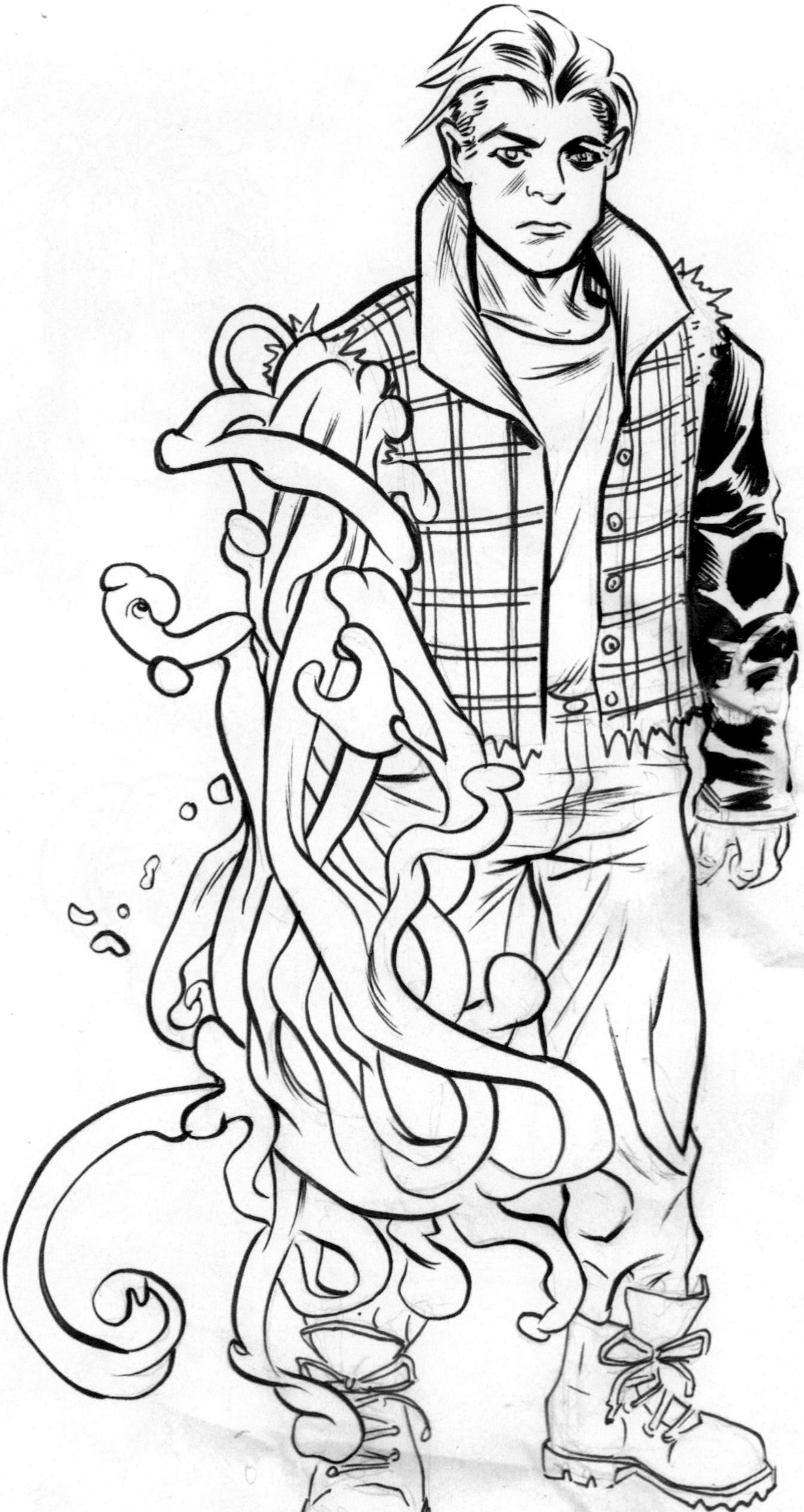

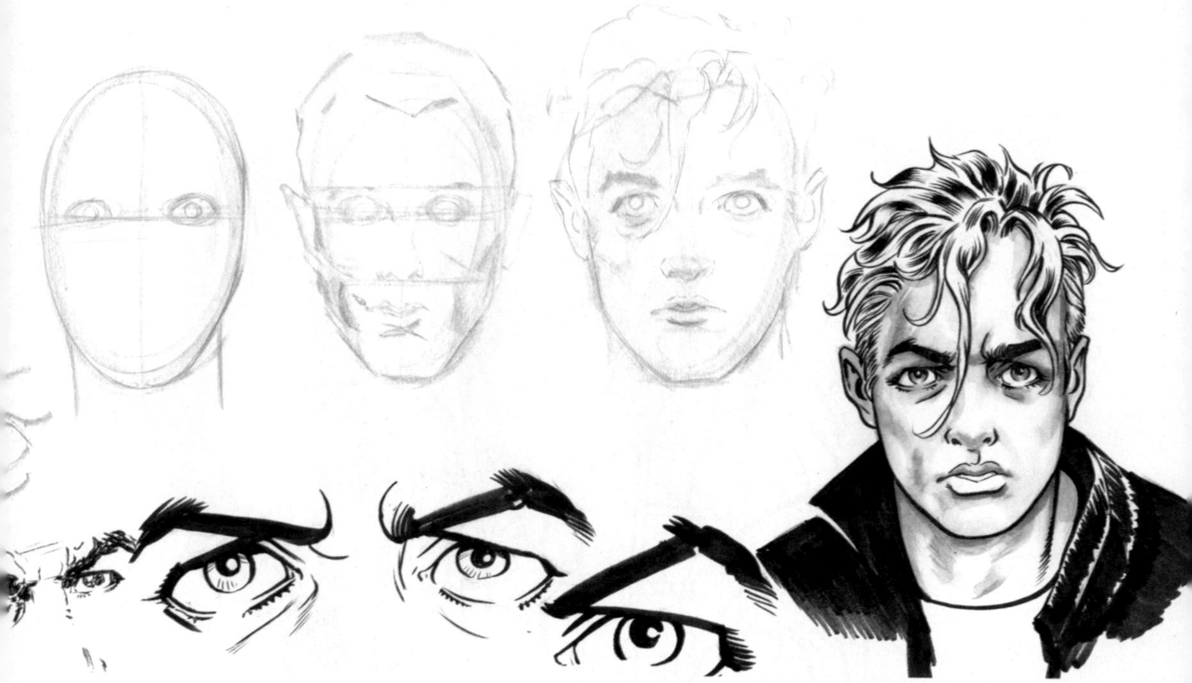

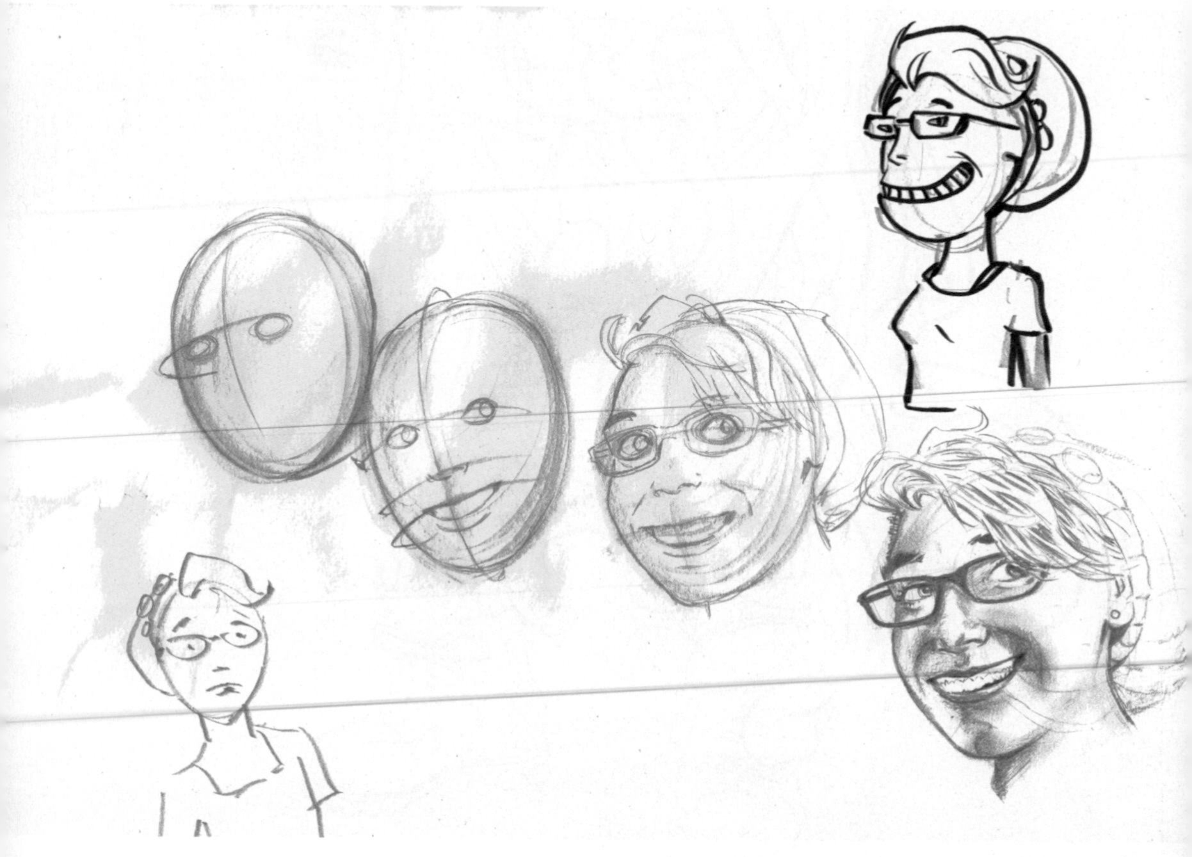

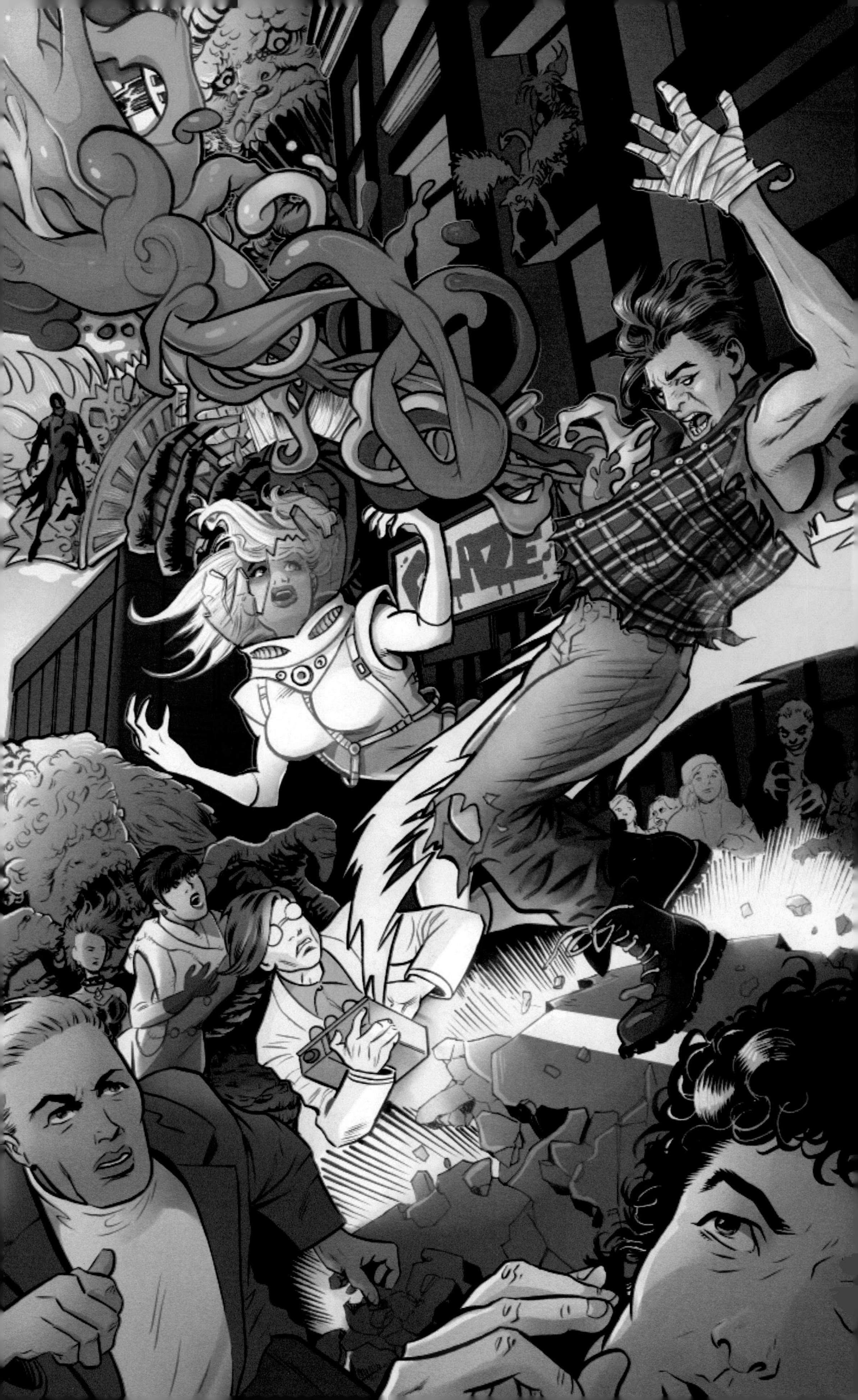

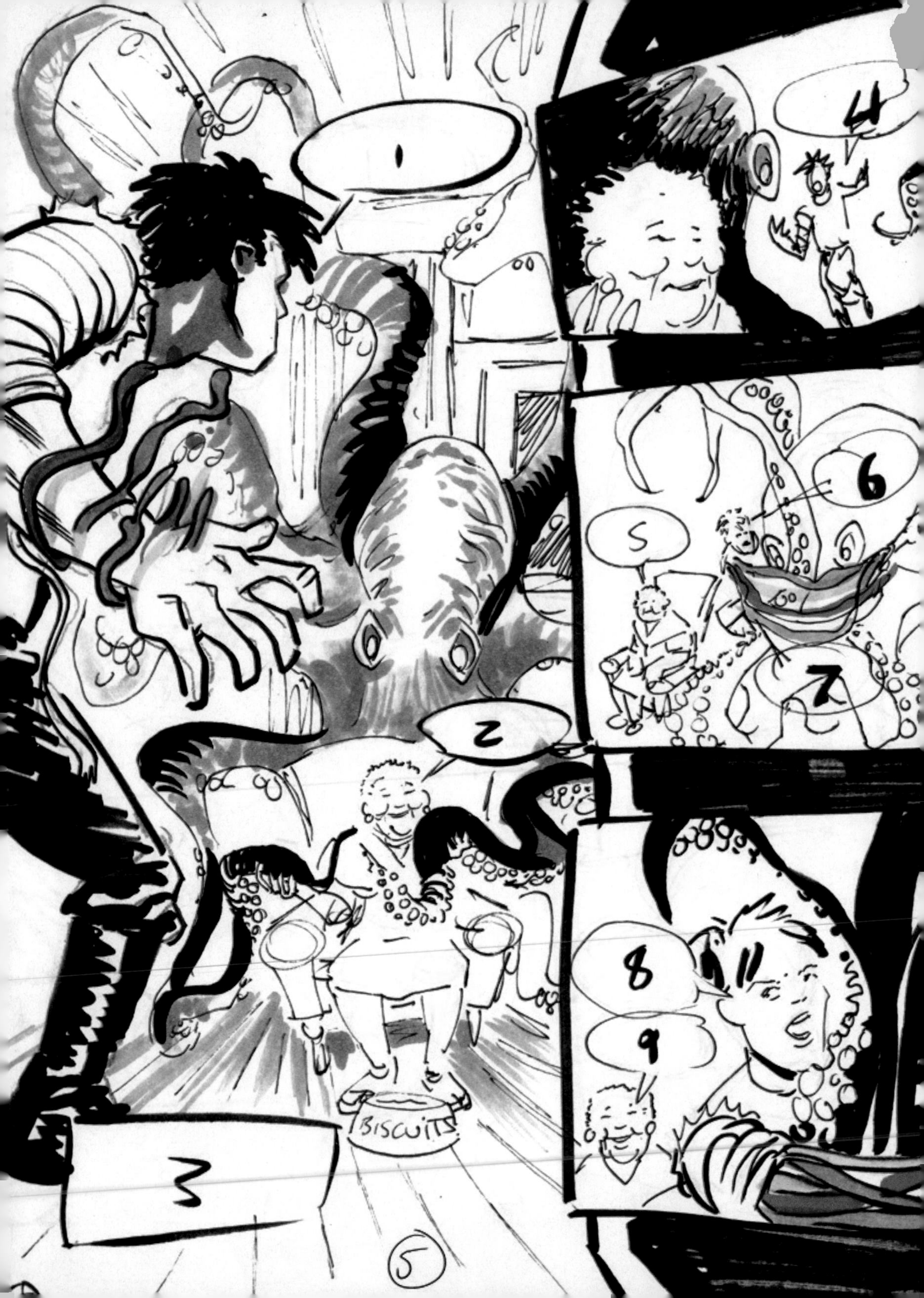
1
2
3
BISCUITS
4
5
6
7
8
9
5

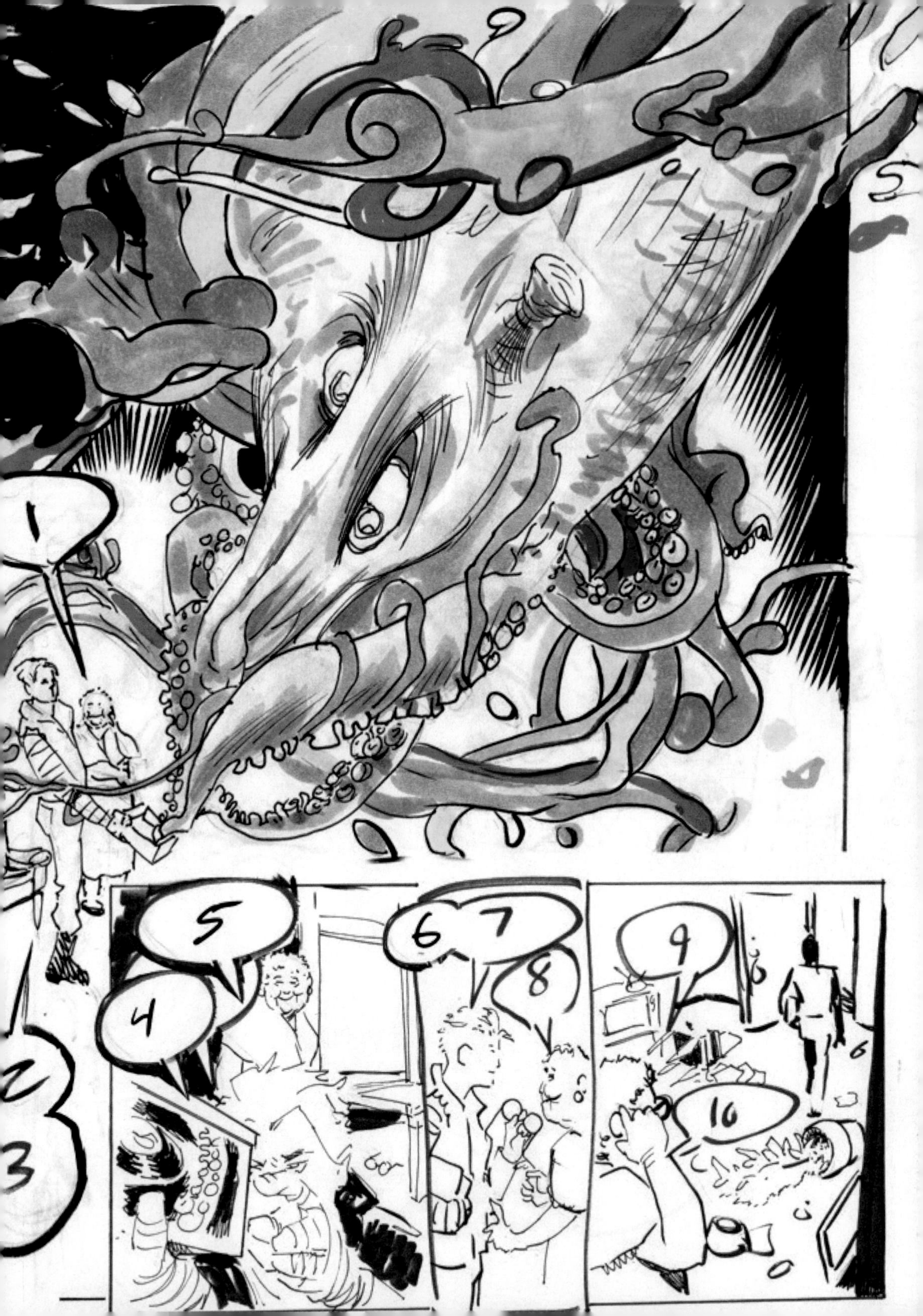
1
2
3
4
5
6
7
8
9
10

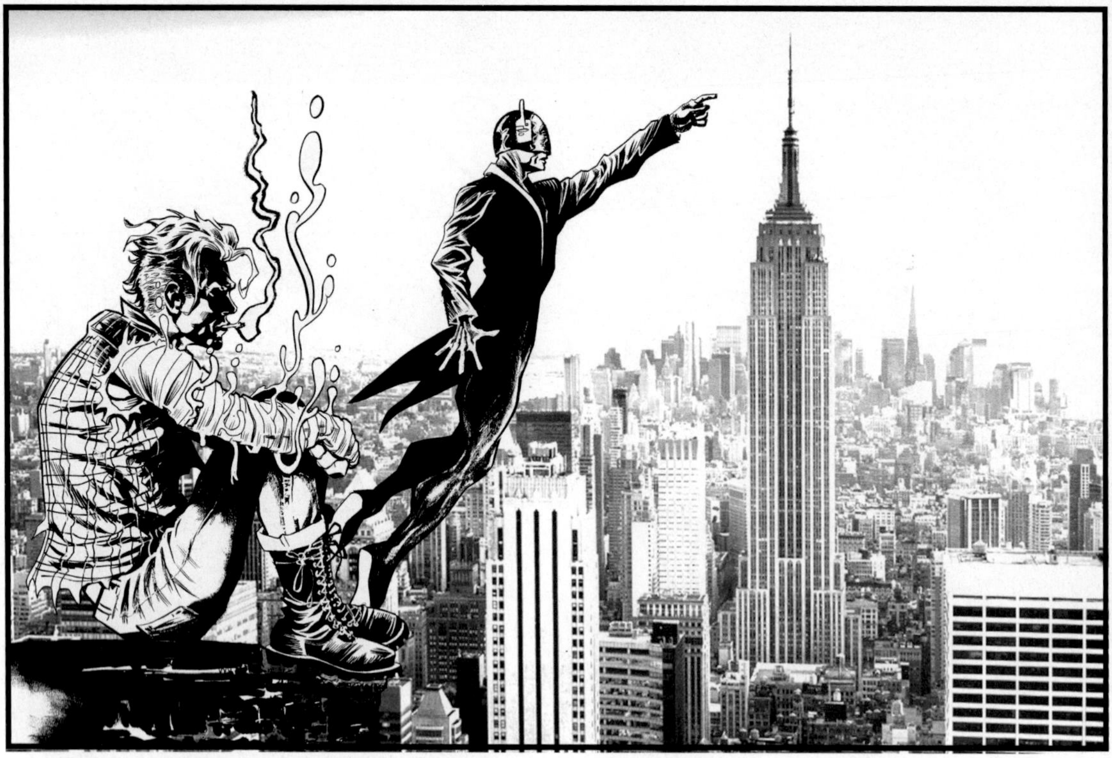

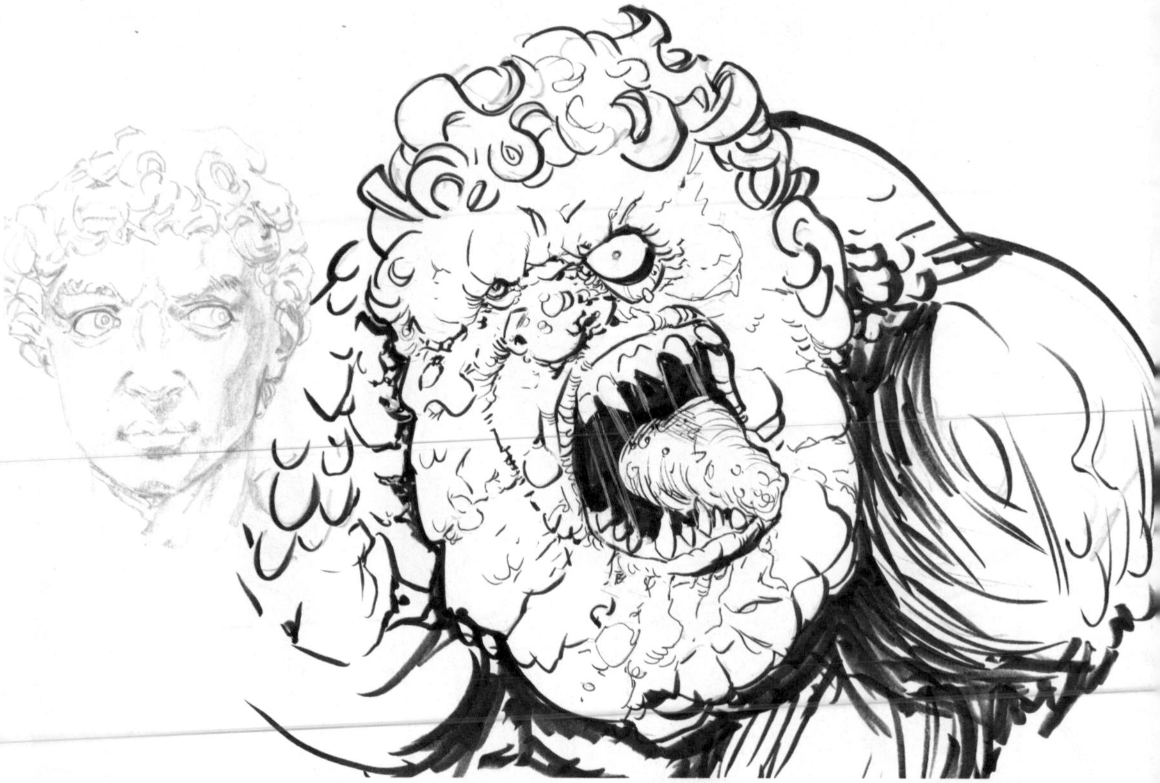